Spanish in Chicago

OXFORD STUDIES IN SOCIOLINGUISTICS

General Editors:
Brook Bolander
Monash University
Adam Jaworski
University of Hong Kong

RECENTLY PUBLISHED IN THE SERIES:
Speaking Pittsburghese: The Story of a Dialect
Barbara Johnstone

The Pragmatics of Politeness
Geoffrey Leech

Language and Superdiversity: Indonesians Knowledging at Home and Abroad
Zane Goebel

Sustaining the Nation: The Making and Moving of Language and Nation
Monica Heller, Lindsay A Bell, Michelle Daveluy, Mireille McLaughlin, and Hubert Noel

Style, Mediation, and Change: Sociolinguistic Perspectives on Talking Media
Janus Mortensen, Nikolaus Coupland, and Jacob Thogersen

Reimagining Rapport
Zane Goebel

Elite Authenticity: Remaking Distinction in Food Discourse
Gwynne Mapes

In Pursuit of English: Language and Subjectivity in Neoliberal South Korea
Joseph Sung-Yul Park

Choreographies of Multilingualism: Writing and Language Ideology in Singapore
Tong King Lee

SPANISH IN CHICAGO

Kim Potowski and Lourdes Torres

OXFORD
UNIVERSITY PRESS

Oxford University Press is a department of the University of Oxford. It furthers the University's objective of excellence in research, scholarship, and education by publishing worldwide. Oxford is a registered trade mark of Oxford University Press in the UK and certain other countries.

Published in the United States of America by Oxford University Press
198 Madison Avenue, New York, NY 10016, United States of America.

© Oxford University Press 2023

All rights reserved. No part of this publication may be reproduced, stored in a retrieval system, or transmitted, in any form or by any means, without the prior permission in writing of Oxford University Press, or as expressly permitted by law, by license, or under terms agreed with the appropriate reproduction rights organization. Inquiries concerning reproduction outside the scope of the above should be sent to the Rights Department, Oxford University Press, at the address above.

You must not circulate this work in any other form
and you must impose this same condition on any acquirer.

Library of Congress Cataloging-in-Publication Data
Names: Potowski, Kim, author. | Torres, Lourdes, 1959– author.
Title: Spanish in Chicago / Kim Potowski & Lourdes Torres.
Description: New York, NY : Oxford University Press, [2023] |
Series: Oxford studies in sociolinguistics |
Includes bibliographical references and index.
Identifiers: LCCN 2022029936 (print) | LCCN 2022029937 (ebook) |
ISBN 9780199326150 (paperback) | ISBN 9780199326143 (hardback) |
ISBN 9780197522882 (epub)
Subjects: LCSH: Spanish language—Social aspects—Illinois—Chicago. |
Spanish language—Variation—Illinois—Chicago. |
Languages in contact—Illinois—Chicago. | Bilingualism—Illinois—Chicago. |
Puerto Ricans—United States—Language. | Mexican Americans—Languages.
Classification: LCC PC4829.I45 P68 2023 (print) | LCC PC4829.I45 (ebook) |
DDC 467/.977311—dc23/eng/20221103
LC record available at https://lccn.loc.gov/2022029936
LC ebook record available at https://lccn.loc.gov/2022029937

DOI: 10.1093/oso/9780199326143.001.0001

Paperback printed by Marquis Book Printing, Canada
Hardback printed by Bridgeport National Bindery, Inc., United States of America

CONTENTS

Acknowledgments   ix

1. Spanish in the U.S. and in Chicago: Contact and Loss   1
   1.1. Introduction   1
   1.2. Visualizations of Contact and Loss   2
   1.3. Latino Chicago   13
   1.4. Mexicans and Puerto Ricans in Chicago: Complex Relationships   23
   1.5. Prior Studies of Spanish in Chicago   31
   1.6. Summary   33

2. **The Chicago Spanish (CHISPA) Corpus**   35
   2.1. Introduction   35
   2.2. Generational Groups   36
   2.3. Regional Origins   40
   2.4. Spanish Proficiency   42
   2.5. Age, Gender, Socioeconomic Status   53
   2.6. Interview Procedures   57
   2.7. Summary   59

3. **Lexical Familiarity**   71
   3.1. Introduction   71
   3.2. Lexical Outcomes of Dialect Contact   71
   3.3. Methodology   79
   3.4. Homeland Speakers   85
   3.5. Chicago Mexicans and Puerto Ricans   89
      3.5.1. Outgroup Lexical Familiarity Scores   89
      3.5.2. Ingroup Lexical Familiarity Scores   91
      3.5.3. Total Lexical Familiarity Scores   93
   3.6. Chicago MexiRicans   96
   3.7. Scores on Individual Items   98

    3.8. Proficiency   106
    3.9. Summary and Conclusions   108

4. **Discourse Markers**   111
    4.1. Introduction   111
    4.2. Discourse Markers in Bilingual Communities   112
    4.3. Methodology   120
    4.4. Overall Frequency of *So* and *Entonces*   125
    4.5. Regional Origin and Generation   126
    4.6. Proficiency   132
    4.7. Functions   137
    4.8. Summary and Conclusions   140

5. **Codeswitching**   145
    5.1. Introduction   145
    5.2. Spanish-English Codeswitching in the U.S.   146
    5.3. Methodology   150
    5.4. Overall Quantity of English   156
    5.5. Number of Codeswitches   162
    5.6. Types of Codeswitches   167
    5.7. Proficiency versus Generation   173
    5.8. Summary and Conclusions   174

6. **Subjunctive**   179
    6.1. Introduction   179
    6.2. The Subjunctive in U.S. Spanish   180
    6.3. Methodology   187
    6.4. Regional Origin   191
    6.5. Generation   192
    6.6. Obligatory Contexts   193
    6.7. Variable Contexts   196
    6.8. Proficiency   197
        6.8.1. Obligatory Contexts by Proficiency Level   200
        6.8.2. Variable Contexts by Proficiency Level   201
    6.9. Proficiency versus Generation   202
    6.10. Summary and Conclusions   203

7. **Phonology**   205
    7.1. Introduction   205
    7.2. Phonological Accommodation in Situations of Spanish Dialect Contact   205
    7.3. Methodology   210

    7.4. Regional Origin   *213*
    7.5. Interlocutor Variety   *227*
    7.6. Connections between /s/ and /r̄/   *231*
    7.7. Qualitative Explorations of Puerto Rican Variation   *233*
    7.8. Summary and Conclusions   *236*

8. **Factors Underlying Spanish Development**   *241*
    8.1. Introduction   *241*
    8.2. Intergenerational Spanish Transmission and Loss in the U.S.   *243*
    8.3. Proficiency Inliers   *248*
        8.3.1. Attitudes about Spanish   *250*
        8.3.2. Language Use in the Home and in Social Networks   *257*
        8.3.3. Order of Acquisition   *272*
        8.3.4. Bilingual Education   *273*
        8.3.5. Travel to Mexico or Puerto Rico   *280*
    8.4. Proficiency Outliers   *283*
        8.4.1. High-Proficiency Outliers ($n = 23$)   *284*
        8.4.2. Low-Proficiency Outliers ($n = 8$)   *289*
    8.5. Summary and Conclusions   *294*

9. **Conclusions**   *299*
    9.1. Introduction   *299*
    9.2. Spanish Proficiency: How to Measure It and Ways to Support It   *299*
    9.3. Summary of Five Linguistic Features   *307*
    9.4. Proficiency Preferable to Generation When Examining Changes in U.S. Spanish   *309*
    9.5. Areas for Future Research   *311*

References   *313*
Index   *329*

ACKNOWLEDGMENTS

We dedicate this book to all U.S. Spanish-speakers, especially those in Chicago who are raising, teaching, and otherwise supporting the bilingualism of new generations. Thank you for entrusting your stories to us. Our primary goal is to support greater linguistic and social justice for all communities, in part through sharing details about the fascinating features of U.S. Spanish and also by educating people about why it's important to fight to raise bilingual children.

Next, we thank DePaul University and University of Illinois at Chicago students who carried out interviews and transcriptions, including those on the following list. You were highly skilled at the "art and science" of the sociolinguistic interview, and this data could never have been collected without your talent and dedication.

Erika Abad	Lillian Gorman	Alba Morales
Doris Alfaro	Sarah Gutierrez	Rosa Ortiz
Leslie Avila	Liz Hernandez	Daisy Perez
Andrea Cristancho	Lisette Jaramillo	Denise Perez
Chris Cashman	Joanna Maldonado	Nancy Perez
Victoria Castro	Kim Manzanares	Mynor Raguay
Nancy Dominguez	Araceli Martinez	Nayeli Rodriguez
Isabel Escarpita	Christina Martinez	Melanie Silva
Monica Garcia	Isabel Matias	Hasalia Torres
	Rocio Miranda	

Graduate students who helped with analyses and/or transcriptions include Clara Azevedo, Laura Bartlett, Clara Burgo, Sabra Duarte, Irene Finestrat Martinez, Kenny Froehlig, Brad Hoot, Sabah Khan, Alicia Luque, Megan Marshall, Janine Matts, L. D. Nicolas May, Glafira Padilla, Ana Rodríguez, Dani Vergara, and a host of people in Kim Potowski's seminars on bilingualism. Thanks to all of you for helping bring this to fruition.

We would like to thank Morgan Edwards, Andrea Olmedo, and Beth Petree for assistance with initial phonological data coding, and David Abugaber for the statistical support and encouragement.

Colleagues who read and/or worked on drafts of different sections of the manuscript include Sonia Barnes, Salvatore Callesano, Danny Erker, Kevin Martillo Viner, Naomi Nagy, Erin O'Rourke, and Isabel Velázquez. We greatly appreciate your critical eyes and expert knowledge. Several anonymous reviewers also provided useful input. Naturally, we authors own any errors and shortcomings.

Many thanks to the folks at Oxford University Press, who have waited patiently for us to finish and whose professional personnel have ushered this manuscript to print. Arturo Olivarez Jr. beautifully executed Kim's idea for the Chicago flag-inspired cover.

This is our love letter to Chicago, the city that we two New Yorkers have each called home since the 1990s. It is a gold mine for the study of many languages, in part because so many wonderful multilingual communities make their lives here. We hope this book provides a good sense of la impresionante fuerza de las comunidades latinas y de la riqueza del español en la Ciudad de los Vientos.

CHAPTER 1
Spanish in the U.S. and in Chicago

Contact and Loss

1.1. INTRODUCTION

Spanish is the second most commonly spoken language in the U.S. after English, estimated by the 2019 Census to be spoken by approximately 42 million individuals. A majority of the U.S. Latino[1] population is of Mexican origin (62%), with Caribbeans forming an additional 18% and Central Americans almost 9%. Linguistic studies on the Spanish spoken by communities around the U.S. continue to proliferate, with scholars documenting how it changes over time as a result of its contact with English as well as due to the reduced quantity and domains of its use. Unfortunately, it is very frequently no longer spoken in families after three or four generations. In addition, speakers of Spanish from different parts of the world come into contact with one another in locations around the U.S., which can have effects on the ways they speak the language. Thus, in many locations around the country, an investigation of Spanish features is simultaneously a study of language contact, of dialect leveling, and of language loss. The relatively large city of Chicago, Illinois, is just such a location. One out of every three inhabitants is Latino, many of whom speak Spanish. Furthermore, since the beginning of the 20th century, the city's Latino population has consisted of significant proportions of both Mexican- and Puerto Rican–origin individuals, giving rise to possible dialect contact phenomena. This makes Chicago an ideal site for our study.

This chapter reviews relevant studies of the outcomes when Spanish speakers have come into significant contact with English speakers and/or with

---

1. We will use this term, alternating with *Hispanic* where we refer to U.S. government data (which use the latter term). We are aware of *Latinx* as a nonbinary alternative.

Spanish in Chicago. Kim Potowski and Lourdes Torres, Oxford University Press. © Oxford University Press 2023.
DOI: 10.1093/oso/9780199326143.003.0001

speakers of varieties of Spanish that are different from their own. It sets a general theoretical stage as well as our research questions about Chicago Spanish, which include phenomena routinely found among native speakers (such as realization of phonological variables, choice of verbal forms, etc.) and the outcomes of waning Spanish proficiency. Our goal is to describe the oral Spanish of three groups of speakers (Mexicans, Puerto Ricans, and MexiRicans) across three generations (first, second, and third), seeking to identify possible patterns of change and propose explanations for them, drawing on previous work in language contact, language loss, and dialect contact.

1.2. VISUALIZATIONS OF CONTACT AND LOSS

We first review general theoretical constructs of language contact, of language loss, and of dialect contact, proposing several visualizations that incorporate all three phenomena. The pattern of immigrant[2] languages in the U.S. typically proceeds in the following fashion. Immigrants arrive in the U.S. monolingual in Spanish. Their children are bilingual in Spanish and English, usually stronger in English, and their Spanish shows signs of contact with English. While some aspects of their Spanish grammar may be very similar or even identical to those of speakers raised in Latin America, there are also noticeable differences in the Spanish of U.S.-raised speakers versus those raised in Latin America. Then the children of U.S.-raised children of immigrants—that is, the grandchildren of the individuals who arrived from Latin America—very frequently have weak Spanish abilities or are monolingual in English; some have only receptive abilities in Spanish. We attempt to represent this process in Figure 1.1 via an analogy that uses colors although the figures appear in black and white; readers may consult the online version to see color figures. Spanish is "Language 1," the immigrant language (blue), and English is "Language 2," the majority language of the U.S. (red). Before we begin, we stress that these visuals are abstractions; they are not meant to fully represent the complexity of the phenomena we seek to understand.

The two nested circles in the middle of Figure 1.1 represent individuals raised in the U.S. bilingually. Their Spanish has "turned purple" because it is in contact with English, in the way that blue turns purple when in contact with red. This is an extreme simplification, one that does not mean to imply that the Spanish spoken in the U.S. is "less Spanish" than that spoken anywhere else. In addition, using a solid purple color is shorthand for several complicated and different processes—it might be more accurate to use a blue circle with flecks of purple and red in it—but we chose the solid color for the purposes of our analogy. We also note that U.S.-raised "purple-speaking" individuals

---

2. Puerto Rico forms part of the U.S. nation-state; thus, many scholars refer to a move from the island to the mainland U.S. as *migration* rather than *immigration*. We use the term *immigration* to mean both migration and immigration, and we use *to the U.S.* to mean both to the country and to the mainland.

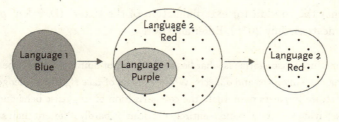

Figure 1.1. Immigrant language contact.

are also in contact with individuals raised in Latin America—including their own parents and others in their communities—whose Spanish still looks very "blue," meaning that it does not evidence much influence from English nor has it diverged from Latin American norms. Just as any shade of purple depends on the proportions of red and blue within it, so do the features of U.S. Spanish depend on the amounts and kinds of Spanish and English constituting it. This process has been referred to as *linguistic convergence*, "the enhancement of inherent structural similarities found between two linguistic systems" (Bullock & Toribio, 2004, p.91). Finally, the far-right circle represents individuals who are largely or totally monolingual in English. There are also stages before this final circle in which the small purple circle within the red one is strongly red in hue.

Going back to the idea of a blue circle with flecks of purple and red in it, and using a different analogy, we are reminded of gemstones. Two different chunks of tourmaline, for example, can have different proportions of aluminum, iron, magnesium, sodium, lithium, and potassium and thus express a fair amount of variation when we shine a light on them from various angles, yet they are both tourmaline. Similarly, two varieties of Spanish in the U.S. can contain different amounts of English-influenced lexicon, outright switching to English, and effects of lack of input in Spanish. Many studies have "shone a light" through the gemstone that is Spanish in the U.S. as it is spoken by the children and grandchildren of immigrants (see Escobar & Potowski, 2015, for review of this body of work), including codeswitching, the use of the subjunctive and other morphology, phonology, and pragmatics.

In Figure 1.1, there was only one variety of the immigrant language. What if there are several varieties of Spanish arriving in a U.S. location? Varieties of Latin American Spanish are frequently described as belonging to one of two broad categories: "highland" or "lowland" (Lipski, 1994) or "Mainlander" or "Caribbean" (Otheguy & Zentella, 2012) based on a series of phonological and morphosyntactic trends in each set of geographical locations. Before continuing with our question, it is important to clarify some concepts about languages and dialects. Scholars have rightly questioned the naming of varieties of any language; it "gets the speaker-language relationship backwards, making the former the conduit for externalization of the latter" (D. Erker, personal communication, July 2015). Erker also notes:

> [An] instinct to categorize is what lies at the heart of binning ways of speaking into named languages and dialects. While scholars of race rightly challenge this instinct, we linguists perpetuate the categorization of linguistic behavior into boxes. Saying someone sounds "entirely Mexican" is hardly different than saying someone looks "completely Latino." It is crucial to distinguish lay impressions of individuals' speech, which are real and worthy of analysis, from what linguists know about linguistic form. We cannot in one breath challenge and problematize the request to explain physical appearance and in the next adopt a rhetoric about linguistic behavior that promotes a similar kind of essentialization. (D. Erker, personal communication, July 2015)

Furthermore, there are important differences in the Spanish spoken at different places around the nation-state that is currently Mexico and in the Spanish spoken at different places around the island of Puerto Rico, such that there is no such thing as "one" Mexican or Puerto Rican Spanish. Despite these complications, and attempting to acknowledge them through this brief disclaimer, we have chosen to use the term *dialect* to refer to the totality of features in a language typically spoken by individuals raised in a particular region or belonging to an identifiable group. Thus, when we refer to a *Mexican speaker* or a *Puerto Rican speaker*, we mean individuals who hail from those regions (or whose families did) and whose Spanish manifests features in proportions that are most common there. As shorthand, *Mexican Spanish* and *Puerto Rican Spanish*, then, refer to the varieties used by these speakers.

Returning to our question of what happens when speakers who use different varieties of a language come into contact with one another. We will refer to this phenomenon as *dialect contact*, and a possible outcome of it is *dialect leveling*. Erker and Otheguy (2016, p. 132) define dialectal[3] leveling as "the intergenerational reduction of regionally differentiated linguistic behavior." We now briefly explore several instantiations of dialect contact by extending our color analogy. One possible set of circumstances is represented in Figure 1.2, where speakers of two or more dialects of the same language come to live together in a place where that language was formerly not spoken (such a place is represented by the empty circle) but becomes dominant in that area. The different dialects blend together to form a new one, which becomes the societally dominant way of speaking.

---

3. Otheguy and Zentella (2012, p. 10) state that the term *dialectal* "avoid[s] the implication that there are Caribbean and Mainland dialects supported by uniquely shared clusterings of features; we claim, much more modestly, that our Caribbean and Mainland speakers simply use subject personal pronouns differently."

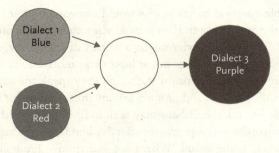

Figure 1.2. New settlement dialect contact.

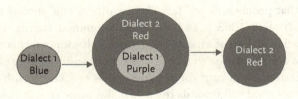

Figure 1.3. Monolingual dialect immigration.

Such situations are frequently referred to as "new towns" (Kerswill & Williams, 2000). Examples include the colonization of Latin America by Spanish speakers (Penny, 2000) and that of Australia by English speakers (Trudgill, 2004).[4] In these instances, the different dialects tend to influence each other more or less mutually, and none of the original dialects remains completely intact; the resulting variety is referred to as a *koine*. Kerswill (2002, p. 9) notes that for a koine to form, the speakers must waive their previous allegiances and social divisions to show mutual solidarity.

A different situation occurs when speakers of one dialect move to an area where another dialect of that same language is spoken. Consider a Spanish-speaking Cuban who moves to Spanish-speaking Mexico or an English-speaking Chicagoan who moves to English-speaking London. This is represented in Figure 1.3. The most typical outcome in this situation is for the relocated adult speakers to acquire some features of the new dialect but largely retain features from their native dialect, represented by the middle circle in which their original "blue" dialect has turned purple as they acquire Dialect 2 features. Their children raised in the new location, however, usually sound like everyone else raised in that location. That is, the children often end up monodialectal in Dialect 2, represented by the red circle in Figure 1.3.

---

4. We do not suggest that Latin America or Australia were devoid of humans with language; obviously, there were abundant speakers of aboriginal/indigenous languages who were relegated to the margins and/or exterminated via colonial processes.

A reasonable question to ask is why would someone bother to change the way they speak when those in their new environment understand them reasonably well? For example, why might a Cuban in Mexico begin to acquire Mexican Spanish features? There are at least three motivations. The first is to promote improved comprehension. Although they speak the same language, there may be Cuban words and pronunciations that are difficult for Mexicans to understand. Second, the Cubans may seek to fit in better within their new surroundings in order to create greater affective bonds with locals and perhaps avoid consistently being asked "Where are you from?" Trudgill (1986) proposed that the fundamental mechanism underlying such processes is *accommodation*, initially proposed by Giles (1970) and summed up by Keller (1994) in the idea that people seek to "Talk like the others talk" during face-to-face interaction. Trudgill (1983, p. 143) described accommodation as "adjustments in pronunciation and other aspects of linguistic behavior in terms of a drive to approximate one's language to that of one's interlocutor, if they are regarded as socially desirable and/or if the speaker wishes to identify with them and/or demonstrate good will towards them." Finally, some speech changes, especially but not only those of younger children, may lie below people's level of consciousness. Delvaux and Soquet (2007), for example, found evidence of unintentional phonetic accommodation to the dialect of a different region of Belgium by adult Belgian French speakers.

The degree to which the Dialect 1–speaking immigrants acquire Dialect 2 is dependent in large part on the age of arrival in the new location, as summarized in Siegel's (2010) review of studies around the world of second dialect acquisition. Other factors include the number of years of residence in the new location, the linguistic distance between the two dialects, the degree of interaction with speakers of Dialect 2, and the desire to integrate with them. This last factor was important in the degree of accommodation toward outgroup dialect use of Spanish subject pronouns found by Otheguy and Zentella (2012) in New York City: Caribbeans with greater "outgroup orientation" were shown to use subject pronouns more like Mainlanders did than other Caribbeans in the city did.

In the next scenario, no one moves anywhere; there are two or more dialects of the same language coexisting in a region. One may be numerically larger and/or enjoy greater status than the other (Figure 1.4). Appalachian English and African American English in the U.S. are two examples of dialects that exist alongside what might be called mainstream U.S. English. Given that language features frequently vary across even small geographic spaces, the difference between what constitutes "having a different accent" or "using different words" versus what constitutes a different dialect is a thorny question that we do not attempt to answer here. While some research on ethnic/social dialects has concluded that individuals cannot be truly bidialectal in them (Labov, 1998; Hazen, 2001), other researchers contend that it is indeed

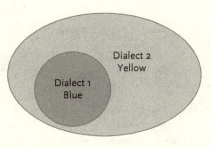

Figure 1.4. Society with 2+ dialects.

possible (Smith & Durham, 2012; Anderson, 2014). The debate may rest largely on a difference in definitions, similar to what occurs with the term *bilingual*, which has been used to refer to a wide variety of linguistic circumstances. We note that the comedic duo Keegan-Michael Key and Jordan Peele exhibit what seems to us to be fluent switching between African American English and mainstream U.S. English, such that they likely meet anyone's definition of *bidialectal*. It is also the case that both Key and Peele were raised by a white mother and an African American father, a situation called *intrafamilial dialect contact*, to which we return later.

Finally, what if speakers from several different dialect groups move to a new location where a different language is spoken? This is the case of Spanish in many U.S. cities. For example, Hirano (2008, 2010) studied speakers from various different English dialect areas who were living and teaching English in Japan, where Japanese is the dominant societal language. Studying more than 10,000 tokens of intervocalic /t/ in words such as *letter, sitting,* and *get it* produced by 39 speakers, she found that a strong social network with native speakers of English from the home country encouraged the use of variants commonly used in the home variety and also hindered the use of variants more commonly used in other varieties. Conversely, a strong social network with native speakers from an outgroup country facilitated the use of variants from that country, and/or suppressed the use of variants from the home English variety. If the children of these speakers also acquired English while living in Japan, it is an empirical question on which variety they might converge.

A similar situation obtains among the Spanish-speaking Salvadorans and Mexicans who live in Houston, Texas, where English is the societal language. In Figure 1.5, the Salvadorans (the smaller, yellow circle labeled Dialect 2) are outnumbered by the Mexicans (the larger, blue circle labeled Dialect 1). The Salvadorans accommodate to the Mexicans on some Spanish features, shown by the green circle. For example, studies have found that Salvadorans in Houston use certain Salvadoran features less frequently than speakers in El Salvador, including the second-person singular subject pronoun *vos* (Hernández,

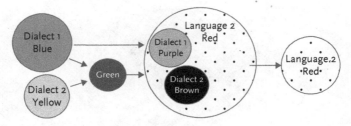

Figure 1.5. One immigrant dialect influences another.

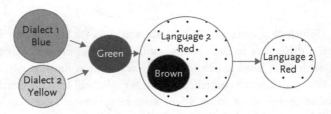

Figure 1.6. Two immigrant dialects influence each other.

2002; Schreffler, 1994)[5] and transitive *andar* (Hernández, 2002);[6] studies on Salvadoran phonological accommodation in Houston are reviewed in Chapter 7. Meanwhile, the Mexicans in Houston have been shown to keep their Spanish dialect features. Both groups are in contact with English (Language 2, the red circle), and their dialects are influenced accordingly: the blue becomes purple, and the green becomes brown. Yet the children of both groups of Spanish speakers frequently end up monolingual in English, the last red circle on the right. Again, though, there are "shades" of brown and purple before red completely takes over the linguistic repertoire of the U.S.-raised communities.

In another scenario, the two immigrant groups exert mutual influence on each other's dialects, which we depict in Figure 1.6. This is not the same as the "New Towns" depicted in Figure 1.2, because in that situation, the arrivals' language became the majority language spoken in all levels of society, meaning that the language continues to grow, change, and eventually coalesce into a new norm or koine; in such a case, the green circle in Figure 1.6 would represent the variety of the new society. But the scenario in Figure 1.6 is different because of the red circle; the two dialects in contact belong to a minority language, one that is not used throughout society and which, similarly

---

5. The *voseo* among U.S. Salvadorans has also been studied by Lipski (1988, 1989), Rivera-Mills (2011), Woods and Rivera-Mills (2010, 2012), and Woods and Shin (2016).
6. Aaron and Hernández (2007) found evidence that some accommodations responded to a desire to avoid being identified as Salvadoran in order to potentially pass as Mexican American and escape notice by U.S. immigration officials.

to other immigrant languages in the U.S. already discussed, eventually dies out altogether. It is a setting of what Otheguy and Zentella (2012, p. 219) called "chronologically relatively shallow contact." In their study of pronouns in New York City, they found that Caribbean and Mainlander Spanish influenced each other, overall the latter were more influenced by the numerically superior Caribbeans. That is, the degree of mutual influence was imbalanced.

To date, the broadest examination of a situation like that in Figure 1.6 is Erker and Otheguy (2016), who studied coda /s/ and subject pronouns in New York City Spanish and then compared their findings to those of three other researchers who examined the same corpus for two additional features: Bookhamer (2013) with the subjunctive and Raña Risso (2013) and Barrera-Tobón (2013) with word order. They found changes in use in five linguistic areas among those who had an average of 22 years of living in New York compared with the recently arrived Latin Americans (Table 1.1).

The authors then asked whether the different linguistic outcomes "represent a disparate list of independent results, or, are they dots that can be connected to reveal a bigger picture?" They proposed that the latter is the correct interpretation and that each result "can be understood as the outcome of contact between (1) Spanish speakers and English speakers, referred to here as linguistic contact, (2) Spanish speakers of different regional origin, which we have called dialectal contact, or (3) some combination of (1) and (2)."

They identified a greater number of effects of contact with English (that is, linguistic convergence) than of dialect leveling (understood as the reduction of regionally differentiated linguistic behavior). In the former category was greater use of subject pronouns, fewer post-verbal subjects, an increased

Table 1.1. SUMMARY OF FINDINGS, ERKER AND OTHEGUY (2016).

Feature	Greater time living in New York City was correlated with:	Change was influenced by contact with:
Expressed pronouns	Increase overall Reconfiguration of constraints Mainlanders decreased	English English Caribbean Spanish
Coda /s/ weakening	Decrease Decreased sensitivity to constraints	Other varieties of Spanish
Subjunctive	Decrease	English
Post-verbal pronouns	Decrease Decreased sensitivity to constraints	English
Word order flexibility	Decrease Decreased sensitivity to constraints	English

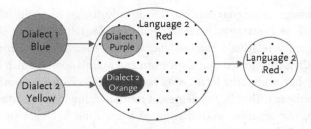

Figure 1.7. Neither immigrant dialect influences the other.

preference for subject-verb-object (SVO) word order, and less use of the subjunctive, while only coda /s/ and Mainlanders' decreased use of subject pronouns were attributed to dialect leveling. Why might there be greater convergence than leveling? The authors note that bilinguals typically seek to lighten the cognitive load created by the competing demands of their two linguistic systems. They do this in part by "modulating the use of . . . features in the direction of analogous structures." When they do so on features that are low in social salience, the "increase in parity between their linguistic systems is acquired at little to no social cost" (144). Thus, it might be predicted that, on a feature that is both (a) analogous in Spanish and English and (b) does not call too much attention, a bilingual might likely converge on English. Erker and Otheguy (2016) explained their findings by proposing that all of the Spanish features they compared are low in social salience (pronouns, the subjunctive, and word order) except for weakened coda /s/, which, despite the numerical preponderance of Caribbeans in New York City, suffers from stigma. They note that variable features like /s/ that elicit strong opinions in monolingual Spanish-speaking communities may or may not retain the same social meanings in the new context, so whether leveling occurs depends in part on how the social meaning of such features is locally (re)defined.

It is also theoretically possible for each immigrant dialect to remain intact before it is lost,[7] particularly if speakers of Dialect 1 and Dialect 2 do not interact with each other (Figure 1.7).

Finally, there is a situation that has been termed *intrafamilial dialect contact*, described in Potowski (2016) as one in which one parent speaks one dialect and the other speaks a different dialect. This is the case for Key and Peele mentioned earlier, who show signs of being bidialectal in African American English and mainstream U.S. English. But unlike the Key and Peele example, where both dialects belong to the majority language of society, what happens when the two parents speak different dialects of an immigrant language that

---

7. It is, of course, also theoretically possible for an immigrant language to not be lost at all. We review cases of stable bilingualism in Chapter 8, but we note here that most immigrant languages in the U.S. meet this fate.

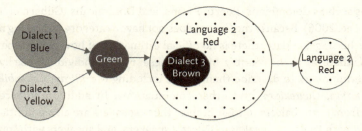

Figure 1.8. Intrafamilial dialect contact.

is not used in wider society? Figure 1.8 shows one possible outcome of intrafamilial dialect contact between a Mexican parent and a Puerto Rican parent raising a "MexiRican" child in Chicago, in which the parents are represented by the blue and yellow circles; the MexiRican individual is the green circle, meaning that they have a combination of Mexican and Puerto Rican features in their dialect of Spanish; and this dialect becomes the brown circle because it is in contact with English.

Tse and Ingram (1987) examined a situation like this involving a young girl's acquisition of two dialects of Cantonese over the period of one year (ages 1.7 to 2.8). She was being raised in an English-speaking area of Canada. The father's dialect had a phonemic distinction between /n/ and /l/ that did not exist in the mother's dialect, which had only /l/. Since the daughter was exposed to two sets of input, the question was whether she would acquire the mother's or the father's dialect or otherwise treat all linguistic input as one dialect with /l/ and /n/ in free variation. The girl clearly recognized the /n/ from her father's dialect and produced words with [n] throughout the recording sessions and with both parents. She treated /l/ and /n/ as being in free variation nearly half of the time and produced many /l/ words with /n/, in violation of both dialects. Therefore, there was no evidence that she had acquired either the mother's or the father's dialect. The authors concluded that she was processing input from both dialects and had not yet separated the two. However, in the later recording sessions, she had begun to converge on her mother's dialect, perhaps due to more frequent interactions with her during the day at home, echoing the findings of Roberts (1997) on the role of female caretakers in the transmission of linguistic features and minority dialect development. Once the girl began schooling in English, her linguistic environment would very likely change considerably, but again, what distinguishes her situation from that of Key and Peele is that there was no variety of Cantonese used widely outside of her home in which she would receive input and onto which she might converge.

Turning to Spanish, given the heterogeneity of origins of Spanish-speaking immigrants around the U.S., it is not surprising to find pairings between individuals from different regional origin groups. In New York City, for example, marriage records from 1991 reveal a high rate of unions between members of groups such as Colombians, Puerto Ricans, and Dominicans (Gilbertson et al., 1996; Lee, 2006). Because the Census does not have a category indicating mixed Latino heritage, to date, there is no official estimation of how many such individuals there are in the country. Many of these "mixed" individuals use hybridized terminology to describe themselves, including *MexiRican*, *ColombiRican*, *CubaDorian*, *Guatexican*, and other combinations. In addition to receiving input from both dialects in their homes, these speakers are also potentially in contact with Dialect 1 speakers, Dialect 2 speakers, and speakers with "purple" Spanish. This is an incredibly complex situation that was described to some extent in Potowski (2016) but which we take up again in this book.

To summarize, in Figures 1.5 through 1.8, we have simplified greatly and attempted to represent visually several possible instantiations of the combination of dialect leveling and linguistic convergence that Spanish in the U.S. can undergo. In this book, we explore the Spanish of three generations of Mexicans and Puerto Ricans in Chicago and of two generations of MexiRicans. Returning to our gemstone analogy, we do this by shining light on speakers' oral Spanish interviews from five different angles—lexical familiarity, discourse markers, codeswitching, subjunctive, and phonology—looking to provide descriptions of general trends in these features and in overall Spanish proficiency. Given that Mexicans predominate numerically among Spanish-speakers almost eight to one in the Chicago area, we might predict a situation like that of Figure 1.5, in which Mexican Spanish influences Puerto Rican Spanish but itself remains largely unchanged. We thus aim to add to the body of work on contact between different varieties of Spanish in the U.S. that has examined the lexicon, discourse markers, phonology, and the use of the subjunctive (reviewed in Chapters 3, 4, 6, and 7, respectively) by examining these features across three generational groups and three regional origin groups. We also add an exploration of speakers' codeswitching, the study of which has not been approached intergenerationally or via regional origin. We also attempt a global evaluation of the Spanish proficiency of all the speakers in our corpus and then consider the role of proficiency in the production of all five these features. Finally, we add an exploration of intrafamilial dialect contact via the MexiRican speakers (Figure 1.8). Following Erker and Otheguy (2016), we also compare our findings from different linguistic subareas, asking whether there are connections between individuals' lexical familiarity, use of *so* and *entonces*, patterns of codeswitching and total proportion of English used, and amount of subjunctive morphology. While we did not attempt to document systematic change across generational time in traditional sociolinguistic fashion by stratifying the sample into gender, age, and socioeconomic status or by comparing constraint hierarchies across different groups of speakers, we hope to paint a portrait of what second generation (G2) and third generation (G3) Spanish looks like. Finally, we present qualitative analyses of what our participants said about how they acquired Spanish in an attempt to understand why some

G2 and G3 speakers develop communicative abilities in the language that are either above or below their generational group's average.

We will now describe Chicago as a Spanish-speaking space to demonstrate its suitability for a study with goals such as ours.

1.3. LATINO CHICAGO

Latinos in the Midwest[8] constitute approximately 9% of the total population in the area and also about 9% of all Latinos in the U.S., according to the 2020 Census. It is the location of the third-largest city in the country, Chicago, which has seen steady growth in its Latino population over the past decades. It has also been home to large Mexican and Puerto Rican communities for more than 50 years, which results in both dialect contact and the existence of "mixed" MexiRican individuals, both of which foster innovative uses of the Spanish language and Latino identity constructions. In this section, we take care to indicate when we are referring to the City of Chicago (Figure 1.9), which measures 228 square miles (589 square kilometers) and in 2019 had a population of 2.7 million, versus the Chicago Metropolitan Statistical Area (described below), with a size of 10,800 square miles (28,120 square kilometers) and a population of 9.5 million.

In 2020, the City of Chicago's Latino population was estimated as 772,791, representing almost one-third (28.6%) of the city and constituting the fifth-largest city in the nation in the number of Hispanic residents, after New York City, Los Angeles, Houston, and San Antonio (Figure 1.10). Figure 1.11 shows the growth in the city's Latino population in the decades since 1970 (data in both figures are from the U.S. Census).

The majority of our study participants lived within the Chicago city limits and, in the case of second- and third-generation speakers, had been raised there. Because not all Latinos in the U.S. speak Spanish, Census data about home language use is useful. According to 2020 estimates, 36% of Chicago residents spoke a language other than English in the home, higher than the national average of 21.5%. The most common non-English language reported in the city was Spanish, spoken by 24% of the overall population. We feel reasonably secure in the conclusion that, given that 29% of Chicago is made up of Latino individuals and that 24% of Chicago is made up of Spanish-speaking individuals, this suggests that 82.7% of Chicago Latinos speak Spanish. We also note that 80.4% of the individuals who report speaking Spanish in the home also report speaking English "very well," meaning that there are many bilinguals in the city.

---

8. We use Escobar & Potowski's (2010) definition of the Midwest as including the nine states of Illinois, Indiana, Iowa, Michigan, Minnesota, Nebraska, North Dakota, Ohio, and South Dakota.

Figure 1.9. City of Chicago.

The next-largest Census-reported area after the city is the county. Chicago's Cook County comes out at number four in the country in terms of Hispanic population (Figure 1.12).

Finally, the Metropolitan Statistical Area (MSA) represents a geographically much larger area and is worth examining as well, because it reflects not only movements of city families to the suburbs[9] but also recent trends of immigrant settlement. In fact, in the year 2000, the number of Latino immigrants coming directly to a Chicago suburb became larger than those coming directly to the city. The Chicago MSA (Figure 1.13), with a population of 9.5 million, includes the Illinois counties of Cook, DuPage, Kane, Lake, McHenry, and Will; the Indiana counties of Jasper, Lake, Newton, and Porter; and Kenosha County in Wisconsin.

---

9. Northern Illinois University has recently begun documenting oral histories of Latinx in the Chicago suburbs; see https://www.chicagolandiaoralhistory.org/.

Table 1.2. THE 10 U.S. METROPOLITAN STATISTICAL AREAS WITH THE LARGEST HISPANIC POPULATIONS.

Metro area	Hispanic population	% Hispanic	Top 3 origin groups
1. Los Angeles–Long Beach–Anaheim, CA	5,959,874	45.1%	Mexican 76.9% Salvadoran 8.1% Guatemalan 5.1%
2. New York–Newark–Jersey City, NY–NJ–PA	4,804,046	25.0%	Puerto Rican 25.0% Dominican 23.0% Mexican 12.3%
3. Miami–Fort Lauderdale–West Palm Beach, FL	2,842,751	46.1%	Cuban 41.6% Colombian 9.2% Puerto Rican 8.4%
4. Houston–The Woodlands–Sugar Land, TX	2,685,133	38.0%	Mexican 73.6% Salvadoran 8.0% Honduran 3.9%
5. Riverside–San Bernardino–Ontario, CA	2,422,979	52.1%	Mexican 86.6% Salvadoran 2.6% Other 2.2%
6. Dallas–Fort Worth–Arlington, TX	2,218,929	29.3%	Mexican 81.7% Salvadoran 4.62% Puerto Rican 2.29%
7. Chicago–Naperville–Elgin, IL–IN–WI	2,137,478	22.6%	Mexican 77.8% Puerto Rican 9.8% Other 12.4%
8. Phoenix–Mesa–Scottsdale, AZ	1,548,788	31.3%	Mexican 85.9% Other 3.6% Puerto Rican 2.9%
9. San Antonio–New Braunfels, TX	1,420,885	55.7%	Mexican 88.3% Other 4.5% Puerto Rican 2.4%
10. San Diego–Carlsbad, CA	1,138,371	34.1%	Mexican 89.0% Puerto Rican 2.2% Other 1.3%

Source: 2020 Census.

City	Latino population	% of city population
New York	2.42 million	28.9%
Los Angeles	1.90 million	48.1%
Houston	1.02 million	44.5%
San Antonio	989,877	64.7%
Chicago	772,791	28.6%

Figure 1.10. Largest Latino populations in U.S. cities.

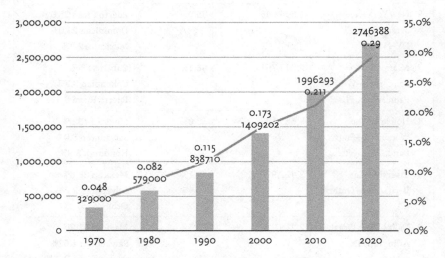

Figure 1.11. Growth in the City of Chicago Latino population, 1970–2020.

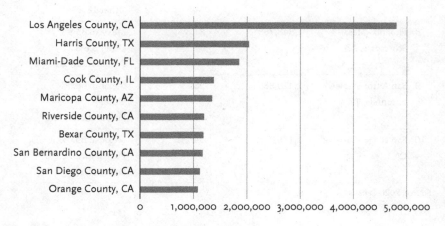

Figure 1.12. Top 10 counties by Hispanic population, 2020.

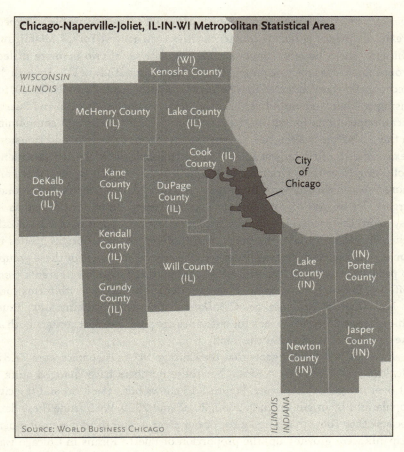

Figure 1.13. Chicago Metropolitan Statistical Area.

Figure 1.14 shows the growth in the Chicago MSA's Latino population in the decades between 1970 and 2020.

In 2020, the Chicago MSA was 22.6% Latino, making Chicago the seventh-largest Hispanic metropolitan area in the country, as shown in Table 1.2. The far right column displays the top three regional origin groups in each location's MSA. We see that eight out of ten of these city areas had predominantly Mexican populations, which is unsurprising given that Mexicans form approximately 63% of the U.S. Latino population.

New York, Miami, and Chicago are the only MSAs whose second-largest origin group represents approximately 10% or more of local Hispanics. That is, the other seven cities have local Latino populations that are dominated by a Mexican presence, and the second-largest group does not reach 10% of the local Hispanic population. This is important for the topic of dialect contact: although Spanish speakers in all ten of these cities likely come into contact with

SPANISH IN THE U.S. AND CHICAGO [17]

speakers of other varieties of Spanish, it would seem reasonable to expect greater frequency of dialect contact in cities such as New York,[10] Miami, and Chicago, where there are more sizable populations of two or more dialect groups. Indeed, as we have noted, the first large-scale study of U.S. Spanish dialect contact was conducted in New York City (Otheguy & Zentella, 2012), focusing on Mainlanders and Caribbeans. Chicago's sizable Mexican and Puerto Rican populations constitute the fourth-largest Mexican-origin community in the U.S. (after Los Angeles, California; Riverside, California; and Houston, Texas) and the fifth-largest Puerto Rican community on the U.S. mainland (following New York, Orlando, Philadelphia, and Miami). In fact, there are more Mexicans in Chicago than in the city of Guadalajara, Mexico, the second-largest city in Mexico, and almost as many Puerto Ricans in Chicago as in Bayamón, the second-largest city in Puerto Rico. In addition to the possibility of dialect contact, the presence of different national-origin groups in a metropolitan area creates greater possibilities for members of these groups to produce mixed-ethnicity children—that is, those who have parents from different Latino groups, many of whom refer to themselves with terms such as *MexiRican*, *SalvaDominican*, *CubaDorian*, and other combinations. Thus, Chicago is an ideal site to look for outcomes of Spanish dialect contact both at the community level and at the family level.

The data in Table 1.2 show that the Chicago MSA's Hispanics were 77.8% Mexican and 9.8% Puerto Rican, but these numbers have changed quite a bit over the past thirty years. Figure 1.15 shows both the MSA and the city populations by origin in 1990, 2000, 2010, and 2020. We include these data because they show that when most of our second- and third-generation participants were growing up, the proportion of Puerto Ricans in Chicago was almost double what it is today.

In summary, Chicago is the fifth-largest city in the nation in terms of its Latino population, Cook County is the fourth-largest Hispanic county, and Chicago's MSA is the seventh-largest. All three areas have become increasingly Mexican since 1990, the MSA to a slightly greater extent.

Chicago is divided into 77 "community areas," as well as into the "South Side" and the "North Side" at Madison Avenue. These two designations have important meanings for residents in both areas. The slightly smaller North Side is home to more transplants from other U.S. locations, students and young professionals, white-collar jobs, and trendy restaurants, while South Side residents typically pride themselves on their tougher blue-collar ethos,

---

10. It is worth noting that Mexicans are now the fastest-growing Latino group in New York City, with a 7.7% increase between 1990 and 2015 compared to 3.0% for Dominicans and −8.3% among Puerto Ricans. By 2036, Mexicans are predicted to surpass Dominicans to become New York's second-largest Latino national subgroup (Center for Latin American, Caribbean, and Latino Studies, 2016).

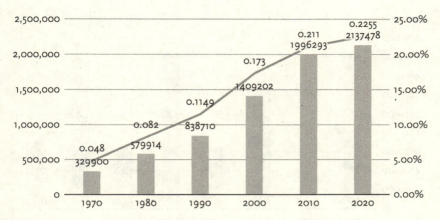

Figure 1.14. Growth in the Chicago MSA Latino population, 1970–2020.

their multigenerational presence in Chicago, and being where "the real meat of Chicago resides . . . the people and neighborhoods who built America with steel mills, won World War II with manufacturing and continue to supply the real muscle for Chicago's economic engine" (Condon, 2005). Baseball is another staunch dividing factor, with the Chicago Cubs playing at Wrigley Field on the North Side and the Chicago White Sox at Cellular Field on the South Side; serious White Sox fans "never, ever set foot in Wrigley Field except very grudgingly for Sox-Cubs games" (Solomon, 2009), and the only thing that seems to unite these sports enemies is their shared hatred of the St. Louis Cardinals.

Figure 1.16 shows the six community areas with the largest Latino populations and how their Census-reported proportions of Mexicans and Puerto Ricans have changed in the 30 years between 1990 and 2020. Of these six areas, two are on the South Side (Pilsen and La Villita, majority Mexican), and four are on the North Side (Hermosa, Humboldt Park, Logan Square, and West Town, which show a greater presence of Puerto Ricans).

There is a considerable amount of excellent scholarly work about Latino communities in Chicago, including book-length studies focusing on Mexicans (Bada, 2014; Farr, 2006; García, 2012; Guerra, 1998; Ramírez, 2011; Zimmerman, 2018), Puerto Ricans (Pérez, 2004; Ramos-Zayas, 2003; Toro-Morn & García, 2019), Mexican and Puerto Rican interactions (Fernández, 2012; De Genova & Ramos-Zayas, 2003; Rosa, 2019) and about Latinos in general (Cruz, 2007; Farr, 2005; Pallares & Flores-González, 2010). We summarize here some salient facts about the history of Mexican and Puerto Rican arrivals in the city. Mexicans began arriving in Chicago in the 1910s, mostly men working in semiskilled and unskilled jobs. During the 1940s, *bracero* workers (a federal program to fill the labor shortage in agriculture because of World War II) began to arrive in the city, and its Mexican population rose to 16,000. Pilsen and La Villita (Figure 1.17) became solidified as Mexican

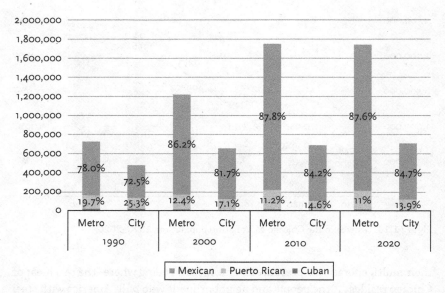

Figure 1.15. MSA and City of Chicago Hispanic populations, percentage by origin. (Sources: Paral, Ready, Chun, Sun 2004, Appendix 2, Table 4; and 2010 and 2020 Census.)

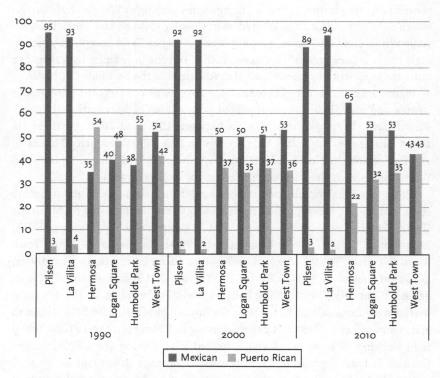

Figure 1.16. Percentage of neighborhood Hispanic populations that are Mexican and Puerto Rican in Chicago's six largest Hispanic communities.

neighborhoods in the 1960s and 1970s and have been close to 90% Mexican since 1990. These areas physically demarcate themselves as Mexican spaces through an archway that reads *Bienvenidos a Little Village* (Welcome to Little Village), multiple colorful murals, and business names reflecting Mexican towns and states. These neighborhoods also proudly boast that 26th Street generates more sales tax than any other area in Chicago except the expensive and touristy stretch of Michigan Avenue called the Magnificent Mile. However, the area is slowly experiencing gentrification and the arrival of vintage clothing stores, upscale restaurants, and white residents.

As for Puerto Ricans, Chicago is home to one of the largest and most organized Puerto Rican communities in the United States. Many working-class Puerto Ricans came to Chicago in the late 1940s and early 1950s as contract workers following the failure of Puerto Rico's modernization project to support the labor needs of the population on the island, known as Operation Bootstrap. A steady stream of migrants continued to arrive up through the 1980s, both for economic reasons and to join family members from earlier migrations. Scholar Ralph Cintrón has described the leadership of the city's Puerto Rican Cultural Center, combined with several social service institutions and affordable housing agencies, as constituting for Chicago Puerto Ricans a "concentration of effort and devotion to the community [that] is completely unusual, completely remarkable, [and] not anything that you see in New York City, Miami, Orlando, or anywhere else around the country" (Agrelo et al., 2019). He further states that when compared with other locations, community members in Chicago are more politically homogeneous in their support of the Puerto Rican independence movement, that the community is smaller and not as widely dispersed as on the East Coast, and that due to their experiences of marginalization and gentrification, Chicago Puerto Ricans "have, over many years, been quite articulate in their analyses of United States colonialism over Puerto Rico."

Chicago Puerto Ricans have tended to live on the city's North Side, where population changes have been more dynamic than on the South Side. Humboldt Park (Figure 1.18), frequently considered the epicenter of the Chicago Puerto Rican community,[11] is demarcated by two enormous steel Puerto Rican flags that arch above Division Street, as well as numerous murals and displays of regional and national flags. Yet the area's proportion of Mexicans has been increasing and the proportion of Puerto Ricans decreasing. For example, as shown in Figure 1.15, in 1990, the Latinos residing in Humboldt Park and Hermosa were approximately 55% Puerto Rican, but by 2000, they shifted to 51% Mexican, and by 2010, Hermosa's Hispanics were 65% Mexican. The only

---

11. There was a thriving Puerto Rican community in Lincoln Park in the 1960s, including the family of former U.S. House of Representatives member Luis Gutiérrez, but they were pushed out by gentrification. Many ended up in Humboldt Park.

Figure 1.17. La Villita neighborhood.

neighborhood that saw its proportion of Mexicans decrease somewhat substantially was West Town, where in 1990, the Hispanic population was 52% Mexican but was 43% in 2010. Due to gentrification, Logan Square has lost more Hispanic residents than of any of the city's 77 community areas: between 2000 and 2014, around 19,200 Hispanic residents moved out of the area, a 36% decrease (U.S. Census Bureau, 2016).

These trends reflect an overall decrease in the proportion of Puerto Ricans in Chicago.[12] Looking again at Figure 1.16, in 1990, three neighborhoods had more Puerto Ricans than Mexicans (Hermosa, Logan Square, and Humboldt Park), but by 2000, this was not the case in any neighborhood. Humboldt Park's population is also 40% African American, meaning that Puerto Ricans here are in greater contact with neighbors who speak English than are Mexicans in Pilsen or La Villita a point we will return to later.

In Chapter 2, we will display the areas where our study participants were raised; there were 56 who grew up on the North Side and 51 on the South Side. We conclude this section with an illustrative quote by Chicago-raised writer Hector Alamo, who described these two regional origin groups and their sense of space and of each other in the city:

> As a North Sider and a Puerto Rican, born and raised a bit in the Humboldt Park area, I'd never been to the South Side, except to go to one of the museums along the lakefront. I only stepped foot in La Villita during a class outing during my last year of college. I came to Pilsen as writer for a predominately Mexican art-activism media company based in the neighborhood, and for a while I was the only writer who discussed Puerto Rican issues and the goings-on in Humboldt

---

12. Chicago's Puerto Rican proportion grew slightly in the aftermath of Hurricane María, with around 1,600 individuals arriving in the city (Spielman, 2017).

Park. Mind you, nearly everyone in the group was Mexican, young and progressive; many were even leftists. And yet, geography and nationalism kept them from exploring much beyond their own Mexicentrism, just as it had kept me from knowing much about their world and their culture. (Alamo, 2017)

1.4. MEXICANS AND PUERTO RICANS IN CHICAGO: COMPLEX RELATIONSHIPS

Puerto Ricans and Mexicans have shared a long and complex relationship in Chicago marked by a history of both collective mobilization and fading animosities. This poem by Alamo (2017) the writer cited above, captures perceptions held by some Mexicans and Puerto Ricans:

> Mexicans hate Puerto Ricans and vice versa
>
> Mexicans think Puerto Ricans are the lazy, gibbering, thieving [n-word] of Latin America
>
> Puerto Ricans think Mexicans are the lazy, gibbering, thieving savages of Latin America
>
> Marriage between the two still remains something of a taboo
>
> Both are glad they're not Haitians
>
> Both are puppets of the same empire
>
> Hondurans hate Mexicans too, and vice versa
>
> And for similar reasons, everybody likes Cubans

If this were the case, we would expect very little interaction between members of the two groups and few attempts to accommodate to each other's dialects. That is, we would expect Figure 1.7 shown earlier. However, Aparicio (1999, 2019) noted that Chicago has a historical trajectory of intra-Latino contact, and according to Pérez (2003), Chicago is in fact the only U.S. city where large numbers of Mexicans and Puerto Ricans have been sharing community space for generations. This section explores Chicago as an urban Latino space by focusing on the coexistence of Mexicans and Puerto Ricans, describing studies of interactions between the two groups and ideologies some hold about each other in order to provide context for understanding the experiences of our participants. That is, to what extent do they interact, and what attitudes do they hold toward each other? This question is beginning to be asked in other areas of the country as well, as seen in a *New York Times* article from 2003 titled "Little but Language in Common; Mexicans and Puerto Ricans Quarrel in East Harlem" (Feuer, 2003) and in syndicated cartoonist

Gustavo Arellano's "¡Ask a Mexican!" from 2011 titled "Do Mexicans Hate Puerto Ricans?" which specifically addresses New York and California populations. The answers to these questions have ramifications for linguistic outcomes of Spanish dialect contact.

The first studies of contact between Mexicans and Puerto Ricans in Chicago came from the field of sociology. E. Padilla (1947) documented early interactions between these two groups via events organized by steel foundries to encourage socializing between male Mexican *braceros* and female Puerto Rican recruited laborers. Almost thirty years later, F. Padilla (1985, no relation to E. Padilla), largely credited with coining the term *latinidad*, examined interactions between the two groups from an institutional perspective, studying how they put aside differences in order to fight for collective benefits. He argued that they forged a "Latino" identity despite their substantial ethnic and cultural boundaries in order to achieve political mobilization. A more recent manifestation of Mexican–Puerto Rican collaboration for political unity is the participation of Puerto Ricans, who by birth are U.S. citizens, in Chicago's pro-immigrant-rights movement. This underlay the chant used by a group of 2007 demonstrators: *¡Boricua y mexicano, luchando mano a mano!* ("Puerto Rican and Mexican, fighting hand in hand!") documented in Rodríguez Muñiz (2010).

However, in other work examining day-to-day interactions, some members of these groups have been found to position themselves as fundamentally different from each other. For example, Pérez's (2003) descriptively titled article "Puertorriqueñas rencorosas y mexicanas sufridas" explored the gendered ways in which these groups articulated their identities. She found that Puerto Rican women accused Mexican women of being *sufridas* (long-suffering) at the hands of abusive husbands, yet the Mexican women considered patience and forgiveness among their virtues. The Mexican women found Puerto Rican women too *rencorosas* (unforgiving), yet the Puerto Rican women were proud of their independence and knowledge of their rights. To date, the most in-depth exploration of Mexican–Puerto Rican social contact in Chicago is De Genova and Ramos-Zayas (2003). They examined how these two groups understood and reproduced differences between each other, and how those differences were linked to a "larger social framework of racialized inequalities of power and opportunity" (p. 2). The term *racialization* refers to the discursive assignment of race-based meanings to a social group. A range of factors emerged as significant in how Mexicans and Puerto Ricans racialized one another, including U.S. citizenship, participation in federal welfare assistance programs, gender and family ideologies, and perceived levels of modernity. Specifically, Mexicans were accused by Puerto Ricans of being illegal immigrants, "taking" all the jobs, and being too docile, "backward," or excessively traditional. Puerto Ricans were criticized by Mexicans for being lazy (mainly for accepting government welfare benefits despite having legal work status) as well as for not maintaining intact families, not attending church, and for being too loud and brash. Thus, it is unfortunately the case that some members of these two groups, in addition to being racialized and negatively stereotyped by the hegemonic Anglo majority, also engage in racializing and negatively stereotyping each other. De Genova and Ramos-Zayas (2003) concluded that Mexicans and Puerto Ricans in Chicago articulate their identities largely through discourses that clearly distinguish them from each other; in other words, part of being Puerto Rican in Chicago is being *not* Mexican, and vice versa.

In addition to these racialized stereotypes, the Spanish language was found to be "an especially salient object around which to produce difference" rather than a uniting factor (p. 145). First-generation Mexicans expected that Mexicans of all generations should know Spanish, including those raised in the U.S., and expressed a sense of betrayal when they did not. They also characterized Puerto Rican Spanish as inferior to Mexican Spanish, a value judgment that many Puerto Ricans shared; Puerto Ricans often claimed that their own group did not speak "proper" Spanish, reflecting internalized linguistic insecurity. Ghosh-Johnson (2005), too, found animosity between Mexican and Puerto Rican high school students in Chicago, who held linguistic ideologies asserting that Mexicans spoke "better" Spanish than Puerto Ricans. The students believed that Mexican families placed more emphasis on Spanish maintenance while Puerto Ricans were "street," which also echoes the "traditional vs. modern/urban" discourses identified by Pérez (2003).[13] Although many first-generation Puerto Ricans expressed concerns about their children's retention of Spanish, the trend was for "urbanized bilingual Puerto Ricans . . . [to demonstrate] greater wherewithal to successfully adapt to the social order of white supremacy and Anglo hegemony in the U.S." (De Genova & Ramos-Zayas, 2003, p. 161). However, despite Mexican wishes to the contrary, what Puerto Ricans and Mexicans had in common was that they were "drawn together by a *latinidad* that actually derived not from shared Spanish language but rather from a shared erosion of Spanish" (p. 168). Potowski (2004) documented precisely such a shift from Spanish to English use across three generations in the city. In summary, despite their common fate of language shift from Spanish to English, De Genova and Ramos-Zayas (2003) found that Chicago Mexicans and Puerto Ricans employed highly divergent discourses about language to fortify the racialized differences between them—discourses about spoken accents, particular words and idiomatic expressions, and perceived "correctness" of Spanish, with Mexican Spanish emerging on top of the hierarchy.

---

13. We do not delve further into Ghosh-Johnson (2005) or her dissertation study because the high school students she studied used English almost exclusively among themselves.

Figure 1.18. Paseo Boricua. (Photos by Kim Potowski.)

More positive manifestations of *latinidad* were found by García and Rúa (2007), who studied participation in two Chicago ethnic festivals, Mexican independence day and the Puerto Rican parade. They noted that "it would be expected that each group would only attend their respective event, oblivious or dismissive of the other" (p. 327), but instead, they found what they termed "complex moments of convergence" (p. 318 and elsewhere). These included the fact that at the annual Fiesta Boricua[14] on Division Street, in addition to the sea of Puerto Rican flags carried by attendees, one can now also see Mexican flags. Figure 1.19 shows such an example from the 2019 Fiesta Boricua.

Meanwhile, on the traditionally Mexican South Side, Puerto Rican Congressman Luis Gutiérrez participated in the Mexican Fiesta del Sol parade on a float decorated with Puerto Rican flags and playing Puerto Rican *plena* music, changing the lyrics of the popular song "Qué bonita bandera" (What a Beautiful Flag) from *la bandera puertorriqueña* (the Puerto Rican flag) to *la bandera mexicana*[15] (the Mexican flag). Similarly, Rosa (2019), in his ethnography of a public high school on Chicago's North Side, describes processes wherein "becoming and unbecoming Mexican, Puerto Rican, Hispanic, Latinx must be reframed as multidimensional processes that demonstrate linkages between diaspora, national (be)longing, and institutional experiences of difference" (p. 72). He argues that Mexicans and Puerto Ricans in Chicago mimic a "close-knit family," whereby they understand, embrace, and even deride their perceived differences. Thus, it may be that the largely negative discourses produced by first-generation immigrant Mexicans and Chicago-raised Puerto Ricans found by De Genova and Ramos-Zayas (2003) are limited to their generational group.

---

14. *Boricua* means Puerto Rican. The term originated in *Boriken*, the word used to refer to the island currently known as Puerto Rico by its original inhabitants, the Taino Indians, before the arrival of the Spaniards.
15. Flags carry important symbolic value among Latinos across the U.S. and are commonly displayed on vehicles and other public and private items. See Potowski (2016) for the ways in which MexiRicans deploy both flags to index a compound ethnic identity.

In order to investigate this further, Potowski (2015) analyzed a subset of interviews from the CHISPA corpus (greater details about the corpus appear in Chapter 2). Specifically, she examined interviews with first-, second-, and third-generation[16] Mexicans and Puerto Ricans who were asked questions about stereotypes that Mexicans and Puerto Ricans invoke about each other, as well as their opinions about each variety of Spanish. Three of the negative stereotypes evidenced in De Genova and Ramos-Zayas's (2003) work emerged with frequency:

- Mexicans as undocumented
- Puerto Ricans as reprehensible for accepting welfare
- Puerto Ricans as too loud and scandalous

Interestingly, however, there was a noticeable shift across generations. G1 Mexicans and Puerto Ricans were more likely to produce these racialized discourses, while the G2 and G3 respondents more often cited "rumors" that these two groups do not get along, either citing personal counter-evidence that these rumors were untrue or reporting that although they had indeed witnessed conflicts between the groups, they themselves had not had any negative experiences with the other group. Thus, while Potowski (2015) found additional evidence of friction between Mexicans and Puerto Ricans in Chicago, these conflicts appeared to be largely restricted to the immigrant groups and to dissipate with successive generations. There are at least two reasons later generations of Mexicans and Puerto Ricans might hold fewer negative attitudes toward the outgroup. First, generation is often correlated with citizenship among Mexicans. Most G2s and, by definition, all G3 Mexicans are citizens, while approximately 30% of all G1 foreign-born Mexican individuals in the city are without documents; all of the Mexicans in De Genova and Ramos-Zayas's (2003) study were G1. Undocumented status could simultaneously elicit greater scorn among Puerto Ricans toward Mexicans because the latter are perceived as "taking" jobs, as well as greater scorn among Mexicans toward Puerto Ricans because if they themselves are undocumented, they are ineligible for public aid, which Puerto Ricans are entitled to receive. A second possible explanation for diminishing animosities is that G1s have spent a relatively smaller proportion of their lives sharing social space with outgroup members, while G2s and G3s have lived their entire childhoods and adult lives in Chicago, many sharing neighborhoods, schools, and workplaces with members of the other group. This increased contact could result in more positive intergroup attitudes. In fact, the very existence of MexiRican individuals to

---

16. Chapter 2 explains the definitions of generational groups used in this book. The abbreviation "G1" refers to first generation, "G2" to second generation, and "G3" to third generation.

be discussed ahead is a result of romantic relationships between Mexican and Puerto Rican individuals.

Regarding language ideologies, recall that De Genova and Ramos-Zayas (2003) found that Mexicans were positioned both by themselves and by Puerto Ricans as possessing both a superior dialect and greater proficiency in Spanish. Potowski's data (2015) revealed a more nuanced mosaic of linguistic ideologies that, again, varied according to generation. Puerto Rican and Mexican individuals, equally distributed across the three generations, were asked whether Mexican and Puerto Rican Spanish were different and, if so, to describe the differences. They were also asked whether one variety of Spanish was "better" than the other. Every single participant could describe the other group's Spanish, and the features of Puerto Rican Spanish frequently mentioned included:

- Puerto Rican coda /s/ weakening: [e.tá] or [eh.tá] for *estás* (you are)
- Lambdacisms: [a.mól] for *amor* (love)
- Velarized /r̄/: [cá.xo] for *carro* (car)

Participants also expressed that Puerto Rican Spanish was *cortado* (cut off) as a result of weakened or deleted intervocalic /d/ (for example, [kom.práo] for *comprado,* bought). Both groups also frequently claimed that Puerto Rican Spanish was spoken at a faster pace, as well as being "hard," "strong," or "loud"—judgments that, again, echo Pérez's (2003) gendered evaluations of Puerto Ricans as *rencorosas*. Fewer descriptions were offered of Mexican phonology, but among them was that it was *cantado* (sung) and spoken at a slower pace.

A third of the participants, when offering descriptions of the other group's Spanish, did so as a criticism. For example, rather than neutrally commenting that coda /s/ was weakened, they claimed that such individuals pronounced words "incorrectly." Yet only one such criticism was about Mexican Spanish;[17] the other criticisms were about Puerto Rican Spanish. Thus, similar to what was found by De Genova and Ramos-Zayas (2003), Potowski found that Puerto Rican Spanish in Chicago suffered from greater stigmatization than Mexican Spanish. Furthermore, it was Puerto Ricans themselves who participated most actively in devaluing Puerto Rican Spanish. The specific negative comments about Puerto Rican Spanish were fairly homogeneous whether they came from Mexicans or Puerto Ricans. Puerto Rican Spanish was described as *machucado* (mashed-up, ground), representing poor pronunciation or even a lack of ability to articulate particular

---

17. This was by a G1 Puerto Rican, who said that Mexicans were *groseros* (foul-mouthed), especially with their frequent use of the word *cabrón* (bastard), which is substantially more offensive in Puerto Rico than in Mexico.

sounds "correctly," and their Spanish was said to be full of "Spanglish." Only two Puerto Rican women were adamant in their rejection of any positioning of their Spanish as inferior. Yet this, too, varied by generation, with criticisms spiking among G2 interviewees. Only three G1s expressed any negative evaluations of outgroup Spanish. But among the second generation, fully half of both groups did so.

A possible explanation is that members of G1, who immigrated as adults, are linguistically secure about their Spanish and do not feel a need to criticize other dialects. G2s as a group are less proficient in Spanish than G1s (we will see ahead that this is true to a statistically significant degree) and often express insecurity about their Spanish. This insecurity among G2s might make them more likely to reproduce prevalent discourses of Spanish hierarchies; that is, Mexicans might more likely be critical of Puerto Rican Spanish and Puerto Ricans of their own Spanish. But why might criticisms of Puerto Rican Spanish drop dramatically among G3 Mexicans? Although all of the G3 participants were able to carry out an interview in Spanish, on average, their proficiency was quite lower than that of their G2 counterparts. In fact, many G3s around the country have shifted entirely to English and develop very little productive capacity in Spanish (see Escobar & Potowski, 2015, for a review). It may be that Spanish no longer figures as prominently in G3 identity constructions, such that there is less at stake for their ethnocultural authenticity that is tied to the Spanish language. That is, many G3 Mexicans simply may not have as much invested in how other groups' Spanish sounds; they may in fact be impressed that anyone in their peer group knows any Spanish at all and may be reticent to criticize its features. Yet the Puerto Rican G3 criticisms of Puerto Rican Spanish remained at about half the participants, perhaps as a vestige of the general stigma assigned to Puerto Rican Spanish.

To what extent are these individuals' social and linguistic prejudices related? That is, social prejudices can shape linguistic ideologies such that a group that is viewed negatively subsequently has its language variety stigmatized as well (as found by Zentella, 1990). As discussed above, in this Chicago corpus, Puerto Ricans' and Mexicans' negative stereotypes about the other group were strongest in G1 and increasingly less present in G2 and G3, while negative linguistic evaluations peaked among G2 and were almost nonexistent among G1 and G3. That is, G1s showed the greatest social friction but the least linguistic friction, G2s showed less social friction but the greatest linguistic friction, and G3s showed little friction of either kind. Figure 1.19 offers a visual display of this relationship, with the most negative attitudes at the top of the y-axis.

Thus, there was no evidence that negative evaluations of Puerto Rican Spanish (lowest among G1s) were consistently related to negative social evaluations of Puerto Ricans (which were high among G1s). The criticisms of

Figure 1.19. Participants carrying Puerto Rican and Mexican flags at Fiesta Boricua, September 5, 2019. (Photo by Kim Potowski.)

Puerto Ricans "mistreating the language" and speaking it *machucado* (mashed-up, ground) are certainly related to an ideology of language standardization (Milroy, 2001) but one that seems to be losing ground in G3, very likely due, in part, to a loosening of the bond between the Spanish language and Latino identity. This decoupling of language from ethnic identity permits a wider variety of individuals to claim *latinidad* but also both reflects and sustains ideologies that permit Spanish loss.

In summary, the social and linguistic sentiments found by Potowski (2015) in Chicago among Mexicans and Puerto Ricans, although more positive than those found by De Genova and Ramos-Zayas (2003) and those expressed in Alamo's (2017) poem with which we began this section, provide a portrait of *latinidad* that includes negative social stereotypes (mostly among G1 individuals) and negative evaluations of Spanish (especially among G2s). However, tensions and negative stereotypes between Mexicans and Puerto Ricans in Chicago appear to be dissipating across generations, which was also captured in Alamo's (2017) conclusion: "Fortunately, much of my accusations carry less weight among the younger generations of Latinos, who are increasingly American-born, American-raised and, thus, more cosmopolitan and multicultural than their foreign-born, nationalistic and monocultural predecessors."

Such conditions, we propose, lead to the kinds of interactions that can generate dialect contact. Indeed, in Otheguy and Zentella's (2012) comparison of Caribbean and Mainlander Spanish speakers in New York City, it was interaction with members of the other group (which they termed "outgroup orientation") that was most correlated with subject pronoun use. As noted by Hernández (2009) in his excellent treatment of social conditions among Salvadorans in Houston, an individual's inclination to accommodate their speech features to those of an interlocutor is closely linked to attitudes toward

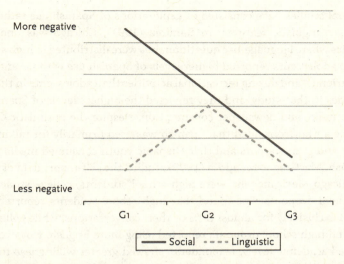

Figure 1.20. Chicago Mexicans' and Puerto Ricans' negative social and linguistic attitudes displayed together. (Potowski 2015.)

the interlocutor's language variety, which often goes hand in hand with attitudes toward the speakers themselves.

1.5. PRIOR STUDIES OF SPANISH IN CHICAGO

Having painted a broad picture of the Chicago neighborhoods where many Puerto Ricans and Mexicans live and some of the discourses they express about each other, we now describe the few studies that have been done on Spanish features in the city. Elías-Olivares et al. (1985) examined the use of the subjunctive in dubative contexts among Mexican-origin residents of Chicago's La Villita neighborhood, finding that normative use of the subjunctive was relatively high. The authors attributed this in part to the continued influx of recent Mexican immigrants to the area. Moreno-Fernández (2005) studied the Spanish lexical availability of Mexican-origin, Chicago-raised high school students in 22 semantic fields including the human body, clothing, parts of the house, and transportation. Of the 20 words most commonly produced in each domain, only 6.5% were Anglicisms, leading the author to conclude that these adolescents' Spanish lexicon was sufficiently solid for communication about general topics. Torres and Potowski (2008) studied the discourse markers *so* and *entonces*, finding that *so* was an integrated core borrowing across three generational groups, although Puerto Ricans used it more frequently than Mexicans. They also found that of several variables analyzed, weaker Spanish proficiency was most strongly correlated with more frequent usage of *so* at the expense of *entonces*.

Several studies have consisted of explorations of Spanish use rather than particular linguistic features. In Ramirez (1991), Chicago was one of 10 U.S. cities where language-use questionnaires were distributed in high schools. Chicago adolescents reported higher levels of Spanish use with parents, with school friends, and during recreational activities than adolescents in the other nine cities in that study, and they reported the highest levels of Spanish television, radio, and newspaper consumption. Despite the optimistic Chicago data, the author concluded that Spanish was used primarily for talking with parents and grandparents and that Hispanic youth consumed media mostly in English. MacGregor-Mendoza (1999) studied the self-report data of almost 300 Chicago Mexicans who were high school students, college students, or high school dropouts. She found that high school students reported using Spanish exclusively for almost 30% of their conversations, while college students and high school dropouts reported using more English. However, with increased academic levels, respondents showed greater willingness to incorporate Spanish in a wider variety of contexts and displayed greater loyalty to Spanish, although loyalty to English was also high, particularly among the dropouts. As a follow-up to Ramirez (1991), Potowski (2004) conducted a survey among 815 Latino high school and college students, asking them how often they spoke Spanish with different people. She found the same thing that has been found everywhere else in the country: a clear and steady decline in Spanish use from first- to second- to third-generation speakers. Gorman and Potowski (2009) found that second- and third-generation Latinos, instead of speaking frequently in Spanish with newly arrived immigrants, in fact reject them as neighbors, friends, and schoolmates for a variety of social reasons.[18] This challenges the notion that there is natural "recontact" (Cisneros & Leone, 1983) with new Spanish-speaking immigrants that necessarily creates opportunities for Chicago-raised individuals to speak Spanish, though we note that many high school students have not yet entered the labor force; we will see in Chapter 9 that the majority of speakers in our corpus did in fact use Spanish at work.

Moving from surveys to more qualitative methods, Parada (2013) investigated the role of birth order and proficiency of children in 18 Chicago families as reported by their mothers. She found clear patterns in both language use and competence: the first- and second-born children reported greater degrees of both than subsequent children. Potowski and Gorman (2011) examined the extent to which the Spanish language plays a role in Chicago *quinceañera* celebrations (a Catholic girl's rite of passage to becoming a woman at age 15). Of the 138 girls surveyed who had *quinceañeras* (the vast majority Mexican, with a few of Puerto Rican, Ecuadorian, and Guatemalan

---

18. Similar findings have been reported in California by Mendoza-Denton (1999) and García Bedolla (2003).

origin), 60% replied that Spanish was useful in their celebrations in order to communicate with family members, understand the mass, offer a short reading from the Bible, and send out invitations. However, they stated that an English-language mass was "acceptable," acknowledging the possibility of being Latina and not knowing Spanish. Although Spanish was not seen as required, the majority of respondents indicated it was important because "the tradition of a *quinceañera* is from a Hispanic background" (p. 81). For another cultural ritual event, Gelb (2005) looked at Spanish in a *santería*[19] initiation. Although the narratives took place in English, the author found significant uses of Spanish terminology (*madrina, botánica, matasano, matanza, santo, diablo, sopera*) and some Hispanicized Yoruba terms (*ocha*, from the Yoruba *orisha*, saint).

In summary, prior studies of Spanish in Chicago are relatively few given the large and long-standing communities it has been home to. They show that Spanish is a vibrant part of the fabric of local Latino communities and that its use is viewed positively but decreases with each generation. Given that 28.8% of the city's Latinos are foreign-born, it seems that, similarly to the case in other cities around the U.S., only new immigration keeps the language vibrant (in our color analogy, the continual influx of blue), because across generations it is shifting from purple to red. In addition, linguistic work in the city has not profitably examined the potential presence of dialect contact between Mexican and Puerto Rican Spanish.

1.6. SUMMARY

Chicago is home to a vibrant Spanish-speaking community of at least three generations, composed primarily of Mexicans and Puerto Ricans, many of whom share community spaces and express positive attitudes toward each other and even have children together. However, we have seen that as in the rest of the U.S., Spanish in Chicago is in a situation of contact (both with English and with other varieties of Spanish) and is frequently lost by the third generation.

The research questions motivating our study of Spanish in Chicago were as follows:

1. How do speakers in different generations and regional origins compare on five Spanish features - lexicon, discourse markers, codeswitching, the subjunctive, and phonology?

---

19. *Santería* is a syncretic Afro-Cuban religion developed from the beliefs of the African Yoruba people with some elements of Catholicism.

2. Which changes seem more attributable to contact with English and which to dialect contact?
3. Of the features that change across generations, do any appear to change in tandem?
4. What factors in the lives of our speakers led to the development of the Spanish they currently speak?

Through an analysis of 124 interviews with Puerto Ricans, Mexicans, and MexiRicans, we ask whether Chicago Spanish undergoes processes more like those alluded to in Figure 1.5, Figure 1.6, or Figure 1.7 and seek to measure with some degree of accuracy the presence of different colors at different points—the amount of blue in the purple or the specks of red it might contain. As we will show in Chapters 3 through 7, the five linguistic features we have chosen to study have been profitably examined in other locations but none within the same corpus and not always across three generations of speakers and/or two different regional origins. Furthermore, no studies besides Potowski (2016) have examined "mixed" individuals such as MexiRicans, who can shed light on intrafamilial dialect contact.

Our speakers' interviews contain not just linguistic features but also narratives about life in Chicago, addressing how the children and grandchildren of immigrants learned Spanish and use it in their daily lives. Harking back to another of our analogies, we treat each interview as if it were a multifaceted gemstone, examining it from many angles, shining light through it, and asking what chemicals and geological forces went into forming it, while also comparing it to other stones in the corpus. We seek to understand the conditions under which the gemstone that is Spanish in Chicago can grow and thrive, with an eye toward contributing to strengthening such conditions for the future.

CHAPTER 2
The Chicago Spanish (CHISPA) Corpus

2.1. INTRODUCTION

This chapter describes the Chicago Spanish corpus, or CHISPA (CHI-cago SPA-nish), and how it was collected and analyzed. We set out to compile a corpus of interviews in Spanish with Mexicans and Puerto Ricans of three generational groups. Initial contacts for participants were made among our undergraduate students at the University of Illinois at Chicago (UIC) and DePaul University as well as via friends and acquaintances throughout the city. Once a person was interviewed, they were asked for recommendations for other potential interviewees. This recruitment through personal networks and subsequent snowballing took place between 2006 and 2010. Early in the process, a young woman showed up for an interview at UIC. We had her listed as Mexican, but during the initial questions, she revealed that one of her parents was Puerto Rican. We decided to interview her anyway, figuring that her data would later be discarded, but we were fascinated by the ways in which her parents' different backgrounds had influenced her life experiences and her Spanish. Thus, we decided to add MexiRicans as a category, which led to Potowski (2016) and the term *intrafamilial dialect contact*. We note that throughout this book, we frequently use the term *Mexican* to refer to individuals born and raised in Mexico as well as their descendants in Chicago, for whom the term *Mexican American* might be more accurate. However, many Latinos in the U.S. in fact prefer the country of origin of their families as ethnic identifier terms (Taylor et al., 2012). Similarly, we use the term *Puerto Rican* to refer to individuals born and raised on the island of Puerto Rico as well as their descendants in Chicago. The majority of individuals we interviewed with one Puerto Rican parent and one Mexican parent seem to prefer the term *MexiRican* (Potowski, 2016).

We describe here the different categories of speakers we sought to represent in a stratified sample, followed by a description of other features that

Spanish in Chicago. Kim Potowski and Lourdes Torres, Oxford University Press. © Oxford University Press 2023.
DOI: 10.1093/oso/9780199326143.003.0002

we did not treat as variables but that provide context for understanding the corpus. We then describe the interview procedures.

2.2. GENERATIONAL GROUPS

Interviews were conducted with a total of 124 individuals belonging to the groups shown in Table 2.1. In sociolinguistic work on Spanish in the U.S., *generation* (abbreviated throughout this monograph as G) has been defined as shown in Table 2.2.

The main determinant of generational category for G1, G1.5, and G2 is the age of arrival in the U.S. This is because there is frequently a relationship between a later age of arrival and greater exposure to and proficiency in Spanish. Individuals raised in Latin America until the age of 12 are considered linguistically mature in Spanish and have mostly converged on the linguistic systems of adults in their community. They have typically attended school in their country of origin and thus received academic instruction in Spanish.

However, there is evidence that after the age of 8, most people will not lose the major morphosyntactic parameters they have acquired in their language, even if they move to an area where the language is not spoken (a review of this work appears in Montrul, 2008), which is why we lowered the age of arrival to 9 to be considered a G1. We underscore the fact that generational categories are merely approximations of life circumstances; there is nothing about turning 10 years old that suddenly makes a person's arrival in the U.S. linguistically different from if they had arrived a week before their 10th birthday. For this reason, in addition to our linguistic analyses by generational category, throughout this book we include additional analyses based on Spanish proficiency level.

We did not have any participants who arrived between 9 and 12 years of age, so the different categorization we are proposing for G1 was relevant to our data only when determining participants' G2 or G3 status via their parents, as we will explain.

Table 2.1. CHISPA CORPUS BY GENERATIONAL GROUPS AND REGIONAL ORIGINS.

	G1	G2	G3	Total
Mexican	12	15	12	39
Puerto Rican	11	16	13	40
MexiRican	—	19	26	45
Total	23	50	51	124

Table 2.2. SOCIOLINGUISTIC DEFINITIONS OF GENERATION CATEGORIES, STUDIES OF U.S. SPANISH.

	Age of arrival/other	
Generational category	Silva-Corvalán (1994) and others	Potowski & Torres (this study)
G1	12+ years	9 years
G1.5	6–11 years	6–8 years
G2	0–5 years, or born in U.S. to G1 parents	
G3	Born in U.S. and at least one parent is G2	

G1 (First Generation)

Among our 23 first-generation (G1) participants, 12 had immigrated from Mexico and 11 from Puerto Rico. For these 23 participants, Appendix A shows their ages of arrival, current age at the time of the interview, the number of years they had been in the U.S. at that time, and what Erker and Otheguy (2020) call PLUS (percentage of life in the U.S.), which is the number of years in the U.S. divided by their age. Only two of the G1 participants had been in Chicago for one year or less, and the remainder (74%) had been there for almost 20 years or more. The average number of years in Chicago was 27.7, and the average PLUS was 56%.

Although, as we have mentioned, G1 participants are usually considered to have arrived in the U.S. with a fully developed Spanish system, we make no claims that they are representative of current systems in their countries of origin, principally given the number of years they have lived in the U.S. with intensive exposure to English.[1] We do, however, consider them an appropriate baseline comparison group for the G2 and G3 participants' language use, given that their Spanish is representative of the linguistic input that their G2 and G3 children and grandchildren receive.

G1.5

There were five G1.5 participants who arrived between the ages of 6 and 8. Given this small *n* size, we collapsed them with the G2 group for our analyses, but we will see that they sometimes evidenced patterns of Spanish use and overall proficiency levels that were slightly higher than the G2 average.

---

1. Length of time lived in the U.S. may influence individuals' Spanish features in noticeable ways (Montrul, 2017).

G2 (Second Generation)

G2 or second-generation individuals are the children of G1 parents.[2] They were either born in the U.S. or arrived before age 6, when formal schooling typically begins. Many (but not all) G2 individuals spend their early childhoods monolingual or very dominant in Spanish—particularly if they are the first- or second-born children—but because they are raised and schooled in the U.S., English typically becomes their dominant language.

Of our G2 participants, 38 were born in Chicago and seven immigrated as children from Mexico or Puerto Rico between 6 months and 5 years of age (recall that information about the ages of arrival, number of years in the U.S., and PLUS is displayed in Appendix A). The remaining 31 individuals in the G2 category were born in Chicago (average age 28) and thus have a PLUS of 100%.

We take a moment to point out that our five G1.5 speakers and our seven foreign-born G2 speakers all arrived before the age of 9. While we did not attempt to rate the English proficiency of any participants, it is possible that these speakers, particularly those who arrived after the age of 7, had English systems that were different from those of the rest of the G2 and G3 speakers.

G3 (Third Generation)

G3 or third-generation individuals were born in the U.S. and raised by at least one G2 parent, who, as we have just seen, by definition was also raised in the U.S. They are the grandchildren of individuals in G1 (although to our knowledge, none of our participants had parents or grandparents who were also in our corpus). We will see in Chapter 9 that many G3 individuals do not receive frequent and consistent input in Spanish, nor do they have many opportunities to interact with people who are monolingual in Spanish.[3]

The CHISPA corpus has a total of 51 G3 participants. We further distinguished two subcategories of G3 individuals based on whether one parent or both parents were G2 (Table 2.3). In other words, having one G2 parent automatically qualifies a person as G3. But while some G3 individuals have one G2 parent and one G1 parent, other G3 individuals have two parents who fit the G2 definition. We applied the label G3:1 to individuals with one G2 parent and another parent who was a G1, and G3:2 to those who had two G2 parents.

---

2. As far as we know, all of our participants had one female parent and one male parent, even if one parent (typically the father) was absent from the home. We were not made aware of any transgender parents or gay couples.
3. While some G2 and G3 individuals around the U.S. live transnationally (Smith, 2006; Farr, 2006), meaning that they spend frequent and extended periods of time in the Spanish-speaking country, none of our participants would be considered transnational by the commonly used definition of the term.

Table 2.3. THIRD-GENERATION SUBGROUPS.

	G3:1	G3:2	Total G3
Mexican	4	8	12
Puerto Rican	6	7	13
MexiRican	12	14	26
Total	22	29	51

We did this because during our initial examination of the G3 interviewees, G3:1 speakers seemed to have stronger Spanish proficiency than their G3:2 counterparts. This is not surprising given that the G1 parent was raised until at least the age of 9 in a Spanish-speaking country and seemed therefore more likely as an adult to have stronger levels of Spanish proficiency, as well as greater inclination to speak it to their children, than their G2 co-parent who was raised in the U.S. We will see that we identified a statistically significant difference in the Spanish proficiency of the 22 G3:1 speakers as compared with the 29 G3:2 speakers.

We mentioned earlier that the different categorization we are proposing for G1s—namely, lowering the age of arrival from 12 to 9 years old—was relevant to our data when determining the G2 or G3 status of speakers. Two of the handful of such cases are as follows. Speaker #82's father arrived from Puerto Rico at age 22 and her mother at age 10. The traditional classification would dictate that her mother was a G2 and therefore that #82 herself was a G3. However, our classification labels her mother a G1 and thus #82 as a G2. In another example, speaker #8's father arrived as an infant (making him a G2) and her mother at age 11. We classified her mother as a G1 and #8 as a G3:1.

These generational categories are by no means simple or homogeneous. Although we will see that our general prediction held that Spanish proficiency declines with each generational group, there were exceptions that we explore in Chapter 9. Furthermore, not all individuals fit neatly into the four generational categories we have identified here (G1, G2, G3:1, G3:2). We experienced complications in determining a participant's generational status in 10 cases. Consider an individual labeled G3:1 because they have one G1 parent and one G2 parent. But what if that G2 parent does not have any contact, leaving only the G1 parent to provide Spanish input? This individual would in fact be more like a G2 in that they were raised in a monolingual Spanish-speaking home. Yet under a strict application of the definition, the G2 parent, although absent, would earn the speaker the label of G3:1. This was the case with one of our participants who was raised by a single mother (according to the U.S. Census in 2011, 82% of custodial divorced parents in the U.S. are mothers).

Another case is that of a G3 with two U.S.-raised parents, but only one was in the home. Should the speaker be labeled a G3:1 based on who was in the home or a G3:2 based on parentage? Again, we applied the parentage definition, and these four speakers were labeled G3:2.

In the other three cases, although when recruiting participants we requested that both parents be Spanish speakers, we ended up with three participants with one non-Latino, non-Spanish-speaking parent.[4] One had a U.S.-born Mexican G2 father and an Irish American mother; we labeled this speaker a G3:2, exactly as we had done with the two individuals who were raised by a single G2 parent. The other two speakers had mothers who had arrived from Mexico in their late teens (that is, they were G1s), so we labeled both of these speakers G2s. This could be considered inconsistent since we did not "bump them up" to G3 status based on the non-Latino parent, but the later age of arrival of these mothers motivated this decision. If there had been more than a handful of speakers in these situations, we would have needed to establish a firmer set of criteria. We also had approximately a dozen participants who had grown up not with a sole parent but with a divorced one and had varying levels of contact with (and thus language input from) the noncustodial parent and their family and/or from one or two stepparents. There were also a few cases of participants' parents coming and going, usually between Puerto Rico and Chicago, during their own childhoods, complicating their own linguistic histories. Finally, although we had no cases like this in our corpus, an individual or one of their parents can be a G1.5, which would complicate classifications.

In the end, given the complications noted here as well as the differences in definitions of generational categories across studies, generational age cutoffs are somewhat arbitrary and not always revealing, even if they are useful in talking about general patterns and language transmission and maintenance versus shift and loss. Our corpus likely reflects many of the complexities found in Spanish-speaking communities around the U.S.

2.3. REGIONAL ORIGINS

There were three regional origin groups; we saw in Table 2.1 that there were 39 Mexicans, 40 Puerto Ricans, and 45 MexiRicans. The most frequently named places within Mexico were in the states of Zacatecas, Guerrero, and Michoacán,[5] and in Puerto Rico, they were Caguas, Arecibo, and Santurce.

---

4. A non-Spanish-speaking parent could also have been Latino, but we did not find this in our corpus.

5. Many Mexican-origin families in Chicago hail from Michoacán, as reflected in the title of Farr's 2006 book, *Rancheros in Chicagoacán*.

Table 2.4. MEXIRICAN GENERATIONAL AND PARENTAL CHARACTERISTICS.

Generational category	Mexican mother	Puerto Rican mother	Total
G2	6	12	18
G3	15	12	27
G3:1	6	9	15
G3:2	9	3	12
Total	**21**	**24**	**45**

The 45 MexiRican speakers in the CHISPA corpus had one Puerto Rican parent and one Mexican parent. The corpus ended up fairly balanced according to parental origins: 21 participants had a Mexican mother and a Puerto Rican father, and 24 had a Puerto Rican mother and a Mexican father (Table 2.4).

As with the corpus in general, when recruiting MexiRican participants, we requested that both parents had been present in the home while the participants were growing up. An absentee parent could have meant that the MexiRican individual was not exposed to one of the dialects and cultures. However, there ended up being 13 individuals who said that, at some point during their childhood, their parents did not live together. Of these individuals, 10 lived with their mothers. For some of these individuals, this circumstance meant very little contact with the father and his culture during their formative years, and for two individuals, it meant no contact with the mother. For a few other participants, however, the father lived nearby and spent significant time with his children. Four individuals had the following circumstance: their mother had married their father, gotten divorced, and remarried another man of the same ethnic background. Two were Puerto Rican women who had each married two Mexican men, and two were Mexican women who had each married two Puerto Rican men. Thus, in these four cases, despite the divorce from the biological father, the participant likely received daily exposure to their father's dialect and culture via their stepfather.

We further note that we do not have direct evidence that the Mexican parent used a predominance of Spanish features common to Mexico or that a Puerto Rican parent used a predominance of Spanish features common to Puerto Rico. Although participants typically stated that this was the case, some mentioned parents who spoke like the other's regional origin group, suggesting that spouses could accommodate to each other's variety. However, for the purposes of this study, we made the assumption that MexiRicans were exposed to substantial quantities of both varieties of Spanish while growing up, which was almost always the case.

2.4. SPANISH PROFICIENCY

Participants' proficiency in Spanish was a variable in our study but one that was determined only after a person had been interviewed. That is, we did not control for this in our study design. Just as second-language (L2) learners vary quite widely in their proficiency in their L2, bilinguals' levels of proficiency in their two languages vary. This strikes us as noncontroversial. However, it is no easy task to operationalize and then rate proficiency in a bilingual language variety in a reliable way. Despite the challenges that we will explore in this section, we sought to rate each of our speakers according to their global Spanish proficiency as represented in their oral interview, in which we attempted to get them to approximate how they naturally used language in their daily life.

We considered applying the Oral Proficiency Interview scale of the American Council on the Teaching of Foreign Languages (ACTFL) (see https://www.languagetesting.com/actfl-proficiency-scale for the 11 levels on this scale) because it is internationally recognized and because both of us have received training on this measure. However, it was created for L2 learners, not for bilingual heritage speakers, and Valdés (1989) and others have questioned its validity with U.S. Spanish. Ultimately, we decided it would be unnecessary to discriminate between so many levels of proficiency. Instead, we developed a simplified scale ranging from 1 (low) to 5 (high). A general description of each of these levels appears in Table 2.5. In general, characteristics that occur at a particular level, such as "compound verb tenses and hypotheticals may be infrequent or absent," are also present at the proficiency levels above it.

These holistic categories are not based on quantitative analyses of specific linguistic features. Rather, they are based on broad, qualitative impressions of speakers' proficiency. We note that in applying this scale, our goal was not to work from a deficit model of proficiency—to describe participants' Spanish in terms of what they do *not* have and *cannot* do—but rather to state what they *are* able to do and also where their language presents simplifications in discourse length, verb complexity, and lexicon. In other words, both of us are strongly opposed to criticizing or shaming U.S.-raised bilinguals for their ways of speaking (see Lynch & Potowski, 2014). As such, we recognize that these categories may be seen as prescriptivist and monolingual in their orientation, although it is far from our intention to promote such a perspective.

Furthermore, we recognize that the use of English by a bilingual does not imply a lack of proficiency in Spanish; a bilingual's languages are not zero-sum. For example, it may be the case that a bilingual, when speaking with another bilingual, says, "Allí entre todos, *you know*, comenzó *like, just being friends* y, se puso *more serious*" ("Among everyone there, you know, it started like, just being friends and, it became more serious") or "Es muy difícil que yo me meta en *that state of mind*" ("It's really difficult for me to get in that state of mind") (both produced by speaker #41, G3 Mexican female), yet if she had

Table 2.5. SPANISH PROFICIENCY LEVELS, ENTIRE CORPUS (*N* = 124).

Level	Description	n
5	Very fluent; largely indistinguishable from a Latin America–raised Spanish speaker. Frequent long stretches of discourse containing compound verb tenses and hypotheticals where necessary. Very infrequent or no use of English.	33
4	Very fluent but distinguishable from a Latin America–raised Spanish speaker. Some long stretches of discourse containing compound verb tenses and hypotheticals where necessary. Relatively infrequent or little use of English.	31
3	Fluent but with fairly frequent grammatical/vocabulary disfluencies and/or influence from English. Compound verb tenses and hypotheticals may be infrequent or absent. Some use of English.	34
2	Halted fluency. Few long stretches of discourse. Some basic verb tenses do not converge on normative paradigm. Frequent use of English.	21
1	Understands what the interviewer asks but answers a third or more of the time in English. Long pauses when producing Spanish.	5
Total		124

been speaking with a Spanish monolingual, she might have rendered them 100% in Spanish. However, it is also true that bilinguals who struggle to express themselves in Spanish often recur to English. There is no reliable way to identify when an English use is crutch-like versus when it is not, but pauses and filled pauses (*um*, etc.) provide a clue that a switch to English was likely due to a lack of ability to say something in Spanish, as in example 1:[6]

1. [Asked to describe how to play marbles]

Había una canica, era una más grande que las otras. Yo sé que después con las chiquititas you had to, mmm . . . le tenías que pegar a la, a la grande y moverla y echarla en un hoyo. (There was a marble, it was larger than the others. I know that then with the little ones, you had to mmm…you had to hit the, the big one and move it and put it in the hole.)

In addition, our speakers sometimes stated directly that they did not know how to say something in Spanish, as in example 2:

---

6. We have deleted the names of all people, streets of residence, and places of work to protect our participants' privacy. We further note that all participants filled out consent forms required by the Institutional Review Board of the University of Illinois at Chicago.

2. [Interviewer: ¿Hay problemas entre los latinos y los blancos o los negros, en general?]

Sí, yo creo que sí. I mean, a veces, um, como dice, los morenos, um, a lo mejor... I don't know how to say it... um... okay, a veces, um, como morenos son los minority y también los latinos como ellos, siempre están, como dice, como los americanos le hacen burla de ellos, entonces, los morenos hacen burla de los latinos, tú sabes. (#38, G2 Puerto Rican female)

[Interviewer: Are there issues between Latinos and white people or black people, in general?] Yes, I think so. I mean, sometimes, um, how do you say, brown people, um, maybe... I don't know how to say it... um... okay, sometimes, um, since brown people are the minority and Latinos too, like them, they're always, how do you say, like Americans make fun of them, so brown people make fun of Latinos, you know.

In Chapter 5, we will share our finding that some speakers whose Spanish we rated at level 4 or 5 had relatively high proportions of English use, suggesting that we may have been reasonably accurate at identifying crutch-like uses of English and that the presence of English material in the interviews did not inappropriately lower the Spanish proficiency ratings we assigned.

Each interview was rated for proficiency independently by both authors; a short sample from each of the five proficiency levels is presented in Appendix B. We coincided on 89% of the participants, a fairly high degree of inter-rater reliability. When our ratings did not match, they almost always differed by just one level, and in those cases, we worked through the interview a second time and came to an agreement on the final rating. We realize that there is a degree of subjectivity in this endeavor, although we note two caveats. First, we have had dozens of bilingual linguistics graduate students evaluate subsets of these interviews as an activity in our university courses, and the ratings have coincided to a great degree. Second, as we will see in a later section, a words-per-minute (WPM) comparison revealed statistically significant differences between the proficiency levels as we identified them, lending a degree of support to our ratings. Even if a different set of criteria were to be developed and applied and the resulting proficiency ratings differed from ours, we feel reasonably certain that the general linguistic trends between proficiency levels that we have identified throughout this book would still hold.

As mentioned in Chapter 1, Spanish proficiency typically declines from G1 to G2 to G3 of immigration to the U.S., which was true in this corpus (Table 2.6).

G1 speakers averaged a proficiency rating of 4.87 out of a maximum of 5.00. The individuals in G2 averaged a Spanish proficiency level of 3.76, while those in G3 were rated slightly lower at 2.77. The differences between all three

Table 2.6. AVERAGE SPANISH PROFICIENCY BY GENERATION.

G	Average proficiency 1 = low, 5 = high
G1 (n = 23)	4.87
G2 (n = 49)	3.76
G3 (n = 52)	2.77
All (n = 124)	3.53

Table 2.7. PROFICIENCY LEVELS OF G3:1 VS. G3:2 SPEAKERS.

G3:1 (n = 24)	3.08
G3:2 (n = 29)	2.52

groups were statistically significant ($F(2, 122) = 51.06$, $p < .001$). The Tukey post hoc analysis indicated that G1s have significantly higher proficiency means (M = 4.87) than both G2s (M = 3.77) and G3s (M = 2.76) and that the G2s (M = 3.77) have significantly higher proficiency than the G3s (M = 2.76) at the .05 level.

However, we must keep in mind that the G3 average proficiency level in this corpus—indeed, in any such corpus—is inflated. This is because there are many G3 individuals around the U.S. who would decline to participate in a study like ours, claiming that they are unable to hold a conversation in Spanish. If we included the very likely ratings of 1 or even 0 of the many such individuals around Chicago who have little to no productive capacity in Spanish, the average would be much lower than the 2.76 we found among these 52 G3 individuals who agreed to speak for an hour in Spanish.

We explained earlier that G3 individuals can have one G2 parent or two G2 parents. Our hypothesis was that G3 speakers with one G1 parent would evidence higher Spanish proficiency than those who had two G2 parents, because the G1 parent would likely be more proficient in Spanish and speak it more in the home than would two G2 parents in their home. Table 2.7 shows that we found evidence supporting this hypothesis.

We see that the 24 G3 speakers who had one G1 parent averaged a Spanish proficiency rating of 3.08 out of 5.00, while those with two G2 parents were rated on average at 2.52, and this difference was statistically significant [($t(52) = 2.28$, $p < .05$)]. We will see in Chapter 9 that grandparents played a

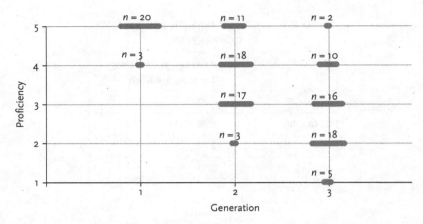

Figure 2.1. Proficiency level by generation. (Horizontal spread indicates the number of individuals at each level, not a difference in ratings.)

very strong role in the Spanish development of G3 individuals, often stronger than that of their parents.

In spite of the generational trend in Table 2.6 showing a clear decline in Spanish proficiency, generation was not always directly correlated with proficiency. Figure 2.1 shows how proficiency levels were spread across generational groups.

It is not surprising that almost all of the individuals (31 out of 33) whose proficiency was rated 5 were G1s or G2s. To develop such strong levels of Spanish, one needs fairly consistent input, which G1s had during their childhoods in Latin America and which many G2s raised in Chicago had via two immigrant parents who likely spoke a lot of Spanish in the home. However, we also see that approximately one third of G2 individuals ($n = 17$) were rated lower, at the level of 3. We explore in Chapter 9 some of the influences on Spanish proficiency outcomes across generational groups. This finding, that Spanish proficiency levels varied relatively widely for individuals in different generational groups, motivated us to incorporate Spanish proficiency as an additional variable in this study. Thus, in addition to looking at linguistic trends across generational groups, we also look at them across Spanish proficiency levels, and we then compare which of the two was more strongly correlated with the linguistic trends.

It was similarly unsurprising that 18 out of the 21 individuals rated at the low Spanish proficiency level of 2 belonged to the G3 group. Recall that G3 individuals have one or two parents who were raised in Chicago, where English is the dominant language, and who consequently are more likely to use English rather than Spanish in the home. A more pleasant surprise for those who work to promote intergenerational Spanish transmission is that there were ten G3 individuals with a relatively high Spanish proficiency level of 4, and two received the highest proficiency rating of 5. How did these grandchildren of immigrants develop such strong levels of Spanish, when the average proficiency for G3s was only 2.76? Chapter 9 will explore in greater detail some of the possible explanations behind these outlying cases, including birth order, the presence of Spanish-speaking grandparents in the home, and periods of time spent in Mexico or Puerto Rico.

A valid criticism of the scale we used is this: Why are three G1 individuals—all of whom were raised monolingually in Mexico or Puerto Rico—rated at a proficiency level of 4? Shouldn't a monolingually raised person be rated at the maximum level on any proficiency measure in their only language? We agree that an individual who is monolingual in a language is indeed a native and fully competent speaker of that language. Competence and proficiency are not exactly the same thing. For example, the ACTFL scale clearly admits that it privileges "educated" ways of speaking. Our scale, with criteria such as "Frequent long stretches of discourse containing compound verb tenses and hypotheticals where necessary" and "Very infrequent or no use of English," can be accused of doing the same thing. Let us consider the three G1 speakers who were rated as 4. One of them had moved permanently to Chicago at age 18 but had also spent three years (seventh, eighth, and ninth grade)[7] in Chicago, which may have been responsible for gaps in her Spanish. Another had arrived from Puerto Rico at age 18 and at the time of the interview had lived 50 years in Chicago, which may have affected her ability to express herself in Spanish. Finally, a 47-year-old woman had arrived from Mexico 21 years earlier, where she had only completed elementary school. Her responses were consistently short and simple, with few of the characteristics of a level 5 proficiency.

Next, we examine proficiency by generation and dialect group in Figure 2.2. We see that in each generational group, Mexicans were rated with higher proficiency levels than Puerto Ricans and MexiRicans, although these differences did not reach statistical significance.

Several possible explanations for this were mentioned in Chapter 1, including the fact that the language ideologies held by G1 Mexicans may make them more likely to insist on Spanish use in the home than their Puerto Rican counterparts, as well as the fact that Chicago residential patterns show that Puerto Ricans more frequently share neighborhoods such as Humboldt Park with English-speaking African Americans, while Mexicans more frequently live in high-density Mexican neighborhoods including La Villita and Pilsen. We have frequently heard the suggestion that the presence of English on the island of Puerto Rico may play a role in this difference in proficiency. While

---

7. In the U.S., students are usually 12 years old at the start of seventh grade, 13 at the start of eighth grade, and 14 at the start of ninth grade, which is the first year of high school.

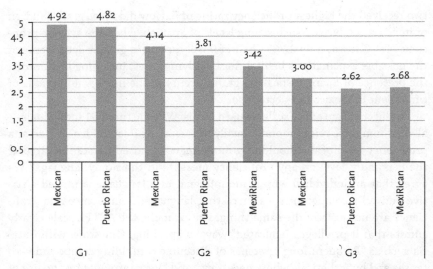

Figure 2.2. Average proficiency per generational and dialect group.

the presence of English on the island is undeniable, we do not believe that this detracts from the Spanish proficiency levels of most Puerto Rican individuals who migrate to the mainland. The G1 Puerto Ricans in our corpus, and the majority of those we have come into contact with over the past 20 years in Chicago, arrived just as monolingual in Spanish as did the G1 immigrants from Mexico. The fact that English lexical borrowings such as *zíper* (zipper) or *matre* (mattress) are common on the island does not mean these speakers have any English proficiency at all. Therefore, we reject the idea that Puerto Rican Spanish "has more English" or is in any way "less Spanish" than that of any other immigrant group from Latin America.

Words per Minute

Before moving on from our discussion of proficiency, we present information on the measure known as words per minute (WPM). Speech rate as measured by WPM has been shown to be closely related to a person's proficiency in a second language (Riggenbach, 1991). This connection has prompted some researchers to use WPM to categorize the overall fluency of bilingual heritage speakers.[8] Polinsky (2008) found that heritage Russian speakers with

---

8. Lexical proficiency tasks such as picture naming are also popular measures of heritage language proficiency (Polinsky, 2006). We examined participants' scores on a lexical identification task (Chapter 3) and found a significant positive correlation with our proficiency ratings.

[48] *Spanish in Chicago*

Table 2.8. THREE EXAMPLES OF THE CALCULATION OF WORDS PER MINUTE (WPM).

		Speech stretch 1	Speech stretch 2	Speech stretch 3	Avg. WPM
Speaker 1	words	115	51	46	123
	seconds	:51	:24	:26	
	WPM	135	128	106	
Speaker 2	words	68	54	40	201
	seconds	:26	:18	:09	
	WPM	157	180	267	
Speaker 3	words	18	13	9	78
	seconds	:17	:07	:09	
	WPM	64	111	60	

the lowest rates of speech as measured by WPM were also more likely to have a verbal system that reduced the gender system from three to two genders. Irizarri van Suchtelen (2016) found that lower WPM rates correlated with a higher rate of use of filled pauses (such as *uh*, *um*, *eh*, which can be signals of disfluency) among heritage speakers but not among first-generation speakers or among homeland monolinguals. He posits that both filled pauses and lower WPM are indicative of the deterioration in automaticity as a consequence of reduced exposure to Spanish.

We analyzed our corpus for WPM in the following way. In each interview, we identified the three longest uninterrupted stretches of speech produced by the interviewee and measured it in seconds. We counted the number of words in each of those stretches of speech and divided that by the number of seconds each one took to produce. Three examples appear in Table 2.8.

We calculated WPM independently of having rated the interviews for proficiency.[9] Figures 2.3 and 2.4 display the average WPM for all 124 participants according to their proficiency levels.

Although it is clear that there was not a one-to-one relationship between overall proficiency and WPM, we do see a general increase in WPM with increased proficiency level and also that everyone with an average WPM of more than 200 had a proficiency level of 3 or higher. The Pearson's product-moment correlation between WPM and proficiency was in fact significant, $r(118) = .32$, $p < .001$, with a medium-sized correlation as per the guidelines in

---

9. Many thanks to Maya Zazhil Fernández for her assistance in calculating WPM.

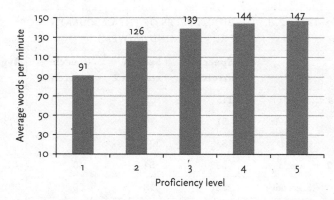

Figure 2.3. Average words per minute by proficiency level.

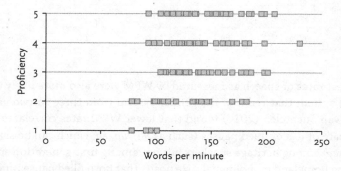

Figure 2.4. Scatterplot, words per minute by proficiency level.

Cohen (1988). Thus, although it may not be apparent to the eye from Figure 2.4, a higher level of Spanish proficiency was correlated with higher WPM.

We then sought to determine whether regional origin groups differed according to their WPM by proficiency level (Figure 2.5). That is, do Mexicans, Puerto Ricans, and MexiRicans, when matched for proficiency or for generation, tend to speak Spanish at different rates?

Our generational analysis proceeded as follows. The fact that there are by definition no G1 MexiRicans means that we could not analyze these two factors under one analysis of variance (ANOVA) model.[10] As such, we performed two ANOVAs, one comparing Mexicans and Puerto Ricans across all three generations and another one comparing Mexicans, Puerto Ricans, and MexiRicans across the second and third generations. A between-participants analysis of

---

10. A reviewer noted that ANOVAs do little to shed light on inter-participant variability. Contemporary linguistics has indeed moved toward mixed-effects regression models; our reliance on traditional ANOVAs throughout this manuscript is a product of having completed the bulk of our analyses between 2006 and 2015.

[50] *Spanish in Chicago*

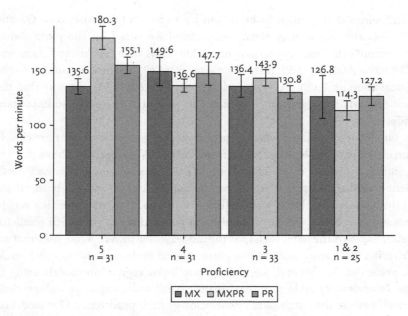

Figure 2.5. Words per minute by regional origin and proficiency level.

variance on WPM with the factors generation (G1, G2, or G3) and regional origin (Mexicans vs. Puerto Ricans) and the within-participant factor generation (G1, G2, and G3) found a significant effect for generation, $F(2,70) = 3.70$, $p = .030$, $\eta_p^2 = .10$. Follow-up t-tests showed that G2 speakers had significantly higher WPMs (M = 147.34, SD = 26.58) than G3 speakers (M = 127.84, SD = 32.13), $t(70) = 2.53$, $p = .042$. However, there was no significant main effect of regional origin, $F(1,70) = 0.37$, $p = .547$, $\eta_p^2 = .01$. Nor was the interaction between regional origin and generation significant, $F(2,70) = 2.60$, $p = .082$, $\eta_p^2 = .07$. This means that Mexicans and Puerto Ricans in the same generational group do not evidence significantly different average WPM. Our second model looked at all three regional origin groups across G2 and G3. A between-participants analysis of variance on WPM with the factors generation (G1, G2, or G3) and regional origin (Mexicans vs. Puerto Ricans) found a significant effect for generation, $F(1, 92) = 6.01$, $p = .016$, $\eta_p^2 = .06$. Follow-up t-tests showed that G2 speakers had significantly higher WPMs (M = 144.52, SD = 29.37) than G3 speakers (M = 144.52, SD = 29.37), $t(70) = 2.53$, $p = .042$. There was no significant main effect of regional origin, $F(2, 92) = 0.27$, $p = .762$, $\eta_p^2 = .01$. Thus, again, the interaction between regional origin and generation was not significant, $F(2, 92) = 0.91$, $p = .405$, $\eta_p^2 = .02$.

In sum, our results show that regional origin was not connected to WPM, but generation was, such that later generations tend to show lower WPM (which is likely correlated to lower Spanish proficiency, as we show below), a difference that seemed to be driven by a steep drop-off between G2 and G3. This conclusion may seem counterintuitive based on the plots above, but we note that the comparison of G1 Mexicans with G1 Puerto Ricans was t(16.63) = 2.06, p = .055, just a hair away from significance. Recurring to the observation noted by Otheguy and Zentella (2012, p. 111), we note that the lack of statistical significance does not suggest that there are no important differences.

Finally, we wondered whether proficiency or generation was more closely correlated with WPM. The results from the ANOVA presented above showed a significant effect of generation on WPM. Because generation and proficiency were correlated, it would not be appropriate to include both effects in the same model due to multicollinearity issues. Our first approach was to run separate models (for proficiency and generation) to see which predictor better explains the data, such that the model with a lower Akaike Information Criterion (AIC) score and a higher percentage of explained variance (R^2) would be preferred. To this end, we ran separate linear regression models using as the dependent variable each participant's WPM and using as an independent variable either the participant's generation or their proficiency. Our model on generation yielded an AIC of 1163.51 and explained 5.32% of variance. By contrast, our model on proficiency yielded an AIC of 1155.31 and explained 10.1% of variance. This suggests that proficiency explains WPM better than generation does. Our second approach to comparing the effects of proficiency and generation involves running a dominance analysis on a linear regression model that includes both proficiency and generation, following a procedure described to account for multicollinearity in regression models (Kraha et al., 2012). Using the *dominanceanalysis* package in R (Navarrete & Soares, 2020), we found that proficiency had an R^2 index of .081, higher than that of generation (.034). Again, this suggests that proficiency explains WPM better than generation does.

We conclude our discussion of WPM by noting that its use as a proxy for linguistic proficiency, especially among heritage speakers, is of limited value. First, some people simply talk at a faster rate than others. This could be based on personality, on age (Verhoeven et al., 2004, found that older people generally speak with a slower rate of speech than younger ones), and/or on gender, given that Whiteside (1996) suggests that males tend to speak slightly faster than females. Second, speaking rate has been found to be related to factors including the length of the turn of speech, familiarity with the interlocutor, and topic. For example, Yuan et al. (2006) found that speech rates rise rapidly for turns from one to seven words, remain level or fall gradually for turns of medium length, and then rise slowly for longer turns. In addition, they found that when talking with strangers or discussing certain topics, people tend to use longer turns but slower speech rates. Finally, some of the speech stretches we analyzed contained English words, the presence of which confounds an analysis of Spanish proficiency. However, given that we did find a correlation between proficiency and WPM, this might be a useful tool to help corroborate proficiency ratings.

We note two final challenges in measuring language proficiency. Other work in Spanish-English bilingual communities has used bilinguals' self-assessments as measures of proficiency, but these are problematic in that they can be influenced by speakers' linguistic insecurities. Finally, we note that language acquisition and proficiency are compounded by language change; that is, which uses represent a lack of proficiency and which uses represent a new variant in U.S. Spanish? Ultimately, all proficiency ratings, including ours, constitute an imprecise endeavor. But U.S. Latino communities usually do not change from "fully proficient" Spanish speakers (whatever that may mean) into non-proficient members in one generation; there are stages of community language loss indicated by the declining proficiency of individual speakers. Our goal was to differentiate in broad strokes the different proficiency levels with which these Chicago-based individuals communicated in Spanish during their interviews.

2.5. AGE, GENDER, SOCIOECONOMIC STATUS

We now briefly describe the corpus according to participants' age, gender, and socioeconomic status, although we did not study their Spanish features according to these variables.

Age

Participants' ages ranged from 18 to 78, with an average age of 30 (SD 13.59). The majority of participants (n = 72, or 58%) were between the ages of 20 and 30. The G1 average age was 48.3, for the G2 speakers it was 28.6, and for the G3 group the average age was 24.4 years. We note that the average age of our second- and third-generation participants at the time the interviews were conducted (between 2007 and 2010) was 26.5. This means that most of them lived the first 10 years of their lives during the years 1985–1995, when the four Chicago neighborhoods of Hermosa, Logan Square, Humboldt Park, and West Town (see Chapter 1) contained a greater proportion of Puerto Ricans than they did in the decades to follow.

Figure 2.6 shows visually the age ranges and frequencies in each generational group. We conducted no analyses with age as a variable, deciding instead to focus on regional background and generation.

To summarize visually our 124 participants according to age, generation, and PLUS, Figure 2.7 plots each participant according to these factors.

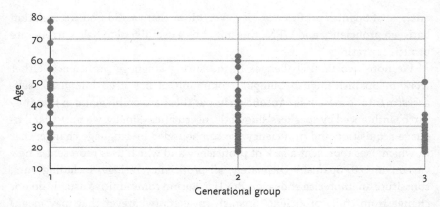

Figure 2.6. Ages of speakers in each generational group.

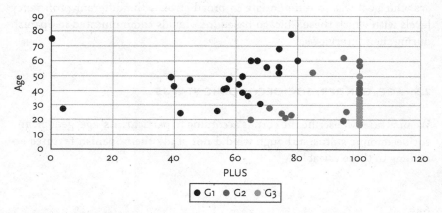

Figure 2.7. Study participants by age, generation, and PLUS (*n* = 124).

Gender

There are 91 females and 33 males in the CHISPA corpus. This predominantly female distribution is likely due to the fact that most interviewers were female and often utilized their personal contacts to locate interviewees. It may also be the case that women, in general, are more willing to participate in research and to talk with other women about the kinds of topics in our interview protocols. The genders were fairly equally distributed among the three generational groups. We conducted no analyses with gender as a variable. Two participants, one woman and one man, mentioned that they were gay, and one of them talked about coming out to their family. Cashman (2018) explores some of the ways in which coming out can affect Latino individuals' identity as well as their Spanish language use; we do not explore this topic here.

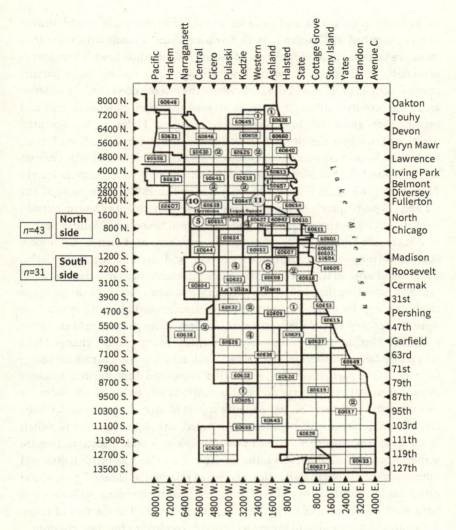

Figure 2.8. Number of participants in each zip code (number is circled) (*n* = 105).

Socioeconomic Status

Most studies explore the effects of socioeconomic status (SES) on language use, following a long-standing tradition in variationist sociolinguistics. This section describes the neighborhoods in which participants grew up, the jobs held by them and their parents, and their schooling experiences in order to demonstrate that the corpus was fairly homogeneous in its working-class origins. As a result, we will not explore SES as a variable in this project.

All 102 G2 and G3 participants grew up in the City of Chicago or in the nearby area of Cicero. Figure 2.8 displays the number of individuals who grew

THE CHICAGO SPANISH (CHISPA) CORPUS [55]

up in each zip code area and includes annotations of the six neighborhood names described in Chapter 1. With few exceptions, Census data show that these are working-class to lower-middle-class neighborhoods with a high concentration of Hispanics. As we will see through their quotes, many participants described problems in the areas where they were raised (such as violence and gang activity), although some mentioned that their neighborhoods had become safer since the time they were growing up. Following the accepted practice of dividing the city into North and South Sides at Madison Street, there were 56 participants who grew up on the North Side and 51 who grew up on the South Side. The North Side traditionally is home to many more Puerto Ricans than the South Side, particularly during the 1990s when most of our G2 and G3 participants grew up. Thirteen of our participants grew up outside the City of Chicago boundaries, including in Westchester and Melrose Park.

Almost all of our G1 participants in the workforce held manual-labor jobs, such as factory workers, restaurant servers, and department store clerks. Similarly, almost all G2 and G3 participants grew up in working-class families, typically reporting that one or two parents worked in a factory, a car garage, a cleaning company, a fast-food restaurant, or similar workplace. A few mothers were elementary-school teachers or secretaries. Many parents held two jobs, and some Mexican parents were undocumented. Many parents changed jobs frequently. Some mothers stayed home for at least a few years to care for young children. Many participants, especially G2s, recounted difficult circumstances including situational poverty and/or the entire family living in one room for several years. However, 30 participants reported attending private Catholic schools for elementary or high school (or both), although some had to switch to public schools due to a decline in the family's economic situation. Despite sometimes harsh circumstances, the narratives are also filled with happy and humorous stories of family parties, cherished relatives, childhood games, and other fond memories. They also offer portraits of tremendous resilience and hard work on the part of these families, who persevered in the face of many difficulties and were able to improve economic conditions for their children.

A measure of the improved social mobility of the G2 and G3 participants compared with that of many of their parents—some of whom had not finished high school—was the rate of postsecondary education. Of the participants, 64 were either attending or had completed a degree at a four-year college, and another 19 were attending or had completed studies at a community college. This totals 67% of our corpus who had some postsecondary education.[11] All but a handful attended a local college or university and lived at home while taking

---

11. Marcia Farr noted that this percentage is higher than among the Chicago Mexican families she researched and posited that postsecondary education negatively affects Spanish proficiency, such that our corpus might reflect lower Spanish proficiency than other Mexican groups in Chicago (personal communication, September 2014).

classes. Some could not complete their postsecondary studies due to financial hardship. Many held jobs while studying, including cell-phone customer service, accounting for a hotel, or general office clerical work. Some complained of work commutes up to two hours long, reflecting a similar admirable work ethic exhibited by many of their parents. Those who had already completed degrees worked in offices, as project managers, and in real estate. Twelve participants had finished high school but did not study further (or had not yet begun to), and they held various jobs including a nurse's assistant, making calls for a collection agency, working in fast food, window framing, or waiting tables.

In sum, we feel that that any differences in SES among our participants are minimal, difficult to tease out, and ultimately would not reveal significant connections to their Spanish, as would probably have been the case if participants were growing up in Latin America or if their families had belonged to the professional classes in Latin America. In other words, it is more likely that their English rather than their Spanish would reflect any differences in education and employment, given that English is the dominant language in Chicago.

2.6. INTERVIEW PROCEDURES

All participants agreed to engage in an oral interview in Spanish "about growing up in Chicago." Interviews lasted from 40 minutes to more than 90 minutes, with an average of approximately one hour. Interviewers did their best to put speakers at ease in the hopes of eliciting as many relaxed and detailed narratives as possible. Many interviewers codeswitched between Spanish and English, which was also common among the G2 and G3 participants (to be explored in Chapter 5). Some interviewers stated explicitly that codeswitching was fine.

Interview questions followed a sociolinguistic protocol (Labov, 1984) and asked about neighborhoods, childhood memories, and dreams, as well as questions related to how participants learned Spanish. Our full list of questions appears in Appendix C. A few questions were added later, including some about ethnolinguistic identity and how Mexicans and Puerto Ricans get along in Chicago.

There were 30 interviewers, 28 women and 2 men (see Table 2.9). All had been raised in the U.S. and were Spanish-English bilinguals. Recruitment for interviewers took place in undergraduate and graduate courses at UIC and at DePaul University. Of the 30 interviewers, 27 (90%) were U.S. Latina women (including coauthor Torres). Of these, all were raised in Chicago, with the exception of one Spanish speaker from New Mexico and Torres (raised in New York). These 27 women carried out 115 of the 124 interviews, or 93% of the corpus. One interviewer was a Chicago-raised Latino male of Mexican background who carried out two interviews. The other two interviewers were Anglo-Americans. One was an undergraduate male in the Teaching of Spanish major who conducted one interview. The other was one of the coauthors (Potowski).

Table 2.9. INTERVIEWERS

	Latina/o	White	Total
Women	27	1	28
Men	1	1	2
Total	28	2	30

Our impressionistic evaluation of the Spanish of all 30 interviewers leads us to categorize them into two general dialect types. Four interviewers of Puerto Rican origin used features common in Puerto Rican Spanish, including weakened coda /s/, subject-verb inversions in questions, and lateralization of /r/. The other 26 interviewers spoke with what can be described as a "general Mainlander" dialect, usually with what would be described as "general Mexican" features, with none of the Puerto Rican features just described.[12] We return to the possible effect of interviewer dialect features on interviewee speech production in Chapter 7, our study of two phonological variables.

Interviewers were provided the list of questions and a document we created called "The Art of the Sociolinguistic Interview," which contained explanations of the project goals, how to transition smoothly between questions, how to avoid asking leading questions, and so on. They were also given a sample interview to analyze which was annotated with comments about what the interviewer had done well (such as follow-up probing questions) as well as opportunities they had missed to ask for additional details. Interviewer candidates then conducted one interview, which they transcribed and submitted to the coauthors, who reviewed it and provided feedback. Despite this training procedure, we did discover some inconsistencies in the interviews, in particular a few questions that were inadvertently not asked of all participants. Interviews were recorded on either a Sony BX or a Sony ICD-BX800 digital voice recorder and later transcribed into Microsoft Word. The interviewers transcribed their own interviews using standard orthography and no linguistic or other annotations such as pauses, laughter, and so on. Over the following four years, the corpus went through three passes of correction and annotations, including removing identifying details and standardizing how filled pauses (such as *um*) were rendered. The CHISPA corpus will be available for consultation at CORPEEU (Corpus del Español en los Estados Unidos) (https://corpus.corpeeu.org/). The corpus will also be partially available on the PRESEEA project website (Proyecto para el Estudio Sociolingüístico del Español de España y de América) (https://preseea.uah.es/).

---

12. The Salvadoran-origin speaker did not weaken any coda /s/, nor did she use *vos*. In fact, we thought she was of Mexican origin until she indicated otherwise.

Table 2.10. NUMBER OF PARTICIPANTS (*N*) FOR EACH ANALYSIS.

Analysis	G1 *n* = 23	G2 *n* = 50	G3 *n* = 51	Total *n* = 124
Lexical familiarity Chapter 3	23	47	51	121
Discourse markers Chapter 4	20	35	35	90
Codeswitching Chapter 5	16	24	24	64
Subjunctive Chapter 6	16	16	16	48
Phonology Chapter 7	14	32	39	85
Underlying factors Chapter 8	23	50	51	124

Some of the interviewees were previously known to the interviewer, but others were strangers. Regardless of degree of familiarity with the interviewer, the majority of participants offered rich narratives with personal details; a few were less forthcoming, sometimes frustratingly so, offering one-word and bare-minimum answers (these were typically young men). The portraits that emerge from this corpus are very textured and revealing. We are honored and humbled to have access to these individuals' stories, and we hope to do justice to them, their families, and their communities by representing and interpreting their experiences.

In summary, we analyzed these interviews for particular linguistic features, that is, *how* participants said things, but also for content, *what* they said about their lives. Each of the five linguistic variables and how it was coded appears in the chapter dedicated to it. The number of participants varies for each analysis (Table 2.10), based on the fact that we selected subsamples for each one at different times.

2.7. SUMMARY

This corpus of 124 speakers in Chicago represents a cross-section of modern *latinidad* in a vibrant U.S. city. All of our analyses come from the interviews except for the lexical analysis, which utilized a picture identification task to be described in Chapter 3. We feel that the corpus reasonably represents Chicago's Spanish-speaking communities and a good deal of their complexity, revealing a fascinating portrait of Chicago Latino life and language.

APPENDIX A
AGE OF ARRIVAL IN CHICAGO AND PERCENTAGE OF LIFE IN U.S. (PLUS), FOREIGN-BORN PARTICIPANTS

G	Participant #/ regional origin	Age at arrival	Current age	Years in U.S.	PLUS
G1	#33 PR	12	60	48	80%
	#92 PR	17	78	61	78%
	#66 PR	18	68	50	74%
	#121 PR	15	56	41	73%
	#118 MX	14	52	38	73%
	#104 MX	17	56	39	70%
	#30 MX	10	31	21	68%
	#51 MX	20	60	40	67%
	#52 MX	21	60	39	65%
	#85 PR	13	36	23	64%
	#117 MX	19	50	31	62%
	#20 MX	15	39	24	62%
	#55 PR	17	44	27	61%
	#116 MX	20	48	28	58%
	#96 PR	18	42	24	57%
	#99 PR	18	41	23	56%
	#17 PR	12	26	14	54%
	#88 MX	26	47	21	45%
	#56 MX	14	24	10	42%
	#122 PR	26	43	17	40%
	#24 MX	30	49	19	39%
	#106 PR	26	27	1	4%
	#91 MX	75	75	.5	0.4%
	Average	**20.6**	**48.3**	**27.8**	**56%**
G2	#13 MXPR	0.5	25	24.5	98%
	#18 PR	3	62	59	95%
	#5 MX	1	19	18	95%
	#71 MXPR	3	24	21	88%

[60] *Spanish in Chicago*

G	Participant #/ regional origin	Age at arrival	Current age	Years in U.S.	PLUS
	#21 PR	8	52	44	85%
	#124 PR	7	44	36	82%
	#7 MX	5	23	18	78%
	#59 MX	5	23	18	78%
	#45 MX	5	21	16	76%
	#15 MX	6	24	18	75%
	#27 MX	8	28	20	71%
	#19 PR	7	20	13	65%
	Average	**5.0**	**30.4**	**25.5**	**82%**

APPENDIX B
EXAMPLES OF ORAL SPEECH AT EACH PROFICIENCY LEVEL (ALL TRANSCRIPTIONS VERBATIM)

Level 5, #96, G1 Puerto Rican female:

Esa historia te va a sonar muy cruel. Mi papá era un hombre de armas tomar y él entendía que si él nos iba tener a nosotras en el medio de una bahía teníamos que saber nadar. No podía ser . . . no podíamos dudar. Así que . . . yo recuerdo de muy chiquita, eh, digamos como en el kindergarten o por allí, ¿no? Eh . . . bueno, en el agua yo siempre estuve, eh, apoyada por mi papá o mi mamá. Y lo que hizo un día mi papá me cogió y me soltó. Y yo caí en el agua y era a nadar. Él quería ver que yo—y así yo aprendí, yo—él me tiró en el agua bien profunda, él allí, pero . . . tuve que salir nadando. Y yo tengo esa memoria y todo—yo cuento esto y la gente se . . . ¿no? Le da horror. Pero sabes que yo lo recuerdo con mucho cariño. Y ese momento lo recuerdo con mucho cariño porque luego yo me sentí como tan orgullosa, ¿no? de, de que ¡sí! Salí nadando, ¿no?

That story will sound very cruel to you. My dad was a formidable man and he understood that if he was going to have us in the middle of a bay we had to know how to swim. It couldn't be . . . we couldn't not. So...I remember, I was very little, um, let's say in kindergarten or around there, no? Um . . . well, in the water I was always, um, held by my dad or my mom. And what my dad did one day he had me and he let me go. And I fell in the water and had to swim. He wanted to see that I---and that's how I learned, I ---he threw me in the very deep water, he was there, but . . . I had to start swimming. And I have that memory and everything---I tell this to people and people get...no? They are horrified. But you know I remember it with a lot of love. And in that moment I remember it with a lot of love because then I was like very proud of myself, no, that that yes! I started swimming, no?

Level 4, #10, G2 Mexican male:

Desde que empezamos nosotros ir a la escuela, am, cuando yo fui a *preschool*, en menos de un mes yo aprendí a hablar más inglés que español. Cuando regresemos de la escuela a casa, siempre estábamos contestando a mi mama en inglés y ella se enojaba porque no entendía lo que estábamos diciendo. Después, nosotros no le queríamos decir nada en español, porque estamos aprendiendo inglés. Entonces cuando vino mi papá del trabajo un día, él dijo que mientras nosotros estemos en la casa siempre vamos a hablar español, conque sea con mamá, o con mi papá, o con amistades, se habla español nada más en la casa. Y afuera de la casa si nosotros queremos estar jugando con nuestros amistades del vecindario, o queremos ir a . . . con amigos de la escuela, cualquier cosa, que podemos hablar lo queramos hablar, pero mientras estemos en la casa se va a hablar puro español. Porque él dijo que el español no quería que se nos olvidara. Y . . . y sí, trabajó, eso fue muy bueno para nosotros.

Since we started school, um, when I went to preschool, in less than a month I learned to speak more English than Spanish. When we returned home from school, we were always answering my mom in English and she would get mad because she didn't understand what we were saying. Then we didn't want to tell her anything in Spanish because we were learning English. Then when my dad came home from work one day, he said that while we were living in the house we always had to speak Spanish, whether with mom, with my dad, or with friends, only Spanish is spoken in the house. And outside the house if we wanted to play with our neighborhood friends, or we wanted to go to . . . with school friends, anything, then we could speak whatever we wanted to speak, but while we were in the house one is going to speak only Spanish. Because he said he didn't want us to forget our Spanish. And... and yes it worked, that was very good for us.

Level 3, #12, G2 Mexican female:

Una vez . . . es que yo traduzco para la mamá. Porque a veces las mamás o los padres no saben hablar inglés. So yo traduzco a los que están diciendo los policía o a otro . . . los niños como yo que estamos ayudando. Yo traduzco para los padres so a veces la mamá empieza a llorar, y yo me siento mal. So, una vez, un sacado . . . yo saqué a uno de los niños malos, lo saqué afuera y yo hablé con él por un buen rato, eran como unos veinte minutos que hablé con él. Y él empezó a llorar. So yo pensé, yo sí pienso que hice un impacto en su vida, porque no lo estaba gritando, pero lo estaba consejeando. So, ojalá que sí hice algo bien. Yo no sé.

One time . . . it's that I translate for moms. Because sometimes the moms or the dads don't know English. So I translate what the police are saying or for other . . . the kids I that we are helping. I translate for the parents so sometimes the mom starts to cry, and I feel bad. So, one time, a taken. . . I took out one of the bad kids, I took him outside and I talked with him for a good long time, it was about twenty minutes that I talked with him. And he started crying. So I thought, I do think I had an impact on his life, because I wasn't yelling at him, rather I was counseling him. So hopefully I did something good. I don't know.

Level 2, #32, G3 MexiRican female:

Well aquí yo trabajo en el centro de educación y siempre, am, siempre trato de ayudar los niños porque los padres a veces no, no saben lo que están haciendo en la escuela y eso para mí . . . algo que, you know, no gasta mucho tiempo pero, ahm, pero ayuda los niños bastante mucho.

"Well here I work in the education center and always, um I always try to help the kids because sometimes the parents don't know what they're doing in school and that for me . . . something that, you know, doesn't take a lot of time but, um, but I help the kids quite a lot.

Level 1, #35, G3 Mexican male:

[Interviewer: "Cuando eras niño, ¿a qué cosas jugabas?"]
　　Ahm, *basketball*, *baseball*, ahm, otras, otros juegos con los niños del *neighborhood*.
　　[Interviewer: "¿Cómo se . . . cuál es el concepto de *basketball*, *baseball*?"]
　　Basketball, ahm, tienes que . . . hay dos equipos y tienes que echar el, el, ahm, la pelota en el *hoop*, [ríe], del otro, ahm, del otro lado.
　　[Interviewer: Y, ¿*baseball*?]
　　Ahm, [ríe] [pause] también hay dos equipos [ríe] y [pausa], *sorry*, hay dos equipos y, ahm, los dos tienen que batear, ahm, una pelota del tamaño pequeño y allí, ahm, [pausa] ahorran puntos. Algo así.

[Interviewer: "When you were child, what kind of things did you play?"]
　　#35: "Ahm, *basketball*, *baseball*, um, other, other games with the neighborhood kids."
　　[Interviewer: "How do you, what is the concept of *basketball*, *baseball*?]
　　#35: "*Basketball*, ahm, you have to . . . . . . there are two teams and you have to throw the, the, ahm, the ball in the *hoop*, [laughs], of the other, ahm, of the other side.

[Interviewer: And, *baseball*?]

#35: Ahm, [laughs] [pause] there are also two teams [laughs] and [pause], *sorry*, there are two teams and ahm, the two have to bat, ahm a small ball and there, ahm, [pause] they get points. Something like that."

APPENDIX C
INTERVIEW QUESTIONS

PREGUNTAS GENERALES

¿Cuántos años tienes?
¿Dónde naciste?
¿Dónde vives ahora? ¿Cuál es el código postal?
¿En qué otros lugares has vivido?

LA FAMILIA

¿Dónde nacieron tu mamá y tu papá? Y ¿tus abuelos?
¿Qué tipos de trabajos han tenido tus padres?
¿Tienes hermanos? ¿Cuántos años tienen y a qué se dedican?
¿Tienes hijos? ¿Cuántos años tienen?

EL VECINDARIO

¿Qué es lo que más te gusta sobre donde vives?
¿Qué es lo que menos te gusta?
¿Te sientes segura/o en tu vecindario? ¿Por qué?
¿Ha cambiado tu vecindario en los últimos años?
¿Qué tal la policía? ¿Crees que ayudan o causan más problemas?
¿Qué cosas buenas ocurren en tu vecindario?
Si pudieras hacer algo para mejorar tu vecindario ¿Qué harías?

LA NIÑEZ

¿Qué jugabas cuando eras niña/o? ¿Cómo se juega? ¿Cuáles son las reglas del juego?
Cuándo eras niño/a, ¿peleabas con otros niños o con tus hermanos?
    ¿Puedes recordarte de una pelea en particular?
¿Puedes contarme una memoria muy linda de cuando eras niño/a?

LA ESCUELA

¿Qué escuelas asististe?
¿Era(n) escuela(s) buena(s) o mala(s)? Por qué?
¿Qué piensas que se podría hacer para mejorar las escuelas?
¿Qué piensas de la educación bilingüe?
¿Quién tiene la responsabilidad de enseñarles español a los latinos?

EL TRABAJO

¿Dónde trabajas?
¿Siempre has tenido este trabajo? Si no, ¿qué otros trabajos has tenido?
¿Usas el español en tu trabajo?
¿Qué te gusta más de tu trabajo?
¿Qué es lo que te gusta menos?
¿Cuál sería tu trabajo ideal?

LAS AMISTADES

¿Quiénes son tus mejores amigos?
¿Qué es necesario para tener una buena amistad?
¿Qué cosas causan problemas entre las amistades?
¿Has perdido un buen amigo? ¿Qué pasó?

LAS RELACIONES AMOROSAS

¿Tienes pareja?
¿Dónde conociste a tu pareja?
¿Cuáles son algunas causas de las peleas entre una pareja?
¿Qué es necesario para tener una buena relación?
¿Por qué crees que tanta gente se divorcia hoy en día?

OTROS TEMAS

¿Qué harías si te ganaras un millón de dólares?
¿Ha habido un momento en tu vida que pensaste que te ibas a morir?
¿Puedes recordar un sueño bonito que has tenido?
¿Y una pesadilla?
¿Qué haces en tu tiempo libre?

EL ESPAÑOL

¿Te acuerdas cómo aprendiste el español? Y ¿el inglés? ¿A qué edades?

¿Decían tus padres algo acerca de la importancia de algún idioma? ¿Qué decían?

¿Estuviste en educación bilingüe algún tiempo? ¿Te acuerdas cuántos años estuviste?

Hoy en día, ¿cuándo y dónde usas español? Por ejemplo, ¿cuánto español usas con tus amigos?

¿Hablan el español diferente los mexicanos y los puertorriqueños? Descríbeme las diferencias.

¿Crees que un español es mejor que el otro? ¿Has escuchado a otras personas decir que un español es mejor que el otro?

¿Crees que los latinos en Estados Unidos deben mantener el español? ¿Por qué? / ¿Quién tiene la responsabilidad de enseñarles el español a los niños?

¿Tienes hijos? ¿Cuánto español saben ahora? ¿Crees que cuando tengan tu edad, van a hablar el español tan bien como tú? ¿Por qué? / Si los tuvieras en el futuro, ¿crees que cuando tengan tu edad, van a hablar el español tan bien como tú? ¿Por qué?

Algunas personas se identifican con términos como *African American*, o *White*, o *asiático*. ¿Hay un término que usas para describirte? El término que usas, ¿depende con quién estás hablando—con otro latino, con un afroamericano, con un blanco? Para ti, ¿qué significa _ [*término*]_? ¿Hay que saber español para ser _[*término*]_? ¿Por qué sí o no?

En tu opinión, ¿es necesario saber el español para ser _[*término*]_?

¿Qué es el *Spanglish*? ¿Qué opinas sobre el *Spanglish*?

SPECIFIC MEXIRICAN QUESTIONS

Tu mamá es [MX o PR] y tu papá es [MX o PR]. ¿Sabes cómo se conocieron? ¿Cómo reaccionaron sus familias cuando se juntaron?

¿Qué influencias mexicanas había en tu casa cuando te creciste? Y ¿puertorriqueñas?

¿Has viajado a [México o Puerto Rico]? ¿Cuántas veces, y por cuánto tiempo? ¿Hay algo que te gusta allá? ¿Algo que no te guste tanto?

¿Qué es lo que más aprecias de la cultura puertorriqueña? Y ¿de la mexicana?

Algunas personas se identifican con términos como *African American*, o *White*, o *asiático*. ¿Hay un término que usas para describirte? El término que usas, ¿depende con quién estás hablando—con otro latino, con un afroamericano, con un blanco? Para ti, ¿qué significa _[término]_? ¿Hay que saber español para ser _[término]_? ¿Por qué sí o no?

En tu opinión, ¿hay algunas características necesarias para que una persona sea considerada _[término]_? ¿Es necesario saber el español para ser _[término]_?

Aquí en Chicago hay muchos mexicanos y muchos puertorriqueños. ¿Has escuchado comentarios negativos que hace un grupo sobre el otro?

¿Qué críticas dicen los mexicanos sobre los puertorriqueños?

¿Qué críticas dicen los puertorriqueños sobre los mexicanos?

En tu experiencia, ¿cómo se llevan estos dos grupos en general?

En tu high school o tu vecindario, ¿hubo problemas entre los dos grupos?

Y tus amigos, en general son ¿de qué grupos étnicos?

APPENDIX C (ENGLISH TRANSLATION)
INTERVIEW QUESTIONS

GENERAL QUESTIONS

How old are you?
Where were you born?
Where do you live now? What is your zip code?
Where else have you lived?

FAMILY

Where were your mother and father born? And your grandparents?
What kind of jobs did your parents have?
Do you have siblings? How old are they and what do they do?
Do you have children? How old are they?

NEIGHBORHOOD

What do you like most about where you live?
What do you like the least?
Do you feel safe in your neighborhood? Why?

Has your neighborhood changed in the recent past?
What about the police? Do you think they help or cause more problems?
What good things take place in your neighborhood?
If you could do something to improve your neighborhood, what would it be?

CHILDHOOD

What did you play when you were a child? How do you play it? What are the rules of the game?
When you were a child did you fight with your siblings or other children? Can you remember a specific fight?
Can you share a nice memory from your childhood?

SCHOOL

What schools did you go to?
Were they good schools or bad schools? Why?
What do you think one could do to improve schools?
What is your opinion of bilingual education?
Who is responsible for teaching Latinos Spanish?

WORK

Where do you work?
Have you always had that job? If not, what other jobs have you had?
Do you use Spanish in your job?
What do you like the most about your job?
What do you least like?
What would be your ideal job?

FRIENDSHIP

Who are your best friends?
What is necessary to have a good friendship?
What kind of things cause problems among friends?
Have you lost a good friend? What happened?

LOVE LIFE

Do you have a partner?
Where did you meet your partner?
What are some of the reasons why partners fight?
What is necessary for a good relationship?
Why do you think so many people get divorced nowadays?

OTHER TOPICS:

What would you do if you won a million dollars?
Has there ever been a time in your life when you thought you were going to die?
Can you recall a good dream you have had?
A nightmare?
What do you do with your spare time?

SPANISH

Do you remember how you learned Spanish? English? At what ages?
Did your parents ever say anything about the importance of a language? What did they say?
Were you ever in bilingual education classes? Do you remember for how many years?
Nowadays, when do you use Spanish? For example, how much Spanish do you use with your friends?
Do Mexicans and Puerto Ricans speak Spanish differently? Describe the differences.
Do you think one type of Spanish is better than any other type? Have you heard people say that one type of Spanish is better than another type of Spanish?
Do you think Latinos in the United States should maintain their Spanish? Why or why not? / Who is responsible for teaching children Spanish?
Do you have children? How much Spanish do they know? Do you think when they are your age, they will speak Spanish as well as you do? Why? / If you have children in the future, do you think that when they are your age, they will speak Spanish as well as you do? Why?

Some people identify themselves with terms such as African American, or White, or Asian. Is there a term you use to describe yourself? Does the term you use depend on who you are talking with – with another Latino, an African American? A white person? What does [term] mean to you?

Does one have to speak Spanish to be [term]? Why or why not?

In your opinion, is it necessary to know Spanish to be___[term] ___?

What is Spanglish? What is your opinion about Spanglish?

SPECIFIC "MEXIRICAN" QUESTIONS

Your mom is [(MX or PR]) and you dad is [(MX or PR]). Do you know how they met? How did their families react when they got together?

What Mexican influences where in your house when you were growing up? How about Puerto Rican influences?

Have you traveled to [México or Puerto Rico]? How many times and for how long? Is there something you like there? Something you don't like?

What do you value the most about Puerto Rican culture? How about Mexican culture?

Some people identify with terms such as African American, or White, o Asian. Is there a term you use to describe yourself? Does the term you use depend on who you are talking with—like another Latino, and African American, a White person? For you, what does the _ [term]_signify? Does one have to know Spanish to be _[term]_? Why or why not?

In your opinion, are there some characteristics one needs to have to be considered a _[term]_? Does one need to know Spanish to be a _ [term]__?

Here in Chicago, there are a lot of Mexicans and Puerto Ricans. Have you heard negative comments one group makes about the other group?

What negative comments do Mexicans make about Puerto Ricans? What negative comments do Puerto Ricans make about Mexicans?

In your experience, how do these groups get along in general?

In your high school or neighborhood, were there problems between the two groups?

And in general, what ethnic groups do your friends belong to?

CHAPTER 3
Lexical Familiarity

3.1. INTRODUCTION

Chapter 1 described several conditions of dialect contact and proposed that Spanish in Chicago might be best described by the situation depicted in Figure 1.5, wherein Mexican Spanish would influence Puerto Rican Spanish but not the other way around. This chapter examines the extent to which Mexicans and Puerto Ricans of different generations are familiar with each other's distinctive lexical items. It also includes an analysis of the lexical familiarity of MexiRicans—individuals with one Mexican parent and one Puerto Rican parent who grew up in a context that has been referred to as *intrafamilial dialect contact* (Potowski 2016). *Lexical familiarity* refers to whether speakers show knowledge of words that differ between Puerto Rican and Mexican Spanish but that have the same referent (e.g., earrings are *pantallas* in Puerto Rico but *aretes* in Mexico). First, we review past studies on lexical outcomes of dialect contact before presenting results of our lexical task of the CHISPA participants.

3.2. LEXICAL OUTCOMES OF DIALECT CONTACT

The vast majority of studies of dialect contact have examined phonological traits, but the lexicon is arguably the most easily acquired of dialect features. For example, Chambers's (1992) first principle of dialect acquisition is that lexical replacement is acquired faster than pronunciation and phonological variants. Lexical items are also likely acquired more quickly than syntax or morphology both in second-language acquisition and in cases of dialect contact. The speed of lexical acquisition is due to at least three factors:

1. Lexical differences are highly salient, even to the most linguistically naive ear. (E.g., *soda* vs. *pop* vs. *Coke* in U.S. English.)
2. Lexical items can be acquired one at a time, unlike a systematic phonological rule. (E.g., a New Yorker might adopt *pop* after moving to the Midwest before showing any evidence of phonological accommodation.)
3. Using a different lexical item can lead to comprehension difficulties. (E.g., a New Yorker, upon arrival to the South, might experience a conversation failure while asking for a "Coke" at a restaurant when the waitstaff replies with "What kind?")

Thomason and Kaufman (1988, pp. 74–78) proposed that even the most casual contact between languages sometimes results in lexical borrowings.

Additional evidence supporting the idea that lexical accommodation is different from that of other linguistic features comes from Nagy (2011). She examined lexical borrowing from a standard language (Italian) into a minority language (Faetar, a variety of Francoprovençal). She found a large degree of lexical borrowing from Italian into Faetar but, interestingly, no correlation between rates of borrowing with age, social class, or sex (which was also found by Zentella, 1990, to be reviewed below). This led her to conclude that lexical change does not necessarily proceed in the same way as phonological change: "It is not surprising that macro-level changes are different for lexical and structural variables, as people continue to regularly acquire lexical items much later in life than they acquire new phonological structures or elements, both in first and second language acquisition" (Nagy, 2011, p. 20).

Nordenstam (1979) studied the long-term linguistic accommodations of 32 Swedish women living in Norway. There is a very high degree of intercomprehensibility between Swedish and Norwegian, leading Trudgill (1986) to propose that this situation is akin to British English speakers who relocate to the U.S. and acquire U.S. English features. This makes Nordenstam's study especially relevant to our study of speakers of different dialects of Spanish coming into contact in Chicago. Nordenstam found that the women's linguistic accommodation began with nouns, particularly those for "typical Norwegian phenomena" and for homonyms—words that sound the same but have different meanings in the two languages. After nouns, accommodation began in the realm of morphology (certain forms of nouns, verbs, adjectives, adverbs, and pronouns). She also found that the majority of her informants began using more Norwegian words than would have been necessary to maintain intelligibility, arguing that this constituted evidence of social motivations for using the Norwegian lexicon.

To our knowledge, Zentella (1990) is the only study to date examining lexical outcomes of Spanish dialect contact in the U.S. She compared lexical familiarity among Puerto Ricans, Dominicans, Colombians, and Cubans in New York City by asking 194 individuals how they referred to 25 objects (displayed in Table 3.1) "in everyday conversation" and whether they knew of any other group's term for each item. The items were selected based on their status as "common objects which are lexically different for one or more of the nationalities studied" (Zentella, 1990, p. 1095). Zentella acknowledged the probable influence of the observer's paradox—that is, the potential influence of the dialect group of the interviewer—but argued that the results constitute "evidence of the speakers' most active vocabulary" (p. 1096) even if it did not represent their complete lexical knowledge.

Zentella found that age, gender, education, number of years in the U.S., and proficiency in Spanish or English were not significantly correlated with subjects' responses but rather that "national origin determines their choice of vocabulary, with some revealing additions and exceptions" (p. 1096). There were five main results, which are displayed alongside the object stimuli in Table 3.1:

1. Majority unity, meaning that the majority of members of all four groups preferred the same term.
2. One group preferring a different word. This means that three of the four national groups gave the same terms more often than any other, but one group preferred another term.
3. An even split between the four groups in their word preferences. For these words, two groups prefer one term, and two other groups prefer one or more different terms.
4. Words with multiple synonyms.
5. Distinct lexicon for all four groups.

The author's conclusions about these five categories of words were as follows. Group 1 words form part of the standard Spanish lexicon in New York. Group 2 words were moving toward, but had not yet reached, convergence (understood to mean everyone using the same word). Here the influence of a larger dialect region was a plausible explanation in the cases of *sidewalk* and *bus*,[1] where the Caribbeans showed uniformity. An even split (group 3) between the four speaker-origin groups suggested no clear regional pattern. As for the two group 4 words with multiple synonyms, *clothes pin* and *hair pin*, Zentella noted that these items are becoming less known because of clothes dryers and new ways of styling hair. Their lower semantic weight is also related to the social variable of gender, because "males were hard pressed to come up with words for these items, since they are linked to the female domains of hairstyling and clothes washing" (Zentella, 1990, p. 1099). Thus, the large

---

1. *Bus* shows considerable variation around the U.S. This book's coauthor Potowski once heard a reporter on a Chicago Univisión newscast say, "Allí está la estación del [bus], donde viene el [bas] a recoger a los niños" (September 8, 2014).

Table 3.1. RESULTS, ZENTELLA (1990).

Group	Items	Variants offered
1. Majority unity	necklace chain necklace purse	collar cadena cartera (although 1/3 of Colombians preferred bolso)
2. One group preferred a different word	orange mattress earrings pepper money jeans	naranja colchón aretes ají dinero yins Puerto Rican exceptions to majority choice: *china, matre, pantallas, pimiento, chavos, mahones.*
	car desk vase	carro escritorio florero Cuban exceptions to majority choice: *máquina, buró, búcaro.*
	sidewalk bus furniture	acera guagua muebles Colombian exceptions to majority choice: *andén, bus, sofá.*[a]
3. Even split	cake garbage can banana	Puerto Ricans and Dominicans prefer one term: *bizcocho, zafacón, guineo*. Other terms: *keik, pastel; latón; plátano, banano.*
	eyeglasses	Puerto Ricans and Cubans prefer one term: *espejuelos.* Other terms: *gafas, lentes.*
	half slip	Puerto Ricans and Colombians prefer one term: *enaguas.* Other terms: *saya, mediofondo.*
	pig grocery store	*puerco, cerdo* *bodega, tienda* The above were most common among all groups. Dominicans produced *puerco* first and *cerdo* last, while Colombians produced *cerdo* first and *puerco* last. Cubans named *bodega* more frequently than *tienda*, while Colombians preferred *tienda.* Puerto Ricans use all 4 terms at similar rates.

[74] *Spanish in Chicago*

Table 3.1. CONTINUED

Group	Items	Variants offered
4. Multiple synonyms	*clothes pin* *hair pin*	Extensive inter- and intra-group variation; 22 variants in total.
5. Distinct lexicon	*kite*	Colombian *cometa*, Cuban *papalote*, Dominican *chichigua*, Puerto Rican *chiringa*.

[a] The author notes that a member of the research team may have mistakenly pointed only to the couch in the photo of "muebles" when interviewing Colombians. As a result, she suspected that *muebles* was really a "majority unity word."

number of competing variants in this category, combined with their low frequency in daily life, suggests that there will not emerge a "winning" variant used by all groups. The same may be true of group 5 (*kite*).

What might explain these findings? According to Chambers (1992), in situations of dialect contact, it is unclear why some lexical items persist and others change: "Instead, there appears to be an element of arbitrariness of the sort despised by linguists and indeed by all scientists" (p. 679). A possible exception is when a word in one dialect is taboo or humorous in another. For example, the Canadian youth he studied quickly acquired the British word *trousers* because the Canadian word *pants* refers to underwear in England. Similarly, Zentella's (1990) interviews with participants contained frequent anecdotes about words that mean one thing in one dialect but something completely different (and often vulgar) in another. Although none of her tested items was taboo in either dialect, it is illustrative to note her suggestion that, for example, Puerto Ricans who are aware that other speakers do not understand *pantallas* for earrings "may switch to *aretes* in their presence, but since *pantallas* has no taboo connotations, most continue to use it. As a result, it was one of the variants most frequently cited as an example of Puerto Rican vocabulary by speakers of the other dialects" (Zentella, 1990, p. 1100). We will see below that there was an item in our lexical identification task, *bizcocho*, that is vulgar in Mexican Spanish.

Another interesting pattern found by Zentella was the use of English terms to avoid confusion. She claims that Latinos in New York "turn to English in order to understand each other's Spanish" (Zentella, 1990, p. 1100). For example, *guagua* means *bus* to most Caribbeans, but for Colombians it refers to a small animal. She suggests that the adoption of *guagua* by Colombians in New York City "is inevitable, if we consider numbers only. On the other hand, the presence of a Colombian homonym in a different semantic field and the similarity of Colombian [bus] to English [bas] may prove effective counterforces" (p. 1100). In other words, Anglicisms can "play the role of neutralizer between competing dialectal variants," acting as the lingua franca and resolving the lexical conflict without favoring one group at the expense of the other (p. 1101). We will see in our Chicago data that both *bus* and *cake* are frequently used in English, with a plausible motivation that these English words avoid confusion among multiple Spanish variants.

Zentella noted that "the total number of people who know and use a term in everyday speech is of critical significance in its extinction or extension," agreeing with Trudgill's (1984) and Labov's (1966) assertions that exposure via personal contact is essential to linguistic accommodation. However, in what was probably Zentella's most important finding, the variants of the most numerous speakers (Puerto Ricans and Dominicans) were in fact *not* the most widely known. What seemed to have a larger effect on people's knowledge of lexical items was class, education level, and race. Only the Dominicans had adopted lexicon from every other group without exception: the Dominican words for *garbage can, sidewalk, money, earrings,* and *blue jeans* were mentioned by Dominicans only, and the majority of Dominicans actually offered more widely known words as their everyday terms for these items. Also, while multiple terms for *kite* were spread out across all groups, the Dominican word *chichigua* was the only one not adopted by any members of other groups. Importantly, and echoing what we reported about Puerto Ricans in Chicago in Chapter 1, many Cubans and Colombians offered harsh criticisms about Dominican and Puerto Rican Spanish, and the Dominicans themselves had internalized negative messages about their own Spanish, with 35% stating that their Spanish is "incorrecto" or "malo." (See Alba, 2009, on the stigma associated with Dominican Spanish.)

These lexical and discursive findings, Zentella argues, add to the evidence from her 1990 study that Colombians, Cubans, and Puerto Ricans "contribute to Dominican linguistic insecurity by their widespread rejection of Dominican Spanish" (Zentella, 1990, p. 1101). She insists that "the process of incorporation, loss, or maintenance is not predictable by a simple mathematical formula which calculates the number of people who know a term versus those who ignore it, because of a number of social and economic realities that impinge upon communication and linguistic change, leveling, and/or diffusion" (Zentella, 1990, p. 1097).

In summary, the lexical variants used by higher-status, more educated, and lighter-skinned Cubans and Colombians in Zentella's New York City study were more widely known than those of Puerto Ricans and Dominicans, who were in fact more numerous in New York but more disadvantaged economically and also discriminated against for their darker skin.

The diverse origins of Spanish speakers in Chicago provide an excellent opportunity to study the lexical outcomes of dialect contact, using methodology similar to that of Zentella (1990) but focusing on the two most numerous groups in the city, Mexicans and Puerto Ricans. We use the terms *outgroup* to mean "of the other group" and *ingroup* to mean "of the same group," such that outgroup for Mexicans refers to Puerto Ricans, and outgroup for Puerto Ricans refers to Mexicans. Similarly, ingroup lexicon for Mexicans means Mexican lexicon, while for Puerto Ricans it refers to Puerto Rican lexicon. With MexiRicans, we do not use either of these terms and refer instead to Mexican and Puerto Rican variants.

We sought to determine whether each group was familiar with the lexicon from the other group and whether this familiarity was connected to regional origin, generational group, and Spanish proficiency. We also wondered about overall lexical scores. Our questions were as follows:

1. Will there be differences in outgroup lexical familiarity scores according to:
    a. Regional origin?
    b. Generational group?
    c. Regional origin and generational group?
    d. Spanish proficiency level?
2. Will Spanish proficiency or generational group be more strongly connected to lexical familiarity scores?

We predicted that Puerto Ricans would show greater familiarity with outgroup lexicon than would Mexicans for three principal reasons. First, Mexicans are far more numerous in Chicago, forming almost 78% of the Chicago Latino community, while Puerto Ricans constitute just 9.8% (see Table 1.2 in Chapter 1). We felt this was a reasonable hypothesis, notwithstanding Zentella's (1990) finding in New York City that the numerical superiority of the Puerto Ricans and Dominicans did *not* lead the Cubans or Colombians to express greater familiarity with Puerto Rican/Dominican lexicon. Second, based on what participants said during their interviews (presented in Chapter 1), we felt that De Genova and Ramos-Zayas's (2003) proposal was correct that Mexican Spanish has greater status in Chicago than Puerto Rican Spanish. This idea is also related to the conclusions of Zentella (1990), who proposed that Puerto Rican Spanish generally suffers from negative stereotypes and stigma. If Mexican Spanish is more prestigious than Puerto Rican Spanish, it seemed reasonable to hypothesize that speakers would show greater familiarity with it in Chicago.

The third factor that led us to formulate this hypothesis is related to the first two: Mexican Spanish is more heavily represented in Spanish-language media available in the U.S. While we could not locate empirical studies about the dialects used in Spanish-language broadcasts in Chicago—research that is sorely lacking around the U.S.[2]—our own viewing of these channels combined

---

2. Dávila (2002) documents the criticisms of U.S. Spanish-language TV programming offered by Latino focus group participants in New York City, who said it was "too Mexican" (and also too white and upper-class). Similarly, Valencia and Lynch (2019)

with the impressions of our linguistics colleagues lead us to propose that a variety of Spanish more closely resembling Mexican Spanish in its phonology and lexicon is what is most often heard on Univisión, Telemundo, and Galavisión, the Spanish broadcasting stations with largest market share in the U.S. That is, our sense is that speech features typical of the Caribbean or the Southern Cone are not frequently broadcast on Chicago television. Furthermore, we believe it is generally accepted among both linguists and laypeople that educated Mexican Spanish is among the most prestigious varieties internationally and closely resembles what might be considered a "standard" dialect used most frequently in formal media broadcasts in the U.S.

It is true that the role of the media in language change is limited. Trudgill (1986, p. 40) and others argue that face-to-face interaction is necessary for accommodation to take place and that people do not accommodate their language to what they hear on television. However, the media can and do contribute to popular acceptance and use of new lexical items. For example, Trudgill (1986) claims that British English has experienced media-driven adoptions of U.S. English phrases such as "Monday *through* Friday" and "Hopefully" as a sentence adverbial, although British English core syntax and phonology[3] are unaffected. Other noteworthy examples of lexical diffusion in the U.S. through television shows include *Seinfeld* words and phrases such as "Yada, yada, yada," "regifter," and "spongeworthy" and *The Colbert Report*'s words "truthiness," "mantasy," and "engayify." Thus, we felt it was reasonable to propose that Puerto Ricans are exposed to significant amounts of Mexican vocabulary (or to non–Puerto Rican, broader pan-Hispanic vocabulary) and would show familiarity with it in our task.

To summarize, the combination of the numerical superiority of Mexicans in Chicago, the greater dialect prestige of Mexican Spanish, and the greater presence of Mexican Spanish in U.S. media led us to predict that Puerto Ricans would evidence a high degree of familiarity with Mexican lexical variants. On the other hand, although Mexicans might come into contact with Puerto Ricans in Chicago, this contact would be far less frequent than that of Puerto Ricans with Mexicans. In addition, if Mexicans are generally confident with the status of their Spanish (see Chapter 1) and encounter it more frequently in the media than Puerto Rican variants, then its speakers would not feel particularly compelled to remember or use Puerto Rican lexical items. Finally, we note that a second hypothesis we held regarding regional origin was that

---

document processes through which Spanish-language broadcasts attempt to "neutralize" regional accents but that typically a "Mexican tonality" prevails and is seen by many as "neutral."

3. Regarding phonology, individual pronunciations and words can be *imitated* from the media but not accommodated to (Trudgill, 1986).

MexiRicans would show greater familiarity with the lexicon of their mother's ethnolinguistic group, based on findings in Potowski (2016).

Regarding generational group, we felt that it would correlate with outgroup lexical scores, but we were unsure how. One hypothesis was that G1 speakers would have greater exposure to outgroup lexicon due to the sheer amount of Spanish use in their daily lives: they tend to speak it more frequently with a wide variety of people belonging to different generations, dialect backgrounds, and so on, around the city. An extension of this is that G2s speak less Spanish and G3s even less, such that lexical scores would be G1 > G2 > G3. A second hypothesis reasoned that G2s, by virtue of having spent their entire childhoods in Chicago, likely had greater exposure to people from the other group than G1s did (all of whom were raised in Latin America until at least age 12, with an average age of arrival of 20) and thus heard outgroup Spanish more, which would lead to greater outgroup lexical familiarity. However, it is also true that G2 youth in Chicago typically speak in English together (Potowski, 2002), so it is parental/adult input that typically constitutes the majority of the Spanish input that G2 children hear. Thus, G2 children would be exposed to outgroup lexicon, albeit only through non-family adults they might have contact with. G3s were raised in Chicago by one or two G2 parents, and their G2 parents may have adopted some outgroup lexicon in their own Spanish by virtue of having spent their own childhoods in Chicago. The prediction here would thus be G3 > G2 > G1 in regard to level of familiarity with outgroup lexicon.

Finally, as we saw in Chapter 2, generational groups can frequently consist of individuals with varying levels of Spanish proficiency, sometimes differing by as much as two levels. We thus hypothesized that Spanish proficiency would be more closely related to overall lexical knowledge than would generational group.

3.3. METHODOLOGY

Participants

Each individual in the CHISPA corpus participated in a sociolinguistic interview in Spanish, described in Chapter 2. At the end of the interview, participants were shown color photos of 10 items that are usually referred to with different words in Mexican versus Puerto Rican Spanish, displayed in Table 3.2. Their responses to these questions are the focus of this chapter.

We do not mean to suggest that any of these words are used exclusively by either Mexicans or Puerto Ricans. For example, *plátano*, *piscina*, and *frijoles* are used widely around the Spanish-speaking world. The point here is that these word pairs form a dialectal division in that most members of each of these groups use one term or the other; evidence for this will be presented in

Table 3.2. ITEMS IN VOCABULARY ELICITATION TASK.

Photo viewed by participant	English	Mexican Spanish	Puerto Rican Spanish
	orange	naranja, mandarina	china
	pacifier	chupete, chupetón	bobo
	bus	camión, autobús	guagua
	eyeglasses	lentes	espejuelos, gafas, anteojos
	earrings	aretes	pantallas
	swimming pool	alberca	piscina
	drinking straw	popote	sorbeto
	banana	plátano	guineo
	kidney beans	frijoles	habichuelas
	cake	pastel	bizcocho

our results from speakers we tested who lived in Mexico and Puerto Rico. We will see that speakers living in Chicago show greater familiarity with outgroup terms than "homeland" speakers in Mexico and Puerto Rico do, which we interpret as an outcome of dialect contact.

Participants were asked to look at the 10 photos in Table 3.2 one at a time and offer the Spanish word they most commonly used for the item. If they could not identify the picture or did not know any Spanish word for the item, the interviewer usually said the word in English. It was hoped that this would jog the participants' memory without resulting in them favoring one Spanish variety over the other. After participants offered a Spanish word, they were asked whether they knew another Spanish word for that item. Most of the time, they were also asked if they knew "who used those words"—that is, with what Spanish-speaking group they associated each lexical item with which they were familiar.

Responses were scored using the following system devised by the authors.[4] The first word offered received 2 points for the dialect it is associated with according to Table 3.2. If a participant offered a second word, it received 1 point for that dialect. If the first word offered was in Spanish but was not one of the variants in Table 3.2, it received no points; a subsequent word that *was* in Table 3.2 received 1 point. Examples 1 through 5 illustrate how five different responses were coded for responses after seeing the picture of earrings.

Example	First word offered	Second word offered	Total points for this item
1	aretes (2 points MX)	pantallas (1 point PR)	2 MX, 1 PR
2	pantallas (2 points PR)	none (0 points MX)	0 MX, 2 PR
3	pantallas (2 points PR)	aretes (1 point MX)	1 MX, 2 PR
4	aretes (2 points MX)	none (0 points PR)	2 MX, 0 PR
5	pendientes (0 points)	aretes (1 point MX)	1 MX, 0 PR

This coding system led to the following possible results. The maximum score for one dialect was 20 points (2 points per word times 10 words), and if this score was achieved, the maximum score for the other dialect was 10

---

4. As explained in Chapter 2, all data were collected between 2006 and 2010, before Fernández Parera (2017) published his study using a four-point scale, but the concept is similar.

points (1 point per word times 10 words). Thus, the maximum total score for each individual was 30 points. We think this coding system represents a slight methodological improvement over Chambers (1992) because our method assigns more value to words offered first. In Chambers's study, responses from subjects who offered both Southern England English and Canadian English words, as some Canadians did, received just 0.5 point in the tally. This is sensible because Cameron's was a study of lexical acquisition, the idea being that if the respondents still had a Canadian word, it was because the English word had not yet ousted it. But we sought to establish participants' familiarity with their own ingroup lexicon as well as with the outgroup lexicon. In our case, the pressure for either Mexicans or Puerto Ricans in Chicago to adopt the others' dialect is not as strong as the pressure faced by the young Canadians relocated to England in Chambers's (1992) study, making it possibly more likely that these Mexicans and Puerto Ricans would be familiar with both terms rather than having one replace the other.

A few questions arise about this methodology. First, assigning 2 points to the first word offered reflects an assumption that it is the word more frequently used by the speaker. But is there reliable evidence that this is true? Matthei and Roeper (1985) argue that the frequency of occurrence of a word affects the time it takes an individual to gain access to that word, which suggests that the first word offered may in fact be the word that is heard and produced with higher frequency by that speaker. Similarly, Porter and Kennison (2010) suggest that words experienced frequently in daily life are responded to faster and recalled better than words experienced more infrequently and that this effect has been observed in a variety of tasks including reading, isolated word identification, and word list recall.

In several instances, however, we saw evidence that the first word produced was not, in fact, according to the participants themselves, typically the first word they would use. Six such examples are shown here; some but not all of these cases involved interviewers of the same dialect background. Regardless, we assigned 2 points to their first response.

Example	Points assigned	
	Mexican	**Puerto Rican**
1. *Es una naranja. En Puerto Rico, le decimos china.* [Interviewer: *Y ¿cuál usa usted más?*] *China.* (#18, G2 Puerto Rican female) It's a *naranja*. In Puerto Rico, we say *china*. [Interviewer: And which one do you use most?] *China.*	2 for *naranja*	1 for *china*

Example	Points assigned	
	Mexican	**Puerto Rican**
2. *Aretes, pantallas.* Yo uso whatever comes out easier. (#40, G3 Puerto Rican female) *Aretes, pantallas.* I use whatever comes out easier.	2 for *aretes*	1 for *pantallas*
3. *Piscina.* [Interviewer:¿Conoces otra palabra?] *Alberca.* [Interviewer:¿Cuál usas más frecuentemente, piscina o alberca?] *Alberca.* (#25, G3 Mexican female) *Piscina.* [Interviewer: Do you know another word?] *Alberca.* [Interviewer: Which one do you use most frequently, *piscina* or *alberca*?] *Alberca.*	1 for *alberca*	2 for *piscina*
4. *Alberca o piscina, yo le digo piscina.* (#15, G2 Mexican female) *Alberca* or *piscina*, I say *piscina*.	2 for *alberca*	1 for *piscina*
5. *Piscina, es la forma correcta para decir alberca. Yo nunca he oído a alguien decir piscina.* (#12, G2 Mexican female) *Piscina*, it's the correct way to say *alberca*. I've never heard someone say *piscina*.	1 for *alberca*	2 for *piscina*
6. *Estos son lentes. Se dice gafas.* [Interviewer: ¿Otro nombre?] *Espejuelos. Para nosotros son espejuelos.* (#92, G1 Puerto Rican female) These are *lentes*. You say *gafas*. [Interviewer: Another name?] *Espejuelos*. For us they're *espejuelos*.	1 for *alberca*	2 for *piscina*

A second question is this: can we be sure that knowledge of an outgroup term is due to contact with members of the outgroup, or could it have come from another source? In most cases, participants stated that their lexical familiarity was a result of contact in Chicago with members of the outgroup. For example, when asked how she knew *autobús*, a G1 Puerto Rican being interviewed by a Mexican stated, "Me parece por haber estado aquí, por conocerlos a ustedes. Si no, solo sabría *guagua*" (It seems to me from having been here, from knowing you all. If not, I would only know *guagua*). But in a few cases, participants stated that they were familiar with outgroup variants from school or television. A Mexican G2, for example, stated: "He escuchado *anteojos* en la televisión, no se qué nacionalidad era" (I've heard *anteojos* on TV, I don't know what nationality it was), while another said, "*Gafas*, lo leí en un libro" (*Gafas*, I read it in a book).

A third and very important question about this lexical task is this: to what extent are speakers' word choices influenced by the dialect of the person with whom they are interacting in that moment? It is notoriously difficult to avoid the problem of interviewer effects. If an individual knows two ways to refer to the same object, it is possible that the first word they produce will depend on the variety of Spanish being spoken by the person interviewing them. For example, both authors are native New Yorkers living in the Midwest. If we were shown a can of a soft drink, we might say "pop" if we had just completed an hour-long interview with someone from the Midwest, but we might produce "soda" if instead we had been speaking with another New Yorker. Similarly, if a Puerto Rican is being interviewed by a Mexican, it is possible that during that time, she will utilize some of the Mexican traits she may have in her repertoire. This idea echoes Grosjean's (1998) and Kroll's (2014) proposals that bilinguals never have any of their languages completely "turned off," but rather the languages are always exerting some degree of influence on each other. It is similarly plausible that individuals who have features from two dialects at their disposal never completely "turn off" one set of features. However, we will see that the majority of speakers vacillated between which variants they offered first—sometimes Puerto Rican, sometimes Mexican—suggesting that influence of the interviewer does not dominate participants' lexical responses.

Short of systematic long-term analysis of naturalistic production, there may not be a viable way to ascertain speakers' lexical knowledge and day-to-day use. Even if each participant were interviewed on two separate occasions, once by a Mexican and once by a Puerto Rican, completing the lexical identification task a second time might show washback effects from having completed it the first time. Given these complications, we emphasize that ours is a measure of *familiarity* with outgroup lexicon. Our findings cannot support any claims about the degree of actual lexical borrowing that might occur in the day-to-day speaking of these individuals. However, it seems logical that being familiar with a word is a necessary precursor to its borrowing and eventual adoption.

Participants

Table 3.3 displays the subset of the CHISPA corpus that was analyzed for lexical familiarity.

Table 3.3. PARTICIPANTS IN LEXICAL IDENTIFICATION TASK (*N* = 121).

G	MX	PR	MXPR	Total
G1	12	11	—	23
G2	13	15	18	46
G3	12	13	27	52
Total	37	39	45	121

This represents the entire CHISPA corpus (described in Chapter 2) except for three speakers who were inadvertently not administered the lexical identification task.

3.4. HOMELAND SPEAKERS

Before exploring Mexican and Puerto Rican lexical familiarity in Chicago, we established a baseline with what we called "homeland" speakers: 15 Mexican college students who never left Mexico and 15 Puerto Rican college students who never left Puerto Rico.[5] We did this for two reasons: (1) to establish that these 10 items are referred to with different terms by most Puerto Ricans and Mexicans, and (2) to determine whether homeland speakers had familiarity with outgroup terms, reasoning that if they did, then the argument that Chicago outgroup lexical scores were the result of dialect contact in the city would not be tenable. We used the same scoring methods described for the CHISPA participants. Results of both homeland lexical familiarity are shown in Table 3.4.

Table 3.4 shows that, as expected, both homeland groups scored the maximum 20 points on ingroup lexicon. Neither group was very familiar with outgroup lexicon, although homeland Puerto Ricans were significantly more familiar with Mexican vocabulary (4.87 points on average) than homeland Mexicans were with Puerto Rican vocabulary (0.80 points on average) ($t(28) = -9.30$, $p < .001$). This supports our choice of these items as common among Mexicans and Puerto Ricans but not among the outgroup. The higher Puerto Rican outgroup score is likely due to differences in diffusion and status of the two dialects in Latin America. The relatively prominent standing of Mexican Spanish in the Spanish-speaking world and the greater diffusion of this dialect across television and movies make it likely that Puerto Ricans on

---

5. Thanks to Luis Ortiz López and to Erika Torres for collecting the data in Puerto Rico, although we very much wanted to do so ourselves during a Chicago winter.

Table 3.4. LEXICAL FAMILIARITY AMONG "HOMELAND" SPEAKERS (MEXICANS AND PUERTO RICANS IN MEXICO AND PUERTO RICO).

Group	Ingroup average score	Outgroup average score
Mexicans in Mexico (n = 15)	20.00	0.80
Puerto Ricans in Puerto Rico (n = 15)	20.00	4.87

the island would be exposed to Mexican/"general" Spanish. Conversely, Puerto Rican Spanish, which tends to be internationally stigmatized (Zentella, 1990, 1997, 2007), is largely unknown in other contexts, perhaps also in part due to the relatively small population of Puerto Ricans—according to the 2010 Census, the island has approximately 3.5 million residents, plus an additional 4.6 million Puerto Ricans living stateside.

We also wanted to see whether any specific lexical items were more or less known by homeland speakers. Given our scoring system of 0, 1, and 2 points, calculating a mean score on each lexical item would result in a range from 0 to 2, which is not terribly revealing. Thus, we chose to report what we call percentage familiarity. Percentage familiarity was calculated as follows. We added all individuals' scores together for each item. At 2 points per first named item, multiplied by 15 people, the maximum composite score for each lexical item is 30. Next, in order to compare the 30 homeland speakers to the 121 individuals in the Chicago corpus—two very different n sizes—the total number of points scored by all participants was multiplied by the maximum score (the maximum score on any item is 2 times n) and then divided by 100. A percentage familiarity score of 40%, for example, does not mean that 40% of the cell knew the item; it means that all speakers in that cell combined scored 40% of the maximum possible score (2 times n) on that item.

Results are displayed in Table 3.5 and Figure 3.1. Looking at the item *bus*, for example, the results should be interpreted as follows. The 15 homeland Mexicans scored 30 total points on the ingroup item, and 30 points is 100% of the maximum of 30 points. These 15 people, however, only scored 2 points total on outgroup vocabulary, and 2 points is 7% of the maximum outgroup score of 30. The 15 homeland Puerto Rican individuals scored 30 points on the ingroup item (100% of 30, the maximum score) and only 8 points on the outgroup item (27% of 30, the maximum score). Because the highest percentage familiarity score was 47%, in Figure 3.1, the *y* axis goes only to 50% so that the small percentage values are more easily visible.

Table 3.5. COMPOSITE SCORES AND PERCENTAGE FAMILIARITY SCORES BY ITEM, HOMELAND SPEAKERS.

	Homeland Mexicans (n = 15)				Homeland Puerto Ricans (n = 15)			
	Ingroup	% Ingroup	Outgroup	% Outgroup	Ingroup	% Ingroup	Outgroup	% Outgroup
orange	30	100%	0	0.0%	30	100%	14	46.7%
pacifier	30	100%	0	0.0%	30	100%	10	33.3%
bus	30	100%	2	6.7%	30	100%	8	26.7%
eyeglasses	30	100%	1	3.3%	30[a]	100%	6	20.0%
earrings	30	100%	0	0.0%	30[b]	100%	12	40.0%
swimming pool	30	100%	7	23.3%	30	100%	5	16.7%
drinking straw	30	100%	1	3.3%	30	100%	1	3.3%
banana	30	100%	1	3.3%	30	100%	0	0.0%
kidney beans	30	100%	0	0.0%	30	100%	4	13.3%
cake	30	100%	0	0.0%	30	100%	12	40.0%
Total, % familiarity	450	100%	12	2.7%	450	100%	72	16.0%

[a] Many homeland Puerto Ricans offered *espejuelos* and *gafas* as their two responses. They may have been familiar with *lentes*, but unfortunately, we did not ask for variants after the first two offered.
[b] Many homeland Puerto Ricans also offered *pendientes*.

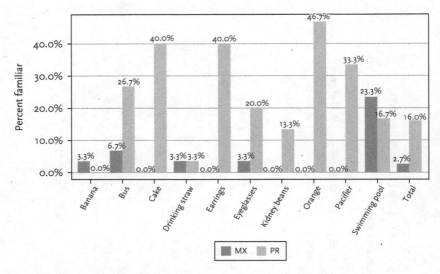

Figure 3.1. Percentage familiarity scores by outgroup item, homeland speakers (*y* axis = familiarity score).

We see that the only Puerto Rican term with which homeland Mexicans showed more than 20% familiarity—the tallest dark grey bar, showing a percentage familiarity score of 23.3% and in this case representing a total of 7 individuals—was *swimming pool*. To our knowledge, the Mexican term for swimming pool, *alberca*, is used only by Mexicans and not by speakers of any other Spanish dialects. This makes *alberca* a minority lexical variant in the Spanish-speaking world. This status as a minority variant, along with exposure to *piscina* in the media and other sources, likely contributes to this high homeland Mexican outgroup score. Yet *popote* (drinking straw) is also uniquely Mexican, but the homeland Mexicans did not show great familiarity with other variants for it (a very low 3% familiarity score). It does not seem likely that *swimming pool* is a much higher-frequency item than *popote*, which might cause homeland Mexicans to show greater knowledge of outgroup terms for swimming pool than for drinking straw.

Homeland Puerto Ricans showed substantial familiarity with the Mexican terms for orange (*naranja*, 47% percentage familiarity score), earrings (*aretes*, 40%), cake (*pastel*, 40%), and pacifier (*chupete/chupetón*, 33%). Of these four words, to our knowledge, the Puerto Rican variants *china*, *pantallas*, and *bobo* are used only in Puerto Rico, making them minority variants.[6] Thus, similarly

---

6. But recall that in New York City (Zentella, 1990), Cubans, Puerto Ricans, and Dominicans knew *china*, and Puerto Ricans, Dominicans, and Colombians knew *pantallas*, probably because they are in contact with speakers from these dialects, unlike the homeland sample.

[88] *Spanish in Chicago*

to what happens with the Mexican word *alberca*, homeland Puerto Ricans may be frequently exposed to outgroup variants for these items. The fourth of these items, *bizcocho*, is also used in the Dominican Republic, but *pastel* is a very common international term for cake.[7] Many Puerto Rican homeland speakers mentioned being exposed to outgroup vocabulary in school (such as *naranja*), on product labels (*frijoles*), and in movies and television (*aretes, chupete, naranja*). *Naranja, pastel,* and *chupete/chupetón* are used in many other Spanish-speaking nations, but as already mentioned, to our knowledge, *aretes* is mostly used only in Mexico.[8] Thus, homeland Puerto Ricans' familiarity with *aretes* is noteworthy.

3.5. CHICAGO MEXICANS AND PUERTO RICANS

3.5.1. Outgroup Lexical Familiarity Scores

Given that our primary question was about knowledge of lexicon from the other group, we present outgroup scores first (Table 3.6 and Figure 3.2) before discussing ingroup and overall scores.

Table 3.6. AVERAGE OUTGROUP LEXICAL SCORES, CHICAGO MEXICAN, PUERTO RICAN, AND HOMELAND SPEAKERS (STANDARD DEVIATIONS IN PARENTHESES).

Mexican		Puerto Rican	
G1 ($n = 12$)	3.75 (2.14)	G1 ($n = 11$)	9.18 (3.54)
G2 ($n = 13$)	3.92 (2.57)	G2 ($n = 15$)	9.47 (2.80)
G3 ($n = 12$)	1.50 (2.44)	G3 ($n = 13$)	8.00 (3.22)
Homeland ($n = 20$)	0.80 (0.94)	Homeland ($n = 20$)	4.87 (1.41)

7. A post on Wordreference.com (2006) about the term *birthday cake* included the following: "Spain: torta. Argentina, Colombia, Peru and Venezuela: torta. Puerto Rico and Dominican Republic: bizcocho. Mexico: pastel." Three homeland Puerto Ricans produced *torta* for cake. When we report the Chicago data, we will explore the fact that *bizcocho* has a vulgar meaning in Mexico. Also, to further complicate this word, *pastel* in Puerto Rico refers to an item similar to Mexican *tamale*.

8. Although a colleague suggested that *aretes* is used in the Dominican Republic as well.

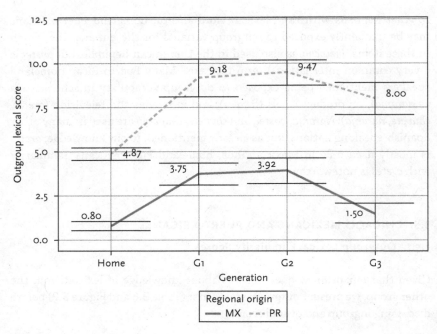

Figure 3.2. Outgroup lexical scores.

We see that five of the six Chicago groups strongly outperform the homeland speakers, which we suggest is due to contact with the outgroup in Chicago. Looking more closely at the Chicago speakers, our first hypothesis was confirmed: a two-way ANOVA on outgroup lexical scores with the between-participants factors of generation (for homeland, G1, G2, and G3 speakers) and regional origin (for Mexican vs. Puerto Rican participants) found a main effect of regional origin, $F(1, 98) = 130.57$, $p < .001$, $\eta_p^2 = 0.57$, such that Puerto Rican participants had significantly higher outgroup lexical scores (M = 7.77, SD = 3.31) than Mexican participants (M = 2.42, SD = 2.35), $t(98) = 11.43$, $p < .001$. There was also a significant main effect of generation, $F(3, 98) = 15.53$, $p < .001$, $\eta_p^2 = 0.32$. Follow-up Bonferroni-corrected t-tests revealed that averaging across regional origin groups, homeland speakers had significantly lower outgroup lexical scores (M = 2.83, SD = 2.38) than G1 speakers (M = 6.35, SD = 3.96), $t(98) = 5.43$, $p < .001$, and than G2 speakers (M = 6.89, SD = 3.86). The G1 and G2 groups did not differ significantly from each other ($p > .05$). The G3 group had significantly lower outgroup lexical scores (M = 4.88, SD = 4.23) than the G2 group, $t(98) = 2.93$, $p = .022$; nonsignificantly lower scores than the G1 group, $t(98) = 2.46$, $p = .073$; and significantly higher scores than the homeland group, $t(98) = 2.93$, $p = .021$. Finally, the interaction of regional origin and generation was not significant, $F(3, 98) = 1.20$, $p = .315$, $\eta_p^2 = 0.04$.

Our finding that Puerto Ricans of all three generations were significantly more familiar with Mexican vocabulary items than Mexicans were with Puerto Rican vocabulary is likely due to the overwhelming numerical superiority of the Mexican population in Chicago and the ubiquitous presence of Mexican Spanish throughout communities and media in the city. We feel this finding is evidence of dialect contact and suggests that accommodation is stronger in one direction—Puerto Ricans toward Mexicans. However, we note that the pattern of differences between Mexicans and Puerto Ricans does not change across the generations; the two lines in Figure 3.2 have the same shape, with the sole difference that Puerto Ricans in G3 do not decline as steeply in outgroup lexicon as do Mexicans.

Regarding generation and outgroup scores, we had two hypotheses: either recency of immigration would correspond to higher outgroup scores due to greater overall levels of Spanish use (G1 > G2 > G3), or the more generational time spent in Chicago, the higher the outgroup vocabulary score would be due to increased length of intergroup contact (G3 > G2 > G1). We see that part of the first hypothesis is sustained: G1 speakers from both groups had significantly higher outgroup lexical scores than G3 speakers. As noted in Chapter 2, the overall proficiency in Spanish of our G3 participants declines, and this decline is likely accompanied by a decrease in input and exposure to Spanish of any variety, but particularly exposure to outgroup varieties. That is, G3s' relatively limited Spanish proficiency appears to be restricted to the variety they learned in the home. However, part of the second hypothesis seems to be supported as well, in that G2 speakers knew slightly more outgroup lexicon than their G1 counterparts did. However, this was by an average of only 0.17 point for Mexicans and 0.29 point for Puerto Ricans, which was not significant. Outgroup scores for Puerto Ricans remained relatively stable from G2 (9.47) to G3 (8.00).

3.5.2. Ingroup Lexical Familiarity Scores

How did speakers in the three generations of Chicago Mexicans and Puerto Ricans score on their own ingroup lexicon, and how do they compare with homeland speakers? Table 3.7 and Figure 3.3 show these results.

We notice that while Mexicans stay fairly uniform on ingroup lexical scores across generations (between 18.6 and 19.4), Puerto Ricans decline from 17.2 to 16.9 and then to 14.5. A two-way ANOVA was performed on ingroup lexical scores, with the between-participants factors of regional origin (Mexican vs. Puerto Rican) and generation (for homeland, G1, G2, and G3 speakers). There was a significant main effect of regional origin, $F(1, 98) = 24.18$, $p < .001$, $\eta_p^2 = .20$, such that Mexicans had higher ingroup lexical scores (M = 19.21, SD = 1.23) than Puerto Ricans (M = 17.26, SD = 3.31), $t(98) = 4.92, p < .001$.

Table 3.7. AVERAGE INGROUP LEXICAL SCORES, CHICAGO MEXICAN, PUERTO RICAN, AND HOMELAND SPEAKERS (STANDARD DEVIATIONS IN PARENTHESES).

Mexican		Puerto Rican	
G1 ($n = 12$)	19.42 (0.79)	G1 ($n = 11$)	17.18 (3.31)
G2 ($n = 13$)	18.69 (0.95)	G2 ($n = 15$)	16.93 (2.52)
G3 ($n = 12$)	18.58 (1.93)	G3 ($n = 13$)	14.54 (3.78)
Homeland ($n = 20$)	20.00 (0.00)	Homeland ($n = 20$)	20.00 (0.00)

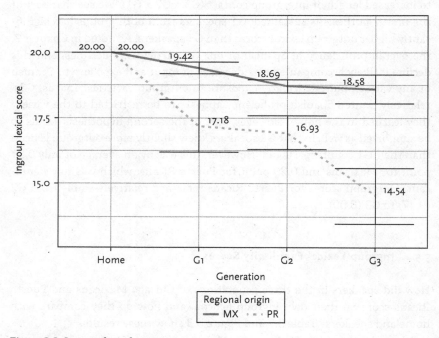

Figure 3.3. Ingroup lexical scores.

There was also a significant main effect of generation, $F(3, 98) = 12.85$, $p < .001$, $\eta_p^2 = .28$. This was qualified by a significant interaction with regional origin, $F(3, 98) = 4.31$, $p = .007$, $\eta_p^2 = .12$. Follow-up analyses revealed that ingroup lexical scores only differed significantly across generational groups within Puerto Rican speakers, such that homeland speakers had significantly higher scores (M = 20.00, SD = 0.00) than G1 speakers (M = 17.18, SD = 3.31), $t(98) = 2.82, p = .005$; and than G2 speakers (M = 16.93, SD = 2.52), $t(98) = 4.02, p = .001$. The G1 and G2 Puerto Rican speakers did not vary significantly with each other ($p > .05$), but each had significantly higher scores than G3 Puerto Rican speakers (M = 14.54, SD = 3.78), for G1 vs. G3: $t(98) = 3.09, p = .014$; for G2 versus G3: $t(98) = 3.02, p = .017$. By contrast, for Mexican speakers, no pairwise comparison between generational groups was significant (all $p > .05$). In sum, these results suggest that generational declines in ingroup lexical scores occur for Puerto Rican speakers but not for Mexican speakers.

Our main takeaway here is that Puerto Ricans score lower on ingroup lexicon than Mexicans do, but as we saw in the previous section, they scored higher than Mexicans on outgroup lexicon. This suggests that dialect contact serves to enhance the linguistic range of Puerto Ricans even when their overall proficiency declines. It also serves as a reminder that what at first glance might appear as a lack of knowledge upon further consideration might actually be an accommodation to another dialect that enriches rather than diminishes their Spanish.

3.5.3. Total Lexical Familiarity Scores

Total lexical scores give a glimpse into speakers' Spanish repertoires. What scores did the three generations of Chicago Mexicans and Puerto Ricans display, and how do they compare to the homeland speakers? Table 3.8 shows all regional origins by generation.

There was no change in total lexical score from G1 to G2. A one-way ANOVA showed a significant effect for generation, $F(2, 73) = 9.95, p < .001, \eta p^2 = .21$. Follow-up t-tests indicated that this significant effect was driven by the G3 group (M = 21.36, SD = 3.03), which had significantly lower total lexical scores than both the G1 group (M = 24.70, SD = 2.79), $t(73) = 3.80, p = .001$, and the G2 group (M = 24.64, SD = 3.23), $t(73) = 3.93, p = .001$. We break total scores down by regional origin (Table 3.9), and Figure 3.4 presents ingroup and outgroup scores together.

Table 3.8. AVERAGE TOTAL LEXICAL SCORES, BY CHICAGO GENERATIONAL GROUP.

G	Total
G1 ($n = 22$)	24.6
G2 ($n = 28$)	24.6
G3 ($n = 25$)	21.4

Table 3.9. TOTAL LEXICAL SCORES, CHICAGO AND HOMELAND SPEAKERS.

Mexican		Puerto Rican	
G1 (*n* = 12)	23.17 (2.17)	G1 (*n* = 11)	26.36 (2.46)
G2 (*n* = 13)	22.61 (2.36)	G2 (*n* = 15)	26.40 (2.87)
G3 (*n* = 12)	20.08 (2.94)	G3 (*n* = 13)	22.54 (2.70)
Homeland (*n* = 20)	20.80 (0.94?)	Homeland (*n* = 20)	24.87 (1.41)

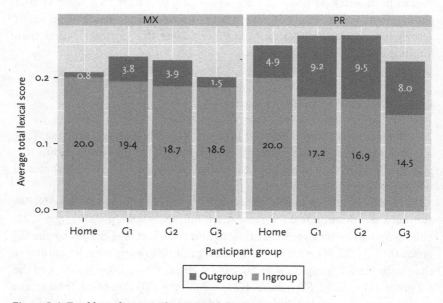

Figure 3.4. Total lexical scores, Chicago and homeland speakers.

We see that for both Mexicans and Puerto Ricans, G1 and G2 speakers actually have higher total vocabulary scores than their homeland counterparts. A two-way ANOVA found a main effect of regional origin, $F(1,98) = 56.51$, $p < .001$, $\eta_p^2 = 0.37$. Follow-up Bonferroni-corrected t-tests revealed that Puerto Ricans had significantly higher total lexical scores (M = 25.10, SD = 3.21) than Mexicans (M = 21.97, SD = 2.78), $t(98) = 3.38$, $p < .001$. Furthermore, our ANOVA also showed a main effect of generation, $F(3,98) = 12.32$, $p < .001$, $\eta_p^2 = 0.27$, such that G1 speakers (M = 24.70, SD = 2.79) and G2 (M = 24.64, SD = 3.23) did not differ significantly from each other ($p > .05$), but each showed significantly higher total lexical scores than G3 (M = 21.36, SD = 3.03) and homeland speakers (M = 22.83, SD = 2.38) (at $p < .05$). No other follow-up pairwise comparisons between generation groups were significant. There was no significant interaction of regional origin and generation, $F(3,98) = 0.64$, $p = .590$, $\eta_p^2 = 0.02$, suggesting that effects of generation group did not differ between Mexicans and Puerto Ricans.

Our results suggest that moving to Chicago results in an increase in knowledge of ways to refer to these items for both Mexican and Puerto Rican G1s but attrition for the third generation. Of these eight groups, G2 and G1 Puerto Ricans showed the greatest familiarity with outgroup lexicon, which, despite their ingroup scores being lower than those of their Mexican counterparts, led to them having significantly higher overall lexical scores than Mexicans. This is interesting because we saw in Chapter 2 that overall proficiency of Puerto Ricans (as measured by applying a modified ACTFL OPI scale to the entire sociolinguistic interview) is lower than average overall Mexican proficiency and also that average Puerto Rican proficiency declines more steeply across the three generations than Mexican proficiency does. Thus, despite lower overall proficiency, Puerto Ricans exhibited higher overall lexical scores on these particular items than Mexicans. Thus, what bolsters Puerto Ricans' lexical scores is their knowledge of outgroup terms.

For a final visual representation of these data, we present Figures 3.5 and 3.6. Mexican scores are along the x-axis, and Puerto Rican scores are on the y-axis. This means that points located close to the diagonal line indicate fairly equal scores for Mexican and Puerto Rican lexicon.

Figure 3.5 shows that Mexicans' scores across all three generational groups stay largely concentrated in the bottom-right quadrant, meaning high Mexican lexical scores and low Puerto Rican scores. One G2 Mexican showed an uncharacteristically high score of 11 on Puerto Rican lexicon, but no such data point occurred in the other two generational groups. Most Mexicans, then, performed largely monodialectally on our lexical task. Similarly, as shown in Figure 3.6, G1 Puerto Ricans were concentrated in the upper-left

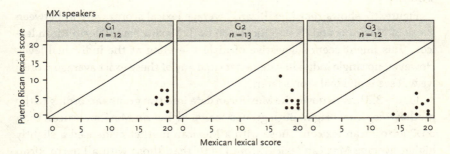

Figure 3.5. Mexican ingroup and outgroup scores by generation.

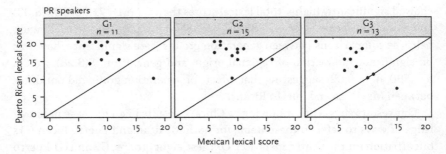

Figure 3.6. Puerto Rican ingroup and outgroup scores by generation.

quadrant, meaning high Puerto Rican scores and low Mexican scores (except for one outlying individual in G1 and another in G3). But among G2 and G3 Puerto Ricans, there was a shift to increased knowledge of Mexican lexicon accompanied by a slight decrease in Puerto Rican lexicon. This suggests that regional origin becomes less strong a predictor of lexical familiarity with increasing generational residence in Chicago and that this is due to changes among Puerto Rican speakers, not among Mexican speakers.

3.6. CHICAGO MEXIRICANS

Now we address the lexical familiarity of MexiRicans. Recall that these individuals, who experience varying degrees of intrafamilial dialect contact, do not have an "outgroup." For most of them, both Mexican and Puerto Rican lexicon was present to some extent in their homes while they were growing up, thus both can be considered ingroup dialects. Based on Potowski (2016), our hypothesis was that MexiRicans would show greater familiarity with the lexicon of their mother's ethnolinguistic group. For ease of comparison, Figure 3.7 the solid line represents Chicago Mexican scores, the small dotted line show Puerto Rican scores, and the larger dashed line represents MexiRicans' scores.

Figure 3.7 shows that MexiRicans' average lexical scores were in between those of Mexicans and Puerto Ricans on both Mexican and Puerto Rican lexicon. This might seem suggestive of dialect leveling at the individual level. However, no single individual demonstrated any of these exact average scores; we will see individual scores later.

Figure 3.8 breaks down the MexiRican data into two groups according to the mother's regional origin. Both groups scored higher on Mexican lexicon than on Puerto Rican lexicon. Those with a Mexican mother evidenced a slightly higher average Mexican lexical score (14.9) than those with a Puerto Rican mother (13.6). The reverse is true of MexiRicans with Puerto Rican mothers;

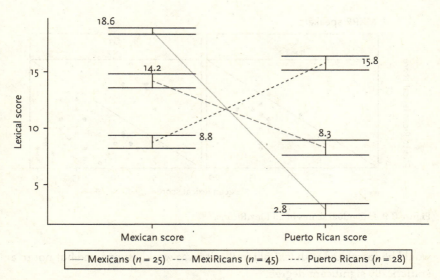

Figure 3.7. Mexican, Puerto Rican, and MexiRican average lexical scores.

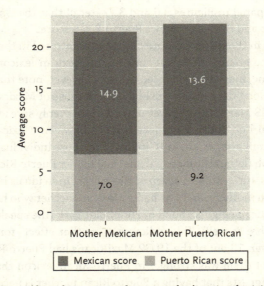

Figure 3.8. MexiRicans' lexical scores according to mother's regional origin.

they knew more Puerto Rican vocabulary (9.2 on average) than those with Mexican mothers (7.0). However, a one-way multivariate analysis of variance (MANOVA) on Mexican scores and Puerto Rican scores with the factor of mother's region of origin (Mexican vs. Puerto Rican) showed no significant differences between the groups, Wilks's Lambda = 0.94, $F(2, 43) = 1.45$, $p = .246$). In summary, the hypothesis that the regional origin of the mother

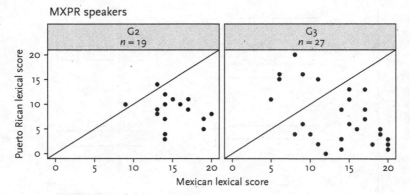

Figure 3.9. Individual scores of all MexiRicans.

would be correlated with lexical familiarity was weakly supported but not to a statistically significant degree.

A bit of additional support for the mother hypothesis comes from Figure 3.9, which presents individual data points from all 45 MexiRicans. This figure should be compared to Figures 3.6 and 3.7—recall that the x-axis represents Mexican scores and the y-axis shows Puerto Rican scores.

MexiRicans in the G2 group were largely concentrated in the bottom-right quadrant of the graph—that is, dominant in Mexican lexicon—or close to the diagonal line, indicating balanced scores. However, note that their Puerto Rican scores (along the y-axis) were higher than those of Mexican G2s (shown in Table 3.9). G3 MexiRicans, however, were more evenly spread on both sides of the diagonal line, indicating more balance between Mexican and Puerto Rican lexical familiarity on these 10 items. Only those individuals in the upper half of the graph (left of the diagonal line) had higher Puerto Rican scores than Mexican scores. Interestingly, seven of these eight individuals had been raised by Puerto Rican mothers, and one had a Mexican mother who had been raised in the Puerto Rican neighborhood of Humboldt Park (the speaker herself had been raised there as well). This indicates a "mother effect" for Puerto Rican lexicon. However, 13 out of the 19 G2 MexiRicans had Puerto Rican mothers, too, yet none of them was stronger in Puerto Rican lexicon than in Mexican lexicon. This suggests that having a Puerto Rican mother is necessary, but not sufficient, to be dominant in Puerto Rican lexicon on these 10 items.

3.7. SCORES ON INDIVIDUAL ITEMS

Data on individual lexical items are interesting for at least two reasons. First, they show specific changes between homeland and Chicago speakers, revealing which items in particular Chicago speakers become more familiar with. Second, these data show changes across generations in Chicago that the aggregate group averages do not reveal. We will report percentage familiarity scores, which were calculated as explained in Section 3.3. Recall our earlier example that a percentage familiarity score of 40% means that all of the participants in that cell scored 40% of the maximum points possible on that item. First we will discuss the scores for all three generations combined, and then we will break down the scores by generation.

Table 3.10 compares all three generations of Chicago Mexicans to homeland Mexicans on both ingroup and outgroup scores on each item.

When looking at the ingroup data in the left half of Table 3.10, we see that for two of the 10 items, *orange* and *cake*, there is zero difference between the percentage familiarity shown by Chicago speakers versus homeland speakers. For the other eight items, there is a drop in ingroup vocabulary scores, ranging from 1 point to a maximum of a 24-point drop for *alberca*. In other words, Mexicans in Chicago scored 24 percentage familiarity points less for *alberca* than their homeland counterparts, suggesting that they acquire *piscina* at *alberca*'s expense. On outgroup lexicon (the right half of Table 3.10), on all 10 items, Chicago Mexicans scored higher than homeland speakers, with the largest increase in familiarity appearing for the items *espejuelos/gafas*, *piscina*, and *habichuelas*. We propose that Chicago Mexicans show greater familiarity with these words because of their contact with Puerto Ricans in the city. However, for six of these words, the Mexicans really did not show great familiarity, averaging 10% or less (*china*, *bobo*, *pantallas*, *bizcocho*, *guineo*, and *sorbeto*). Regarding the item *swimming pool*, as stated earlier, *alberca* is a minority variant used only in Mexico, so it is not surprising that Chicago Mexicans scored double that of the homeland Mexicans on their familiarity with *piscina*. Interestingly, *alberca* showed the lowest ingroup familiarity average among Chicago Mexicans (76%).

Table 3.11 makes the same comparison for Puerto Ricans: all three generations of Chicago Puerto Ricans and homeland Puerto Ricans on both ingroup and outgroup scores by individual lexical item.

Just as with the Mexicans, we see that there is a drop in ingroup vocabulary scores for all 10 lexical items, ranging from 5 points for *pacifier* to a maximum of a 31-point drop for *orange*. That is, Puerto Ricans in Chicago are, on average, 31 percentage points less familiar with *china* than their homeland counterparts, 30 percentage points less familiar with *espejuelos/lentes*, and 27 percentage points less familiar with *pantallas*. For outgroup lexicon, however, on nine out of the 10 items, Chicago Puerto Ricans scored higher than homeland speakers, with the largest increase in familiarity obtaining for *frijoles*, *plátano*, *lentes*, and *autobús*. For some reason, Chicago Puerto Ricans were slightly less familiar with the Mexican variants *chupete/chupetón* than homeland Puerto Ricans were. Unlike the Mexicans, who showed 10% or less familiarity with six items, the Puerto Ricans did not average less than 19% familiarity on any

Table 3.10. PERCENTAGE FAMILIARITY SCORES ON INDIVIDUAL LEXICAL ITEMS, MEXICANS.

Item	Ingroup vocabulary			Outgroup vocabulary		
	Chicago MX % In	Homeland MX % In	Difference, Chicago–Homeland	Chicago MX % Out	Homeland MX % Out	Difference, Chicago–Homeland
orange	100.0	100	0.0	10.6	0	10.6
pacifier	96.0	100	-4.0	7.0	0	7.0
bus	98.7	100	-1.3	20.4	6.7	13.7
eyeglasses	97.3	100	-2.7	30.0	3.3	26.7
earrings	97.4	100	-2.6	4.0	0	4.0
swimming pool	75.4	100	-24.6	47.5	23.3	24.2
drinking straw	89.0	100	-11.0	9.6	3.3	6.3
banana	94.6	100	-5.4	4.0	3.3	0.7
beans	96.0	100	-4.0	17.5	0	17.5
cake	100.0	100	0.0	8.1	0	8.1
Average	94.4	100	-5.6	15.8	4.0	11.9

Table 3.11. PERCENTAGE FAMILIARITY SCORES ON INDIVIDUAL LEXICAL ITEMS, PUERTO RICANS.

Item	Ingroup vocabulary			Outgroup vocabulary		
	Chicago PR % In	Homeland PR % In	Difference, Chicago–Homeland	Chicago PR % Out	Homeland PR % Out	Difference, Chicago–Homeland
orange	68.0	100	-32.0	70.6	46.7	23.9
pacifier	96.1	100	-3.9	28.4	33.3	-4.9
bus	84.5	100	-15.5	56.4	26.7	29.7
eyeglasses	69.3	100	-30.7	53.8	20.0	33.8
earrings	73.4	100	-26.6	44.9	40.0	4.9
swimming pool	89.7	100	-10.3	19.2	16.7	2.5
drinking straw	83.3	100	-16.7	28.2	3.3	24.9
banana	82.1	100	-17.9	34.7	0.0	34.7
beans	88.2	100	-11.8	51.2	13.3	37.9
cake	84.8	100	-15.2	56.5	40.0	16.5
Average	81.9	100	-18.1	44.4	24.0	20.4

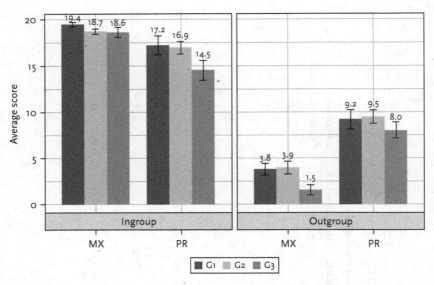

Figure 3.10. Average scores on ingroup and outgroup vocabulary, Chicago only.

outgroup item—and it is no surprise that the lowest score was on the Mexican item *swimming pool*, because *alberca* is limited to Mexican Spanish. If we ignore *swimming pool*, Chicago Puerto Ricans show between 28% and 70% familiarity with the Mexican variants.

Now we examine the generational responses by lexical item. First, for a clearer view of the overall generational patterns, Figure 3.10 presents side by side the data we saw earlier in Table 3.10 but without the homeland speakers' data.

Figure 3.10 reminds us that the relatively low ingroup Puerto Rican familiarity rates should be understood in light of the group's high outgroup familiarity rates: their overall lexical scores are higher in spite of their lower ingroup scores.

Table 3.12 presents the Mexican data organized by two categories of outgroup vocabulary scores: scores that decreased from G1 to G3 and scores that exhibit an irregular pattern. Ingroup scores are not included here because, with the exception of *swimming pool*, ingroup scores were always above 92% (and for half of the items, ingroup scores reached a 100% familiarity rate).

We see in Table 3.12 that for the first six items listed, Mexicans' knowledge of Puerto Rican variants decreases across generations. While for some words (*pacifier, earrings, banana*), it decreased by less than 15 percentage points, which is relatively little, these words did not have very high scores to begin with. But even the relatively low degree of familiarity dropped to zero for G3 speakers. The table clearly confirms our observation that Mexicans prefer their own lexical items across the board. As for the words that did not show a

[102] *Spanish in Chicago*

Table 3.12. MEXICAN CHANGES IN OUTGROUP PERCENTAGE FAMILIARITY SCORES ACROSS GENERATIONS.

			G1	G2	G3
Decrease	> 15 percentage points	beans	29	23	0
		eyeglasses	42	31	17
		drinking straw	17	8	4
	< 15 percentage points	pacifier	13	8	0
		earrings	8	4	0
		banana	8	4	0
Irregular changes		orange	4	19	8
		bus	21	23	17
		swimming pool	38	77	25
		cake	8	12	4

Table 3.13. PUERTO RICAN CHANGES IN OUTGROUP PERCENTAGE FAMILIARITY SCORES ACROSS GENERATIONS.

			G1	G2	G3
Increase	> 15 percentage points	orange	59	70	81
		eyeglasses	32	60	65
Decrease	> 15 percentage points	pacifier	55	23	12
		earrings	64	43	31
	< 15 percentage points	bus	64	53	54
		beans	59	50	46
Irregular changes		cake	45	67	54
		banana	32	40	31
		drinking *straw*	23	33	27
		swimming *pool*	27	30	0

decline in familiarity scores with each generation but rather a more irregular pattern, we do notice that in all four cases (*orange, bus, swimming pool, cake*), it was G2 speakers who showed the highest familiarity.

Next, we examine lexical scores in the same way for Puerto Ricans (Table 3.13).

Table 3.13 shows that outgroup scores for *orange* and *eyeglasses* actually increased as generation increased. Perhaps for G3 Puerto Rican speakers, the Mexican variants of these items are higher in frequency. However, most changes were decreases or showed an irregular pattern, which suggests that each word has its own story and requires further analysis (recall Chambers's statement cited in Section 3.1 that there is often arbitrariness regarding why some lexical items persist and others change in situations of dialect contact). We also note that of the four words that showed an irregular pattern, two were the same words that showed irregular patterns for Mexicans (*cake* and *swimming pool*), and again it was G2 speakers who showed the highest familiarity.

There are two items that seem to offer a clear explanation for the scores shown here. The first is *banana*. Among homeland Puerto Ricans, 100% referred to the photo of the yellow fruit with the word *guineo* and thus had a zero score for the word *plátano*; this is because on the island, the word *plátano* refers to a green plantain, not a yellow banana. But Chicago Puerto Ricans scored 36% familiarity on *plátano*, suggesting contact with Mexicans. Another interesting example is the Puerto Rican variant for *cake*, which is *bizcocho*. In Mexico, this word can mean *vagina* or can be used as a vulgar flirtatious comment about a woman's attractiveness.[9] Recall Zentella's (1990) finding that if a word is taboo in one dialect, lexical accommodation can be accelerated. Several Chicago Puerto Ricans stated that they were aware that *bizcocho* had a taboo meaning among Mexicans, and such a taboo likely facilitates familiarity with, and even possible shifting to, the Mexican variant *pastel*. Yet *pastel* in Puerto Rico refers to a completely different food item resembling a Mexican *tamal*, which complicates matters even further, as demonstrated in the following exchange with a G1 Puerto Rican woman:

[Interviewer shows photo of birthday cake.]
INTERVIEWEE: Para mi es *bizcocho* pero yo se que pa' los Mexicanos son *pasteles*. Pero *pasteles* para mi es otra cosa. (For me it's *bizcocho*, but I know for Mexicans they're *pasteles*. But *pasteles* for me is something else.)
INTERVIEWER: ¿Qué es? (What is it?)
INTERVIEWEE: Para mi los *pasteles* son como tamales pero tamales son mexicanos, *pasteles* son puertorriqueños, pero el *bizcocho* le llamaba *pasteles*, para nosotros es *bizcocho* cake. (For me *pasteles* are like tamales but tamales are Mexican, *pasteles* are Puerto Rican, but *bizcocho* they called it *pasteles*, for us it's *bizcocho* cake.)

9. In a similar vein, it would be interesting to study whether the verb *coger*, which in Puerto Rico and the majority of Spanish-speaking varieties means to take or grab but in Mexico is a vulgar term for sexual intercourse, is used less frequently by Chicago Puerto Ricans than by homeland Puerto Ricans.

In summary, across the three generations, Puerto Ricans in Chicago seem to be keeping *bobo, piscina, guagua, habichuelas, bizcocho,* and *guineo* but replacing *china, anteojos/espejuelos/gafas, pantallas,* and *sorbeto* with Mexican variants. Perhaps *orange, eyeglasses, earrings,* and *drinking straw* are higher-frequency items and, as a result, Puerto Ricans are hearing the Mexican equivalents for these words more frequently than they hear the other items. We consulted the Corpus del Español NOW (News on the Web, https://www.corpusdelespanol.org/now), but this can only tell us how frequent these items are in Spanish print media, which is very likely not the primary source of our participants' Spanish input. Additionally, the item *china* returns more than 100,000 hits, but all are related to the Asian country and not the fruit. Therefore, we can only speculate as follows:

- *Pacifier* is not a very common word (which might lead to retaining the first-learned word, *bobo*).
- *Bus* is a very common referent in a city like Chicago, so it is unclear why Puerto Ricans hold on to *guagua*—perhaps as a marker of Puerto Rican identity. *Guagua* is a distinctively Caribbean word which almost all other national groups recognize as such and thus has a highly marked social significance.
- *Beans* are commonly referred to in the Puerto Rican dish *arroz con habichuelas*, so we were not surprised that Puerto Ricans across generations hold on to *habichuelas*; they likely associate *frijoles* with Mexican food. We note that according to Hernández (2002), despite holding negative attitudes toward Salvadoran Spanish, Mexicans in Houston have acquired the use of Salvadoran lexical items for foods such as *curtido* (cabbage relish) and *pupusa* (thick round flatbread), even though phonological and grammatical levels of Mexican Spanish do not seem to be affected by contact with Salvadoran Spanish speakers. Thus, food items seem to constitute a unique lexical category because they often reflect regional cuisines.

Finally, we compare MexiRicans with Mexicans and with Puerto Ricans on their percentage familiarity scores with each item (this is presented visually in the figures included in Appendix A). For nine out of the 10 lexical items, MexiRicans evidenced familiarity scores in between those of their Mexican and Puerto Rican counterparts. For example, the word used by Mexicans to refer to a drinking straw is *popote*. G2 Mexicans showed 88% familiarity with this term, Puerto Ricans showed 33% familiarity, and MexiRicans were in the middle with 67%. The only exception was *piscina*, on which G2 MexiRicans scored lower than the other two G2 groups. We see in Figure 3.10 that the same pattern holds for G3 speakers: on all 10 items, G3 MexiRicans were in between the scores of generationally matched Mexicans and Puerto Ricans.

In summary, MexiRicans' lexical familiarity on both Mexican and Puerto Rican variants were in between those of Mexicans and Puerto Ricans. Overall, MexiRicans scored like Mexicans in that they have much higher Mexican than Puerto Rican scores, but they looked like Puerto Ricans in that their Puerto Rican scores never dropped below 23% familiarity. Only four items experienced a steep drop in familiarity from G2 to G3 among MexiRicans: the Mexican variants for *pacifier*, *earrings*, and *eyeglasses* and the Puerto Rican variant for *drinking straw*. These drops are attributable to the fact that some individuals did not know any Spanish word for these items, which is observable in the fact that the score for the opposite variant did not increase. We saw that *earrings* and *drinking straw* were being lost by G3 Mexicans and Puerto Ricans, too, many of them offering no Spanish word at all for these items.

Finally, we note that in some cases, participants offered outgroup vocabulary *before* ingroup vocabulary. This was most common for Puerto Ricans (n = 75 tokens) on the words *lentes*, *naranja*, *aretes*, *camión*, and *pastel* (regarding *pastel*, we noted earlier that the Puerto Rican variant for cake has a different, vulgar referent for many Mexicans). Mexican speakers offered outgroup variants first only 18 times, and 90% of those were *piscina*. We also note that *bus* and *cake* were frequently offered in English, echoing Zentella's (1990) finding that Spanish speakers in the U.S. sometimes "use English to understand each other's Spanish."

3.8. PROFICIENCY

Recall from Chapter 2 that both authors independently rated each speaker for Spanish proficiency using a scale of 1 (very weak) to 5 (very strong). In Figure 3.11, we compare speakers' proficiency ratings with their overall lexical scores. For both Mexicans and Puerto Ricans, Spanish proficiency and lexical scores were significantly positively correlated, $r(74) = .35$, $p = .002$, with a medium to large effect size as to the guidelines from Cohen (1992). That is, higher proficiency corresponded to higher total vocabulary scores. Among MexiRicans, Spanish proficiency and lexical scores were also significantly positively correlated, $r(43) = .58$, $p < .001$, with a large effect size according to Cohen's guidelines (1992).

This largely unsurprising finding suggests that overall level of proficiency is positively related to lexical knowledge, echoing Polinsky's (2008) finding of a robust connection between speakers' proficiency in their heritage language and their lexical knowledge in that language. It also lends support to our proficiency ratings (Chapter 2).

Our question now is whether this correlation is stronger than that of generation. It would not be appropriate to include both generation and proficiency within the same models, because these two factors are correlated (see

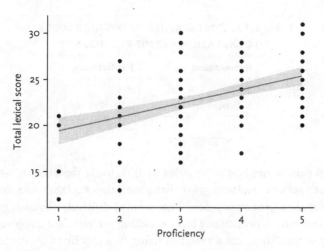

Figure 3.11. Total lexical score and proficiency.

Table 3.14. CORRELATION OF OUTGROUP SCORES TO GENERATION VERSUS PROFICIENCY.

	Generation	**Proficiency**
AIC	431.7 3.2% of variance	433.2 0.6% of variance
R^2	.020	0.04

Chapter 2), leading to multicollinearity issues. Thus, our first approach was to run separate models (for proficiency and for generation) to see which predictor better explains the data, such that the model with a lower AIC score and a higher percentage of explained variance (R^2) would be preferred. Our second approach is to compare the effects of proficiency and generation via a dominance analysis on a linear regression model that includes both proficiency and generation, following a procedure described to account for multicollinearity in regression models (Kraha et al., 2012). This was done using the *dominance-analysis* package in R (Navarrete & Soares, 2020).[10] The results for outgroup lexicon appear in Table 3.14.

For outgroup lexical scores, our model on generation yielded an AIC of 431.7 and explained 3.2% of variance. By contrast, our model on proficiency yielded an AIC of 433.2 and explained 0.6% of variance. The dominance analysis

---

10. We will repeat these two statistical analyses in the remainder of this monograph every time we compare the effects of proficiency and generation, but henceforth we will report only the AIC and the R^2 index values without repeating this explanation.

Table 3.15. CORRELATION OF INGROUP SCORES TO GENERATION VERSUS PROFICIENCY.

	Generation	**Proficiency**
AIC	376.5 6.8% of variance	374.2 9.5% of variance
R^2	0.035	0.063

found that proficiency had an R^2 index of .004, lower than that of generation (.020). Both sets of results suggest that generation explains outgroup lexical score better than proficiency does. This seems intuitively obvious, given that homelanders have a proficiency level at ceiling yet very low outgroup scores. Outgroup scores, then, are a result of living in a city like Chicago in contact with the speakers from the other group.

Table 3.15 shows our two comparative analyses of ingroup scores.

Here our model on generation yielded an AIC of 376.5 and explained 6.8% of variance, but our model on proficiency yielded an AIC of 374.2 and explained 9.5% of variance. Similarly, the dominance analysis also found that proficiency had an R^2 index of .063, higher than that of generation (.035). Both sets of results suggest that for ingroup lexicon, proficiency explains speakers' scores better than their generation does.

3.9. SUMMARY AND CONCLUSIONS

In our study of lexical familiarity, both Mexicans and Puerto Ricans showed greater outgroup lexical knowledge than homeland speakers who remained in Mexico or Puerto Rico. In all three generational groups, Puerto Ricans showed a greater familiarity with outgroup lexicon than Mexicans did, supporting our hypothesis that in Chicago's context of dialect contact, Puerto Ricans are accommodating more to Mexican lexicon than the other way around. Mexicans in Chicago show the same pattern of knowledge of outgroup lexicon as Puerto Ricans do, just to a smaller extent: G1 speakers know more outgroup words than those who never left Mexico; G2 knows slightly more than G1; and G3 declined (in the case of Mexicans, almost to zero).

A major conclusion from Zentella's (1990) study of four Latino communities in New York was that a dialect's prestige rather than the relative size of a population had a more significant impact on the direction of accommodation. In our case, it is difficult to separate the impact of population proportion versus dialect prestige since Mexican Spanish enjoys both demographic dominance and greater prestige in Chicago, as well as greater prominence in Chicago's Spanish-language media.

Among MexiRicans, we observed the same tendency attesting to the greater status and preponderance of Mexican Spanish in Chicago. All MexiRicans were slightly more familiar with Mexican lexicon than with Puerto Rican lexicon, but those with Puerto Rican mothers showed slightly greater familiarity with Puerto Rican words than those with Mexican mothers, suggesting a slight "mother effect" in intrafamilial dialect contact.

In terms of how generational group correlates with outgroup lexical familiarity, we found a more complex pattern. G2 speakers had the highest outgroup lexicon compared with G1 and G3, but the difference was not statistically significant. Since G2 speakers have spent their entire lives in Chicago, with likely greater exposure to outgroup Spanish than their G1 parents, this may account for the slightly higher outgroup lexicon. G3s did not have higher outgroup scores than G2 as we predicted, though, presumably because their overall Spanish had declined and eroded their lexicon such that whatever they did know was only in the ingroup dialect. The G1 data also provided evidence that even when immigration to the U.S. occurs after adulthood, familiarity with other variants can displace homeland variants.

As for the relationship between Spanish proficiency and lexical familiarity, we saw that proficiency was correlated with overall lexical scores. This finding also reminds us of the importance of looking broadly at Spanish proficiency: Puerto Ricans had lower ingroup lexical scores than Mexicans but higher overall lexical scores, which suggests accommodation to Mexican Spanish rather than telling us anything about their own Spanish proficiency. One question that emerges is the degree to which this larger range of lexical familiarity that Puerto Ricans evidence is a temporary effect that will diminish, or whether over time one of two varying lexical items (probably the Mexican one) is preferred at the expense of knowing the other. A central factor, however, is whether G4 individuals will know any Spanish at all. Given the fact that 53% of G3 U.S. Hispanics say that they do not speak Spanish "very well" or "well" (Pew Research Center, 2012), to us it seems doubtful that many G4 speakers would score very high on our measure on either ingroup or outgroup lexicon.

Finally, we note two more trends. First, while proficiency was the best predictor of total lexical scores, generation was the best predictor of outgroup scores. Second, although tendencies did emerge for familiarity with individual words, the more mixed results with other words supported findings by Zentella (1990) and Chambers (1992) that some lexical items simply have their own story. A particular item's frequency, connotations, relationship to other words, stigmatization, gendered nature, and so on, can lead to a trajectory that distinguishes it from general tendencies. For example, we saw that *bizcocho* (*cake* in Puerto Rico) is embarrassing for Mexicans, similarly to *pants* for the British in Chambers (1992), and *pacifier* is rather infrequent, as was *hair clip* in Zentella (1990), and similarly possibly gendered if women are more engaged in caring for babies.

We conclude this chapter by noting that the lexicon has not received as much attention as other aspects of Spanish in the U.S., despite the fact that it might offer a useful lens to gauge language contact and other issues such as maintenance, shift, and dynamic bilingualism. Future research can be enhanced by greater attention to how to best capture and measure lexical familiarity. Possibly fruitful areas might involve more laboratory-type tasks, including measuring participants' reaction times, or, in a very different approach, long-term ethnographic observations of speakers during their day-to-day activities within their communities.

APPENDIX A
PERCENTAGE FAMILIARITY SCORES: MEXICANS, PUERTO RICANS, AND MEXIRICANS

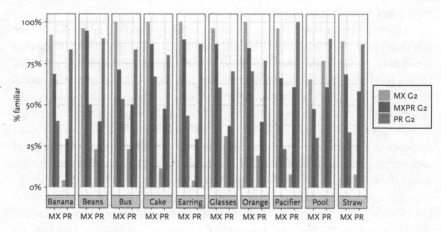

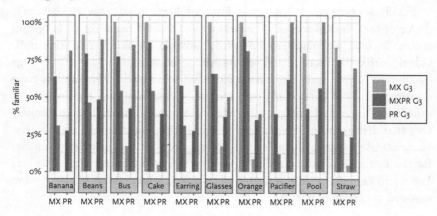

[110] *Spanish in Chicago*

CHAPTER 4
Discourse Markers

4.1. INTRODUCTION

Discourse markers are linguistic particles that contribute to overall coherence by signaling relationships across them. Although not all researchers agree on how exactly to define them, there is consensus that they serve a pragmatic function. For example, they can signal topic shifts, hold a speech turn, introduce new information, present tag questions, and denote register and style differences (Sánchez-Muñoz 2007). Common discourse markers in English include *you know*, *I mean*, *well*, and *so*. As proposed by Fuller (2003,p. 186), a particle functions as a discourse marker if two criteria are met upon removal of the discourse marker: the semantic relationship between the elements connected by the marker does not change, and the utterance remains grammatical. Take, for example, invented examples (1), (2), and (3), where the italicized particles meet both of these criteria:

(1) We left super late. *Anyway*, she told us we should call her when we got home.
(2) They didn't want them to, *you know*, find out where it was.
(3) I couldn't hear a thing, *so* I told him to turn it up, *right*?

Discourse markers have been shown to be acquired relatively early by both monolingual and bilingual children (Andersen et al., 1999; Brizuela, et al., 1999). There have been multiple studies about discourse markers in the last two decades in pragmatics, contact linguistics, bilingualism, and second language acquisition. Among other things, these particles can shed light on language evolution and change, stylistic variation, and codeswitching and language-mixing patterns.

After reviewing studies on discourse markers among bilinguals, this chapter examines discourse markers in the CHISPA corpus. Specifically, we compare patterns of use of *so* and *entonces* among Mexican, Puerto Rican, and MexiRican speakers of different generational groups who have varying Spanish proficiency levels. As with all five of the linguistic features we study in this monograph, we seek to explore two main questions. The first is whether regional origin groups show different patterns of use and, if so, whether they become more like each other across generations. If they begin to converge in their features, it may be attributable to dialect contact. The second question is whether generational group and Spanish proficiency are correlated with the use of particular features and, if so, whether one is more strongly correlated than the other.

4.2. DISCOURSE MARKERS IN BILINGUAL COMMUNITIES

Early studies of language contact suggested that function words such as discourse markers were less likely to be borrowed than content words such as nouns and verbs, but researchers have indeed found borrowings of discourse markers. According to Mougeon and Beniak (1986), this practice seems to be associated with situations of "intense" language in which bilinguals regularly use the two languages. These authors analyzed the use of *so* in the speech of Canadian bilingual adolescents categorized as either low, middle, or high users of French. They discovered that mid-level users of French use *so* more frequently than the low and high users. The authors proposed that a relatively balanced level of bilingualism is a prerequisite for the borrowing of core lexical items such as discourse markers; thus, a high frequency of *so* usage could be taken as an indicator of balanced bilingualism in that region.

Since then, at least three kinds of discourse marker systems have been found when languages are in contact: (1) the two sets of discourse markers coexist, (2) similar markers from each language acquire differentiated meanings, or (3) the markers from one language may replace those of the other language, either partially or totally. Studies that exemplify each outcome are displayed in Table 4.1.

Coexistence, Similar Functions

Hill and Hill (1986) studied *mexicano*, the term used by many speakers of Náhuatl to refer to their language, which is being lost in many areas of central Mexico. The authors found that speakers manipulate how much Spanish they use depending on the situation, topic, and interlocutors, because while Spanish is seen as the language of power, it is simultaneously considered a

Table 4.1. SUMMARY OF SELECTED BILINGUAL DISCOURSE MARKER FINDINGS.

Outcome	Study	Languages
Coexistence, similar functions	Hill and Hill (1986)	Náhuatl + Spanish
	Brody (1987, 1995)	Tojolba'l Maya + Spanish
Coexistence, differentiated functions	Solomon (1995)	Yucatec Maya + Spanish
Replacement, partial	Rooij (2000)	Shaba Swahili + French
	Hlavac (2006)	Croatian + English
Replacement, total	Fuller (2001)	Pennsylvania German + English
	Goss and Salmons (2000)	Texan German + English

polluting entity. They examined a range of particles, including discourse markers, interjections, conjunctions, and exclamations, finding much evidence of phonological and syntactic convergence and coexistence of discourse markers with similar functions. Also finding coexistence of material from both languages, Brody (1995) found that in Tojolba'l Mayan, Spanish markers sometimes appeared alone or alongside a Mayan marker, and they were usually not in complementary distribution; that is, markers from both languages seemed to fulfill similar roles. She suggested that the Spanish markers might be used to emphasize or highlight a point in the text and perhaps represented speakers' "emblematic forays" into the more prestigious, dominant language (Spanish). She also speculated that this kind of discourse marker doubling might be a step in a process of language change where native markers are eventually replaced and lost, although this outcome had not come to pass in Tojolba'l or any of the indigenous languages she studied.

Coexistence, Differentiated Functions

Can two bilingual discourse systems coexist indefinitely? Solomon (1995) argues that they can if they acquire differentiated functions. She found that in Yucatec Maya, the Spanish marker *entonces* (then, so) coexists with the Maya discourse marker *ka* (and then). Her data come from one Yucatec Maya narrative produced by a 44-year-old male farmer. Upon close examination of this narrative, she found a differentiation of functions: *entonces* was usually used to distinguish narrative sections (a global function), for example, the orientation from action sequences, while *ka* served to foreground actions and states in narrative episodes within episodes (a local function) and also acted as a subordinator and coordinator between events to establish temporal connections. Her study suggests that in some cases, differentiated functions can become apparent only when both local and global functions of discourse markers are identified. Since Solomon's analysis is based on only one narrative, further research is needed to determine the degree to which her findings are generalizable.

Partial or Total Replacement

Several researchers posit a process that begins with coexisting discourse markers and proceeds until the partial or complete replacement of one set of bilingual markers. Goss and Salmons (2000) report a case of complete replacement of a discourse-marking system in Texan German varieties in contact with English, where German is the subordinate language used less with each generation. English discourse markers enter German speech through codeswitching in the speech of bilinguals. These discourse markers coexist for some time with the German ones, but eventually the English discourse markers replace German markers completely in the language of bilingual speakers.

Similarly, Fuller (2001) studied English-origin discourse markers in Pennsylvania German. She outlined a gradual process of adaptation to an English-language discourse-marking system. Based on this process, she argued (similarly to Brody, 1995, with Tojolba'l Mayan) that the use of bilingual markers without a complementary distribution of functions does not bode well for maintenance of the subordinate-language discourse-marking system and that only when doublets assume different functions can both discourse-marking systems survive. Similarly, Hlavac (2006) describes how English markers replace Croatian markers in the speech of Croatian-English bilinguals born in Australia to Croatian parents. Examining the frequency and functional versatility of English-language markers in Croatian speech, he found that English discourse markers co-occur with Croatian ones. The English-language markers that appear to be replacing Croatian forms are those that are performing more than one function, while the Croatian forms that they replace have fewer functions. For example, *yeah* is a discourse marker that conveys affirmation but also has non-affirmative functions such as turn termination. The Croatian marker *da* similarly expresses affirmation but does not have non-affirmative functions in monolingual Croatian. However, for some bilingual speakers, *da* is beginning to acquire non-affirmative functions, yet this development is not halting the preference for *yeah* among bilingual speakers. Hlavac concludes that linguistic and pragmatic factors influence selection of these forms in bilingual speech.

In a study of the use of French discourse markers in Shaba Swahili conversations, Rooij (2000) also noted that French markers were replacing Shaba

Swahili markers. He found that French markers are used to mark what speakers are saying and create contrasts between languages so that listeners are cued about how to understand the utterance. However, he pointed out that for bilingual speakers who control both languages well, French discourse markers are used for effect alongside Swahili markers. For bilingual speakers who can still distinguish the two systems of markers, they are examples of codeswitching. Rooij found, however, that speakers who are experiencing language loss in their first language may experience the elimination of some native discourse markers in their speech.

In summary, in situations of language contact, discourse markers probably enter the language as codeswitches, then become borrowings. There is evidence that speakers who are most bilingual introduce the markers, which are then taken up by speakers who are less proficient in the two languages (Mougeon & Beniak, 1986). There is also evidence that less proficient bilinguals may use the markers differently from the way more proficient bilingual speakers use them. Furthermore, the discourse markers may acquire differentiated functions (Solomon, 1995); they can mean the same things such that speakers use them in doublets (Hill & Hill, 1986; Brody, 1987, 1995); or the discourse markers from one language partially replace the markers from the other (Rooij, 2000; Hlavac, 2006) or even result in the total disappearance of native markers (Goss & Salmons, 2000; Fuller, 2001). It is important to recognize that the value attached to the two languages must be considered when analyzing the motivation behind the borrowing or codeswitching of the dominant-language discourse markers. For example, in the research surveyed here, the valued languages are Spanish, English, and French (i.e., the majority languages in their respective regions), whereas the languages with less societal value are Náhuatl, Maya, Croatian, Shaba Swahili, and U.S. varieties of German (i.e., the minority languages).

The fact that discourse markers show sensitivity to language contact makes them an ideal candidate for our study of Spanish in Chicago, where Spanish is under intense pressure from English. Discourse markers may also be a fruitful site for possible effects of dialect contact. If first-generation Mexicans and Puerto Ricans in the U.S. are found to use discourse markers differently but subsequent generations use them more similarly, this might constitute evidence either of a degree of leveling as a result of contact between speakers from the two groups or of the effects of contact with English. On the other hand, if subsequent generations were to continue to show differences in discourse marker use, we might conclude that these markers are not responsive to pressures of dialect contact.[1] Finally, it is novel to examine discourse

---

1. Our robust findings from Chapter 3 that many speakers know outgroup lexicon suggest that there is in fact contact between speakers of the two regional origin groups.

marker use among MexiRicans, who experience intrafamilial dialect contact. In this chapter, we address these questions via an examination of *so* and *entonces* in Chicago Spanish, following an exploration of discourse markers in U.S. Spanish.

To date, we have found seven published studies examining discourse markers in U.S. Spanish, summarized in Table 4.2. The final column compares the findings of each of these studies to those presented in Table 4.1.

In Brentwood on Long Island (a suburb of New York City), Torres (2002) carried out a cross-generational analysis of three groups of Puerto Rican Spanish-English bilinguals: Spanish-dominant, English-dominant, and relatively balanced. She observed that it was easily detachable forms such as *you know* that were the most common English-language discourse markers in the Spanish narratives of all three groups of speakers. She agreed with previous proposals that these markers enter the language more easily than other particles because they have the least effect on syntax, yet they are highly salient participation markers and thus can be used to mark the attitude or involvement of the speaker. She found that in Spanish narratives, speakers from all generations used the same set of bilingual discourse markers (*so/entonces*, *tú sabes/y'know*, *and/y*), but language proficiency affected both the frequency and the function of English discourse markers; as proficiency in English increased, so did the frequency of their use. Although English and Spanish markers were not used in complementary distribution, their functions did differ in each group; Torres found a higher frequency and less restrictive use of English discourse markers as proficiency in Spanish decreased. She argued that English-language markers probably first entered Spanish through codeswitching and then became borrowings. She concluded that the high frequency of *so* qualified it as a fully integrated borrowing. Traces of its use as a codeswitched element were found only in the Spanish narratives of the English-dominant speakers; in 25% of the tokens from G3 speakers' narratives, it appeared as part of a codeswitched utterance. This was never the case for the other two groups, where *so* was always surrounded by Spanish.[2] In summary, *so* and all the English-language discourse markers studied in Torres (2002) were found to coexist with Spanish-language markers that encode similar information and functions, similarly to the coexisting marker systems found by Hill and Hill (1986) and Brody (1987, 1995).

Aaron (2004) studied the distribution of *so* and *entonces* in New Mexican bilingual speech. She found that *so* was used by more than half the study participants. Focusing on the speakers who used both *so* and *entonces* in their

---

2. Similarly, Silva-Corvalán (1995, p. 269) argued that *so* has almost completely replaced *así que* in the speech of even Spanish monolingual Mexican Americans in Los Angeles and can be considered a core borrowing.

Table 4.2. STUDIES OF DISCOURSE MARKERS IN U.S. SPANISH.

Study Speakers, location	Discourse markers	Conclusions	Comparison with previous outcomes
Torres (2002) Puerto Ricans, New York	*so/entonces* *tú sabes/y'know* *and/y*	All speakers use the same group of Spanish and English discourse markers, but each group has its own pattern of use. High frequency of *so* even among Spanish monolinguals seems to qualify it as a fully integrated borrowing.	Coexistence, same functions
Aaron (2004) New Mexico	*so/entonces*	Both markers perform the same discourse functions	Coexistence, same functions
Said-Mohand (2008) Various dialect groups, Miami	*so/entonces*	As Spanish proficiency decreased, so did use of *entonces*. *So* is an integrated loan in the speech of high-Spanish-proficiency speakers.	Functions not studied
Lipski (2005) Recordings of bilingual speakers from across the U.S.	*so*	*So* was very frequent in the Spanish of bilinguals of high, middle, and low Spanish proficiency	Functions not studied
Torres and Potowski (2008) Mexicans, Puerto Ricans, MexiRicans, Chicago	*so/entonces*	*So* was a core borrowing for all groups, but Puerto Ricans and MexiRicans used *so* more than Mexicans, and G3 speakers used *so* more than the other two generation groups.	Coexistence, slightly differentiated functions
Flores-Ferrán (2014) Puerto Ricans, New York, and Puerto Rico	all discourse markers used by speakers in narratives	New York–raised speakers used English discourse markers much more than island-raised counterparts.	Coexistence, same functions
Kern (2020) Mexican Americans, southern Arizona	*like, como, como que*	Bilingual speakers use *like* as a discourse marker more frequently than any of the Spanish equivalents, and its use is conditioned differently in each language.	Coexistence, different functions

narratives, Aaron found the distribution of use of the two markers to be very similar in the following four contexts: (1) introducing a result, (2) introducing a conclusion, (3) following a conclusion, and (4) marking progression. Similarly to Torres (2002), Aaron did not make a case for specialized function of the use of these two markers, arguing instead that they both perform the same discourse functions. She concluded that it is unlikely that *so* will replace *entonces*. However, since Aaron did not track the patterns of use of *so* and *entonces* across generations of New Mexican speakers, or with speakers of different age groups, further study is required.

Said-Mohand (2008) studied the impact of English on the Spanish of young bilingual students (37 females and 19 males) in heritage Spanish courses in Miami. He measured their Spanish proficiency via the number of "errors" in 10 areas (including verb agreement, use of the subjunctive, lexical density, prepositions, and preterite vs. imperfect use); examples of errors included "la coche de mi padre" and "él compralo para su amigo."[3] He found a positive correlation between language proficiency and use of *entonces*, where use of *entonces* decreased as proficiency decreased. In a mirror-like pattern, he found a negative correlation between proficiency and use of *so*, where use of *so* increased as Spanish proficiency decreased. Like Torres (2002) and Aaron (2004), Said-Mohand (2008) argued that *so* is an integrated loan in the speech of high-Spanish-proficiency speakers, and like Torres (2002), he found that in English-dominant speakers, use of *so* was within codeswitched clauses.

Lipski (2005) sought to develop a typology of borrowing and switching by studying the incorporation of *so* and similar items into the Spanish of U.S. bilingual speakers. Reviewing cases of *so* reported in published papers and in interviews he and his students had collected over several years, Lipski found *so* in the Spanish discourse of bilinguals of high, middle, and low Spanish proficiency. He proposed that the incorporation of *so* and other function words should be considered differently from the borrowing of lexical items because they occur below the level of speaker awareness. Similarly to Mougeon and Beniak's (1991) proposition, Lipski (2005) argued that "*so* insertion" in a situation of intense language contact may suggest the degree to which all bilingual speakers are experiencing acculturation, regardless of their levels of proficiency. The other studies cited here found *so* at all proficiency levels, too, but they looked more closely to reveal differences in the proportions and functions of its use.

---

3. Said-Mohand (2008), aligned with our assertion in Chapter 2 that measuring language proficiency is an arduous task, recurred to Fernández's (1997) definition of an error as a production that "any native speaker would not doubt in calling ungrammatical or unacceptable in a particular context."

Torres and Potowski (2008) examined the use of *so* and *entonces* in Chicago (similar to what we report in this chapter but with a much smaller sample size of *n* = 51). They looked at 23 Mexicans, 17 Puerto Ricans, and 11 MexiRicans distributed across three generational groups. They studied four functions, which, based on Travis (2005; to be explained in more detail), were called *result*, *conclusion*, *trailing*, and *move*. They found that *so* was a core borrowing for all groups but that Puerto Ricans and MexiRicans used *so* significantly more than Mexicans (approximately 80% of the time vs. only 34% for Mexicans) and G3 speakers used *so* more than the other two generation groups (86% for G3, 50% among G2, and 60% among G1). However, there were too few speakers per cell to compare generational differences across each of the three regional origin groups, which the present study aims to address. They also found that *so* was greatly preferred (almost 75% of the time) for three out of the four functions they studied (result, conclusion, trailing), while *entonces* was used half the time for one of the functions (move). This led the authors to conclude that the two discourse markers would coexist for some time.

Flores-Ferrán (2014) identified 73 different discourse markers in the speech of a group of 17 Puerto Ricans (13 raised in New York and four raised in Puerto Rico), including many doublets such as *so entonces* and *so anyway*. The New York–raised speakers used English discourse markers at a rate of 23%, explainable by their intense contact with English, while their island-raised counterparts did so only 1.4% of the time. However, the proportions of discourse markers used for the four different functions identified by the author (connectives, causatives, participatory, and clarification) did not differ very much between the two groups.

Finally, Kern (2020) looked at the use of *like* in English and *como*, *como que*, and *like* in Spanish in the speech of 18 bilinguals from southern Arizona. He found that *like* in English was much more frequent (average frequency 360 tokens per 10,000 words) and occurred in many more syntactic positions than its Spanish equivalents (average frequency of *como* at 56 tokens per 10,000 words and of *como que* at 8 tokens). *Like* in English and *como* in Spanish were conditioned differently from *como que* and *like* in Spanish. While *like* in English and *como* in Spanish were used as discourse particles clause-internally, the use of *como que* in Spanish was very infrequent, and *like* in Spanish was never used. Gender did not have significant correlations with linguistic production, but the percentage use of *como* and all the Spanish variants was positively correlated with Spanish dominance.

In summary, we see that these studies document more frequent use of English markers and a decline in the frequency of Spanish markers as Spanish-language proficiency decreases and that *so* seems to be the most frequently integrated discourse marker across communities. Regarding *so* and *entonces*, we notice a fairly stable pattern of coexistence, either with the same functions (Aaron, 2004; Flores-Ferrán, 2014) or slightly differentiated functions

(Torres, 2002; Torres & Potowski, 2008). We sought to explore the use of *so/entonces* in a larger subsection of the CHISPA corpus than previously analyzed, determining the overall proportions as well as the distribution of functions for three generations of speakers belonging to three regional origin groups. We were guided by the following questions:

1. Will there be differences in discourse marker use (overall and by function) according to the following?
   a. Regional origin
   b. Generational group
   c. Regional origin and generational group
   d. Spanish proficiency level
2. Will Spanish proficiency or generational group be more strongly connected to discourse marker use?

Given our 2008 finding that Puerto Ricans and MexiRicans used *so* significantly more than Mexicans, we expected this pattern to hold cross-generationally in this larger corpus. In addition, based on Potowski (2016), we predicted that MexiRicans' patterns would follow those of their mother's regional origin group more closely than that of their father's group. As for generational group, our hypotheses were based on previous findings that all point to a greater use of *so* than *entonces* across generations in U.S. Spanish (Torres, 2002; Aaron, 2004; Said-Mohand, 2008; Lipski, 2005; Torres & Potowski, 2008; Flores-Ferrán, 2014). Our previous study in 2008 also led us not to expect different distributions of functions by generational group. Given that we found proficiency in Spanish to decline with generation, we expected that with each generational group, the proportional use of *entonces* would decrease for all three regional origin groups. In other words, we predicted that *so* is introduced among Spanish-dominant bilinguals, is used liberally among G2 proficient bilinguals, and is used even more among G3 speakers whose Spanish is the weakest of the three groups. We also felt that proficiency would be more closely tied to discourse marker use than generational group would.

4.3. METHODOLOGY

Participants

We selected 91 interviews at random from the CHISPA corpus to represent our regional origin groups and generational groups as shown in Table 4.3.

Of the MexiRicans in this subset, there were 12 with a Mexican mother and 17 with a Puerto Rican mother.

Table 4.3. SUBSET OF CHISPA CORPUS ANALYZED FOR DISCOURSE MARKER STUDY.

	MX	PR	MXPR	Total
G1	11	10	n/a	21
G2	10	12	13	35
G3	10	9	16	35
Total	31	31	29	91

Coding

We read all transcripts and extracted all uses of *so* ($n = 1{,}473$) and *entonces* ($n = 1{,}005$). Of these 2,478 tokens, we eliminated 231. This included tokens surrounded by English ("It's not all the same dialect *so* he kinda gets confused"); uses of *entonces* with a temporal function ("Vivimos allí desde entonces"), and the doublet *so entonces*. We also excluded tokens of *so* and *entonces* adjacent to English words, including the following.

a. Tokens preceded by English, as in examples (4) and (5):

(4) Para mí es muy importante no identificarme como una hispana o Hispanic porque para mí estas palabras son de el gobierno y está . . . hay un . . . estas palabras son resultadas de colonialism and oppression. **Entonces** para mí es muy importante para identificar como una latina y como MexiRican porque es la representación de mis culturas diferentes, pero no es Mexican and Puerto Rican, es MexiRican. (#46, G3 MexiRican female)

For me it's very important that I do not identify as "hispana" or Hispanic because for me these words come from the government and it's . . . there's a . . . these words are a result of colonialism and oppression. **So** for me it's very important to identify as a Latina woman and as MexiRican because they represent my different cultures, but it's not Mexican and Puerto Rican, it's MexiRican.

(5) As long as you correct me, I don't care, you can make fun of me. **So** yo creo que depende de ti como persona y tu ambiente. (#17, G1 Puerto Rican female)

As long as you correct me, I don't care, you can make fun of me. **So** I think that it depends on you as a person and your environment.

b. Tokens followed by English, as in examples (6) and (7):

(6) No habla español muy bien, **so** go figure. (#48, G2 Mexican female)

She doesn't speak Spanish very well, **so** go figure.

DISCOURSE MARKERS [121]

(7) Pero **entonces** it was okay. (#49, G3 MexiRican female)

But **then** it was okay.

In (4) through (7), the discourse marker sits at the switch point between Spanish and English. It is not possible to determine whether they are the trigger for or the result of a language switch. For example, it could be argued that in (4), *entonces* triggered the switch back to Spanish and that in (6), *so* triggered the switch to English (Aaron, 2004; Said-Mohand, 2008; and others have found that discourse markers frequently prompt codeswitches). We made the conservative choice to eliminate them so as not to confound them with codeswitching.

The remaining 2,247 tokens of *so* and *entonces* were coded as fulfilling one of the five functions displayed in Table 4.4. We chose these categories based mostly on Travis (2005), who studied conversations among Colombians[4] and identified the meanings of discourse markers by looking at the conditions under which they appeared, specifying three core meanings for *entonces*: to mark a result, to mark a conclusion, or to indicate progression. What these core meanings have in common is that "what follows *entonces* is uttered because of what has been said in the preceding discourse" (Travis, 2005, p. 224). Travis argues that, like *so* in English, *entonces* was originally a temporal adverb meaning "en ese momento" (e.g., "Me dijo que llegaría a las seis y media así que decidí servir la cena entonces") but that it has acquired various meanings and functions over time. Currently, the discourse-marking functions of *entonces* in Colombian Spanish are much more frequent than its temporal function.[5] Our categorizations of *so* and *entonces* are derived from Travis's exhaustive study.

The first function—result—was applied when the discourse marker signaled that the first proposition was the cause of the second proposition. This function can be seen with *so* in example (8) and with *entonces* in example (9). In these examples, *so* and *entonces* function similarly to introduce something that is a direct consequence of the previous statement.

(8) Y entonces por ser yo la bebé de mi casa y la más pequeña, la única nena, pues mi papá le decía a mi hermano, "Si algo le pasa a la nena es problema tuyo." **So** él siempre tenía que estar conmigo, como quien dice, y estar pendiente. (#26, G1 Puerto Rican female)

---

4. Our speakers were not of Colombian origin, but Travis (2005) is the most comprehensive examination of Spanish discourse marker functions to date.

5. As mentioned earlier, we eliminated from our analysis the tokens of *entonces* with a temporal function. These were very few, similar to what was found in Colombian Spanish by Travis (2005). Aaron (2004) found a high frequency of *entonces* (31%) with temporal meaning in her New Mexico data, but she acknowledges that the topic of her interviews, how things use to be in another time, accounted for this high frequency.

Table 4.4. POSSIBLE FUNCTIONS OF *SO* AND *ENTONCES* (BASED ON TRAVIS, 2005)

Function	Definition
1. Result	Introduces a consequence or a result. There is a causal relationship between the two propositions.
2. Conclusion	Introduces a conclusion; that is, the proposition introduced by the discourse marker sums up the propositions that came before it.
3. Move	Marks a progression, moves the narrative along. Does not imply consequence, result, or conclusion. Can often be replaced with *and*.
4. Trail	Ends a turn or changes the subject.
5. Other	Temporal functions.

And then because I was the baby in my house and the youngest, the only girl, well my dad would tell my brother, "If something happens to the girl it is your problem." **So** he always had to be with me, as they say, and he had to be attentive.

(9) . . . muchas veces, aquella es tu amiga pero no le gusta la otra muchacha que tú tienes y luego este va y siempre tira sus, sus chismecitos y luego muchas veces va y le dice una cosa a la otra y la otra se cree que la otra lo dijo y **entonces** empieza la envidia. (#18, G2 Puerto Rican female)

. . . many times someone is your friend but she doesn't like the other girl that you have and then um she goes and always spreads gossip and then a lot of times she goes and tells something to the other one and the other one thinks that the other one said it and **so** the envy starts.

Under the second function—conclusion—the proposition introduced by the discourse marker sums up the propositions that came before it. Examples (10) and (11) are conclusions introduced by *so* and *entonces*, respectively.

(10) Mis papás, yo creo que también al otro lado se ponen un poquito . . . a veces, nerviosos cuando están hablando inglés porque no es su primera lenguaje y aprendieron a hablar inglés cuando ya eran mayor de edad como 20 o 21 años **so** ellos tienen acento cuando hablan. (#11, G2 MexiRican female)

My parents, I think that they also, on the other hand, get a bit . . . sometimes, nervous when they are speaking English because it is not their first language and they learned to speak English when they were already older, around 20 or 21 years, **so** they have an accent when they speak.

(11) . . . vine aquí a Chicago y en todo los letreros de las lavanderías . . . puse más atención y vi que no nada decía wachetería o sea todo decía lavandería o

DISCOURSE MARKERS [123]

laundromat **entonces** me pareció como una diferencia muy grande. (#5, G2 Mexican female)

... I came here to Chicago and on all of the signs of the laundromats ... I paid more attention and saw that they didn't say *wachetería* or rather they said *lavandería* or *laundromat* **so** it seemed to me like a big difference.

There was sometimes strong overlap between the two categories of result and conclusion. For example, in examples (5) and (6), it might be argued that *so* is introducing a result instead of a conclusion. We determined that the category conclusion would be used when the discourse marker occurred at the end of a turn containing several propositions and for which the use of the discourse marker appeared to be offering a concluding remark.

The third function—move—was used to mark a progression that simply advanced the narrative. The proposition introduced by this marker was not the consequence, result, or conclusion of the proposition(s) before it. These uses appear for the most part semantically empty and in many cases can be replaced by *y* (and). Examples (12) and (13) demonstrate this function, (12) with *so* (the speaker describes her recently married Puerto Rican mother's move to Mexico to live with her Mexican husband, which we include at greater length for its narrative interest) and (13) with *entonces*.

(12) ... decidió que sí le gustaría ir a conocer otro lugar y se fueron a vivir a México, pero ella no sabía que iba a llegar a vivir a un rancho **so** dice que cuando ella llegó allí, los primeros meses le fue mal, porque ella tuvo que lavar en el río, tuvo que aprender a hacer tortillas. Iba ella bien blanquita con sus uñas largas y su pelo largo y cuando fuimos a Puerto Rico a que mis abuelitos me conocieran, mi abuelo ni la reconoció porque iba con sus trenzas así enrolladas como la India María [laughs] y ella me tenía envuelta en un rebozo, y pues eso no acostumbran a ver eso allá en Puerto Rico. (#13, G2 MexiRican female)

... she decided yes she would like to get to know another place and they went to live in Mexico but she didn't know that she was going to live on a ranch **so** she says that when she got there, the first months were hard because she had to wash clothes in the river and learn how to make tortillas. She was all white with her long nails and her long hair and when we went to Puerto Rico so that my grandparents could meet me, my grandfather didn't even recognize her because she had her braids rolled up like India María [laughs] and she had me wrapped up in a shawl, and well they weren't used to seeing that in Puerto Rico.

(13) ... este, queríamos verlo porque era como un túnel, teníamos que pasar ese túnel y en ese túnel bien metido adrento de la tierra era un nightclub, uh-huh, **entonces** este, tenía el stage y tenían muchas cosas buenas allí. (#18, G2 Puerto Rican female)

... um, we wanted to see it because it was like a tunnel, we had to pass through this tunnel and this tunnel was really buried underground, it was a nightclub, yes, **so**, um it had a stage and lots of good things there.

Discourse markers placed in the fourth category—trailing—serve to end a turn or change the subject. Trailing (or stand-alone) *so* is quite common in monolingual English (Raymond, 2004) but was very infrequent in our corpus, and trailing *entonces* is rare in monolingual Spanish. Examples of trailing *so* and *entonces* are presented in examples (14), in which the speaker was finishing a comment about feeling less accepted for being MexiRican than for being gay, and (15).

(14) . . . yo no quería estar con latinos porque ellos, porque ellos me miraban . . . como soy una, no soy normal, **so**. (#42, G2 MexiRican male)

. . . I did not want to be with Latinos because they looked at me . . . like I'm a . . . I'm not normal, **so**.

(15) [Interviewer: ¿Pero con quién lo aprendiste (español)?]

Pues no había otro idioma que se hablara, español **entonces**. (#30, G1 Mexican male)

[Interviewer: But with whom did you learn it (Spanish)?]

Well they didn't speak any other language, Spanish **then**.

Finally, the fifth category was labeled "other." We used this label for any uses that did not fit into the previous four categories. Only 5% of the corpus fell into this category, all of which were the adverbial use of *so* (we found no cases of an adverbial function of English *so* imported into Spanish, as in "estaba so grande") and the temporal use of *entonces* as stated earlier. These uses will not receive further attention.

As noted earlier, some of the instances of the discourse markers could arguably fit into more than one category, particularly result or conclusion; Otheguy and Zentella (2012, p. 47) remind us that there is often an "unavoidable element of judgment" when making such decisions. The two of us coded all the tokens individually and then discussed the cases where we disagreed, which were fewer than 10% of all cases. We reviewed these examples in the context of the larger narrative and then came to an agreement on the most appropriate category.

4.4. OVERALL FREQUENCY OF *SO* AND *ENTONCES*

Figure 4.1 shows the overall distribution of the two discourse markers in the CHISPA corpus.

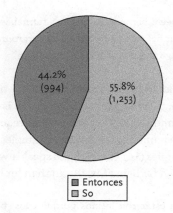

Figure 4.1. Overall distribution of *so* and *entonces*.

Of the 2,247 tokens, $n = 1{,}253$ (56%) were *so*, and $n = 994$ (44%) were *entonces*. Unlike in Torres and Potowski (2008), where *so* was used overall three times more frequently than *entonces*, we see here that the difference between overall use of *so* and *entonces* was not statistically significant: individual speakers' proportions of *so* use (relative to that individual's total uses of either *so* or *entonces*) were, on average, not significantly different from 50% as determined by a one-way Wilcoxon signed rank test, $V = 2028$, $p = .769$. This test was performed in lieu of a t-test because a Shapiro-Wilk normality test indicated that our results did not follow a normal distribution, $W = 0.82$, $p < .001$, most likely due to the substantial number of participants who used *so* either 100% or 0% of the time.

These divergent findings between our study and Torres and Potowski (2008) may be due to the larger sample size here ($n = 92$) compared to the previous study ($n = 51$). We also had a slightly higher proportion of proficiency level 5 speakers in the present study (23 out of 91, or 25%) compared to the first study (11 out of 51, or 22%) and, similarly, proportionally fewer proficiency level 1 and 2 speakers (15 out of 91, or 17%) than in the first study (13 out of 51, or 26%). We will see that higher proficiency in Spanish was correlated with lower use of *so*; thus, the combination of these two factors may account for the higher proportion of *entonces* and the lower proportion of *so* in this study.

4.5. REGIONAL ORIGIN AND GENERATION

The discourse marker use of Puerto Rican–origin and Mexican-origin speakers of all generational groups is displayed in Figure 4.2.

We see that Puerto Ricans distinguished themselves by using *so* more frequently than Mexicans, and a Mann-Whitney U test confirmed that

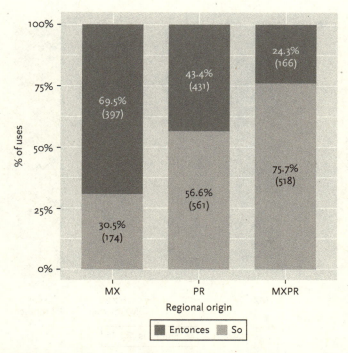

Figure 4.2. Proportion of discourse marker use, Mexicans and Puerto Ricans.

individuals' average proportions of *so* use differed significantly between the two ethnic groups, $U = 294$, $p = .008$.

Next, we examine the use of discourse markers among MexiRicans according to mother's regional origin. Figure 4.3 shows group-level proportions and raw token counts for *so* and *entonces*, but note that sample size differences between MexiRicans with Mexican versus Puerto Rican mothers make a comparison of raw token counts problematic. We have included Mexican and Puerto Rican speakers' data for comparative purposes. Recall that G1 MexiRicans do not exist, so data from the G1 Mexicans and the G1 Puerto Ricans are omitted here.

Figure 4.3 shows several interesting things. First, when considering aggregated group counts, MexiRicans with a Mexican mother used almost double the proportion of tokens of *so* (63.8%) compared with Mexicans (33.7%). That is, MexiRicans with a Mexican mother do not look at all like Mexicans in their discourse marker use; their usages are similar to those of Puerto Ricans (who, as a group overall, used *so* 66.2% of the time). However, a Mann-Whitney U test comparing individual speakers' proportions of *so* use did not reach significance, $U = 92$, $p = .155$. In addition, MexiRicans with a Puerto Rican mother used a higher proportion of *so* (82.9%) than those with a Mexican mother did (63.8%) in the aggregated group counts. Although analyses of

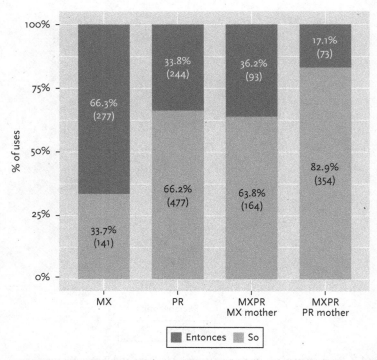

Figure 4.3. Average discourse marker use, all G2 and G3 Mexicans and Puerto Ricans and all MexiRicans according to mother's regional origin.

individuals' average proportions of *so* use comparing G2 and G3 Mexicans versus MexiRicans with Mexican mothers weren't statistically significant, $U = 100.5$, $p = .891$, the overall trend suggests against a conclusion that high *so* use constitutes a feature particular to MexiRican Spanish—in other words, MexiRican Spanish is not a coherent dialect on this feature. It does suggest that both parents exert influence on MexiRicans' Spanish development, the mother perhaps slightly more strongly than the father.

Also regarding MexiRicans with a Puerto Rican mother, we found that individual speakers in this group used almost the same average number of tokens of *so* (22.1) as Puerto Ricans did (22.7). This might seem to suggest that having a Puerto Rican mother leads to the development of a discourse marker system that more closely resembles that of Puerto Ricans. However, this conclusion cannot be sustained in strong form because it is not the case that these 16 MexiRican individuals each produced approximately 20 tokens of *so*. Two speakers with Puerto Rican mothers were in fact majority *entonces* users, while six speakers with Mexican mothers were majority *so* users. Even so, there was a tendency for speakers with Puerto Rican mothers to be majority *so* users ($n = 14$ people out of 17). We also note in Figure 4.3 that as a group, MexiRicans with a Puerto Rican mother had an even greater proportional use

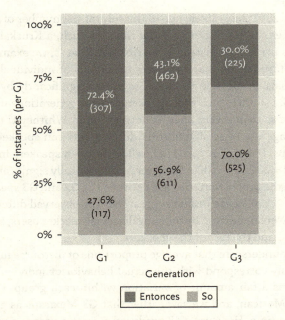

Figure 4.4. Percentage of *so* and *entonces* use by generation, with raw token counts in parentheses.

of *so* (82.9%) than Puerto Ricans did (66.2%). It is not clear why this might be the case. One possibility is different social networks among MexiRicans with a Puerto Rican mother, rather than the effect of their fathers' input per se.

When looking at *so* and *entonces* by overall proportions, we see noticeable differences by generation (Figure 4.4). In these and all subsequent comparisons of generational groups, we must bear in mind that there are 14 more participants in G2 ($n = 35$) and in G3 ($n = 35$) when compared to G1 ($n = 21$). This is because MexiRican G1s do not exist, as explained in Chapter 2. Thus, overall number of tokens generated by G1s will be lower. Percentages are displayed in Figure 4.4, with raw token counts in parentheses.

We see in Figure 4.4 a steady decline in the proportion of *entonces* from 72.4% in G1 to 43.1% in G2 and down to 30.0% in G3, whose proportion is the mirror opposite of that of G1 speakers. Thus, the biggest users of *so* were G3s, for whom *so* constituted 70% of all of their discourse markers, followed by G2s (57%) and G1s (28%).

Note, however, that Figure 4.4 only shows aggregate counts for each generation, leaving the possibility that these observed differences were driven by outliers within each group. To guard against this possibility, we compared individual speakers' proportions of *so* use (relative to that individual's total uses of either *so* or *entonces*) across the three generation groups. A Shapiro-Wilk normality test indicated that these values did not follow a normal distribution,

DISCOURSE MARKERS [129]

$W = 0.82$, $p < .001$, most likely due to the substantial number of participants who used *so* either 100% or 0% of the time. As such, a Kruskal-Wallis rank sum test was performed instead of an ANOVA. That is, we examined the average percentage use of *so* and *entonces* for groups of individuals. We found that individuals' proportion of use of *so* varied significantly by generation, $H(2) = 14.56$, $p < .001$, such that speakers in later generations used a higher proportion of *so* than earlier ones. Follow-up Mann-Whitney U tests showed that percentage use of *so* significantly differed between speakers in the G1 and G2 groups, $U = 149$, $p < .001$, as well as between speakers in the G1 and G3 groups, $U = 207.5$, $p = .006$. However, no statistically significant difference was found in the proportion of *so* use between the G2 and G3 speaker groups, $U = 724.5$, $p = .190$. These results suggest that the observed differences in *so/entonces* use were not driven by outlying discourse marker users, at least when comparing G1 and the rest of the speakers.

To further underscore that average proportions of discourse marker use do not necessarily correspond with the actual behavior of individuals, we note that there was a fair amount of variation within each group. For example, #48 is a G2 Mexican, and we saw earlier that G2 Mexicans as a group used *so* 34% of the time. However, #48 produced a greater proportion of *entonces* (n = 52 tokens, or 98%) than *so* (n = 1 token, or 2%). In addition, there were some cases of both discourse markers being used in the same utterance, as in examples (17) and (18).

(17) Porque ya la familia ya es tan grande **so** [result] solamente los niños y **entonces** [move] a cada uno les regala mis padres. (#89, G2 Puerto Rican female)

Because already the family is already so big **so** only the kids and **so** my parents give a gift to each one.

(18) Porque nuestros hijos casi todos tienen la misma edad, **so** [result] siempre se han criado juntos y . . . Ellas vivían aquí, pero se han . . . se han . . . cambiado a otros vecindarios. **Entonces** [result] siempre hemos mantenido nuestro . . . amistad. (#53, G2 Mexican female)

Because our kids are almost all the same age, **so** they've always grown up together and . . . They lived here, but they've . . . they've . . . moved to other neighborhoods. **So** we've always maintained our . . . friendship.

This suggests that a high frequency of use of *so* in a particular category does not necessarily mean that *entonces* is being replaced in that category or in any other. This variation only indicates that if we are observing a change to a system where *entonces* is replaced by *so*, it is occurring very gradually, and both forms will be used for some time to come.

Thus far, we have established that Puerto Ricans use *so* more than Mexicans in Chicago. Now we explore discourse marker use across regional origins and generational groups together. Figure 4.5 shows these results. At first glance, we notice the following: G1 Mexicans and Puerto Ricans are similar in using *entonces* the majority of the time (69.0–78.4%). It is in G2 and especially G3 where Puerto Ricans increase their proportion of *so* use, to 54.2% and 82.4%, respectively. MexiRicans stay at approximately 25% *entonces* use in both generational groups. When examining these values statistically, we found a significant effect for regional origin, $\chi^2(1) = 13.47$, $p < .001$, such that Puerto Rican speakers used a higher proportion of *so* than Mexican speakers, $z = 3.00$, $p = .003$. There was also a significant effect of generation, $\chi^2(2) = 7.76$, $p = .021$, such that (aggregated across regional origins) G1 showed a lower proportion of *so* use when compared with G2, $z = 2.12$, $p = .002$, and with G3, $z = 3.00$, $p = .008$. By contrast, there was no significant difference between G2 and G3, $z = 0.27$, $p = .961$. Finally, there was a significant interaction of regional origin and generation, $\chi^2(2) = 12.79$, $p = .002$, such that Mexican and Puerto Rican

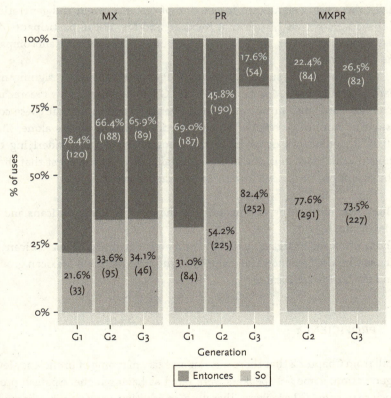

Figure 4.5. Percentage of each discourse marker, all groups and generations.

participants differed significantly in G1, $z = 2.06$, $p = .040$, and G3, $z = 2.08$, $p = .038$, but not G2 ($p > .05$).

When following up this interaction in the other direction (i.e., comparing across generations within each regional origin), Mexican participants showed a significant difference between G1 and G2, $z = 2.75$, $p = .016$, but not between G1 and G3 or between G2 and G3 (all $p > .05$). Meanwhile, Puerto Rican participants showed a significant difference between G1 and G3, $z = 2.35$, $p = .050$, but not between G1 and G2 or between G2 and G3 (all $p > .05$). These results suggest that discourse markers are not responding to any pressures of dialect contact: Puerto Ricans are not becoming more like Mexicans in using lower proportions of *so* across generations. In fact, their proportion of *so* use increases significantly between G1 and G3. Nor are Mexicans looking more like Puerto Ricans in using more *so* as their generational group increases.

For our second model comparing all three regional origin groups across G2 and G3, we found no significant main effect of regional origin, $\chi 2(2) = 2.37$, $p = .305$. There was, however, a significant main effect of generation, $\chi 2(1) = 8.80$, $p = .003$, such that G2 showed a lower proportion of *so* use than G3. Finally, there was a significant interaction of regional origin and generation, $\chi 2(2) = 15.03$, $p < .001$, such that Mexican and MexiRican participants differed significantly in G3, $z = 2.52$, $p = .032$, but no other pairwise subcomparisons were significant ($p > .05$).

To summarize our statistical findings: Puerto Ricans show significantly greater use of *so* than Mexicans in G1 and G3. MexiRicans show greater use of *so* than Mexicans but not more than Puerto Ricans. Note that these conclusions do not always align with our intuition from the figures alone, since statistical significance depends on the amount of variance underlying the averaged values shown in the figures. Overall, our results suggest that these eight groups can be divided into three general behaviors:

- Those who used *so* the vast majority of the time (G3 Puerto Ricans and all MexiRicans).
- Those who used *so* and *entonces* approximately equally (G2 Puerto Ricans).
- Those who used *entonces* the majority of the time (all three Mexican groups and the G1 Puerto Ricans).

4.6. PROFICIENCY

Recall from Chapter 2 that there was not an exact mapping of proficiency level to generation; some G3 speakers were rated as having higher Spanish proficiency than some G2 speakers. Therefore, in addition to examining discourse

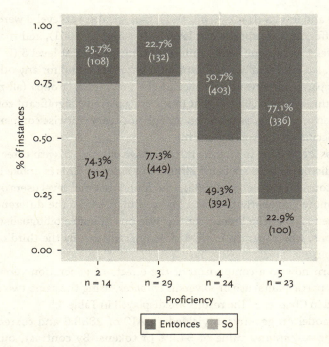

Figure 4.6. Percentage of each discourse marker by proficiency level.

marker use by generation, we looked at overall use of *so* and *entonces* by proficiency level. Figure 4.6 shows these results.[6]

In Figure 4.6, we see a clear pattern similar to what we saw with generational groups: when considering aggregated counts within groups, higher Spanish proficiency was linked to greater use of *entonces* relative to *so*. The 43 speakers rated at proficiency levels 2 and 3 showed much proportionally larger uses of *so* (74% and 77%, respectively) compared with the 24 speakers rated at level 4 (49%) and the 23 speakers rated at level 5 (23%).

We turn now to inferential statistics to determine whether or not these patterns were driven by outliers within each group. As before, a Shapiro-Wilk test revealed that individuals' proportions of *so* use were not normally distributed, $W = .83$, $p < .001$. As such, a Kruskal-Wallis rank sum test was performed (in lieu of an ANOVA) to compare speakers across proficiency levels. We found a significant difference in the use of *so* across proficiency levels, $H(3) = 20.55$, $p < .001$. Follow-up Mann-Whitney U tests revealed that speakers at proficiency level 2 were significantly different from speakers at level 4 ($U = 236$,

---

6. There was one proficiency level 1 individual in the subcorpus whom we removed from this analysis.

p = .040) and level 5 (U = 274, p < .001); that speakers at level 3 were significantly different from speakers at level 5 (U = 528, p < .001); and that speakers at level 4 were significantly different from speakers at level 5 (U = 411.5, p = .003). No statistically significant difference was found for any other pairwise comparisons between the rest of the proficiency groups (all p > .05). Overall, these results suggest that proficiency played a significant role in the proportion of *so/entonces* use, even though not every pairwise comparison between specific groups was significant.

Groups 2 and 3 are in fact the mirror image of group 5, with three-fourths of their discourse markers being either *so* or *entonces*. This is unlike the findings of Mougeon and Beniak (1986), who found that mid-level users of French used *so* more frequently than the low and high users. The difference likely lies in the fact that the French context was one of stable bilingualism across generations, while Spanish in the U.S. is typically lost by the third or fourth generation.

We turn now to a comparison of the effects of generation versus proficiency in participants' use of *so* versus *entonces*, using the same two analyses described in Chapter 3. The results are displayed in Table 4.5.

Our model on generation yielded an AIC of 2888.6 and correctly predicted the *so/entonces* value of 64.2% of tokens. By contrast, our model on proficiency yielded an AIC of 2802.0 and an accuracy of 66.8%. This suggests that proficiency explains the use of *so* versus *entonces* use better than generation does. Our second approach found that proficiency had a McFadden index (R^2M) of .088, higher than that of generation (.052), again suggesting that proficiency explains the use of *so/entonces* better than generation does.

Finally, we saw earlier in Figure 4.5 that Puerto Ricans used *so* far more overall than Mexicans. However, we must determine whether these Puerto Ricans used *so* more than their Mexican counterparts because they were less proficient in Spanish. Thus, we sought to compare a subgroup of Mexicans and Puerto Ricans at comparable levels of proficiency. The proficiency ratings with enough speakers of each group to allow for a reasonable comparison were levels 3 and 4, where there were 15 Mexican speakers and 16 Puerto Ricans,

Table 4.5. CORRELATION OF USE OF *SO* TO GENERATION VERSUS PROFICIENCY.

	Generation	**Proficiency**
AIC	2888.6 64.2% of tokens	2802.0 66.8% of tokens
R^2	.052	.088

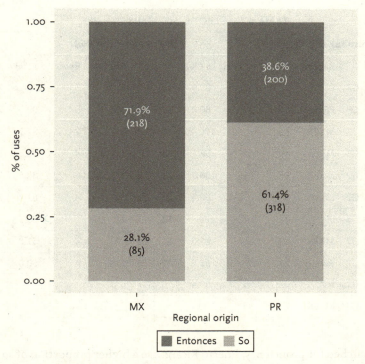

Figure 4.7. Proportion of discourse markers, Mexican and Puerto Rican speakers, proficiency levels 3 and 4 only.

so we collapsed these two groups for this analysis. Since this is not the exact same number of speakers in each group, Figure 4.7 presents both the number of tokens and their relative percentages.

We see that among speakers at proficiency levels 3 and 4 only, *so* formed almost two-thirds (61%) of Puerto Ricans' discourse marker use but only slightly less than one-third (28%) of that of Mexicans, and these proportions are not very dissimilar from when all proficiency levels were compared in Figure 4.7, where the proportions were 57% (Puerto Ricans) and 31% (Mexicans). We also averaged the number of tokens per speaker at these two proficiency levels and found that Puerto Ricans used *so* approximately three times more (an average of 19.9 tokens per speaker) than their proficiency-matched Mexican counterparts (5.7 tokens). This difference was statistically significant, as revealed by a Mann-Whitney U test (used in lieu of a t-test due to non-normality in the data), U = 67.5, p = .039. This provides some support for the argument that *so* constitutes a more prominent feature of mainland Puerto Rican Spanish than of U.S. Mexican Spanish, independently of speakers' Spanish proficiency. To summarize thus far, then, proficiency is more strongly correlated to use of *so* than generation, but even when they

Table 4.6. STRONG *SO* USERS (*N* = 20).

By number of tokens (*n*)						By proportion (%)					
#	G	Region	Prof.	*so* (*n*)	*so* (%)	#	G	Region	Prof.	*so* (%)	*so* (*n*)
8	G3	PR	2	93	98.9	14	G2	MX	3	100	24
123	G3	PR	4	84	80.0	15	G2	MX	5	100	28
11	G2	MXPR	3	65	100	40	G3	PR	2	97.1	34
61	G3	MXPR	4	52	98.1	19	G2	PR	4	96.8	31
81	G2	MXPR	3	49	96.1	72	G2	MXPR	3	87.5	24
36	G2	PR	3	41	80.4	17	G1	PR	4	81.6	38
77	G2	PR	4	41	100	55	G1	PR	5	65.1	43
73	G2	MXPR	3	40	81.6	18	G2	PR	4	51.8	56
115	G2	PR	2	39	31.5	47	G2	MX	4	50.0	24
12	G2	MX	2	36	97.4						
42	G3	MXPR	2	36	100						

are matched for proficiency, Puerto Ricans use a higher proportion of *so* than Mexicans.

A final way that we explore discourse marker use is by examining which speakers produced the greatest sheer numbers of *so* as well as the greatest proportions of it—that is, speakers who evidenced a use of *so* of more than 50% of their discourse markers, regardless of the *n* size of tokens. We identified the 10 individuals who produced the greatest number of tokens of *so*. Two individuals produced 36 tokens each, tying for 10th place, so they are both included and bring us to a total of 11 speakers. These individuals appear in the left half of Table 4.6. We see that not only did they each produce 36 or more tokens of *so*, but this *so* use constituted 80% or more of their total discourse marker use[7] (signaled in the shaded *n* column).

In the right half of Table 4.6, we present information about nine additional individuals whom we have included in this analysis because while their total number of tokens of *so* did not make the top 10, it constituted more than 50% of their total discourse marker use (signaled in the % column), and in addition, each person produced a total number of tokens of 24 or greater. We chose this number because 24.6 was the average total number of tokens produced (SD 22.5); we did not see benefit in analyzing individuals with high percentages of *so* use but only a handful of total discourse marker tokens. Thus, similarly

---

7. With the exception of one individual, #115, for whom it was a much lower 31.5%.

to the 11 individuals on the left, these nine individuals constitute relatively strong users of *so* in both proportion and number of tokens.

Immediately noticeable is that of these 20 high *so* users, half (*n* = 10) are Puerto Ricans, and almost a third (*n* = 6) are MexiRicans. Only four Mexicans (#12, #14, #15, and #47) are on this list. In addition, the majority of high *so* users (*n* = 13) are G2, and only five are G3s. Curiously, two high-proportion *so* users, #17 and #55, are G1s, and both are Puerto Rican. The fact that they have strong Spanish proficiency levels rated at levels 4 and 5 suggests that *so* is common even for high-proficiency Puerto Ricans in Chicago.

4.7. FUNCTIONS

Recall that based on Travis (2005), we identified five functions for these discourse markers: result, conclusion, moving the story forward, trailing, and other. Figure 4.8 shows the proportion of each discourse marker within each of the five functions.

We see that *so* was preferred for 65.2% of all results, for 65.5% of all conclusions, and for 90.6% of trails. These high percentages lend support to Torres

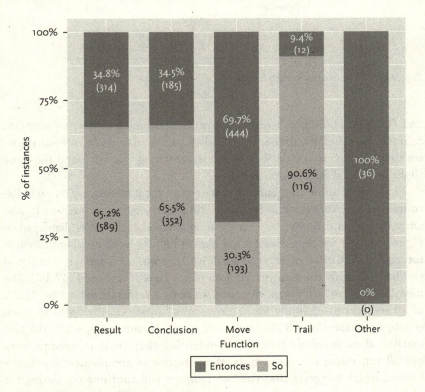

Figure 4.8. Functions by discourse marker.

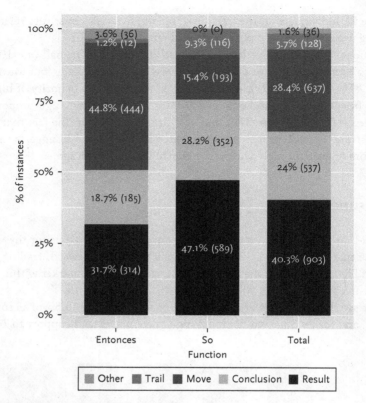

Figure 4.9. Discourse markers by function.

and Potowski's (2008) conclusion that *so* has become a borrowing into U.S. Spanish. Also similarly to that study, only for the function of move was *entonces* strongly preferred (69.7% of the time), meaning that we found the same slight functional distribution as before.

Next, we examine the functions carried out most commonly by each discourse marker. That is, what functions did *so* carry out most frequently, and what functions did *entonces* execute most frequently? This is displayed in Figure 4.9. We see that *entonces* did almost half its work moving discourse forward (44.8% of all *entonces* tokens), while *so* was used primarily to signal results in roughly the same proportion of the time it was used (47.1%). The next-largest function for *entonces* was marking a result (constituting 31.7% of all *entonces* uses), while for *so* the second-largest function was to mark conclusions (forming 28.2% of all uses of *so*). In summary, while the two markers show preferred functional tendencies, they are both used to carry out all functions; in other words, they are not in complementary distribution, which suggests that the two markers will continue coexisting for some time.

[138]   *Spanish in Chicago*

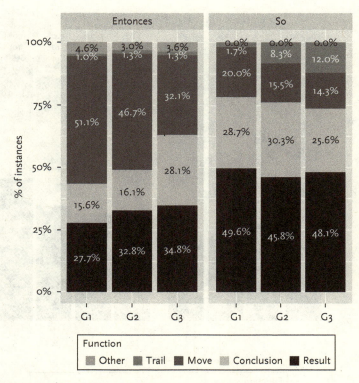

Figure 4.10. Proportional distribution of functions across generations.

Next, we examine whether there were differences in the ways in which *so* and *entonces* were used (that is, the functions they fulfilled) by each of the three generational groups. Figure 4.10 shows these proportions.

The distribution of functions of *so* and *entonces* across generations was fairly similar. For example, in all three generational groups, the use of *entonces* to mark a result accounted for between 28% and 35% of all uses of *entonces* and for 46% to 50% of all uses of *so*. Thus, it is not the case that different generations are using these discourse markers proportionately for different functions. This distinguishes our findings from those of Hlavac (2006), who found that Croatian speakers in Australia were increasingly using *da* for new (non-affirmative) functions. Thus, the functions of the two discourse markers appear to be in a relatively stable state across generations in Chicago.

For our final analysis, we look at the distribution of functions of *so*/*entonces* by proficiency level (Figure 4.11).

We do not see any major difference between functional distribution by proficiency and by generation. For maximum clarity, Appendix A shows side by side the functional distributions of *so* by generational groups compared with

DISCOURSE MARKERS [139]

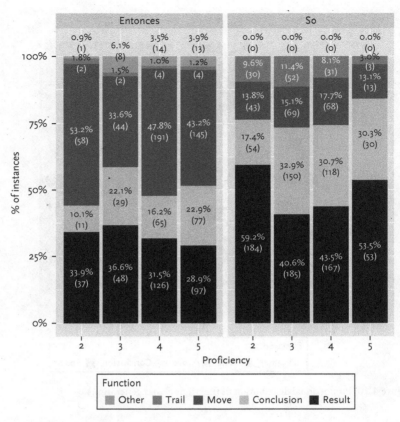

Figure 4.11. Functions by proficiency level.

proficiency levels, while Appendix B does so for *entonces*. Thus, these discourse markers were used broadly in the same ways by different generational groups and proficiency levels.

4.8. SUMMARY AND CONCLUSIONS

We explored the use of the discourse markers *so* and *entonces* among a subset of 91 speakers in the CHISPA corpus. We found a slightly greater proportional use of *so* than *entonces*, but this difference was less that what we found in our previous study (Torres & Potowski, 2008): 55% of all tokens were *so*, and 44% were *entonces*. As we predicted based on our prior work, Puerto Ricans used *so* proportionally more than Mexicans, and this difference was statistically significant. For some assurance that the difference between the two regional groups was not a function of proficiency differences, we looked at a subset of speakers from the two regions who shared proficiency levels (3 and 4). Here we saw that *so* formed almost two-thirds (61%) of Puerto Ricans' discourse marker use but only slightly less than one-third (28%) of that of Mexicans. We were thus more confident in our finding that Puerto Ricans use *so* more than Mexicans. Our hypothesis concerning MexiRican discourse marker behavior was that MexiRican patterns would follow those of their mother's regional origin group more closely than that of their father's group. This hypothesis was not completely borne out, although MexiRicans with a Puerto Rican mother did use a higher proportion of *so* than those with a Mexican mother.

Proportional use of *so* increased with generational group, but when we looked more closely at each generational group, we noticed that there was a fair amount of variation within each one. We also looked at the interaction of regional origin and generation and found that Mexicans and Puerto Ricans differed significantly in G1 and G3 but not in G2. That is, the two groups were very different in G1, became more alike in G2, and then diverged again in G3. This means that we did not find evidence that dialect contact is impacting usage of discourse markers: Puerto Ricans are not becoming more like Mexicans in using lower proportions of *so* across generations, nor are Mexicans looking more like Puerto Ricans in using *so* more as their generational group increases. We also predicted that the proportional use of *so* would decrease with increased Spanish proficiency level, which was borne out: the highest-proficiency speakers used *so* proportionally less than the other groups, and higher Spanish proficiency was linked to greater use of *entonces* relative to *so*.

As expected, we found slight functional distributions of *so* and *entonces* as we had in the 2008 study: while both *so* and *entonces* were used for all functions, *so* was preferred for all functions except for moving discourse forward, where *entonces* was strongly preferred. However, we found no evidence of strict complementary distribution, since both markers were used for all functions, and we also found the same functional distribution across all generational groups and proficiency levels. A future study could examine the distribution of functions of *so* and *entonces* by individual speakers.

As we saw in the introduction, there is evidence that coexisting discourse-marking systems tend to survive only when they are used for different functions (Fuller, 2001), and since we have found no evidence of differentiation of functions, *entonces* may not survive in Chicago Spanish. The status of borrowed particles may be different in situations of stable bilingualism versus situations where language attrition is under way; unfortunately, it will be challenging, if not impossible, to study whether both *so* and *entonces* will coexist indefinitely in Chicago Spanish, because the language is very rarely transmitted beyond the third generation. That is, *entonces* can only survive if Spanish does.

APPENDIX A
FUNCTIONAL DISTRIBUTION OF *SO*, PROFICIENCY VERSUS GENERATION

Proficiency Generation

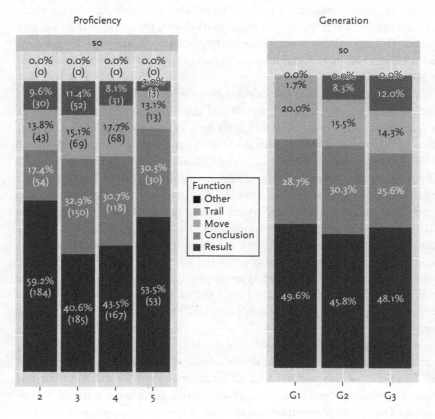

[142] *Spanish in Chicago*

APPENDIX B
FUNCTIONAL DISTRIBUTION OF *ENTONCES*, PROFICIENCY VERSUS GENERATION

Proficiency Generation

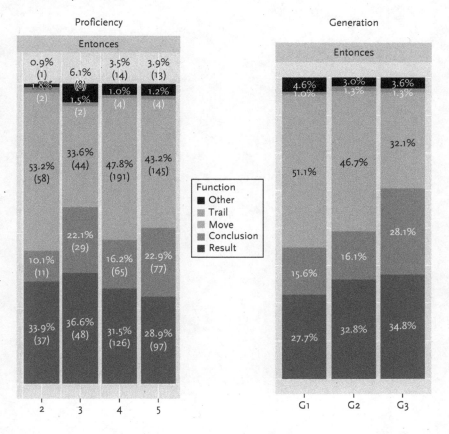

DISCOURSE MARKERS [143]

CHAPTER 5
Codeswitching

5.1. INTRODUCTION

Codeswitching, the use of two or more languages in a communicative act, is a common practice when speakers in a community have more than one language at their disposal. While once thought to be a random practice by speakers who lacked proficiency in one or both of their languages, it is now recognized to be a complex, rule-governed mode of communication (Bullock & Toribio, 2009). Among the many studies on codeswitching in multilingual communities around the world, some have sought to identify syntactic constraints (Becker, 1997; Sankoff & Poplack, 1981; Timm, 1975), while others explore functions and social motivations (Bailey, 2000; Huerta-Macias & Quintero, 1992; Valdés, 1976) and attitudes toward codeswitching (Cooper, 2013; Hidalgo, 1986, 1988; Anderson & Toribio, 2007).

This chapter[1] offers an analysis of codeswitching among 64 Puerto Ricans, Mexicans, and MexiRicans from three generational groups in the CHISPA corpus, looking at overall frequency and proportions of different types of codeswitching. We found that both overall frequency and frequency by codeswitching type varied by regional group, by generation, and by Spanish proficiency level. We compare our findings with those of other research on U.S. Spanish.

---

1. An earlier version of this chapter was published as Torres and Potowski (2016). We have added here one variable (Spanish proficiency level), several new comparisons, and new statistical analyses.

5.2. SPANISH-ENGLISH CODESWITCHING IN THE U.S.

In Poplack's (1980) study of codeswitching among Puerto Ricans in New York City's El Barrio, she and her team gathered audio recordings of informal conversations among 20 bilingual speakers through participant observation and sociolinguistic interviews. Her analyses of these data led her to propose two constraints on bilingual codeswitching: the free-morpheme constraint and the syntactic-equivalence constraint. The free-morpheme constraint posits that codeswitching cannot occur between a bound morpheme and a free morpheme—for example, *bailanding (dancing) does not occur, because -ing is a bound morpheme in English. The syntactic-equivalence constraint stipulates that codeswitching can only occur at points where the surface structure of each of the two languages is the same. Poplack also discussed a sociolinguistic pattern of syntactic switch points: she argued that those speakers who had the strongest proficiency in both Spanish and English tended to produce intrasentential switches (i.e., those that occur within a sentence). These switches typically require more facility with both of the languages,[2] because in order to carry out the switch successfully, the syntax of both languages must be respected. Therefore, they are considered a "riskier" type of codeswitching than intersentential switches, which occur at the sentence boundary.

A few years later, Silva-Corvalán (1983) focused on eight Mexican American adolescents in Los Angeles, California, who were English-dominant but engaged in codeswitching. She found that both the quantity and the quality of their codeswitching differed from those of more balanced bilinguals. These speakers codeswitched primarily to fill in memory gaps, to compensate for lacking Spanish-language words and phrases, and to evaluate and clarify messages. Their codeswitching was often marked by pauses, hesitations, and other means of editing. The speech of the English-dominant participants also evidenced some violations of the syntactic-equivalence constraint. For example, an English-dominant speaker stated, "El último juego de mi junior year era el más . . . *excited juego* de mi vida" (The last game of my junior year was the most . . . excited game of my life). Spanish and English have different noun phrase rules for adjective placement, and the construction *excited juego* violates Spanish rules, since in Spanish adjectives usually follow the noun they modify. Silva-Corvalán (1983) concluded that the codeswitching that English-dominant speakers engage in is significantly different from that engaged in by more balanced bilinguals and proposed that it be referred to with a different term: *code-shifting*.

Lipski's (1985) study of codeswitching was based on two data sets. One consisted of 30 hours of Spanish-English bilingual speech collected from

---

2. Norteir (1990) also found that proficiency correlated with type of codeswitch in her study of Dutch-Moroccan Arabic speakers.

Mexican American radio programs broadcasted in Houston with 22 speakers who ranged in age from 16 to 60. The other included three hours of spontaneous conversations recorded in Texas. The combined data set included 4,000 examples of language switching. Lipski coded for 20 constituent switch points, the most frequent of which were prepositions, sentences, coordinating conjunctions, and tag phrases. He noted that when comparing his findings to those of Poplack (1980), he found that "the degree of correspondence is quite high, despite the different classificatory schemes which have been utilized" (Lipski, 1985, p. 25) and also despite the fact that one community was Mexican and the other Puerto Rican. In Poplack's data, 77.2% of the switches were intrasentential, while 20.3% were sentential and 22.5% were tag switches. In Lipski's data, 74.6% were intrasentential switches, while 15.7 were sentential and 9.8% were tag switches.

In her long-term ethnography of 37 children in the same Puerto Rican community where Poplack (1980) conducted her study, Zentella (1997) analyzed the speech of five girls. Her data reaffirmed the free-morpheme constraint and the syntactic-equivalence constraint. She also coded the data for 28 different switch points, and her results overlapped with those of Poplack (1980) and Lipski (1985). Overall, Zentella found that of 1,685 codeswitches produced by the five girls, 23% were intersentential and 77% were intrasentential.

Interested in what he termed "low-fluency bilinguals"—those who use Spanish infrequently or not at all and may not be in contact with fluent bilingual speakers—Lipski (2009) compared codeswitching in three language pairs (Spanish + Portuguese, Spanish + Italian, and Spanish + English) in which each language is progressively more dissimilar to Spanish. He proposed that less fluent speakers favor *congruent lexicalization*. Congruent lexicalization is when two languages share grammatical structures that can be filled lexically with elements from either language and usually occurs when the languages in contact share similar morphosyntactic structures and cognates (Muysken, 2000). Although these language pairs are progressively more dissimilar, Lipski claimed that situations of intense contact can bring about the type of congruent lexicalization usually found only in switching between very similar languages. He found that low-fluency speakers exhibited a great range of switch types not usually seen with fluent bilinguals; they switched all types of constituents and fragments of constituents, as would be expected only in cases of congruent lexicalization.

In a subsequent study, Lipski (2014) compared the codeswitching of what he called Spanish heritage or "low-fluency" speakers with that of more balanced Spanish-English bilinguals. The low-fluency speakers were Sabine River Spanish speakers from northwestern Louisiana, a region where not many fluent Spanish speakers remain. Among the low-fluency speakers, Lipski found many cases that violated the norms of typical codeswitching by more fluent bilinguals. For example, in example (1), a semi-fluent speaker switches between a pronominal subject and predicate, and in example (2), a switch occurs between the infinitive marker and the infinitive. Both of these switches are typically considered infelicitous.

(1) Well, {some // vinieron} de Texas, de México.

Well, some came from Texas, from Mexico.

(2) I used {to // andar} de noche, pero las dos de la mañana venía patrás la casa.

I used to walk at night, but at two in the morning I came back home.

The author found that low-fluency speakers exhibited characteristics of congruent lexicalization and produced what he called "ragged" switching. Although the type of congruent lexicalization that he described is most frequently found in contact situations with languages that share considerable lexical and syntactic structures (e.g., Spanish and Portuguese), Lipski again claimed that it may also arise in the case of relatively more dissimilar languages (English and Spanish) under situations of intense contact. He called for more studies on codeswitching among low-fluency bilinguals.

In summary, this body of research on Spanish-English codeswitching in the U.S. shows that the more balanced bilinguals exhibited the patterns displayed in Table 5.1, while both the quantity and the quality of codeswitching among non-fluent bilinguals were different and sometimes violated common constraints observed among the more fluent bilinguals.

To date, no study has compared the quantity or types of codeswitching produced by members of different regional origin groups living in the same city. Doing so intergenerationally provides an opportunity not only to look at codeswitching behavior across apparent time but also to look for potential outcomes of dialect contact. For example, if G2 Mexicans and Puerto Ricans are found to codeswitch differently but those in G3 are more similar to each other, we might be able to propose that this convergence was a result of dialect contact. However, although English proficiency likely plays no role in any differences between G2 and G3 (given that all Chicago-raised individuals

Table 5.1. COMPARISON OF TYPES OF CODESWITCHING AMONG "BALANCED" BILINGUALS.

Study	Group	Intrasentential	Intersentential	Tags
Poplack (1980)	Puerto Ricans	77.2%	20.3%	22.5%
Lipski (1985)	Mexican Americans	74.6%	15.7%	9.8%
Zentella (1997)	Puerto Ricans	77.0%	23.0%	1.8%

are likely to develop the same levels of English), it could be due to decreased Spanish proficiency.

Our research questions about codeswitching in the CHISPA corpus were as follows:

1. Will there be differences in overall English use, number of codeswitches, and types of codeswitches according to the following?
   a. Regional origin
   b. Generational group
   c. Regional origin and generational group
   d. Spanish proficiency level
2. Will Spanish proficiency or generational group be more strongly connected to overall English use and number of codeswitches?

We predicted that G2 speakers would produce patterns of codeswitching similar to those displayed in Table 5.1 because they tend to be the most fluent bilinguals, that is, with strong levels of both Spanish and English. We also expected that G3 speakers would produce the greatest quantity of English, followed by G2 and G1. In addition, despite the general correlation between proficiency and generation (shown in Chapter 2), in the case of the quantity of English produced during an interview, proficiency in English is clearly as relevant as proficiency in Spanish, and proficiency in English is related to generational group in the following ways. G1 speakers are dominant in Spanish, and many have relatively little command of English. G2 speakers tend to be more balanced in their bilingualism, although for some, their English is considerably stronger; however, they are presumably equally as proficient in English as G3s. Thus, if we consider four individuals all with a Spanish proficiency rated at level 5 but belonging to different G groups, we assume their English proficiency would compare as follows:

Spanish proficiency level rated at level 5	*Assumed English proficiency*
G1 = G2	G1 < G2
G2 = G3	G2 = G3

We would thus predict that the G2 speaker might use more English or engage in a greater amount of codeswitching because their English is stronger, and obviously not because their Spanish is any weaker, than that of the G1 speaker. We might not, however, make this prediction when one speaker is a G2 and the other a G3; the English proficiency of these two generational groups is very probably the same, that is, as native-like as anyone raised in Chicago.

Finally, we point out that the amount of English used in an interview is not synonymous with the number of codeswitches the interview contains. It may be the case, for example, that a speaker uses a large number of English words but these are contained in infrequent turns. Another speaker may codeswitch a great deal more frequently but using shorter English chunks. This is why we will examine both. With regard to types of codeswitches, given that G2 speakers tend to have stronger bilingual skills than G1 or G3 speakers, we expected them to engage in intrasentential switching more frequently than the other two generational groups. Similarly, we expect speakers with higher Spanish proficiency to engage in one-word and two-or-more-word intrasentential codeswitching more frequently than those with lower Spanish proficiency. We did not have strong hypotheses about the three regional origin groups' rates of English use or codeswitching.

5.3. METHODOLOGY

Participants

This analysis is based on a subsample of the CHISPA corpus consisting of 64 interviews distributed equally across the eight generational and regional categories displayed in Table 5.2. We chose these speakers randomly to fill the generational and regional origin categories.

It is important to keep in mind that unlike the naturalistic data in the studies by Poplack (1980), Lipski (1985), and Zentella (1997), our data were collected with sociolinguistic interviews. While these attempted to elicit natural conversation, we cannot claim that they are equal to observed interactions taking place in a community. As explained in Chapter 2, we conducted the interviews in Spanish, and participants were asked to speak in Spanish as much as possible, even if that was not the language they were more comfortable speaking. Using mostly Spanish for an extended conversation was not unfamiliar to many of our participants, who noted that they had family members and acquaintances who were Spanish-monolingual or Spanish-preferring. Interviewers also told interviewees that any use of English would be understood. All the interviewers were fluent in Spanish and raised in the U.S., so

Table 5.2. SUBCORPUS: REGIONAL BACKGROUND AND GENERATIONS.

	MX	**PR**	**MXPR**	**Total**
G1	8	8	—	16
G2	8	8	8	24
G3	8	8	8	24
Total	24	24	16	64

they were also native English speakers. This fact was known by the interviewees, either because they had a previous relationship with the interviewer or because the interviewer made this known before the interview began.

Many participants engaged in codeswitching throughout the interview. In our readings, we did not notice salient qualitative or quantitative differences in the amount of codeswitching in the interviews conducted by known versus unfamiliar interviewers.

Coding

Both authors read each transcript and noted all uses of English material. These uses were categorized into the categories described in the sections that follow.

Proper Nouns

Proper nouns, including proper names, are nouns that are normally singular (*Humboldt Park*, *Burger King*, *Mexico City*, *Laura*) and do not take an article. They designate a particular being or thing and in English are typically capitalized. We omitted these from our analysis.

Intrasentential Codeswitching

Intrasentential codeswitching refers to switches that occur within a sentence (or a clause, if the utterance is not a complete sentence). As stated earlier, this type of switch has generally been regarded as requiring high proficiency in the two languages, because it entails a more complex mixture of the two languages and may potentially result in ungrammatical sequences in one or both of the languages (Lipski, 1985; Norteir, 1990; Poplack, 1980).

Intrasentential switches can consist of one word or of two or more words. Classifying one-word switches has been amply discussed in the literature (Myers-Scotton, 1993; Poplack, 1980; Poplack et al., 1988) because there is no agreed-upon method of distinguishing between a one-word codeswitch and a borrowing. A common definition of the difference holds that a borrowing is adapted phonologically and morphologically to the host language, while a codeswitch is not. The borrowing is said to become part of the lexicon of the host language, while the one-word codeswitch retains its original sound and structure and is not considered part of the host language. Two examples of material from Spanish used in English are offered to illustrate this difference. The food item *tamales* is quite common in U.S. English, and most speakers have adapted it to English phonology [tʰəmɑliʲz] and even morphology, referring to one *tamal* as a "tamalee." In addition, many people with no knowledge of Spanish or contact with Spanish speakers or cultures use this word or at least know what it means. Thus, it appears to be a borrowing into English. On the other hand, we have heard people speaking English insert the word *chancla* (sandal, flip-flop) using native Spanish phonology. It is our sense that people with no knowledge of Spanish or much contact with Spanish speakers or cultures do not recognize or use this word at all; only bilingual/bicultural individuals do so, typically when referring to the humorous stereotype that Latina mothers discipline their children with a *chancla* (a cursory Internet search of the word *chancla* reveals how common this trope is). Despite being common among Latinos, *chancla* constitutes a one-word codeswitch into English.

This distinction between codeswitching and borrowing is important because it implies a different relationship between the languages. Even so, some linguists have argued that a one-word codeswitch is indistinguishable from a borrowing (Gardner-Chloros, 2009; Myers-Scotton, 1992) and even make the case for treating single-word switches as lexical borrowings (Varra, 2013). In the case of U.S. Spanish, when a single English word appears frequently and is also often surrounded by Spanish, we can be more confident that it is a borrowing into Spanish rather than a one-word codeswitch. As we argued in Chapter 4, this appears to be the case with the discourse marker *so* in our corpus. Discourse markers have been shown to make up a large proportion of one-word codeswitches in several corpora (Lipski, 1985; Poplack, 1980; Torres, 2002), so they are typically categorized separately from one-word switches.

In conclusion, in our analysis, we make no attempt to determine whether a one-word codeswitch is in fact a borrowing. We decided to count as a codeswitch every English word (that was not *so* or a proper noun) surrounded by Spanish or a pause. After determining that a codeswitch was intrasentential, we categorized it as either a one-word or a two-or-more-word switch; the discourse markers *you know* and *I mean* were counted as one word. Examples of one-word switches include:

Creo que sería un *waste*.	I think it would be a waste.
Y aquí el *season* cambia de calor a frío.	And here the season changes from hot to cold.
Y lo vi en el *alley*.	And I saw him in the alley.
Pero a veces, *you know*, no sabe una palabra.	But sometimes, you know, he doesn't know a word.

Examples of two-or-more-word switches include:

Dos hermanos que somos *full blooded*.	Two siblings who are full blooded.

Digo "soy latina" *or something like that.*   I say "I'm Latina" or something like that.

Cuando estaba en *high school.*   When she was in high school.

We would like to point out several additional points about the coding of *so*. All tokens of *so* received one of three different codings. Where it was surrounded by English, it was simply counted as an English word in that turn of speech ("He asked me, **so** I told him the truth"). When *so* was surrounded by Spanish and a pause, it was considered a borrowing and not a codeswitch ("Llegó a los seis meses, **so** se crió aquí"). This is consistent with our argument in Chapter 4 that *so* frequently functions as a borrowing into Spanish. However, when *so* was adjacent to Spanish material on one side and English material on the other side, as in "Me gradué, so I'm what they call, ya soy lo que se llama alumna" (I graduated, so I'm what they call, I'm already what they call alumna) (#37, G3 MexiRican female), we no longer considered that token a borrowing because it did not meet the criterion of being surrounded by Spanish. Instead, we counted it as one of the words within the two-or-more-word codeswitch. Finally, in the example *so you know*, one could argue that the discourse marker *you know* is a borrowing, in which case the token *so you know* would constitute a three-word Spanish borrowing, but we did not choose this route, instead counting *you know* as a one-word codeswitch.

Intersentential Codeswitches

An intersentential codeswitch occurs at the sentence boundary. Since people do not speak with punctuation that clearly indicates sentence boundaries, we did our best to identify these boundaries by ear based on intonation and pauses. Some examples of intersentential codeswitches include:

Pues primeramente sacar todas las gangas. *Um, basically, that's it.*

Well, first get rid of all the gangs.

¿Que si me gusta [el spanglish]? No, porque es hablar una o hablar otra. Pero, no lo pueden mezclar, no. *That's a no no.*

Do I like [Spanglish]? No, because you speak one or the other. But, you can't mix it, no.

Y ahora el hijo mío me mira y me dice, "Why do I have to speak Spanish? No quiero hablar el español."

And now my son looks at me and says [. . .] I don't want to speak Spanish.

There were sometimes cases of intra- and intersentential codeswitches in the same turn, such as:

[Interviewer: ¿Dónde usas el español?] En iglesia, en la casa. [Pause] *I use it here . . . I would say forty percent of the time,* cuarenta, porque mi esposo nomás habla español, *you know.*

The speaker switched to English ("I use it here") after a sentence boundary, which was coded as an intersentential codeswitch. However, she then switched back into Spanish ("porque mi esposo") and into English again ("you know"). The use of *you know* was coded as a one-word intrasentential codeswitch.

After a codeswitch was coded as intersentential or intrasentential, we counted the number of English words it contained. Although we do not attempt to categorize motivations for codeswitching, sometimes a reasonable explanation seemed evident. Some one-word codeswitches appeared to be lexical items that the speaker was more accustomed to saying in English, such as in examples (11) through (14).

(11) Nos ponía la ropa en *layaway*. (#43, G2 Puerto Rican female)

She always put our clothes on layaway

(12) Hago *bookkeeping*, entonces. (#17, G1 Puerto Rican female)

I do bookkeeping, so.

(13) Por ejemplo no tenía que hacer un *internship* que casi todos los, um, las personas en *college* tienen que hacer. (#37, G3 MexiRican female)

For example you didn't have to do an internship which almost all, um, people in college have to.

(14) Está en un *freshman center* porque en Cicero tenemos muchos jóvenes tienen un *building* para los *freshmen* solamente y ya de ahí para la *high school* que es de *sophomore* hasta *senior*." (#69, G2 MexiRican male)

She's in a freshman center because in Cicero we have a lot of young people they have a building just for the freshmen and from there to high school which is from sophomore to senior.

Some English words were quite common across generations of speakers in the corpus, including *high school, building, basement,* and *alley.* There were also numerous semantic extensions such as *colegio* for college and *grados* for grades. We present a list of neologisms from the CHISPA corpus in Appendix A. Oteguy and Garcia (1993) noted that some neologisms in U.S. Spanish may in fact refer to new concepts, meaning that the "equivalent" word in Spanish really is not equivalent at all because the referent is different. Along these lines, it seems likely to us that *callejón* has a different semantic referent from *alley* and that *secundaria/preparatoria* is contextually different from a U.S. *high school*.

As for two-or-more-word switches, the motivations for switching languages in examples (15) and (16) also seem to present ready explanations:

(15) Each house, cada casa era veinticinco dólares. (#43, G2 Puerto Rican female)

Each house, each house was twenty-five dollars.

(16) Me dicen que si por favor if I could help translate. (#17, G1 Puerto Rican female)

They ask me if please if I could help translate.

In (15), the speaker seems to have begun in English, realized that the expected language of the interview was Spanish, and so started over in Spanish. In (16), it seems likely that the speaker is indirectly quoting the person or people who asked whether she could help translate. However, in the majority of cases, such as (17) and (18), there is no clear reason the speaker used English instead of Spanish.

(17) Que la familia te dé el support. (#17, G1 Puerto Rican female)

That your family gives you support.

(18) Me fui con él a los dos días de graduación, and my parents cried. (#43, G2 Puerto Rican female)

I left with him two days after graduation, and my parents cried.

Based on the totality of their interviews, it seems unlikely that the speakers who produced (17) and (18) did not know how to say in Spanish the words produced here in English, nor does it seem that these English uses constitute neologisms à la Otheguy and Garcia (1993). Zentella (1997) showed that 75% of the codeswitches in her corpus consisted of words that the Puerto Rican girls actually did know how to say in the other language. Similarly to the vast majority of researchers on this topic, we do not attempt to explain the "whys" behind the codeswitches in our corpus.

First we present overall percentage of English, then the types of codeswitches (intrasentential one-word, intrasentential two-or-more-word, and intersentential) according to regional origin, generation, and proficiency.

Table 5.3. AVERAGE TOTAL NUMBER OF WORDS PRODUCED.

Regional origin	Mexican	4,566
	Puerto Rican	4,529
	MexiRican	4,470
Generation	1	4,470
	2	4,751
	3	4,343
Proficiency	5	4,639
	4	4,571
	3	4,320
	2 + 1	4,550

5.4. OVERALL QUANTITY OF ENGLISH

In order to examine the proportion of English use, first we needed the total number of words produced by each interviewee (excluding proper nouns and tokens of *so* surrounded by Spanish). We present in Table 5.3 the average total number of words produced, which showed no clear patterns by regional origin, by generation, or by proficiency level.

To arrive at the percentage of English use, we counted the number of English words each interviewee used and divided this into the number of words they produced in total. Figure 5.1 shows the average percentage of English words by regional origin group.

We see that when combining speakers of all generational groups and proficiency levels, MexiRicans used the highest proportion of English, followed by Puerto Ricans and then Mexicans. These differences were not significant.

By Generation

Figure 5.2 shows the average proportion of English words according to generational group.

Figure 5.2 suggests a clear linear increase in the percentage of English words. This was supported by a one-way between-participants ANOVA on the percentage use of English during the interview, which found a significant effect of generation, $F(2, 61) = 4.57$, $p = .014$, $\eta_p^2 = .13$, such that later generations showed higher percentage use of English during the interview

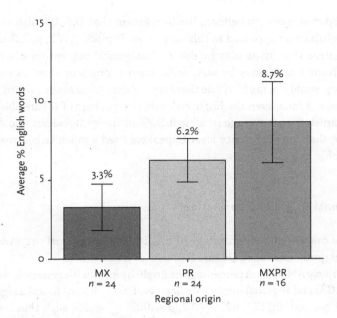

Figure 5.1. Percentage of English words by regional origin.

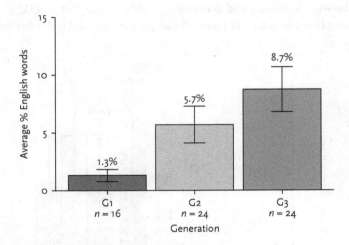

Figure 5.2. Percentage of English words by generational group.

than earlier ones. This supported our hypothesis that with each subsequent generation there would be an increase in the amount of English used in the interview.

We pause here to make an important observation. Even among this subcorpus of G3 speakers, the average percentage of English use is only 8.7%, with a maximum of slightly more than 10%. This is not as high as what some critics of U.S. Spanish seem to believe. The impression that U.S. Spanish is riddled with English is unsupported in this corpus. As Poplack (1982, p. 22) explains, this negative stereotype may be due to "categorical perception whereby deviation from a norm may be seen as far more prominent than its negligible frequency would warrant." While there is an obvious increase in use of English across generations, even the English-dominant speakers of G3 are able to produce Spanish for an average of almost 90% of their interviews (we do note, however, that the proficiency level 1 speakers used a much larger proportion of English).

By Regional Origin and Generation

Next, we calculated the percentage of English use by regional origin and generational group combined (Figure 5.3).

A two-way ANOVA on percentage of English words with generation (for G1, G2, and G3) and regional origin (Mexican vs. Puerto Rican) found a significant effect of generation, $F(2, 42) = 7.12$, $p = .002$, $\eta_p^2 = .25$, such that later generations showed a higher percentage use of English. We found no significant effect of ethnicity, $F(1, 42) = 2.68$, $p = .109$, $\eta_p^2 = .06$, and no significant interaction between ethnicity and generation, $F(2, 42) = 0.07$, $p = .931$, $\eta_p^2 < .01$, suggesting that Mexican and Puerto Rican participants did not differ between

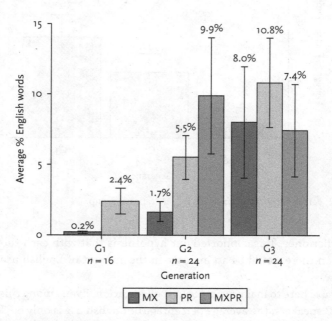

Figure 5.3. Percentage of English words by regional origin and generational group.

each other significantly in terms of percentage of English use. Thus, speakers in later generations use significantly more English than those in prior generations, and despite Puerto Ricans having an average percentage of English use higher than that of their Mexican generational counterparts, there was so much variability that this regional origin difference did not reach significance.

Comparing all three ethnic groups across G2 and G3, a two-way ANOVA found no significant effects for either generation, $F(1, 42) = 1.50$, $p = .228$, $\eta_p^2 = .03$; regional origin, $F(2, 42) = 0.92$, $p = .405$, $\eta_p^2 = .04$; or the interaction between generation and regional origin, $F(2, 42) = 1.22$, $p = .305$, $\eta_p^2 = .05$. This means that all three regional origin groups experienced similar changes across generations, and there were no significant differences between Mexicans, Puerto Ricans, and MexiRicans at G2 or G3.

By Proficiency Level

Finally, we calculated the proportion of English use by proficiency level (Figure 5.4).

We notice in Figure 5.4 the same linear increase in percentage of English use as we did with generation: as proficiency decreases, percentage of use of English increases. A one-way between-participants ANOVA on the percentage of English words in the interview and the effect of proficiency level (with proficiency levels 1 and 2 collapsed into one group due to small sample sizes) found a significant effect such that higher Spanish proficiency was associated with less use of English, $F(3, 60) = 6.41$, $p < .001$, $\eta_p^2 = .24$.

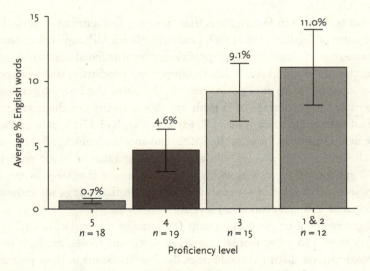

Figure 5.4. Averages of percentage of English words by proficiency level.

Table 5.4. CORRELATION OF USE OF ENGLISH TO GENERATION VERSUS PROFICIENCY.

	Generation	Proficiency
AIC	446.6 13.0% of variance	437.4 22.3% of variance
R^2	.066	.159

As we did for lexicon and discourse markers, we then asked whether proficiency or generation is more closely correlated with the proportion of English used, using the same two analyses described in Chapter 3. The results are displayed in Table 5.4.

Our model on generation yielded an AIC of 446.6 and explained 13.0% of variance. By contrast, our model on proficiency yielded an AIC of 437.4 and explained 22.3% of variance. This suggests that proficiency explains proportion of English use better than generation does. In our second model, we found that proficiency had an R^2 index of .159, higher than that of generation (.066). This agrees with the result of our model comparison approach in suggesting that proficiency explains percentage of English use better than generation does.

We note that any analysis using averages does not show individuals' behaviors. In other words, none of these 64 individuals produced a percentage of English use of exactly 0.7%, 4.6%, 9.1%, or 11.0%, the average values displayed in Figure 5.4. We can more clearly see individual variability in percentage of English use across proficiency ranges in the scatterplot shown in Figure 5.5.

What is clear from Figure 5.5 is that there is a fair amount of variation in the amount of English used at each proficiency level. Although the differences in percentage of English use by proficiency level reached statistical significance, this scatterplot reminds us to temper any conclusion that in a conversation intended to be entirely in Spanish, the lower the Spanish proficiency, the greater the percentage of English use; this is clearly not the case. One individual with proficiency level of 4, for example, had a 31% rate of English usage in her interview, another had 12%, and another had 8%, all three values well above the 4.6% average and also above the rates of many proficiency level 3 speakers. This also provides some reassurance that large proportions of English use did not unwarrantedly downgrade the ratings we assigned to participants' Spanish proficiency levels.

Might regional origin group count for some of the variation within proficiency levels? In other words, at a given proficiency level, might it be that the Mexicans are distinguishable from the Puerto Ricans in their percentage of English use and thus influence the average for the group? Looking at

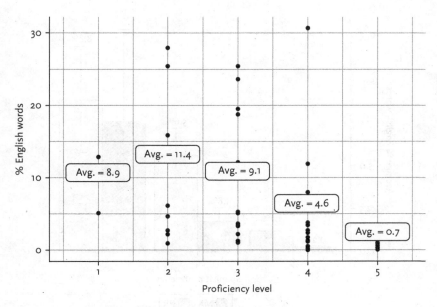

Figure 5.5. Percentage of English words by proficiency level.

Table 5.5. DISTRIBUTION OF SPEAKERS WITH EACH PROFICIENCY LEVEL BY REGIONAL ORIGIN GROUP IN THE CODESWITCHING SUBCORPUS (SPEAKERS IN SHADED CELLS WERE SELECTED FOR COMPARISON).

Proficiency level	Mexican n	Puerto Rican n	MexiRican n	Total n
1	1	1	0	2
2	2	4	4	10
3	4	5	6	15
4	7	6	6	19
5	10	8	0	18

Table 5.5, we can see that there were only two speakers at proficiency level 1 and 10 speakers at proficiency level 2 (and the latter were not evenly distributed across the three regional origin groups). Therefore, we conducted this comparison on proficiency levels 3, 4, and 5 only. Additionally, there were no MexiRican speakers at proficiency level 5, so we restricted this analysis to Mexicans and Puerto Ricans only. Thus, this subanalysis was conducted only on those speakers in the shaded cells of Table 5.5.

Figure 5.6 shows the average percentage of English use by Mexicans and Puerto Ricans at proficiency levels 3, 4, and 5.

CODESWITCHING [161]

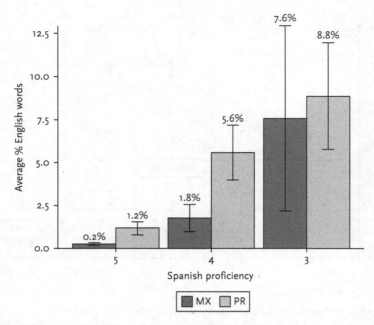

Figure 5.6. Percentage of English use by proficiency level and regional origin group, proficiency levels 3, 4, and 5.

Among speakers of the same proficiency levels, in every generational group Puerto Ricans showed higher rates of average English use. However, this did not reach significance: a two-way between-participants ANOVA on percentage of English use with the factors regional origin (Mexican vs. Puerto Rican participants) and proficiency (levels 3, 4, and 5) found no significant effect for regional origin, $F(1, 34) = 1.92$, $p = .175$, $\eta_p^2 = .05$. We did find a main effect of proficiency, $F(2, 34) = 8.73$, $p = .001$, $\eta_p^2 = .34$. There was no significant interaction for regional origin and proficiency, $F(2, 34) = 0.44$, $p = .646$, $\eta_p^2 = .03$. In sum, this means that Puerto Ricans and Mexicans experienced similar increases in the amount of English they used as their proficiency declined. Although there seems to be quite a bit of height difference in the figure between Mexicans and Puerto Ricans at each proficiency level, there is also a lot of variance (and a relatively small number of speakers), such that these regional origin differences within each proficiency level did not reach significance.

5.5. NUMBER OF CODESWITCHES

There were a total of 3,802 codeswitches in this subcorpus of 64 speakers. As we did for English use, we present these findings by regional origin, by

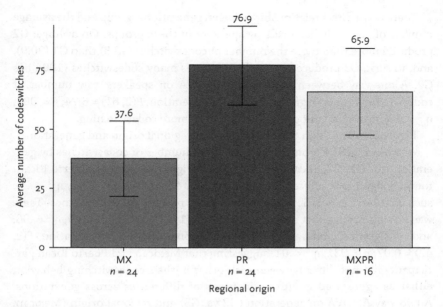

Figure 5.7. Average number of all codeswitches by regional origin.

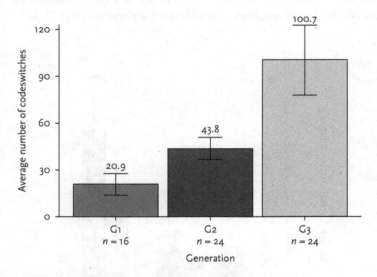

Figure 5.8. Average number of codeswitches by generational group.

generation, by regional origin and generation, and finally by proficiency. Figure 5.7 shows the average number of codeswitches by regional origin.

We see that Puerto Ricans engaged overall in more codeswitching than the other two regional origin groups. Figure 5.8 shows number of codeswitches by generational group.

There was a direct relationship between generational group and the average number of codeswitches made by speakers in these groups. On average, G2 produced more than twice the number of codeswitches (43.8) than G1 (20.9), and, in turn, G3 produced more than twice as many codeswitches (100.7) as G2. A one-way between-participants ANOVA on speakers' raw number of codeswitches found a significant effect of generation, $F(2, 61) = 6.74, p = .002$, $\eta_p^2 = .18$, such that later generations showed more codeswitching.

Figure 5.9 focuses on the combination of regional origin and generation.

A two-way ANOVA on participants' total number of codeswitches by generation (for G1, G2, and G3) and regional origin (Mexican vs. Puerto Rican) found a significant effect of generation, $F(2, 42) = 7.12, p = .002, \eta_p^2 = .25$, such that later generations showed a higher number of codeswitches. There was no significant effect of regional origin, $F(1, 42) = 2.68, p = .109, \eta_p^2 = .06$, and no significant interaction between regional origin and generation, $F(2, 42) = 0.07, p = .931, \eta_p^2 < .01$, suggesting that Mexican and Puerto Rican participants did not differ between each other in their codeswitching behavior, either as aggregated groups or in terms of differences across generations. A two-way ANOVA on generation (G2 vs. G3) and regional origin (Mexican, Puerto Rican, and MexiRican) found a significant effect of generation, $F(1, 42) = 5.69, p = .022, \eta_p^2 = .12$, such that G3 showed more codeswitches than G2 overall. We found no significant effects of regional origin, $F(2, 42) = 1.21$,

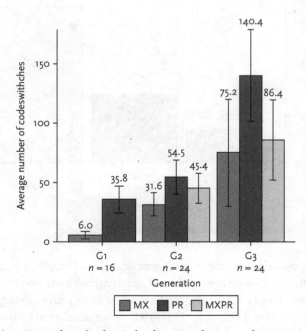

Figure 5.9. Average number of codeswitches by regional origin and generation.

$p = .309$, $\eta_p^2 = .05$, and no significant interaction between generation and regional origin, $F(2, 42) = 0.37$, $p = .691$, $\eta_p^2 = .02$.

In sum, our hypothesis that G3 participants would switch more frequently, followed by G2 and then G1, was borne out and to a statistically significant degree. We also found that in each generation, it was Puerto Ricans who codeswitched the most, followed by MexiRicans (for G2 and G3), and Mexicans codeswitched the least, but these differences did not reach statistical significance. In addition, none of our findings suggests influence of contact between dialects; the different regional origin groups are not becoming more alike across generations.

Figure 5.10 shows our final analysis for this section: the average number of codeswitches by proficiency level. A one-way ANOVA of proficiency (levels 1 and 2 were grouped into one category due to low sample sizes) found no significant effect for proficiency, $F(3, 60) = 9.33$, $p < .001$, $\eta^2 = .32$. This may seem surprising given how different the four groups look. Closer inspection revealed that speakers at proficiency level 1 or 2 had significantly more codeswitches (M = 141.75, SD = 133.89) than speakers at level 3 (M = 69.27, SD = 57.35), $t(60) = 2.82$, $p = .033$; at level 4 (M = 41.21, SD = 28.96), $t(60) = 4.10$, $p = .001$; and at level 5 (M = 15.50, SD = 20.19), $t(60) = 5.10$, $p < .001$. No pairwise comparisons between speakers at levels 3, 4, or 5 were significant (all $p > .05$). This suggests that codeswitches are significantly higher only for speakers at the lowest proficiency levels. A possible conclusion here is that people codeswitch a lot and very likely in a crutch-like manner when they have low Spanish proficiency, but when their Spanish proficiency is strong, their codeswitching

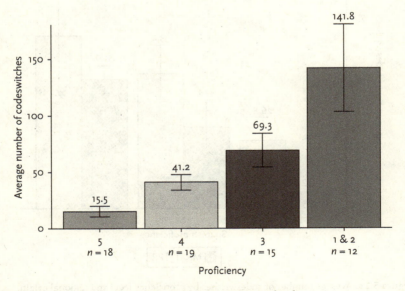

Figure 5.10. Average number of codeswitches by proficiency level.

is a stylistic choice that doesn't vary between intermediate versus advanced speakers.

We next ran a comparison on proficiency levels 3, 4, and 5 only (as before, there were no MexiRican speakers at the proficiency level of 5, so we restrict this analysis to Mexicans and Puerto Ricans only). This is shown in Figure 5.11. What we found is that Puerto Ricans at each proficiency level produced on average a greater number of codeswitches than Mexicans did. A two-way ANOVA on the total number of codeswitches with regional origin (Mexican vs. Puerto Rican) and proficiency (levels 3, 4, and 5) found a significant effect for regional origin, $F(1, 34) = 4.68$, $p = .038$, $\eta_p^2 = .12$. A follow-up t-test found that Mexican speakers (M = 23.52, SD = 24.63) showed significantly fewer codeswitches than Puerto Rican speakers (M = 46.00, SD = 37.49), $t(34) = 2.16$, $p = .038$. Our ANOVA also found a significant effect for proficiency, $F(2, 34) = 8.17$, $p = .001$, $\eta_p^2 = .32$. Follow-up t-tests showed that level 5 speakers (M = 15.50, SD = 20.19) showed significantly fewer codeswitches than level 4 speakers (M = 41.85, SD = 28.97), $t(34) = 2.61$, $p = .035$, and than level 3 speakers (M = 60.56, SD = 38.99), $t(34) = 3.84$, $p = .002$. Level 3 and level 4 speakers did not vary significantly between each other ($p > .05$). Finally, our ANOVA showed no significant interaction between regional origins ($p > .05$). In all, these results suggest that Puerto Ricans codeswitch more than Mexicans and that participants with the highest proficiency level codeswitch

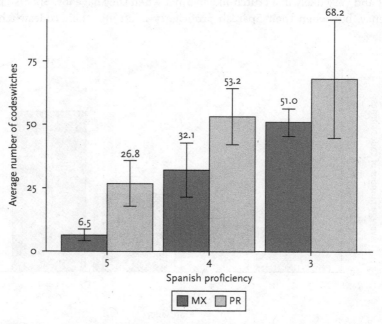

Figure 5.11. Average number of codeswitches by proficiency level and regional origin.

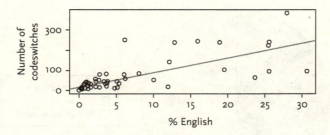

Figure 5.12. Percentage of English use and total number of codeswitches.

less than speakers at lower proficiency levels, but these effects of regional origin and of proficiency do not interact.

Before moving on to our analyses of the different types of codeswitching, we wondered whether the percentage of English used in the interview would correspond to the overall number of codeswitches produced. This relationship is shown in Figure 5.12.

We found a significant correlation between percentage of English use and total number of codeswitches, $r(62) = .74$, $p < .001$, with a large effect size as per Cohen's (1988) guidelines. As we noted earlier, the great majority of the 64 speakers in this subcorpus have a percentage English rate of lower than 10%; what we see here is that the majority of these individuals codeswitched 50 times or fewer. This correlation was surprising because, as noted earlier, a single codeswitch can consist of one word or many; the maximum length in our corpus of a two-or-more-word stretch of English was 271 words, but the average length was 7.62 words (with SD of 16.60).

5.6. TYPES OF CODESWITCHES

We turn now to our final question about the three types of codeswitches and how frequent each was in our subcorpus. Figure 5.13 displays the proportion of intrasentential one-word switches ($n = 1,459$), intrasentential two-or-more-word switches ($n = 1,948$), and intersentential switches ($n = 395$) for all 64 speakers.

Approximately half of all the codeswitches were two or more words, and another 40% were one word. Adding one-word and two-or-more-word codeswitches together, we see that 90% of all codeswitches were intrasentential, and the remaining 10% of codeswitches were intersentential.

Next, we looked at each of the three types of codeswitching according to generational group (Figure 5.14). Recall that we are reporting the average number of each kind of codeswitch with no regard to the number of English words contained in those switches.

CODESWITCHING [167]

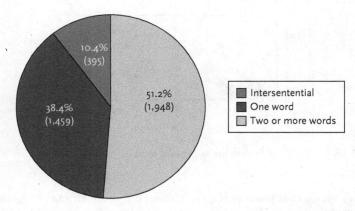

Figure 5.13. Proportions of types of codeswitching among all tokens (*n* = 3,802).

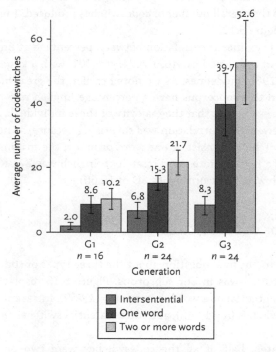

Figure 5.14. Average number of each type of codeswitch produced by generational groups.

Speakers in G3 produced both the most intrasentential and the most intersentential codeswitches. In fact, G3 speakers produced on average 52.6 switches of two or more words, which was more than double the rate of the other two groups. This prompted us to examine the data in a slightly different way, using proportions of each type of switch instead of averages (Figure 5.15).

[168] *Spanish in Chicago*

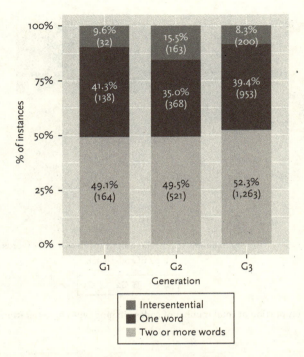

Figure 5.15. Proportion of codeswitching types produced by each generational group.

What we see in Figure 5.15 is that of all the G3 speakers' codeswitches, 52% were two or more words. This is not substantially greater than the 49% proportion evidenced by G1. Therefore, the fact that G3 speakers' average number of two-or-more-word codeswitches was so high compared with that of the other two groups (as seen in Figure 5.13) simply reflects the fact that their *proportion* of two-or-more-word codeswitches was slightly higher, and they had a higher total number of codeswitches. What we also see is that G1 speakers, when they codeswitched at all, tended to use intrasentential switches (one word and two or more words). This contradicted our hypothesis that G1 speakers would stick with intersentential codeswitches since these are relatively less complex or risky. However, as seen in Figure 5.14, G1 speakers' use of codeswitching overall was very low, perhaps constituting an avoidance of complex or risky codeswitching behaviors in general.

An intergenerational comparison according to the kind of codeswitch appears in Figure 5.16.

Of all the one-word codeswitches in the entire corpus, only 9.5% were produced by G1 speakers, 25.2% by G2 speakers, and more than half (65.3%) by G3 speakers. The two-or-more-word switches and intersentential switches followed a similar pattern. It is thus not the case that an overwhelming proportion of a particular kind of codeswitch was produced by one generational

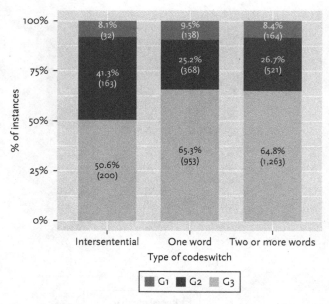

Figure 5.16. Proportion of total number of codeswitching types by generation.

Table 5.6. TYPES OF CODESWITCHES, THIS STUDY'S "BALANCED BILINGUALS" COMPARED WITH THREE EARLIER STUDIES.

Study	Intrasentential	Intersentential	Tags
Poplack (1980)	77.2%	20.3%	22.5%
Lipski (1985)	74.6%	15.7%	9.8%
Zentella (1997)	77.0%	23.0%	1.8%
This study	88.3%	11.7%	N/A

group, although G3 did produce a majority of the one-word switches and of the two-or-more-word switches.

We pause here to compare our findings to those of Poplack (1980), Lipski (1985), and Zentella (1997). For ease of reference, we reproduce Table 5.1 here as Table 5.6 and include our findings only from speakers who were likely "balanced" bilinguals like those studied in those three earlier publications, that is, our speakers who met two criteria. First, they were either G2 or G3 (these two generational groups have strong levels of English), and second, they also had levels of Spanish proficiency rated at 3, 4, or 5.

Our finding that the majority of codeswitches were intrasentential is similar to those of the earlier studies, although our 88% was higher than their approximately 75%. However, unlike Poplack (1980), we did not find that those speakers with the strongest proficiency in Spanish and English (our G2 speakers) tended to engage in intrasentential switching the most. In our corpus, the G3 speakers, those with the lowest proficiency in the Spanish language, produced considerably more instances of two-or-more-word intrasentential codeswitches. This may be because G3 speakers were placed in a situation in which they were expected to speak their less dominant language, so they frequently switched to English when their verbal skills in Spanish where insufficient to communicate their meaning. This is similar to the findings of Silva-Corvalán (1983) and Lipski (2009, 2014).

Now, in Figure 5.17, we turn to the number and types of codeswitches produced by each generational group and regional origin group to see whether, in a particular generational group, any regional origin speakers acted differently from the others.

First, a mixed-effects ANOVA on the overall number of codeswitches with generation (G1, G2, or G3) and regional origin (Mexicans vs. Puerto Ricans) found a significant effect for generation, $F(2,42) = 6.21, p = .004, \eta_p^2 = .23$, such that later generations showed a higher number of codeswitches overall. There was also a significant effect for type of codeswitch, $F(2, 84) = 11.11, p < .001, \eta_p^2 = .21$, such that intersentential codeswitches ($M = 6.25, SD = 13.00$) were

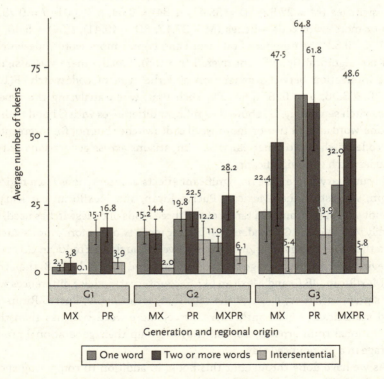

Figure 5.17. Average number of each type of codeswitch by generation and regional origin.

significantly less common among them than either one-word codeswitches (M = 23.23, SD = 35.65), $t(84) = 3.57$, $p = .002$, $d = 1.27$, or two-or-more-word codeswitches (M = 27.77, SD = 44.24), $t(84) = 4.47$, $p = .001$, $d = 0.66$. The numbers of one-word and two-or-more-word codeswitches were not significantly different overall ($p > .05$). Finally, there was a significant interaction between generation and the type of codeswitch, $F(4, 84) = 3.20$, $p = .017$, $\eta_p^2 = .13$, such that, when analyzing the type of codeswitch separately, G3 showed significantly more tokens than G2 for one-word switches, $t(93.5) = 2.40$, $p = .018$, $d = 0.70$, and for two-or-more-word codeswitches, $t(93.5) = 3.05$, $p = .003$, $d = 0.65$, but not for intersentential switches ($p > .05$). There were no significant effects or interactions from regional origin, suggesting that Mexican and Puerto Rican participants did not vary between each other significantly in terms of their codeswitching behavior.

Next, a mixed-effects ANOVA on the number of codeswitches, according to generation (G2 vs. G3) and regional origin (Mexicans vs. Puerto Ricans vs. MexiRicans) found a significant effect for generation, $F(1,42) = 5.69$, $p = .022$, $\eta_p^2 = .12$, such that later generations showed a higher number of codeswitches overall. There was also a significant effect for type of codeswitch, $F(1.76, 73.78) = 15.18$, $p < .001$, $\eta_p^2 = .27$, such that intersentential codeswitches (M = 7.56, SD = 13.22) were significantly less common than either one-word codeswitches (M = 27.52, SD = 36.41), $t(84) = 3.64$, $p = .001$, $d = 0.73$, or two-or-more-word codeswitches (M = 37.17, SD = 49.41), $t(84) = 5.40$, $p < .001$, $d = 0.82$. The number of one-word and two-or-more-word codeswitches was not significantly different overall ($p > .05$). Finally, there was a significant interaction between generation and the type of codeswitch, $F(1.76, 73.78) = 3.96$, $p = .028$, $\eta_p^2 = .09$, such that, when analyzing the type of codeswitch separately, G3 showed significant differences with G1 and with G2 for one-word and for two-or-more-word codeswitches but not for intersentential codeswitches. No other pairwise comparisons across generations or type of codeswitch were significant.

In summary, there were no significant effects or interactions from regional origin, suggesting that Mexican, Puerto Rican, and MexiRican participants did not vary significantly in terms of the three kinds of codeswitches used, but readily visible is the G3 tendency to use far more two-or-more-word switches than the other two generational groups. Even though Puerto Rican G3 speakers evidenced greater average numbers of this kind of switch (61.8) than their G3 MexiRican (48.6) and Mexican (47.5) counterparts, these differences were not significant. Thus, it is not the case that, for example, Puerto Rican G3s used statistically significantly more two-or-more-word switches than their generational counterparts, nor did they drive up their generational group's average in a pronounced way.

As we have done throughout this book, in addition to comparing speakers from different generational groups, we also compared them according to

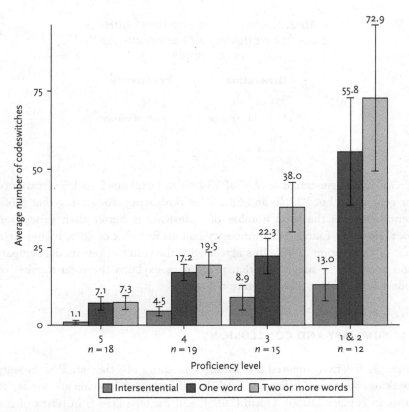

Figure 5.18. Average number of each type of codeswitching by proficiency level.

their Spanish proficiency. Figure 5.18 shows the average number of tokens of the three different types of codeswitching according to proficiency level. We see that as proficiency in Spanish declines, speakers use a greater number of two-or-more-word codeswitches. This is a corollary to Figures 5.14 and 5.15, which showed codeswitching types by generation. We continue to point out that Spanish proficiency does not exactly map onto generation, but given that the differences in proficiency levels across generational categories were shown to be statistically significant, it is not surprising that the codeswitching behaviors of generational groups and of proficiency level groups are more or less the same.

5.7. PROFICIENCY VERSUS GENERATION

We now ask whether proficiency or generation is more strongly correlated with the codeswitching patterns exhibited in this subcorpus using the same two tests described in Chapter 3. Results are found in Table 5.7.

Table 5.7. CORRELATION OF TOTAL NUMBER OF CODESWITCHES WITH GENERATION VERSUS PROFICIENCY.

	Generation	Proficiency
AIC	734.45 18.1% of variance	723.46 28.8% of variance
R^2	.098	.205

Our model generated an AIC of 734.45 and explained 18.1% of variance for generation but 723.46 and 28.8% for proficiency, suggesting that proficiency explains the total number of codeswitches better than generation does. Next, we found that proficiency had an R^2 index of .205, higher than that of Generation (.098). This agrees with the result of our model comparison approach in suggesting that proficiency explains the total number of codeswitches better than generation does.

5.8. SUMMARY AND CONCLUSIONS

First, we briefly compared our findings to those of other studies. Broadly speaking, our more "balanced" English and Spanish bilinguals are similar to those in Poplack (1980), Lipski (1985), and Zentella (1997) in terms of the proportions of types of codeswitches. However, unlike Poplack (1980), we did not find that those speakers with the strongest proficiency in Spanish and English (our G2 speakers) tended to engage in intrasentential switching the most. In our corpus, the G3 speakers, those with the lowest average proficiency in Spanish, produced considerably more instances of two-or-more-word intrasentential codeswitches. This may be because G3 speakers were placed in a situation in which they were expected to speak their less dominant language, so they frequently switched to English when their verbal skills in Spanish where insufficient to communicate their meaning. This is similar to the findings of crutch-like codeswitching by Silva-Corvalán (1983) and Lipski (2009, 2014). Similarly, we predicted that with each generation, the amount of English used would increase, since speakers have more interactions in English and tend to be more comfortable speaking in English. This hypothesis was confirmed. A similar hypothesis was confirmed for proficiency: as Spanish proficiency increases, less English is produced.

MexiRicans produced the most English, and Puerto Rican G1 and G2 participants produced more English than Mexicans, but surprisingly, G3 Puerto Ricans' rate of English use was very close to (less than 1% greater than) that of G3 Mexicans. However, when we analyzed percentage of English use by proficiency for levels 3, 4, and 5 for Mexicans and Puerto Ricans, we found that Puerto Ricans consistently had higher rates of English use. It seems fair to conclude that the Spanish of Puerto Ricans is more likely to include English-language words and phrases. In general, however, in spite of stereotypes of a U.S. Spanish overrun by English, participants in this subcorpus overwhelmingly spoke in Spanish across their interviews. As expected, G3 used the most English, but even then, 89% of their interviews were in Spanish. Use of English for G1 was negligible.

Findings about overall number of codeswitches mirrored those just summarized for percentage of English use. As expected, G3 participants switched more frequently, followed by G2 and then G1. Similarly, participants with lower Spanish-language proficiency codeswitched more frequently than did those with stronger Spanish proficiency. G1 Puerto Ricans codeswitched more than G1 Mexicans, G2 and G3 Puerto Ricans codeswitched more than MexiRicans, and Mexicans codeswitched the least, even though the differences among the three groups did not reach statistical significance. We shared in Chapter 1 the documented ideologies that Mexicans retain Spanish longer and have higher proficiency than other Latinos; our codeswitching data may be a reflection of this, although both fluent and nonfluent speakers codeswitch, and codeswitching does not necessarily lead to less speaking in Spanish. Finally, our findings do not present any evidence of contact between dialects; the different regional origin groups are not becoming more alike across generations.

Rates of intrasentential versus intersentential codeswitching presented more complex results. Research suggests that strong bilinguals are generally more likely to engage in intrasentential switching, so we expected G2 and G3 speakers with higher Spanish proficiency to engage in intrasentential codeswitching more frequently than their generational cohorts (assumed to have the same level of English proficiency) with lower Spanish proficiency. As we expected, rates of intersentential switching—the simpler type of switching—increased linearly with each succeeding generation as proficiency decreased. However, rates of intrasentential switching were the opposite of what we expected for both one-word and two-or-more-word codeswitches. In fact, G3 produced almost twice as many intrasentential two-or-more-word codeswitches as G2, who produced almost twice as many codeswitches as G1 speakers. Examining the data by proportion of codeswitching types rather than average number of codeswitches yielded a less dramatic difference among the three groups' intrasentential switches. Nonetheless, G3 participants still had a larger proportion of two-or-more-word switches, which is counter to what we expected. In sum, our G3 speakers used a higher percentage of English and a higher percentage of all codeswitching types. This may be because their relatively lower proficiency in Spanish required them to rely on English more often to express themselves.

The fact that speakers of all proficiency levels engaged in intrasentential codeswitching, which is considered by many scholars to be the type more associated with speakers who are fairly proficient in both languages and not with those on the lower end of the proficiency spectrum, needs to be explored further. It is possible that what looks like the same behavior across generations actually involves different processes conditioned by proficiency; it might be the case that G3 speakers were resorting to English because their relatively lower proficiency in Spanish required them to rely on English more often to express themselves. That is, intrasentential codeswitching for G3 individuals may be motivated by L1 erosion. Other studies in language-attrition situations have also demonstrated intrasentential switching. For example, a study of Arabic-French bilinguals in Morocco (Bentahila & Davies, 1995) found that older balanced bilinguals favored one-word switching while the second-generation speakers, who were dominant in Arabic, tended to engage in intrasentential codeswitching more frequently. A study by Bolonyai (1998) showed a significant increase in intrasentential codeswitching as U.S.-raised Hungarian children moved toward English. Lindsey (2006) also found that low-level Spanish heritage language learners produced an unexpected number of intrasentential switches in synchronous chat conversations with other students.

A future study could examine whether the amount of codeswitching changes as the interview progresses and/or whether speakers' codeswitching patterns are sensible to those of the interviewer.

APPENDIX A
NEOLOGISMS IN THE CHISPA CORPUS

Example in CHISPA	**Meaning in English**	**General Spanish**
More than one token		
la escuela ir a/estar en la escuela pagar (para) la escuela	school (college) go to/be in school pay for school	estudiar estudiar pagar los estudios
factoría	factory	fábrica
ganga/ganguero	gang/gang member	pandilla/pandillero
grado	grade	año escolar
hacer dinero	to make money	ganar dinero
principal (de una escuela)	principal (of a school)	director/a de una escuela
escribir papeles	write papers	escribir trabajos/ensayos (académicos)

Example in CHISPA	Meaning in English	General Spanish
actualmente "Actualmente, una es menor que yo." (#21, G2 Puerto Rican female)	actually (in fact) "Actually, one is younger than me"	de hecho
atender "El high school que yo atendí fue . . ." (#93, G3 Mexican female)	attend "The high school I attended was . . ."	asistir
introducir "Las personas en la clase se introducían"	introduce "The people in the class introduced themselves"	presentarse
bildin "Viví en un bildin" (#31, G3 Puerto Rican female)	building "I lived in a building"	edificio
trabajar "El aire acondicionado no trabaja" (#77, G2 Puerto Rican female)	to work "The air conditioning doesn't work"	funcionar
One token		
directó "Me lo directó a mí" (#2, G3 Mexican female)	directed "He directed it at me"	dirigió
reflecta "Reflecta el impacto" (#1, G2 Mexican female)	reflects "It reflects the impact"	refleja
quitear "El janitor se quitó" (#66, G1 Puerto Rican male)	to quit "The janitor quit"	dejar
yarda "Pero la yarda es puertorriqueña" (#33, G1 Puerto Rican female)	yard "But the yard is Puerto Rican"	jardín
trostiar "Primero trostiar una persona" (#18, G2 Puerto Rican female)	to trust "First trust a person"	confiar en

Example in CHISPA	Meaning in English	General Spanish
envolverse "Empecé a envolverme" (#17, G1 Puerto Rican female)	to get involved "I started to get involved"	involucrarme
aprochar "No saben cómo aprochar al maestro" (#19, G2 Puerto Rican female)	to approach "They don't know how to approach the teacher"	llegarle
frisar "Lo que no dejó que yo me frisara" (#39, G2 Puerto Rican female)	to freeze "What kept me from freezing"	congelarse
plesentes "No las quiero recordar, no son momentos plesentes" (#39, G2 Puerto Rican female)	pleasant "I don't want to remember them, they're not pleasant moments"	placenteros
gasten "Que pues sí que gasten tiempo con ellos" (#85, G1 Puerto Rican male)	spend (time) "Well yeah that they spend time with them"	pasar
comfortable "Se siente más comfortable en español" (#41, G3 Mexican female)	comfortable "She feels more comfortable in Spanish"	cómodo/a

CHAPTER 6
Subjunctive

6.1. INTRODUCTION

Research on L1 acquisition has provided evidence that subjunctive morphology emerges around 2 years of age in direct and indirect commands and that it is used robustly to refer to present and past events by three and a half years old (Aguado, 1988; Cortés & Vila, 1991; Hernández-Pina, 1984; López-Ornat et al., 1994). However, acquisition of all parameters of the subjunctive system in both variable and obligatory contexts is a process that can span an additional seven years, that is, up to 12 years of age (Blake, 1980, 1983; Montrul, 2009).

The Spanish subjunctive has been examined in bilingual communities across the U.S., including the Southwest (Guitart, 1982; Martínez-Mira, 2009), Miami (Lynch, 2008), New York City (most recently, Viner, 2016, 2017, 2018, 2019), and California (Silva-Corvalán, 1994; Gutiérrez, 2003; Acevedo, 2000). The majority of these studies examine three generations of speakers but from homogeneous national origin groups (e.g., all Cubans or all Mexicans). More recently, Viner (2016, 2018, 2019) compared six different national origin groups, but they belonged to only one or two generational groups. Here we combine these two approaches: we examine subjunctive use across three generations of Spanish-English bilinguals with Mexican and Puerto Rican origin residing in Chicago.[1] As we have done in previous chapters with lexicon, discourse markers, and codeswitching, our goal is to determine whether there are differences according to regional origin, generation, and level of Spanish proficiency.

---

1. We did not include MexiRicans in this analysis; it is a viable area for future research. This chapter is based on Villegas et al. (forthcoming).

6.2. THE SUBJUNCTIVE IN U.S. SPANISH

Studies on U.S. Spanish find that the subjunctive is used less frequently than in other Spanish-speaking locations, both in contexts that categorically require it as well as in variable contexts (Silva-Corvalán, 1994). We briefly describe these two contexts using examples from the CHISPA corpus. Some contexts strongly favor the subjunctive, such as embedded clauses that contain verbs of obligation (1) or desire (2), in temporal clauses where the embedded event has not occurred yet (3), or in purpose clauses (4):

(1) Siempre nos hacen que *hagamos* el extra más. (#116, G1 Mexican female)

They always make us do [SUBJ] more.

(2) Porque él dijo que el español no quería que se nos *olvidara*. (#10, G2 Mexican male)

Because he said he didn't want us to forget [SUBJ] Spanish.

(3) Siempre nos decía desde chiquitas que "cuando *agarren* trabajo te van a dar el trabajo porque hablas dos idiomas." (#26, G3 Mexican female)

Since we were little he always told us that "when you get [SUBJ] a job they're going to give you the job because you speak two languages."

(4) Ellos vivían el verano entero en Puerto Rico para que *supieran* lo que es Puerto Rico, lo que es vivir en Puerto Rico. (#21, G2 Puerto Rican female)

They lived in Puerto Rico for the whole summer so that they would know [SUBJ] what Puerto Rico is, what it is to live in Puerto Rico.

In other contexts, there is a fair amount of variation between subjunctive and indicative, such as in concessive clauses (5), uncertainty clauses (6), or possibility clauses (7).

(5) Él también lo disfruta aunque él *sabe* [*sepa*, SUBJ] que no sé nada de deportes. (#20, G1 Mexican female)

He also enjoys it even though he knows [IND/SUBJ] that I don't know anything about sports.

(6) No pienso que *va* [*vaya*, SUBJ] a hacer nada. (#82, G2 Puerto Rican female)

I don't think he's going to do anything.

(7) Todos tienen su diferente acento, sus formas de vivir, tal vez *sean* [*son*, IND] un poco diferentes. (#5, G2 Mexican female)

Everyone has their different accent, their ways of living, maybe they are [SUBJ/IND] a little different.

However, returning to examples (1)–(4), in at least one monolingual Spanish-speaking location, a decrease in subjunctive use has been noted. Gallego (2016) examined subjunctive production among 224 monolingual high school educated women and men in Rosario, Argentina. Participants completed a task producing sentences in response to prompts including *¿Qué le recomendás?* (What do you recommend?) and *¿Qué es lo más/menos importante?* (What is the most/least important?) The author found a clear age and gender effect: females 50 and older produced the subjunctive on average five or more times in their responses, but the 18-to-30-year-old females and males produced it fewer than one time on average, opting to use other constructions such as the infinitive (*Te recomiendo hacer ejercicio* [I recommend that you to do exercise]). Additionally, participants completed a second task that required selecting one of two versions of a sentence, one containing the indicative and one with the subjunctive (*Mi hermana quiere que le traigamos/traemos regalos* [My sister wants us to bring gifts]). While the contexts of volition and recommendation elicited the subjunctive form 100% of the time (except among 18-to-30-year-old males, who averaged a still very high 90%), the context of uncertainty (*No creo que el problema de la seguridad se solucione/soluciona pronto* [I don't believe that the security problem is going to be solved soon]) led to the highest degree of indicative selection, although five out of the six groups still selected the subjunctive on average more than four times out of five in this context. The author states that these findings suggest "an incipient tendency . . . to accept [the indicative] in some contexts in which the subjunctive would be considered normative." Finally, Gallego (2016) noted that the semantic categories showing less subjunctive production and selection were the same as those evidenced by the 20 speakers who originated from 10 different countries in Gudmestad's (2010) study.[2] Similarly, a comparative study by Schwenter and Hoff (2020) looked at subjunctive usage in nominal clause complements across Argentine, Mexican, and Peninsular Spanish. They argued that despite prescriptive grammar's insistence that some verbs always call for the subjunctive and others the indicative, variability was the norm for the 22 verbs they compared using data from an online mega-corpus. They found that the subjunctive was most productive in Argentina (which is curious given the findings of Gallego, 2016, just cited), followed by Mexico and then Peninsular Spain. In other words, inherent variability was present within

---

2. Argentina, Chile, Colombia, Costa Rica, the Dominican Republic, Guatemala, Mexico, Peru, Spain, and Puerto Rico.

and across dialects. The authors affirmed the need for studies of subjunctive usage within and among different varieties.

It is not surprising to see the subjunctive lose ground given tendencies in other Romance languages. In their study of Portuguese, Spanish, Italian, and Canadian French, Poplack et al. (2018) found that despite a great deal of variability within and across all four languages, there is a process of desemanticization that "has gone to completion in Italian, Portuguese and French," such that the subjunctive is "indisputably the least productive in French" (248), while Spanish uses it the most. Finally, we note that subjunctive use has declined in Spanish varieties in contact with other languages. For example, Crespo del Río (2022) notes that several studies of Peruvian Spanish have documented an increase of indicative usage in contexts where grammar guides call for use of the subjunctive and that this tendency is especially prominent in those Spanish varieties that are in contact with Quechua and other indigenous languages that do not have subjunctive forms.

In light of the variation of subjunctive in monolingual and bilingual Spanish-speaking communities, U.S. Spanish provides a fertile context for research because the U.S. is an English-dominant society, where there is little if any normative pressure on Spanish. In addition, in some locations such as Chicago, there is not only direct contact between Spanish and English but also between different varieties of Spanish. In fact, the majority of studies on the subjunctive in U.S. Spanish have examined its use cross-generationally within one sole dialect group. For example, Torres (1989) compared subjunctive use in obligatory contexts[3] between four G1 island-raised Puerto Ricans and six G2 speakers raised in East Harlem, New York. She found that while there was some variation within each group for a number of categories, overall the G2 speakers used the subjunctive less and in fewer semantic contexts compared with their G1 counterparts. Contexts such as conditional clauses, doubt clauses, and clauses with indefinite antecedents showed the most variation for G2 speakers.

Silva-Corvalán (1994), considered a canonical cross-generational study of U.S. Spanish subjunctive use, studied 50 Mexican-origin Spanish speakers in Los Angeles, identifying five tense systems that systematically decreased in complexity. Speakers with system I, the most complete tense system, had productive use of all four subjunctive forms (present, present perfect, past, plusquamperfect). Speakers with systems II and III used all forms except for the present perfect subjunctive. Speakers with system IV showed productive use of only the present subjunctive, and speakers with system V lacked all subjunctive forms. The author found a strong connection between system and generational group. Systems I and II were exhibited by G1 speakers and some

---

3. Henceforth, we use this term as shorthand to refer to what grammars of Spanish typically specify.

highly proficient G2 speakers; no G2 speakers evidenced system I. Systems II–V were evidenced by G2 and G3 speakers and were interpreted as a systematic simplification of Spanish, with the use of the present perfect subjunctive (*que hayas visto*, that you have [SUBJ] seen) proving to be a clear indicator separating G1 speakers from G2 and G3 speakers. Some low-proficiency Spanish speakers did not produce subjunctive forms at all. The results of this study show that each G group used less subjunctive than the one before it (G1 > G2 > G3); similar results were found by Lynch (1999) among three generations of Miami Cubans. Silva-Corvalán claimed that although they did not produce the subjunctive, "I have enough evidence to assume that most of the bilingual speakers at the lower levels of the Spanish proficiency continuum *understand* the meaning of these tense forms" (p. 26; emphasis added).

Montrul (2007) sought to test Silva-Corvalán's (1994) assumption. She gave two tasks to 20 bilingual U.S.-raised college students. All were G2 speakers with varying degrees of proficiency raised in the Chicago area. They scored less accurately on both tasks compared with native speaker participants.[4] For example, bilinguals more frequently rated as "logical" sentences such as *Cada año, Ana se alegra cuando le aumenten el sueldo* (Every year, Ana is happy when they increase her salary), although it is actually illogical; the subjunctive *aumenten* should have triggered a future meaning.[5] Although ours is a study of production and not comprehension, it is worth underscoring that if subjunctive production is declining, Montrul's (2007) findings suggest that the meanings encoded by this morphology are lost as well. More closely related to our current study is Montrul's (2007) additional finding that speakers' overall proficiency as measured by a modified Diplomas de Español como Lengua Extranjera (DELE) exam (which did not require production or interpretation of the subjunctive) was correlated to their accuracy on two subjunctive interpretation tasks. That is, overall proficiency in Spanish was found to be likely positively correlated with normative subjunctive interpretation and use.

Montrul (2009) again examined the production and interpretation of the subjunctive/indicative contrast among G2 undergraduate students using three different tasks. On the first task, only the advanced-Spanish-proficiency bilinguals produced the subjunctive as frequently (56% of the time) as the native speakers (58%). The intermediate- (31%) and low-proficiency speakers

---

4. Native speakers were defined as individuals raised to adulthood in a Spanish-speaking country.

5. It may be argued that the triggers used in this study, including *cuando* (when), *de manera que* (so that), and restrictive relative clauses (*Necesito un libro de cuentos para niños que tenga/tiene ilustraciones de Miró, pero no sé si hay uno* [I need a children's storybook that has illustrations by Miró, but I don't know if there is one]) are less frequent overall; these same speakers may have responded differently to prompts involving semantic domains shown to be the most robust with the subjunctive, such as volition and recommendation (as shown by Gudmestad, 2010; Gallego, 2016).

(19%) produced subjunctive significantly less frequently and also produced the indicative in contexts in which the subjunctive is considered obligatory (e.g., *Es importante que tú *pones [pongas, SUBJ] escuela antes de salir de fiestas con tus amigos* [It's important that you put school before going out partying with your friends]).[6] The second task, requiring participants to fill in blanks with verbs in either indicative or subjunctive to complete sentences, showed the same pattern: native speakers and advanced-proficiency U.S.-raised bilinguals produced the subjunctive according to normative grammar 98% to 99% of the time, while the intermediate- and low-Spanish-proficiency speakers did so less frequently (61% and 39%, respectively). The third task was based on the one used in Montrul (2007), and the findings were similar: intermediate-proficiency bilinguals showed an ability to discriminate between indicative and subjunctive with *cuando* clauses, but both the intermediate- and low-proficiency groups tended to accept subjunctive sentences as logical regardless of clause type, although it is again worth asking whether clauses using *de manera que* constitute an accurate means by which to measure these speakers' interpretation of subjunctive morphology, since it may not be a phrase that they heard frequently.

In addition to looking at subjunctive production cross-generationally, Viner (2016, 2018, 2019) compared six different varieties grouped into two regions: Caribbeans (Puerto Rican, Dominican, and Cuban) and Mainlanders (Mexican, Ecuadorian, and Colombian). The two generational groups were those raised in Latin America and having immigrated to New York after the age of 16 (referred to as G1s in the nomenclature of our study) and those raised in New York and having been born in the city or having arrived before the age of 3 (also called G2s). All three of these studies used semi-controlled sociolinguistic interviews from the Otheguy-Zentella corpus (Otheguy & Zentella 2012). We will now describe this body of work with a fair amount of detail due to its high relevance to our study; results of all three studies are also displayed in Table 6.1.

Viner (2016) examined nine obligatory contexts in the speech of 26 G1 speakers (a group composed of 13 Mainlanders -449 tokens- and 13 Caribbeans -556 tokens-) and of 26 G2 speakers (a group also composed of 13 Mainlanders -434 tokens- and 13 Caribbeans -298 tokens-). The nine obligatory contexts included purpose/contingency such as *para que canten* (so they sing), temporal adverbial clauses with future reference such as *cuando canten*

---

6. However, some of the uses that the author considered non-normative "errors" may not have been so. For example, *trabajaba* was considered a mood error in *Me encantaría si me pagaran mucho y trabajaba lo menos posible* (I would love if they paid me a lot and I worked as little as possible). Yet the speaker could have meant "and I would work as little as possible," a context in which several Latin American varieties of Spanish have been shown to use the imperfect indicative. That is, *Me encantaría* may not have governed *trabajaba* in this utterance.

Table 6.1. SUMMARY OF FINDINGS: SUBJUNCTIVE USE ACROSS TWO GENERATIONS AND SIX DIALECT GROUPS (VINER 2016, 2018, 2019).

Year	Context	% subjunctive use				
2016	9 obligatory contexts	G1: 98%			G2: 86%*	
		Mainland	Caribbean	Mainland	Caribbean
		99%	99%	94%	88%
2018	10 optional contexts	G1: 66%			G2: 47%*	
		Mainland	Caribbean	Mainland	Caribbean
		65%	63%	45%	54%
2019	Comment clauses	G1: 86%			G2: 65%*	
		Regional percentages not reported but not significantly different			

* = p < .001

(when they sing), and causative clauses such as *hace que canten* (makes them sing). The author found a statistically significant drop in the use of the subjunctive from G1 (90%) to G2 (86%), F (1, 50) = 13.7, p = .001, but no significant difference according to geographical region. Another finding was that the G1 group produced 100% subjunctive use in a total of five contexts, while G2 speakers did so for just three contexts, and these contexts were not in the same rank order.

Using a subcorpus of the same stratification of generation and region just described for the 2016 study, Viner (2018) examined 10 optional contexts including concessive clauses such as *Aunque yo esté/estoy con mi papá* (Even if I'm with my dad) and comment clauses such as *No me importa lo que piensen/piensan otras personas* (I don't care what other people think). Similarly to his 2016 study, the author found a statistically significant drop in the use of the subjunctive from G1 (66%) to G2 (47%), F (1, 50) = 13.5, p = .001, but again no significant difference according to regional origin. Another difference that reached significance between the two generational groups was the rank order of syntactic and semantic contexts. For example, G1 speakers used the subjunctive 88% of the time in comment clauses, but G2 did so only 65% of the time.

Finally, Viner (2019) analyzed the transcripts of 18 G1 speakers and 18 G2 speakers in his study of comment clauses. Once more, he found a statistically significant drop in the use of the subjunctive from G1 (86%) to G2 (65%), X^2 (1, N = 194) = 12.3, p < .001, but no significant difference according to regional origin, gender, tense, or verb negation. Although both generational groups used significantly more subjunctive following impersonal matrix clauses compared to personalized ones, there was a rearrangement of the constraint hierarchy of mood. The author argued that this shift in the constraint hierarchy may be the first finding of its kind in U.S. Spanish.

In sum, two consistent findings emerged from the three Viner studies. First, as a group, G2 speakers used significantly less subjunctive than G1 speakers. This was also found by Silva-Corvalán (1994) and Torres (1989). Second, there were no statistically significant differences between Mainlanders and Caribbeans, although in the 2016 study, it was descriptively noticeable that Caribbean speakers declined in obligatory subjunctive use quite a bit more than their Mainlander counterparts (but they actually outscored them in optional contexts). Viner (2017) is yet another study that found no statistically significant differences between Mainlanders and Caribbeans, specifically in rates of subjunctive use in 18 optional and obligatory contexts. We do not report more extensively on this study because it was limited to 26 G2 speakers, making no comparisons with G1 speakers. We further note that to the best of our knowledge, there is no evidence that speakers in Mexico and Puerto Rico use the subjunctive similarly (or differently) in obligatory or variable contexts; Gudmestad (2010, p. 36) notes that geographical variation of mood distinction has not been extensively documented.

The present study seeks to add to knowledge of U.S. subjunctive use by comparing one Mainland group (Mexicans) and one Caribbean group (Puerto Ricans), as in Viner (2016, 2017, 2018, 2019), but with the addition of a third generational group, as in Silva-Corvalán (1994). We consider this a potentially fruitful avenue of study given that G3 speakers have already been found to use less subjunctive (Silva-Corvalán, 1994) than G2s. In addition, while the differences in regional origin found by Viner (2016, 2017, 2018, 2019) did not reach statistical significance, they were still large enough to merit notice and suggest that further study is warranted. It may be that focusing on a larger *n* size of one sole group of Mainlanders (in our case, Mexicans) and one group of Caribbeans (Puerto Ricans) will lead to different results from those found by Viner (2016, 2017, 2018, 2019). It may also be that a significant difference between these two groups is found between our G2s but that this difference disappears or levels out, that is, is not found between G3s (a group not studied by Viner).

These questions lead to the following research questions for the current study:

1. Will there be differences in subjunctive use in obligatory and variable contexts according to the following?
   a. Regional origin
   b. Generational group
   c. Regional origin and generational group
   d. Spanish proficiency level
2. Will Spanish proficiency or generational group be more strongly connected to subjunctive use?

Table 6.2. NUMBER OF PARTICIPANTS BY GENERATION AND REGIONAL GROUP.

Regional group	G1	G2	G3	Total
Mexican	8	8	8	24
Puerto Rican	8	8	8	24
Total	16	16	16	48

6.3. METHODOLOGY

Participants

We analyzed a subset of 48 transcripts from the CHISPA corpus. Table 6.2 shows the general characteristics of the subsample, which was chosen at random to fill the cells according to regional origin and generation.

Following Viner (2016, 2017, 2018, 2019), we extracted all subjunctive tokens along with their contexts. We then re-examined each transcript to extract all indicative tokens that appeared in the same contexts. This resulted in a total of 1,420 tokens. Next, all tokens were labeled for context and lexical governor where applicable. Once each token was labeled, we calculated the frequency of subjunctive use for G1 participants in each context to determine obligatory and variable subjunctive contexts. A context was categorized as obligatory (O) if G1 participants produced the subjunctive 90% or more of the time in that context. Any context in which subjunctive usage was below 90% was categorized as variable (V). The final coding step was to label G2 and G3 tokens as belonging to O or V. No evaluative judgment of accuracy or grammaticality was assigned. This coding procedure gave rise to the Os in Table 6.3 and the Vs in Table 6.4, which follow Viner's naming conventions for the contexts.

Our coding of contexts as either O or V ended up corresponding to those of the New York speakers in Viner (2016, 2018, 2019) in all but two cases.[7] Comment clauses (*es bueno que* [it's good that], etc.) made up an O for our G1 speakers but were a V in Viner's data. This is likely due to the fact that Viner's data contained affirmative *gustar* clauses (e.g., *me gusta que* . . . [I like that . . .]) under comment clause, but none of our G1 speakers produced a subjunctive verb following an affirmative *gustar* clause, so *gustar* clauses were not included in our data set. The second difference was that hypothetical

---

7. We also coded hypothetical *como si* clauses ($n = 4$); however, this context was not included, following Tagliamonte's (2012) recommendations to include only contexts with 10 or more tokens.

Table 6.3. OBLIGATORY SUBJUNCTIVE CONTEXTS (O)*.

Context	# of tokens	Example from CHISPA corpus
Causative clause	12	"*Esa es la mayor satisfacción que yo tengo. No le hace que te hayas ido . . .*" (#52, MX G1 female) That is the greatest satisfaction that I have. It wasn't that you [her son] had to leave.
Comment clause	162	"*Es importante que la gente en general sepa español.*" (#96, PR G1 female) It is important that people in general know Spanish.
Indirect command	36	"*Pues decir que pusieran más policías que cuidaran y que hubieran juntas . . .*" (#116, MX G1 female) I would say that they put more police to watch [the neighborhood] and that [the neighbors] were together.
Protasis clause with hypothetical conditional	84	"*Pues más fácil a aprender a esa edad que, que si estuvieran más avanzados en la edad.*" (#85 PR G1 male) It is easier to learn [Spanish] at this age than if they were older.
Purpose/contingency adverbial clause	167	"*Más que todo pagar la casa para que mi esposo no tuviera que trabajar tanto*" (#20, G1 MX female) Above all, I would buy the house so my husband would not have to work so much.
Temporal adverbial clause with futurity	70	"*Cuando muera aquí lo enterramos.*" (#33, PR G1 female) When he dies we will bury him here.
Volitional/influential noun clause	153	"*No lo quieren hablar porque no quieren que los corrijan ellos.*" (#52, MX G1 female) They do not want to talk [in Spanish] because they do not want to be corrected.

Note. * Subjunctive use in obligatory contexts appeared 90%+ among our G1 speakers

como si (as if) clauses ended up being V in our data but were O in Viner's data. This difference is likely due to the fewer number of tokens produced by G1 participants in this context in the current study (G1 *n* = 5, out of which 4 were subjunctive) compared with Viner (2016) (G1 *n* = 29, of which 28 were subjunctive) and not to a systematic difference between speaker groups. While the token count for the G1 group is low according to the threshold used in Tagliamonte (2012), the total number of tokens produced by G1, G2,

Table 6.4. VARIABLE SUBJUNCTIVE CONTEXTS (V)*.

Context	# of tokens	Example from CHISPA corpus
Adjective clause with nonexistent/indefinite antecedent	180	"*Puede ser una persona que conozcas mañana no sé y resulte ser mejor persona que una que has conocido.*" (#56, MX G1 male) It could be a person that you meet tomorrow, I don't know, that turns out to be a better person than someone you already know.
Apodosis clause with hypothetical conditional	31	"*Si me vuelven por atrás . . . yo me vendría para acá.*" (#55, PR G1 male) If I were to do it again…I would come here.
Hypothetical *Como si* clause	36	"*ahora si yo voy a mi pueblo es como si estoy en Chicago*" (#92, PR G1 female) Now if I go to my town [in Puerto Rico] it's as if I am in Chicago.
Locative clause	22	"*[ella] fue supervisora en el hospital donde trabajó durante muchos años.*" (#24, MX G1 female) [She] was a supervisor at the hospital where she worked for many years.
Modal clause	132	"*No lo rechazo, es que no es lo que yo digo.*" (#96, PR G1 female) I don't reject it, it is just not what I say.
Negated noun clause	82	"*No te podría [decir] que hay algo en específico que no me gusta.*" (#17, PR G1 female) I could not tell say that there is something specific that I don't like.
Possibility clause	68	"*Tengo bastantes amistades, pero sí, hay un grupo de amigos con los cuales tal vez me frecuento un poquito más seguido.*" (#30, MX G1 male) I have plenty of friends, but there is one group of friends that I might spend a little more time with.
Protasis clause with concessive	35	"*Porque la ventaja de ellos es que lo hablan, aunque a veces saben que no lo hablan bien.*" (#52, MX G1 female) The good thing about them is that they speak [Spanish] even when they know that they don't always speak well.

(*continued*)

Table 6.4. CONTINUED

Context	# of tokens	Example from CHISPA corpus
Subordinate clause after *depende*	16	*"Dependiendo de la persona que tú conoces"* (#56, MX G1 male) It depends on the person that you know.
Uncertainty clause	97	*"No creo que se le olvidó."* (#116, MX G1 female) I do not believe that he forgot it.

Note. * Subjunctive use in variable contexts appeared <90% among our G1 speakers

and G3 in the subcorpus (*n* = 36) does exceed that, so we decided to include this context in the analysis.

At this point it is worth discussing the idea of obligatory or variable use of the subjunctive since the definition of these categories varies across studies. In some studies of mood selection these categories are based on prescriptive grammar, but in other cases including Viner (2016, 2018, 2019) and our present study, the categories derive from language use data. In her dissertation on mood choice in New York Spanish, Birnbaum (2019) does not divide linguistic contexts into optional and obligatory categories. She argues that mood choice is related to linguistic context availability (in other words, whether or not subjunctive-inducing contexts are available):

> "The idea at the heart of this a typical perspective is that all of the contexts in these two categories are variable, meaning that the speaker is always faced with a choice—the choice to use the Subjunctive or the Indicative mood, depending on the type of message that s/he wishes to express. The result is that speakers are consistent with respect to both their mood and linguistic context preferences." (p. 9)

Thus, Birnbaum analyzes the distribution of subjunctive and indicative forms as well as the distribution of nine linguistic contexts in the speech of all participants. She argues that subjunctive and indicative variants can be found in similar expressions, in any or all of the nine linguistic contexts she studies. While not all linguistic contexts occur to the same degree in everyone's speech, subjunctive rates and linguistic context availability are highly correlated. In particular, she found that women, younger speakers, and New Yorkers (long-term residents or New York raised) have lower subjunctive rates than men, newcomers to New York and older participants. Furthermore, she found that "some of the same groups are subjunctive-inclined and linguistic context-inclined (that is, a same linguistic context tends to occur more in their speech), while others behave differently with respect to the two" (187).

Here, we take G1 participants' mood selection data as a baseline for comparison. Obviously, ranges such as "over 90%" (and not 100%), indicate that language use is always variable and absolutes can only be found in prescriptive grammars. The fact that not all studies agree on the classification of obligatory and optional contexts is another indicator that variability is always at play in mood selection. Studies such as Poplack et al. (2018) remind us of the inherent variability of the subjunctive across Romance languages as well as the ongoing grammaticalization of the subjunctive, leading to a declining production of the subjunctive with different rates of productivity across Italian, Portuguese, French, and Spanish. We also see a declining use of the subjunctive in a number of studies of monolingual Spanish and Spanish in contact with other varieties. What we seek to capture and compare here are usage patterns for particular groups (i.e., generation, regional group, proficiency level) in a particular moment in time and to do so in a way that allows us to compare our data to previous studies which coded the data similarly.

6.4. REGIONAL ORIGIN

Subjunctive use by regional origin (Figure 6.1) shows that the Mexican individuals not only produced more qualifying tokens, but they also used the subjunctive for a greater proportion of them (73.9%) compared with the Puerto Rican speakers (61.0%).

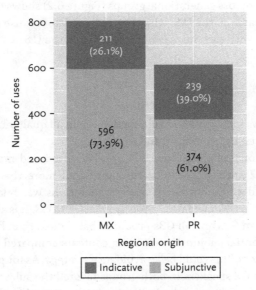

Figure 6.1. Indicative and subjunctive use in all qualifying tokens by regional origin (all generational groups).

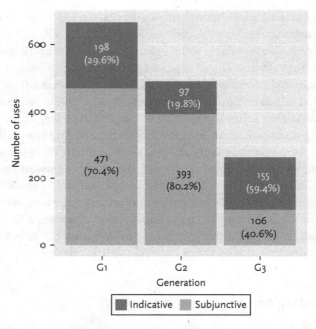

Figure 6.2. Indicative and subjunctive use in all qualifying tokens by generation.

6.5. GENERATION

Subjunctive use across generational groups (Figure 6.2) shows the same trends as in other research in the U.S. which we reviewed above: use of the subjunctive diminishes with each increasing generation in the U.S.

Generation and Regional Origin

Figure 6.3 shows indicative and subjunctive use in all qualifying tokens -both O and V contexts- by generation and regional origin.

In both regional origin groups, G1 speakers produced more subjunctive tokens than G2 speakers, who in turn produced more than G3 speakers. Puerto Ricans' decrease in tokens across generations was relatively gradual, while the Mexicans dropped precipitously from G2 to G3. It is also noteworthy that Puerto Rican G2s and all G3s produced half or less than half of the total number of potential subjunctive-eliciting contexts compared with the other groups of speakers. This could be an avoidance strategy. As for proportions, we see that G1 and G2 speakers in both groups favored the subjunctive (ranging from 68.5% to 87.5%) over the indicative in these combined O and V contexts. Among G3s, however, Mexicans showed only a slight preference for the

[192]   *Spanish in Chicago*

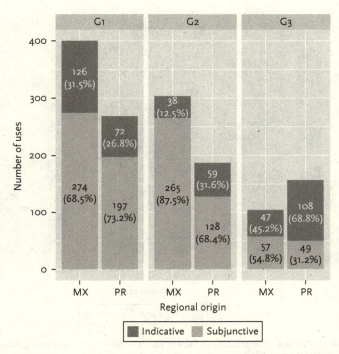

Figure 6.3. Indicative and subjunctive use in all qualifying tokens by generation and regional origin.

subjunctive (54.8%), while Puerto Ricans strongly preferred the indicative (68.9%).

Recall that we are also interested in whether subjunctive use is different depending on the obligatory or variable nature of the context. Based on Silva-Corvalán's (1994) findings, we hypothesized that subjunctive use in O contexts would be highest among G1, would decline among G2, and would be lowest among G3. Figure 6.4 provides a side-by-side visual comparison of the proportion of subjunctive use by Mexicans and Puerto Ricans across generations in both O and V contexts.

It is evident that subjunctive use varies not only across generations but also by context. Next, we consider whether generational and/or dialectal differences emerge for subjunctive and indicative usage in O and V contexts separately.

6.6. OBLIGATORY CONTEXTS

Figure 6.5 extracts only the O contexts. The *y*-axis shows the number of tokens, which allows us to see subjunctive versus indicative use more clearly.

SUBJUNCTIVE [193]

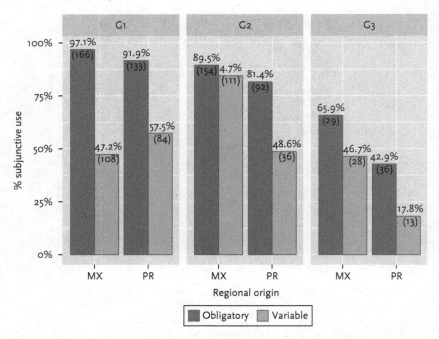

Figure 6.4. Percentage of Mexican and Puerto Rican subjunctive use across generations in both obligatory and variable contexts.

We see in Figure 6.5 that Mexican speakers produced fairly similar numbers of O contexts in G1 (n = 161 subjunctive and n = 5 indicative, total n = 171) and in G2 (n = 172) but dropped to a total of only n = 44 contexts in G3. Puerto Rican speakers declined more steadily across generations in the number of O contexts produced (from 123 to 113 to 84). We also see that our hypothesis held for both groups: Puerto Ricans' subjunctive use declined from 92% in G1 to 81% in G2 and 43% in G3, while that of Mexicans went from 97.0% to 89.5% to 65.9%. In examining these differences statistically, a 3 (generation) times 2 (regional origin) between-participants ANOVA on individuals' percentage production of subjunctives in obligatory contexts reached significance for generation, $F(2, 42)$ = 13.55, $p < .001$, $\eta_p^2 = .39$, but not for regional origin, $F(1, 42)$ = 3.44, $p = .071$, $\eta_p^2 = .08$. There was no interaction between regional origin and generation, $F(2, 42)$ = 0.34, $p = .716$, $\eta_p^2 = .02$. Consistently with Viner (2016, 2018, 2019), then, the lack of an interaction indicates that the overall pattern of change across generations for Mexican and Puerto Rican participants is not different and does not warrant separate analyses.[8]

---

8. With more speakers per group, we might have found significant differences between groups, although based on this current data set, we would expect differences only in V contexts and not in O contexts based on the increase in the percentage of

[194] *Spanish in Chicago*

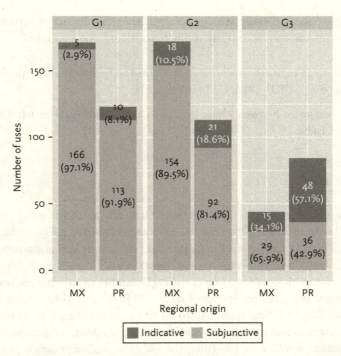

Figure 6.5. Number of tokens of indicative and subjunctive produced in obligatory contexts by generation and regional origin (each column totals 100%).

Given the lack of significance, we now collapse regional origin to consider differences between generations (it is worth noting descriptively that Mexican speakers in all generational groups used a slightly higher proportion of subjunctive tokens than their Puerto Rican counterparts; this may be because in each generational group, Mexican speakers evidenced slightly higher proficiency than did their Puerto Rican counterparts). Following up the main effect of generation in Os, Bonferroni-corrected t-tests revealed that G3 (M = 54.81%, SD = 32.07) produced the subjunctive significantly less in obligatory contexts than did G1 (M = 94.09, SD = 8.27), $t(42)$ = 5.02, $p < .001$, and G2 (M = 84.67, SD = 20.16), $t(42)$ = 3.69, $p = .002$. By contrast, the G1–G2 difference was not statistically significant ($p = .570$). Thus, only G3s were significantly different from the other two groups in their use of subjunctive in O contexts. In addition, the observed variability in subjunctive use as measured by SD increased across generations, indicating that G3 mood grammar is less homogeneous than that of G1 and G2.

subjunctive tokens used by Mexican G2s in variable contexts compared with the steady decline evidenced for Puerto Rican participants across G groups.

We also note that there are signs of avoidance of subjunctive structures by the participants who did not use it much, including this example:

(1) *Lo puedo reconocer cuando lo oigo . . . pero no es tan extensivo que lo quería que ser* (*sea*, SUBJ). (#14, G2 Mexican male)

I can recognize it when I hear it . . . but not as extensive as what I would want it to be.

6.7. VARIABLE CONTEXTS

We now examine the variable contexts (V) such as *Puede que le interesa/ interese la oferta* (It could be that the offer interests them). Figure 6.6 shows the number and proportion of indicative and subjunctive tokens across generations and regional groups in variable contexts.

Both groups showed a decline in the total number of variable contexts produced across generations, Mexicans from 229 in G1 to 131 in G2 down to 60 in G3 and Puerto Ricans from 146 to 74 to 73. As for the proportion of subjunctive use, no clear pattern was evident among the Mexican groups: G1 used the subjunctive 47.2% of the time, the G2 speakers surprisingly jumped to

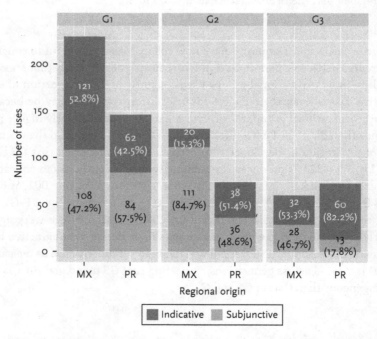

Figure 6.6. Proportion use of indicative and subjunctive mood in variable contexts by generation and regional origin.

[196] *Spanish in Chicago*

84.7% subjunctive use, and G3s were back down to G1 levels at 46.7%. Puerto Ricans, on the other hand, showed an intergenerational decline of subjunctive use in variable contexts (from 57.5% to 48.6% to 17.8%). A notable deviation from the expected pattern was that G2 Mexicans had a stronger preference for the subjunctive than G1 Mexicans in variable contexts. However, we will argue that this is an artifact of grouping speakers by generation as opposed to Spanish proficiency.

In assessing these differences statistically, a 3 (generation) times 2 (regional origin) between-participants ANOVA on individuals' percentage production of subjunctives in variable contexts revealed a main effect for generation, $F(2,41) = 9.98, p < .001, \eta_p^2 = .33$, and regional origin, $F(1, 41) = 6.01, p = .019, \eta_p^2 = .13$, but no interaction between regional origin and generation, $F(2, 41) = 1.87, p = .167, \eta_p^2 = .08$. Follow-up t-tests revealed that Mexicans produced a gerater percentage use of the subjunctive in variable contexts (M = 59.35%, SD = 31.13) than Puerto Ricans (M = 41.62%, SD = 26.37), $t(41) = 2.45, p = .019$. However, we are reluctant to interpret this result at face value because later analyses suggest that this difference is driven by lack of homogeneity in participants' proficiency within the generation groupings for variable contexts and not by true differences between regional groups' use of the subjunctive. Therefore, in the following analyses, we combine Mexican and Puerto Rican speakers to consider the role of generation and obligatory/variable context.

As for the main effect of generation in Vs, follow-up Bonferroni-corrected t-tests revealed that G3 speakers (M = 30.79%, SD = 28.69) produced the subjunctive in variable contexts significantly less than G2 speakers (M = 70.24%, SD = 27.82), $t(41) = 4.45, p < .001$, and also less than G1 speakers (M = 52.21%, SD = 19.97), $t(41) = 2.52, p = .047$. Meanwhile, the G1–G2 difference was not significant at $p = .167$. In addition, the larger variance found in G1 and G2 in the Vs as compared with the Os further corroborates the coding of these contexts as variable.

Although generation provides a proxy for linguistic change over time, the large amounts of variance around mean rates of subjunctive use suggest that generation, at least among G2 and G3 speakers, may not be the most appropriate metric. To account for this, we now present an analysis of subjunctive use in Os and Vs by proficiency.

6.8. PROFICIENCY

Recall that each speaker's Spanish proficiency was rated on a scale of 1 (lowest) to 5 (highest) as described in Chapter 2. As noted earlier, although proficiency in the CHISPA corpus clearly declined across generations, there were individuals with Spanish proficiency that was either higher or lower than their G group average. Table 6.5 shows what the proficiency distributions ended up being for

Table 6.5. PROFICIENCY LEVELS OF *N* = 64 SPEAKERS IN THE SUBJUNCTIVE CORPUS.

Proficiency	Level 5	Level 4	Level 3	Level 2	Total
Mexican *n*	11	6	6	1	24
Puerto Rican *n*	7	7	5	5	24
Total	18	13	11	6	48

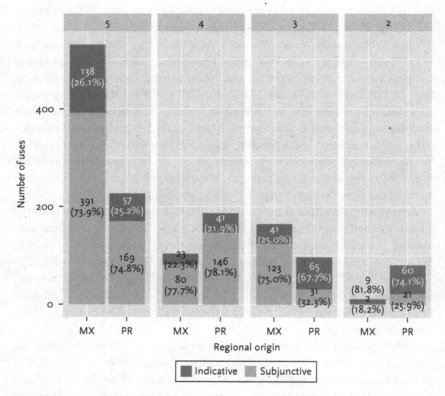

Figure 6.7. Number of indicative and subjunctive tokens by regional origin and proficiency level (columns total 100%).

the subcorpus we had selected at random to represent all regional origins and generations.

Figure 6.7 shows the number of indicative and subjunctive tokens produced by proficiency and regional origin in O and V contexts combined, while Figure 6.8 shows percentages of O and V separately. We will compare these two figures with their analogous G analyses that were presented in Figures 6.2 and 6.3.

[198] *Spanish in Chicago*

We notice the following from Figure 6.7. First, Mexicans with a Spanish proficiency level of 5 were largely responsible for the total number of qualifying tokens ($n = 529$), but this was also the largest group of speakers ($n = 11$), so we would expect more tokens here. Their proportion of subjunctive use, however, was relatively the same as that for level 5 Puerto Ricans (close to 74%). At proficiency level 4, too, Mexicans and Puerto Ricans used the indicative and the subjunctive in proportions similar to each other. It is at level 3 where we see that Mexicans remained close to three-quarters use of the subjunctive, but Puerto Ricans declined to one-third, and at proficiency level 2, both groups were close to just 20% to 25% subjunctive use.

Figure 6.8 shows the proportions of subjunctive use in each context by regional origin and proficiency.

In Figure 6.8, we notice the following. Again, speakers with proficiency levels of 5 and 4 from both regional origins looked the same at 90.4% to 95.1% subjunctive use, although Puerto Ricans produced fewer tokens. It was in proficiency level 3 where Mexicans dropped to 79.3%, and the Puerto Ricans dropped even further to 46.5% subjunctive use. They are more or less the same again at proficiency level 2. Thus, when Figure 6.3 showed that Mexican G2s had a fairly high proportion of subjunctive use (87.5%), we see now that this was due to their high levels of proficiency. Essentially, the analysis by G is

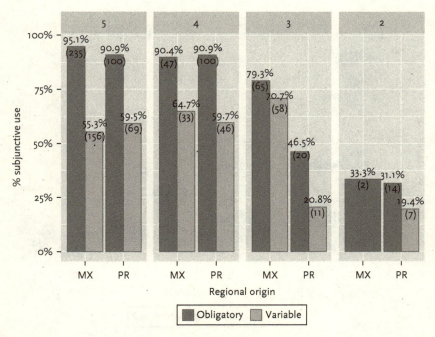

Figure 6.8. Proportion of indicative and subjunctive tokens by regional origin and proficiency level.

SUBJUNCTIVE [199]

misleading, because some of the Mexican G2 speakers had proficiency levels of 4 and thus behaved more like G1s. This finding offers support to Erker and Otheguy (2016), who claim that the Spanish of some G2 speakers is not "incomplete" and that it shares more similarities with a homeland variety than it has differences. Our data suggest that this is true for the use of the subjunctive, when G2 speakers had a proficiency level of 5 or 4.

We would have liked to examine whether Mexican and Puerto Rican participants could be considered independent when grouped by proficiency, but due to low participant numbers per cell, we did not have the statistical power to do so. Therefore, in subsequent sections, Mexicans and Puerto Ricans will be combined to examine subjunctive and indicative use across proficiency levels as in the analysis by G.

6.8.1. Obligatory Contexts by Proficiency Level

To see the proportions more clearly, Figure 6.9 shows only O contexts with the number of tokens on the *y*-axis.

A two-way ANOVA on the percentage of subjunctive use in obligatory contexts found a significant effect of proficiency, $F(3, 39) = 15.43$, $p < .001$, $\eta_p^2 = .54$. Follow-up Bonferroni-corrected t-tests revealed that speakers

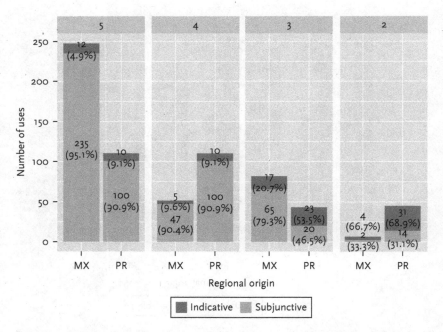

Figure 6.9. Obligatory contexts, number of tokens of indicative and subjunctive by regional origin and proficiency level.

with a proficiency of 2 (M = 32.39%, SD = 28.11) used the subjunctive significantly less than those with a proficiency of 4 (M = 91.70%, SD = 9.33), $t(39)$ = 4.97, p < .001, and with a proficiency of 5 (M = 92.63%, SD = 8.41), $t(43)$ = 6.50, p < .001, but not significantly less than speakers with a proficiency of 3 (M = 58.31%, SD = 30.09), $t(39)$ = 2.08, p = .265. Speakers with a proficiency of 3 used the subjunctive significantly less than those with a proficiency of 4, $t(39)$ = 4.33, p < .001, and those with a proficiency of 5, $t(43)$ = 4.64, p < .001. The difference between speakers with a proficiency level of 4 and those at level 5 was not significant (p = .999). There was no significant effect for either regional origin or the interaction of proficiency by regional origin, p > .05. That is, Mexicans and Puerto Ricans did not differ at each proficiency level in their subjunctive use. In addition, we still see a large amount of variance at the lowest proficiency levels.

6.8.2. Variable Contexts by Proficiency Level

When the participants are separated by proficiency level, we see a steep decline after level 5 in the number of tokens produced (see Figure 6.10). However, when it comes to percentage, the decline in subjunctive use occurred only at level 2 with a very substantial drop.

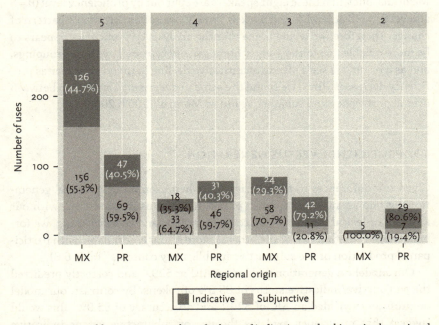

Figure 6.10. Variable contextx, number of tokens of indicative and subjunctive by regional origin and proficiency level.

A two-way ANOVA revealed a significant difference for subjunctive use at different proficiency levels, $F(3, 38) = 4.60$, $p = .008$, $\eta_p^2 = .27$. Bonferroni-corrected t-tests revealed that speakers with a proficiency of 2 (M = 16.71%, SD = 11.83) used the subjunctive significantly less than speakers with a proficiency of 4 (M = 65.86%, SD = 25.88), $t(38) = 3.37$, $p = .010$, and those with a proficiency of 5 (M = 57.84%, SD = 25.84), $t(38) = 2.90$, $p = .038$. No other pairwise comparisons were significant (all $p > .05$). There was no significant effect for either regional origin or the interaction of proficiency by regional origin, $p > .05$.

Interestingly, the least amount of variability was found for speakers with low proficiency, suggesting that at the lowest level of proficiency (which was one Mexican speaker and five Puerto Rican speakers), they were more consistently defaulting to using the indicative instead of the subjunctive in variable contexts. However, the very low number of participants at proficiency level 2 means that these conclusions remain speculative.

To summarize, the quantitative analyses by generation and proficiency presented here reveal a fairly consistent pattern. For both Os and Vs, the latest generation (G3) and the lower proficiency levels 2 and 3 showed a significant decrease in their use of the subjunctive. However, we cannot assume homogeneity of proficiency within each G group. The benefit of using proficiency as opposed to generation is even more evident when looking at variable contexts. In variable contexts, Mexican G2s showed a higher use of subjunctive than G1 Mexicans, but when these eight speakers are split out by proficiency level ($n = 3$ at level 5, $n = 3$ at level 4, and $n = 2$ at level 3), we see a more stable pattern of change. Therefore, we would argue that the analysis by proficiency appears to be more reliable due to the greater homogeneity captured by these groupings, and as a result, we see a steady quantitative decline in mood grammar as proficiency decreases. Thus, we found the same unsurprising correlation between overall proficiency and subjunctive use as Montrul (2007, 2009).

6.9. PROFICIENCY VERSUS GENERATION

Given the differences in subjunctive use when examining speakers' generational group versus their Spanish proficiency, and as we have done with our analyses of lexical familiarity, discourse markers, and codeswitching, we formally tested whether one or the other is more strongly correlated with participants' production of the subjunctive in obligatory contexts (Table 6.6).

Our model on generation yielded an AIC of 529.4 and correctly predicted the subjunctive/indicative status of 83.5% of tokens. By contrast, our model on proficiency yielded an AIC of 520.1 and an accuracy of 85.9%. This would suggest that proficiency explains the use of subjunctive versus indicative better than generation. Our second approach found that proficiency had an

Table 6.6. CORRELATION OF TOTAL NUMBER OF CODESWITCHES WITH GENERATION VERSUS PROFICIENCY.

	Generation	**Proficiency**
AIC	529.4 83.5% of tokens	520.1 85.9% of tokens
R^2	.063	.067

R^2M of .067, higher than that of generation (.063). This agrees with the result of our model comparison approach in suggesting that proficiency explains the use of mood better than generation does.

Thus, we argue that when studying features of U.S. Spanish, overall Spanish proficiency as measured holistically based on at least 30 minutes of quasi-naturalistic informal conversational speech may be a better predictor than generational level. This is quite logical when we consider that proficiency is not always directly correlated with generational level, as shown in the CHISPA corpus overall (see Chapter 2).

6.10. SUMMARY AND CONCLUSIONS

We compared the use of the subjunctive across three generations and proficiency levels of Mexicans and Puerto Ricans in Chicago. Previous studies of Spanish in the U.S. focused on differences across either generations or regional groups; we combined these approaches and also considered proficiency independently of generation. Statistical tests showed that for mood selection, Mexicans and Puerto Ricans did not need to be analyzed as independent groups; their proportions of indicative and subjunctive use looked the same in G1, thus there was no need to test whether they were becoming more alike in subsequent generations. Descriptively, we found that among proficiency level 3 speakers, Mexicans used a higher proportion of subjunctive than Puerto Ricans, but the two groups used very similar proportions of indicative and subjunctive at all other proficiency levels.

As in other studies of U.S. Spanish (Viner, 2016, 2017, 2018, 2019; Silva-Corvalán, 1994), we found a general increase in use of the indicative as generation increased, except among G2 Mexicans. However, this was explained by the fact that many G2 Mexicans had strong Spanish proficiency levels on par with their G1 counterparts. As we found for lexicon (Chapter 3), discourse markers (Chapter 4), and codeswitching (Chapter 5), proficiency was more highly correlated to subjunctive use than generation was. This trend of declining subjunctive use is similar to what has been found in monolingual

Spanish contexts (Gallego, 2016; Gudmestad, 2010; Schwenter & Hoff, 2020) and in other Spanish contact varieties (Crespo del Río, 2022). That the indicative is being used in what have usually been considered obligatory subjunctive contexts suggests that Spanish may be moving along the continuum that has been traversed by other Romance languages and that it is accelerated by contact with English and/or reduced use of Spanish (as argued by Silva-Corvalán, 1994). Furthermore, it suggests that the use of the indicative where subjunctive morphology might be expected does not suffer from strong stigma; recall Erker and Otheguy's (2016) prediction that a feature for which (a) Spanish and English are analogous and (b) the feature does not call too much attention, a bilingual might likely converge on English.

Similarly to Viner (2016, 2017, 2018, 2019), we did not find differences in proportions of subjunctive use between regional groups, even though we restricted the analysis to a single country of origin from each region. Future work could examine internal variables such as negation, verb type, and so on, and include a logistic regression to examine the role of all variables.

CHAPTER 7
Phonology

7.1. INTRODUCTION

In this chapter we examine several phonological realizations in the Spanish of a subgroup of Mexicans, Puerto Ricans, and MexiRicans in the CHISPA corpus.[1] Unlike Chapters 3, 4, and 5, which examined Spanish features that were possibly sensitive to proficiency in Spanish, for this analysis we do not posit that proficiency will be correlated to speakers' phonological production. Although U.S.-raised Spanish speakers have been found to differ on several features (see Ronquest & Rao, 2018), they are not among those we study here.

First, we review in more detail studies of phonological outcomes with a particular focus on Spanish before discussing our research questions, methodology, and findings. After presenting findings about the two features we studied, we follow up with a qualitative review of narratives in an attempt to understand the factors that may have been involved, finding reasonable explanations in some cases but not others.

7.2. PHONOLOGICAL ACCOMMODATION IN SITUATIONS OF SPANISH DIALECT CONTACT

Phonological accommodation may occur when speakers of phonologically different varieties of the same language come into contact with each other. Possible outcomes of this contact include: (1) there can be an increase in the frequency of a variant that was already part of a speaker's speech repertoire;

---

1. This chapter is based on O'Rourke and Potowski (2016). The present version includes two new elements: statistical tests in R and comparative qualitative analyses of several Puerto Rican individuals who used many versus few of the features we study.

(2) the use of a variant could be decreased, usually a stigmatized one; and/or (3) new features absent from a speaker's repertoire may be introduced. An important factor that impacts accommodation is the salience of a feature—the degree to which speakers are aware of it. Some features come to be so salient that they act as linguistic stereotypes. For example, we saw in Chapter 1 that in Chicago, interviewees frequently mentioned coda /s/ weakening, lambdacisms, and velarized /r̄/ as typical features of Puerto Rican Spanish, meaning that they are highly salient in this location.

Several studies of Spanish phonological accommodation have looked at the situation we represented with Figure 1.3 in Chapter 1: when speakers of one dialect move to a place where a different dialect of that language is the main variety spoken in society. For example, there has been work on the phonology of Spanish-speaking immigrants from various locations to Mexico City (Pesqueira, 2008; Rodríguez Cadena, 2006; Serrano, 2002) as well as Dominicans in Puerto Rico (Pedraza & Ortiz López, 2016). Hernández-Campoy (2010) examined more temporary accommodation via analyzing formal recordings of three politicians from Murcia, Spain, when speaking locally versus in Madrid.

There have also been studies carried out within contexts such as those represented in Chapter 1 via Figures 1.5 and 1.6, for example, among speakers of Salvadoran and Mexican Spanish in the U.S. Aaron and Hernández (2007) examined coda /s/ (hereafter "/s/") reduction patterns in Salvadoran Spanish in Houston, where Mexicans form the predominant Spanish-speaking group. While in most Mexican varieties of Spanish the /s/ is retained, in Salvadoran Spanish degrees of /s/ reduction and deletion are common. The authors found a pattern of /s/ reduction inversely related to length of time in Houston: the longer speakers had lived in Houston, the less likely they were to reduce or delete /s/. The authors attribute this accommodation to the salience and prestige of /s/ in the community, arguing that Salvadorans sense that their Spanish is stigmatized in Houston and accommodate to Mexican Spanish in this feature.

Also in Houston, Hernández (2009) tested the degree to which Salvadorans accommodated their speech when interacting with an outgroup member—a speaker of Mexican Spanish—versus when speaking to an ingroup Salvadoran Spanish speaker. He further divided the Houston Salvadorans according to their neighborhoods, one with a Latino population that was 90% Mexican and the other where Salvadorans formed 22% of the local Latino population. He measured the rates of word-final nasals, which Salvadoran speakers tend to velarize (*pan* > *paŋ*) but which is uncommon in Mexican Spanish. First, overall he found that the choice of word-final nasal was "undeniably sensitive to the physical space": the velar (i.e., Salvadoran) variant was used 23% of the time in El Salvador, 14% in the more Salvadoran Houston neighborhood, and only 3% in the Mexican Houston neighborhood. In addition, in the Salvadoran neighborhood, each speaker was interviewed twice and overall produced higher rates of velarization when interviewed by a fellow Salvadoran (22%) compared with when interviewed by a Mexican (8%). Finally, younger arrivals velarized less frequently than those who immigrated later in life, regardless of the regional origin of the interviewer.

However, in Lorain, Ohio, where Puerto Ricans are the numerically dominant Spanish speakers, Ramos-Pellicia (2007) found no evidence that newly arrived Mexicans accommodated to Puerto Rican phonological features. Why is this outcome so different from the clear Salvadoran accommodation to Mexican Spanish found in Houston (Hernández 2009)? It may be related to the negative ideologies among Mexicans that Puerto Rican Spanish is inferior to their own variety.

Finally, Erker and Otheguy (2016) examined the weakening of coda /s/ among Caribbean- and Mainlander-origin speakers in New York City. They found clear regional differences among newcomers, but region of origin ceased to statistically differentiate the /s/ production of longtime residents; the two groups of speakers became more like each other over time.

These studies demonstrate that in dialect contact situations, a variety of factors condition accommodation: size of populations, prestige of their varieties, regional origin of the interlocutor, and age of arrival of speakers. It is no surprise that /s/ is a frequent subject of studies of dialect contact, given that it reasonably neatly divides Caribbean from Mainlander varieties. For example, in most varieties of Mexican Spanish, /s/ is maintained as a sibilant.[2] Serrano (2002) found that among speakers in Mexico City, there was an /s/ weakening rate of only 3%, while Puerto Rican Spanish and other Caribbean varieties exhibit frequent aspiration and elision of /s/, which is conditioned both phonologically and socially (Terrell, 1977; López-Morales, 2003; Cameron, 2000). Among Puerto Ricans living on the mainland U.S., realizations of /s/ have also been found to vary according to phonological, social, and stylistic constraints (Ma & Herasimchuk, 1971; Poplack, 1980; Lamboy, 2004; Ghosh-Johnson, 2005; Otheguy & Zentella, 2012; Ramos-Pellicia, 2012). Otheguy and Zentella (2012, p. 115) argue that in New York City, weakened /s/ is less prestigious than its sibilant variant, which, as we saw in Chapter 1, appears to be the case in Chicago as well.

Another potentially interesting site of accommodation between Puerto Rican and Mexican Spanish speakers is trilled /r̄/ (hereafter "/r̄/"). In Spanish, /r̄/ is found in word-initial and syllable-initial positions after alveolar consonants *l*, *n*, and *s*, as in *ropa* (clothes), *alrededor* (around), *Enrique*, and *Israel*. It is also found contrastively between vowels, as in *carro* (car) compared to

---

2. Some regional Mexican dialects weaken /s/, including along the coasts of the states of Guerrero and Veracruz. However, only two of our participants or their families hailed from these regions.

single-tap /ɾ/ caro (expensive).[3] Mexican Spanish, like the vast majority of Spanish dialects, pronounces /r̄/ as trilled, with some assibilated, affricate, and retroflex regional variants. However, Puerto Rican Spanish can evidence a velar realization, /r̄/ as [x], whereby barra and baja sound very similar (Lipski, 2011).[4] However, we note that Delgado-Díaz and Galarza (2015) showed that Puerto Rican listeners can more accurately distinguish the difference between such minimal pairs (e.g., Ramón, man's name, vs. jamón, ham) than listeners from other Spanish dialect origins can. It seems that in the Spanish-speaking world, only Puerto Rican Spanish shows velarized /r̄/ (Delgado-Díaz & Galarza, 2015; Megenney, 1978, p. 72; Valentín-Márquez, 2015). How frequently do Puerto Ricans velarize /r̄/? Medina-Rivera (1999) reported 9.3% velarization for speakers in Caguas, although this was based on impressionistic categorization. In Valentín-Márquez's (2015) acoustic study of speakers from Cabo Rojo, velar tokens accounted for 15.8% of the data, but including all post-alveolar allophones increased the velarization rate to 19.7%. Studies suggest that Puerto Ricans stigmatize velarized /r̄/ as a trait belonging to rural contexts and low socioeconomic status (López-Morales, 2003; Medina-Rivera, 1999), but some attribute to it the positive association of being "typical" of Puerto Rico (Valentín-Márquez, 2015).

Thus, the two phonological features we selected for our analysis were /s/ and /r̄/.[5] These two features exhibit variants that clearly distinguish Puerto Rican Spanish from Mexican Spanish. Obviously, sibilant /s/ and trilled /r̄/ are not uniquely "Mexican features" and in fact are frequently present in Puerto Rican Spanish as well as in varieties of Spanish around the world. For ease of reference, we use "Mexican" to distinguish these two realizations from their "Puerto Rican" counterparts, which, again, are not limited to Puerto Rico, although velarized /r̄/ does seem to be used only by Puerto Rican Spanish speakers.

---

3. The single-tap /ɾ/ also has a trilled variant in syllable- and word-final coda position, which may be considered a stylistic variant used for increased emphasis, as in parte (part), pronounced [paɾte] or [par̄te] (see Hualde, 2014, for further description). This was not examined in the present study; only phonemically contrastive trills and trills in obligatory strengthening contexts were analyzed, since syllable-final neutralization results in a different distribution of allophonic variants (Valentín-Márquez, 2007; Simonet et al., 2008; Luna, 2010).

4. The voiceless velar fricative [x] is used to represent the posteriorizing nature of this process. However, several phonetic variants may be included in this grouping, including the uvular trill [ʀ] and voiced and voiceless uvular fricatives [ʁ] and [χ].

5. To hear examples of /s/ weakening, readers can search YouTube for videos of interviews with Puerto Rican singer René Pérez ("El Residente") from the group Calle Trece; in his interview with Juan González in 2013, he velarizes some tokens of /r̄/ as well. For additional examples of velarized /r̄/, consult the University of Iowa's site http://dialects.its.uiowa.edu/ under Países > Puerto Rico > Arecibo > Anécdota (note that at the time this went to press, a browser other than Chrome was required for the proper functioning of the Flash Player).

Taking heed of the findings of Hernández (2009) that the features utilized by the interviewer might affect speakers' realizations, we sought to explore whether Mexicans display more Puerto Rican features when speaking to Puerto Ricans or, in a more likely scenario given the numerical predominance of Mexicans and the higher status of Mexican Spanish, whether Puerto Ricans display more Mexican features when speaking with Mexicans. If either of these outcomes obtains, it may constitute evidence of a process of accommodation. We note that for MexiRicans, there is no "outgroup" dialect, because both Puerto Rican and Mexican Spanish were present in the speakers' homes. Thus, in addition to examining rates of /s/ weakening and /r̄/ velarization, we asked whether MexiRicans demonstrated a greater preponderance of features that corresponded with the dialect of the mother's regional origin group. We were unable to analyze MexiRican data according to whether the interviewer was Mexican or Puerto Rican due to the relatively small number of Puerto Rican interviewers. Finally, we examined whether /s/ and /r̄/ realizations occurred in any pattern in relation to each other.

Our research questions were as follows.

1. Will there be differences in the realizations of /s/ and /r̄/ according to the following?
   a. Regional origin
   b. Regional origin and generational group[6]
   c. Interlocutor
   d. Interlocutor and generational group
2. To what extent will /s/ weakening and /r̄/ velarization occur together?

We hypothesized that given the status of Mexican Spanish and the numerical dominance of Mexicans in Chicago (despite the fact that the proportion of Puerto Ricans among Chicago Latinos was twice as large when many of our participants were growing up), our Mexican participants would not change on either feature across generations or according to interlocutor. On the other hand, we thought that Puerto Rican speakers would reduce use of weakened /s/ and velarized /r̄/—that is, use Puerto Rican variants less frequently—when speaking with Mexican interviewers. We also thought that Puerto Ricans would weaken /s/ less and velarize /r̄/ less from G1 to G2 to G3, showing a generational accommodation to Mexican Spanish. We hypothesized that this might happen (despite the findings presented in Chapter 2 that negative

---

6. Unlike in previous chapters, we did not attempt an analysis by generational group alone, given that Mexicans and Puerto Ricans are so starkly different phonologically that putting speakers of all generational groups together would not reveal much of interest.

attitudes about the outgroup variety dissipated across generations) due to the sheer numerical dominance of Mexicans in the city.

7.3. METHODOLOGY
Participants

We selected at random a subgroup of 88 individuals from the CHISPA corpus, choosing speakers with recordings of sufficient quality and who were spread out among the three different regional origin groups and generational categories. The two regional origin groups were further subdivided according to whether the dialect origin of the interviewer was the "same," such as when a Mexican interviewed another Mexican, or "different," such as when a Puerto Rican interviewed a Mexican. These characteristics are displayed in Table 7.1.

The subcorpus of MexiRicans selected for this analysis were also subdivided according to the ethnolinguistic origin of the mother (shown in Table 7.2).

Table 7.1. MEXICAN AND PUERTO RICAN PARTICIPANTS.

Dialect origin, speaker	n	Dialect origin, interviewer	n	Generation	n
Puerto Rican	24	Same (PR)	9	G1	4
				G2	2
				G3	3
		Different (MX)	15	G1	4
				G2	6
				G3	5
Mexican	19	Same (MX)	9	G1	3
				G2	3
				G3	3
		Different (PR)	10	G1	3
				G2	5
				G3	2
Total	43	Same	18	G1	14
		Different	25	G2	16
				G3	13

[210] *Spanish in Chicago*

Table 7.2. MEXIRICAN PARTICIPANTS.

Dialect origin, mother	n	G	n
Puerto Rican	22	G2	11
		G3	11
Mexican	23	G2	8
		G3	15
Total	45	G2	19
		G3	26

We pause here to point out an important area for future research. We did not gather two recordings with the same person, one time interviewed by a "same" dialect interlocutor and then again by a "different" dialect interlocutor. That is, we have no direct evidence for whether any individuals changed the way they spoke with different interlocutors. As noted earlier, Hernández (2009) found higher rates of nasal velarization among Salvadorans in Houston who were interviewed by a Salvadoran versus when they were interviewed by a Mexican. This methodology was also employed by Smith and Durham (2012), who examined lexical, phonological, morphosyntactic, and phonetic variables among speakers in two different conversations, first with a standard Scottish English speaker and subsequently with a Shetland Islands dialect speaker. They found that half of the speakers switched dialect features according to the interlocutor; the other half exhibited monodialectal behavior. Similarly, Holliday (2014) studied 260 declarative clauses produced by a mixed-race African American and white male speaking with African American versus white interlocutors. She found that although he produced no stereotypical African American syntax features (such as deleted copula *be* and third-person –s) with either type of interlocutor, when speaking with African Americans he showed greatly increased pitch fall rate and use of falsetto, two features identified with African American English (Wolfram & Schilling-Estes, 2006).

However, we note that Foreman (2003) carried out a double interview procedure with U.S. English speakers who had moved to Australia, one conducted by a U.S. English speaker and the other by an Australian English speaker, but she found that the interlocutor's dialect did not affect speakers' phonological realizations. Although multiple interviews with interlocutors who spoke different dialects would have provided us with more reliable evidence of phonological accommodation, the fact that large proportions of our corpus had "same" and "different" interviewers is a step toward direct evidence of whether speakers accommodate to their interlocutor, and some statistically significant patterns did emerge.

As stated in Chapter 2, the type of microphone and recording equipment varied, which affected the amount of background noise on the recordings. However, differential behavior between these dialect groups was salient enough to be identified. Future work would be supported by a more fine-grained acoustic study. All recordings were transferred to a computer at a 44.1-Hz (16-bit) sampling rate and analyzed as .wav files. The analysis of the recordings was conducted in *Praat* (Boersma & Weenink, 2020) for annotation and segmentation of the sound files to determine word and syllable boundaries. All sound tokens were played in *Praat* and coded as described below.

Coding

Minutes 10:00–20:00 of each recording were extracted. After 10 minutes of conversation, speakers have ideally become accustomed to the interview process and equipment and are using a more relaxed, informal speech style. The first half of this section was coded for the two phonemes under study and generated an average of 72 tokens of /s/ per speaker (SD = 27). However, in the case of /r̄/, 10 minutes was sometimes not enough to generate our 10-token minimum, so additional segments were coded as follows: the second five minutes of the 10-minute extraction; then, if necessary, 10-minute segments until the end of the recording; and finally, the initial 10 minutes of the recording were coded if needed.

A *Praat* script was used to extract all coding. The words in which the /s/ or /r̄/ appeared were noted, along with the following sound and the location of the sound in relation to the stressed syllable. The following instances of /s/ were eliminated from our final corpus:

- Word-final /s/ preceding a vowel (e.g., *las otras*), since resyllabification might affect or precede aspiration.
- /s/ preceding an /r̄/ (e.g., *las rojas*), since it is a context where both voicing and elision are common and it is difficult to distinguish spectrographically with the following segment even in cases of maintenance (Navarro Tomás, 1967; Hualde, 2014).
- Word-final /s/ followed by /s/ in the onset of the next word (e.g., *las sopas*), since it is difficult to delineate the end of the coda and the beginning of the following consonant.

All remaining instances of /s/ (6,320 tokens) and of /r̄/ (1,287 tokens) were coded according to the following criteria:

- The presence of a sibilant realization of /s/ was coded as s-s, including voiceless and voiced realizations [s] and [z].

- Any weakened realization of /s/ was coded as s-0, including aspirated [h] and elided or null [Ø] realizations. That is, we did not distinguish between weakened and elided /s/, even though Bullock et al. (2014) pointed out that among Dominicans, the use of [h] may in fact be an accommodation away from [Ø] toward sibilant /s/.[7] Thus, there was a fair amount of variability that we were not capturing with this method, but it permitted a general contrast between weakened and non-weakened /s/, which proved to be fruitful.
- For /r̄/, velarized realizations were coded as r-x, while any non-velar realizations were coded as r-rr, which included trills, single taps, assibilated, and retroflex variants. All tokens occurred in syllable-onset position.[8]

We also examined three prosodic factors: word stress, position in relation to the stressed syllable, and position with respect to the end of a syllable, word, or phrase. Also, in a subset of cases in which /s/ was followed by a consonant, tokens were coded for voicing and consonant class (obstruent or sonorant) of the following consonant. However, the findings from these analyses were in line with previous studies and are therefore not reported here. Other potentially related factors such as place and manner of articulation need to be explored, although a larger data set is needed in order to balance the number of tokens across speakers.

We present in the following order the results of /s/ and /r̄/: regional origin, generation, generation and regional origin together, and interlocutor's variety (first by regional origin and then by generation and regional origin together).

7.4. REGIONAL ORIGIN

We first present the rates of /s/ weakening and /r̄/ velarizations according to speakers' regional origin (Table 7.3). As predicted, overall maintenance of /s/ was high among Mexicans (90.9%) and lower among Puerto Ricans (42.1%).

Mexican speakers weakened /s/ at an average rate of only 9.1%. One might have expected a 0% /s/ weakening rate among these non-coastal Mexican speakers, but as we saw earlier, a certain amount of weakening in fact occurs

---

7. Similarly, aspiration was interpreted as maintenance among speakers from Buenos Aires in Mexico City (Pesqueira Barragán, 2012) and as weakening among Salvadorans in Texas (Hernández & Maldonado, 2012).

8. This procedure made an initial velar/non-velar division, although the r-rr group still might include a large range of other variant realizations. Acoustic cues in the waveform and spectrogram such as the presence or absence of high-frequency noise and formant transitions were used as secondary confirmation of segment identity as available. Again, there was a good deal of variability that we were not capturing by using this method, but clear differences between the Puerto Rican and Mexican groups were still observable.

Table 7.3. WEAKENING OF /S/, MEXICANS AND PUERTO RICANS.

Group	Tokens (n)	Average rates across speakers	
		Sibilant avg % (SD)	Weakened avg % (SD)
Mexicans (n = 19)	1,421	90.9 (5.7)	9.1 (5.7)
Puerto Ricans (n = 24)	1,749	42.1 (35.6)	57.9 (35.6)

even among speakers from the interior of the country (Serrano, 2002, found a 3% weakening rate). Because /s/ weakening among Mexicans is unexpected, we take a moment here to explore what we found. First, three speakers accounted for 43.0% (n = 58) of all the 135 weakened tokens: 153-MG (n = 19, 14.1%), 20-EJ (n = 17, 12.6%), and 25-BF (n = 22, 16.3%). The remaining 16 speakers have fewer than 10 tokens each of weakened /s/, including eight speakers with fewer than five tokens and one speaker with zero tokens. Second, we examined the particular items in which Mexicans weakened /s/. These are displayed in Appendix A. Overall, the most frequent instances were observed word-finally before a consonant. Nouns showed more instances of weakening, although some specific words showed greater instances of weakening word-internally (e.g., *mismo* and *estar*). In terms of following-consonant quality, weakening occurred more frequently before voiceless consonants word-internally but before voiced consonants word-finally. These rates may also be due to trailing off during speech production, speech errors, or (particularly among later generations) a lack of morphology or a form that appears to be lexicalized with weakening. For example, one of our G3 Mexican speakers typically did not weaken /s/—exhibiting a 94.8% maintenance rate—but still produced *otro(s) países*, which may mirror the structure "other countries" in English, which does not have a plural inflection on the modifier. In some cases, such as with the word *mismo* (same), it was pronounced without a sibilant (*mi[s]mo*) by a G1 Mexican speaker who otherwise predominantly showed sibilant production (87.3% maintenance). This suggested that a lexicalization of the non-sibilant pronunciation might be in progress.

The 24 Puerto Rican speakers weakened /s/ at an average rate of 57.9%. However, Figure 7.1 presents a closer examination showing how many individuals weakened at different percentage rates, reporting data in deciles. In Figure 7.1, "10%" represents speakers whose data fell between 10% and 19%, "20%" represents data between 20% and 29%, and so on. We see that 75% of these Puerto Rican speakers (18 out of the 24) were either regular weakeners or regular maintainers: they weakened 80% or more of the time (n = 11 in the

[214] *Spanish in Chicago*

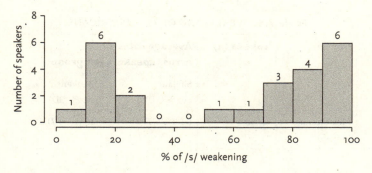

Figure 7.1. Rates of /s/ weakening among Puerto Ricans (number of individuals).

"80%" plus "90%–100%" categories) or maintained 80% or more of the time (n = 7 in the "20% or less" categories).

As suggested by Tagliamonte (2014), we used multiple statistical methods to corroborate our findings: a generalized estimating equation (GEE) analysis and a variable rules (VARBRUL) analysis. Of the two analyses, the GEE can be considered more conservative; while VARBRUL takes into account only fixed factors, in the GEE analysis, we have also included speaker as a random factor in order to account for individual variation. The VARBRUL findings are not reported here. The GEE is a mixed model similar to the generalized linear model. This analysis was chosen because the data are binary and the model includes subject as a random factor, taking into account multiple observations per speaker (i.e., that the data are correlated) and significant variation between speakers (i.e., there is less reliance on normality within a given group). The analysis was conducted in R using the *geepack* package (Yan, 2002; Yan & Fine, 2004; Halekoh et al., 2006), with *p* values calculated using the *joint_tests* function from the *emmeans* package (Lenth, 2020). In particular, the working correlation matrix was set to "Exchangeable" and the type of model was "Binary logistic." The reference was the Puerto Rican variant in order to calculate the likelihood of producing a weakened /s/ (or in the subsequent analyses, a velarized /r̄/). In this analysis, the exponentiate of the beta estimate, or Exp(B), indicates the increased odds that the variant will be produced for the given level of the factor. Significance is interpreted as probability values at $p \leq .05$.

A significant effect was found for the factor of group (Mexican, Puerto Rican) ($p < .001$); the parameter estimates show that the odds increased nearly 14 times for the realization of a weakened /s/ by the Puerto Rican group, Exp(B) = 13.72. As we suggested earlier, a more fine-grained acoustic analysis could determine if there was a qualitative difference between Mexican and Puerto Rican weakening, such as more use of aspiration versus full deletion, but this finding confirmed the very basic distinction noted earlier that Puerto Ricans weakened /s/ more frequently than Mexicans.

Table 7.4. WEAKENING OF /s/, MEXIRICANS.

Group	Tokens (n)	Average rates across speakers per group	
		Sibilant avg % (SD)	Weakened avg % (SD)
MexiRicans (n = 45)	3,150	84.8 (24.7)	15.2 (24.7)

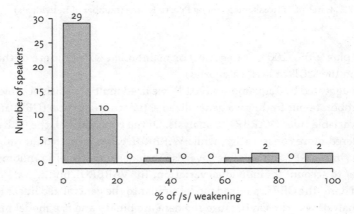

Figure 7.2. Rates of /s/ weakening among MexiRicans.

As for MexiRicans, of the total number of tokens (n = 3,150), this group showed 83.7% maintenance of /s/ overall.

As we see in Table 7.4, the average /s/ maintenance across the 46 MexiRican speakers was 84.8% (SD = 24.7%). In this way, their pattern looked more like the Mexican group than the Puerto Rican group. Figure 7.2 shows the number of MexiRicans who weakened /s/ in various proportions.

The vast majority of MexiRican speakers (n = 39) weakened at rates below 20%, and 29 of them weakened at a rate of less than 10%. It is worth noting, however, that all five of the individuals who weakened /s/ at rates of 60% or higher were raised by Puerto Rican women. Thus, having a Puerto Rican mother appears to be necessary (but not sufficient) for a MexiRican individual to develop a pattern of a high rate of weakened /s/, yet some MexiRicans with Puerto Rican mothers were in the category of < 20% weakened /s/.

This provides a segue into our examination of whether mother's regional origin group exerted an influence overall on /s/ behavior (Figure 7.3).

Figure 7.3 shows that, unlike in Potowski (2008), there did not appear to be an effect for mother's regional origin group. Rates of /s/ weakening only varied by approximately 7 percentage points between those with a Mexican

[216]   Spanish in Chicago

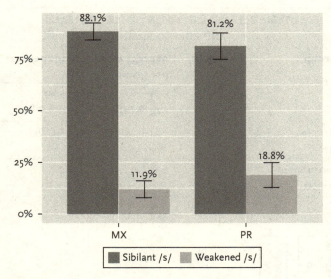

Figure 7.3. MexiRican /s/ by mother's regional origin group.

mother (11.9%) and those with a Puerto Rican mother (18.8%). The GEE analysis of mother shows no significance ($p = .332$). This may be due to two factors: the greater number of speakers in the present study (45) compared with the previous one (27) and the use of acoustic analysis to support the categorization of variants instead of a series of impressionistic ratings in the previous study.[9]

Now we examine /r̄/ velarizations by regional origin group. There were a total of 617 tokens of /r̄/ among Mexicans and Puerto Ricans, with an overall higher usage of the trilled variant of /r̄/ among Mexicans (98.5%, $n = 271$) than Puerto Ricans (85.4%, $n = 292$). Table 7.5 shows the average rates of alveolar and velar realizations by dialect group.

As expected, almost all tokens of velarized /r̄/ (50 out of 54) were produced by Puerto Ricans. A statistical comparison was not carried out because such an analysis would be appropriate only if more tokens had been produced by the Mexican group.

We now explore /r̄/ velarization in a bit more depth. We did not expect a single token of [x] among the Mexican speakers, but there ended up being four. One was *nos rentamos* (we rent) made by a G1 speaker. The remaining

---

9. In particular, impressionistic ratings rely on similarity between raters who need to have a high degree of agreement in what the phonological categories (and their cutoffs) should be, which requires similar levels of proficiency and exposure to the items in question. Acoustic analysis is less reliant on subjective evaluation (albeit by trained professionals) since the acoustic cues remain static and therefore observable, segmentable, and measurable.

Table 7.5. VELARIZATION OF /R/, MEXICANS AND PUERTO RICANS.

Group	Tokens (n)	Average rates among speakers per group	
		r-rr avg % (SD)	r-velar avg % (SD)
Mexicans (n = 19)	275	98.0 (7.0)	2.0 (7.0)
Puerto Ricans (n = 24)	342	83.8 (27.2)	16.2 (27.2)

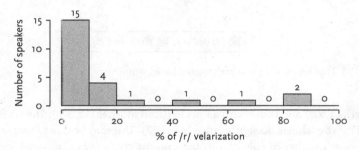

Figure 7.4. Rates of velar /r̃/ among Puerto Ricans.

three were made by the same G3 male: one in *la razón* (the reason) and the other two in the word *puertorriqueños* (Puerto Ricans). His first mention of *puertorriqueños* was realized with a velar /r̃/, which we think may have been a performative use of this variant to represent what he considered a prototypical Puerto Rican accent. But almost half a minute later, the same word was realized with a non-velar /r̃/; and approximately 4.5 minutes later, *puertorriqueños* was again produced with a velar /r̃/. The variation suggests that this speaker used both pronunciations for this lexeme. Given this low number of tokens, we did not analyze Mexicans' production of /r̃/ any further.

Among all 24 Puerto Rican speakers, velar /r̃/ was produced at a rate of 16.2%, which was similar to the 15.8% rate found by Valentín-Márquez (2007) in Cabo Rojo. But again, group averages obscure individual variation, shown in Figure 7.4.

Figure 7.4 shows that 13 speakers did not produce any tokens of velarized /r̃/ (0%), seven speakers produced it at rates between 1% and 29%; three speakers did so between 40% and 89%; and one speaker weakened at a rate of 90%.

Finally, looking at the MexiRicans, they produced a total of 670 tokens of /r̃/. Of these, overall 12 (1.8%) were velarized. Table 7.6 shows the use of /r̃/ variants among the MexiRicans, averaged across speakers.

Table 7.6. VELARIZATION OF /R/, MEXIRICANS.

Group	Tokens (*n*)	Average rates across speakers per group	
		r-rr avg % (SD)	**r-velar** avg % (SD)
MexiRicans (*n* = 45)	670	97.9 (7.9)	2.1 (7.9)

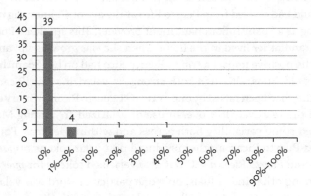

Figure 7.5. Rates of velarized /r̄/ among MexiRicans.

The MexiRican speakers velarized /r̄/ at an average rate of 2.1%. Thus, similar to their /s/ usage, their /r̄/ velarization looks more like that of the Mexican group than like the Puerto Rican group. This finding constitutes another difference between the Puerto Rican and MexiRican groups, even those with a Puerto Rican mother: what was used variably among Puerto Rican speakers showed nearly categorical lack of use among MexiRicans. Figure 7.5 shows the number of MexiRican speakers who produced velar /r̄/ at different rates.

Only two MexiRican individuals, both G3s with Puerto Rican mothers, produced velarized /r̄/ at rates above 20%. We looked at their transcripts and background information for potential explanations. Both grew up in or very near the Puerto Rican neighborhood of Humboldt Park. One of these participants was raised primarily by her Puerto Rican grandparents (which makes her profile more like that of a G2 speaker). She noted the strong Puerto Rican influence of her upbringing:

> Mis abuelos me criaron, so ellos me criaron bien tradicional. Y como me crié con mi familia puertorriqueña, pues eso, tengo más influencia con la cultura puertorriqueña. (#16, G3 MexiRican female)

PHONOLOGY [219]

My grandparents raised me, so they raised me very traditionally. And since I was raised with my Puerto Rican family, well that, I have more influence with the Puerto Rican culture.

She had several notable Puerto Rican phonological features, including weakened /s/ at a rate of 98.3%; lateralized coda /ɾ/ (*sentir* > *sentil*, to feel; *fuerte* > *fuelte*, strong), and velarized word-final /n/ (*sin* > *siŋ*). She was also aware that because she was raised by her Puerto Rican grandfather with whom she is still connected, her Spanish sounds more Puerto Rican. The other speaker was categorized as G3 because her Mexican father was G2, but her Puerto Rican mother was in fact G1 and had arrived from Puerto Rico at the age of 11 knowing no English, thus serving as a Spanish-dominant input provider. This speaker's Puerto Rican maternal grandfather lived in the home when she was growing up, and she also described the positive impact a trip to Puerto Rico had on her Spanish when she was 8 years old. Thus, although both strong /r̄/-velarizing MexiRican speakers were G3s, they had been raised by one or two G1 Puerto Rican primary caregivers.

Despite the relatively low overall use of velarized /r̄/ among MexiRicans, we observed some variability both across and within speakers. For example, a G3 with a Puerto Rican mother produced non-velar tokens of *puertorriqueños* (*n* = 5) and *Puerto Rico* (*n* = 1) but also velarized tokens for *puertorriqueño* (*n* = 2). Among other individuals, only one particular word was velarized. For example, one speaker produced all non-velar tokens with the exception of the word *carro* (car), which was velarized.

The role of the mother's regional group among MexiRicans is addressed quantitatively for /r̄/ in Figure 7.6.

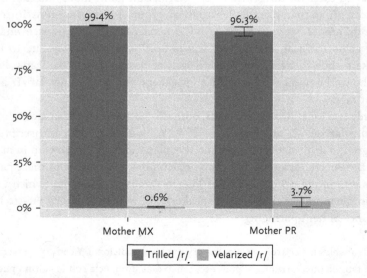

Figure 7.6. MexiRican /r̄/ by mother.

[220] *Spanish in Chicago*

Similar to what we found with /s/, MexiRicans with a Puerto Rican mother were more likely to produce velarized /r̄/ than those with a Mexican mother. A GEE analysis of mother shows marginal significance when this factor is considered alone (p = .073). Parameter estimates give a 4.5 times increase in odds of producing a velarized /r̄/ when the mother is Puerto Rican, Exp(B) = 4.548. Although this does not reach significance, the fact that 9 of 12 velar /r̄/ tokens (75% of them) were produced by MexiRicans with a Puerto Rican mother suggests an influence of the mother's dialect. Our sample may not be large enough to see a statistical effect. It is important to consider other possible contributing factors in addition to the mother's dialect, such as exposure to Puerto Rican Spanish within the community and other social networks, although it is also true that Chicago-raised peers tend to speak with each other in English (Potowski 2004).

Regional Origin and Generation

We now ask whether regional origin and generation are correlated with /s/ and /r̄/ realizations. We start with /s/. Figure 7.7 shows only a very small difference between the three generations of Mexican speakers.

All three generations of Mexican speakers showed maintenance of /s/ at nearly 80% or above, but there is a slight increase in the group average from 88.5% among G1 to more than 91% among G2 and G3. These results were not significant (p = .201). Thus, as we predicted, there was no trend of Mexicans

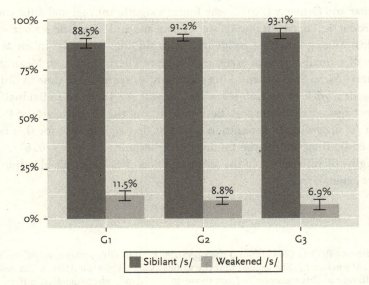

Figure 7.7. Mexican /s/ by generation.

PHONOLOGY [221]

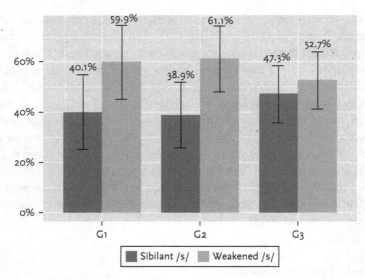

Figure 7.8. Puerto Rican /s/ by generation.

accommodating to Puerto Ricans on these features across generations. Counter to our prediction, however, the Puerto Rican groups also showed very little variation across generations (Figure 7.8).

G1 and G2 speakers showed higher rates of weakening (around 60%) compared with the G3 group (closer to 50%). This is similar to findings in New York City by Lamboy (2004), where first-generation male Puerto Ricans retained /s/ more than second-generation females and males, and to those by Erker and Otheguy (2016), who found a significant regional difference in /s/ production between immigrant Caribbeans and Mainlanders but which was lost among longtime residents.[10] Our findings might be taken as evidence of a small degree of accommodation of Puerto Ricans to Mexican /s/ as Puerto Rican Spanish-speaking communities spend more time in Chicago interacting with Mexicans. However, we will see that the individual data suggest against this interpretation. In addition, the GEE analysis of Puerto Rican /s/ according to generation does not find significance for this factor (p = .854). Thus, unlike the findings of Erker and Otheguy (2016), region of origin still differentiated the /s/ production of Chicago-raised individuals across generations.

---

10. Ramos-Pellicia (2012) found the opposite trend in Ohio, where only the G3s favored /s/ weakening. She argued that the values assigned to aspiration versus deletion are different in this community from those on the island, where deletion is more stigmatized than aspiration.

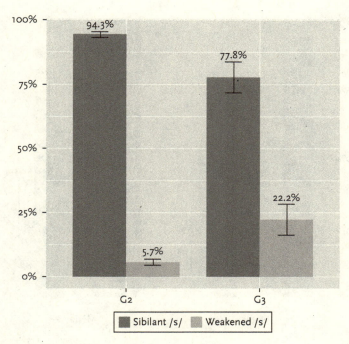

Figure 7.9. MexiRican /s/ by generation.

Variants of /s/ by Generation, MexiRicans

Figure 7.9 shows the MexiRicans' use of the two /s/ variants by generation, which revealed a difference.

On average, the 26 speakers in G3 weakened /s/ considerably more than the 19 speakers in G2, which is similar to the findings of Ramos-Pellicia (2012) among Puerto Ricans, who found that first- and second-generation speakers preferred /s/ retention while the third-generation speakers were more likely to delete /s/. A GEE analysis of generation reveals significance for this factor ($p < .001$), with parameter estimates showing nearly five times greater odds of /s/ weakening for the G3 group compared with the G2 group, $\text{Exp}(B) = 4.790$. However, as was the case for Puerto Ricans, we are disinclined to believe that this is due to intergenerational accommodation to Mexicans, because the high rate of weakening appears to be due to five G3 speakers who weakened at 60% or above, while the remaining 21 G3 speakers displayed lower rates of weakening similar to the G2 speakers.

When we examine /s/ behavior by generation and mother combined, we once again see the higher rate of /s/ weakening of the G3 group (Figure 7.10).

Figure 7.10 shows that the highest rate of /s/ weakening was among those G3s with a Puerto Rican mother. That is, there initially appeared to

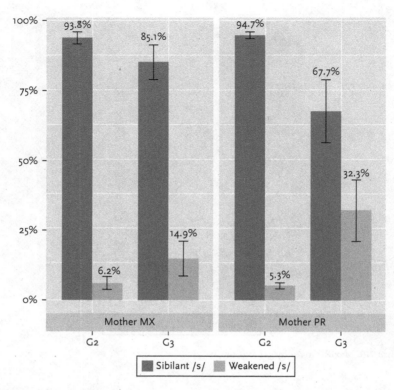

Figure 7.10. MexiRican /s/ by generation and mother's ethnolinguistic group.

be a "mother effect" among the G3 speakers. Nonetheless, a GEE analysis reveals significant differences for the main effect of generation ($p < .001$) but not for that of mother ($p = .303$); the interaction between factors generation and mother is also not significant ($p = .146$). This suggests that the apparent "mother effect" may be due to simple intragroup variation, as noted below.

Although the overall rates of /s/ weakening among G2 MexiRican speakers was fairly low (all below 20%), it is worth describing some of the individual variation. Among the G2 speakers with a Puerto Rican mother, eight of them weakened at a rate of 5% or less, two weakened between 7% and 9%, and one weakened at a rate of 15%. Among the G2 speakers with a Mexican mother, six weakened /s/ at a rate of 0% to 6%, and the other two weakened at a rate of between 14% and 17%. It is among the more frequently weakening G3 speakers that a more detailed examination is warranted of /s/-weakening behavior, as shown in Figure 7.11.

We see in Figure 7.11 that the average /s/-weakening rate for G3 speakers with a Mexican mother was 14.9%. Figure 7.11 shows that 13 of these 15 speakers weakened at a rate of less than 20%. However, although Figure 7.10 also showed the average weakening rate for the 11 G3 speakers with a Puerto Rican

[224] *Spanish in Chicago*

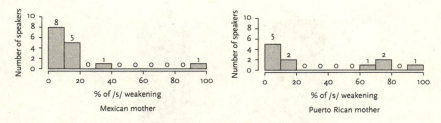

Figure 7.11. Rates of /s/ weakening, G3 MexiRicans (number of individuals).

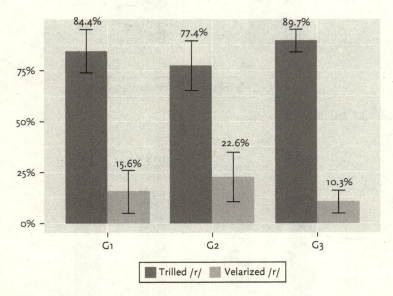

Figure 7.12. Puerto Rican /r̄/ by generation.

mother at 32.2%, the majority of them weakened at a rate of 10% to 19% or below, as appears in Figure 7.11. In other words, the behavior of just four "Puerto Rican mother" G3 speakers was responsible for raising the group average.

Now we move on to /r̄/ by generation. As we noted earlier, the Mexican speakers did not produce enough tokens for an analysis, so Figure 7.12 shows the tokens produced by Puerto Ricans.

Average rates of velar /r̄/ are at or above 15% for G1 and G2; the G3 group shows a drop to 10.3%. However, the differences between G groups were not significant ($p = .582$).

As for MexiRicans, examining /r̄/ behavior by generation reveals a similar pattern to that seen with /s/, which is displayed visually in Figure 7.13.

Figure 7.13 shows that G3 MexiRicans velarized /r̄/ at a low average rate of 3.7%. A statistical analysis for generation as a factor was not performed because there were no instances of velar /r̄/ within the G2 group.

PHONOLOGY [225]

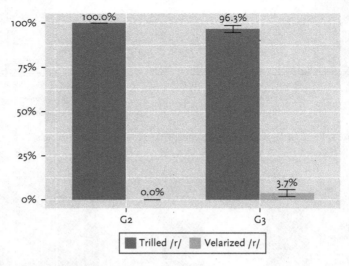

Figure 7.13. MexiRican /r̄/ by generation.

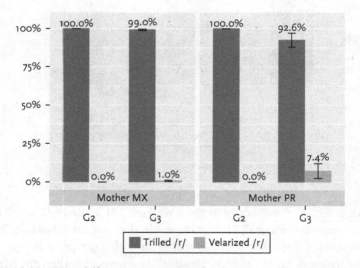

Figure 7.14. MexiRican /r̄/ by generation and mother (average across speakers).

The interaction of generation and mother can be observed in Figure 7.14.

Figure 7.14 shows that it was the G3 speakers with a Puerto Rican mother who showed the most use of velar /r̄/. A GEE analysis including both generation and mother was not conducted since there were no instances of velarization among G2 speakers. However, a GEE analysis of just the G3 group was conducted with mother as a factor and found significance ($p = .032$) with around six times the odds of producing a velar /r̄/ when the mother was Puerto Rican, Exp(B) = 5.712.

Table 7.7. REGIONAL ORIGIN AND GENERATION.

	s-s			r-rr		
Group	**G1**	**G2**	**G3**	**G1**	**G2**	**G3**
Mexican	88.5%	91.2%	93.1%	98.7%	100%	94.0%
Puerto Rican	40.1%	38.9%	47.3%	84.4%	77.4%	89.7%
MexiRican	N/A	94.3%	77.8%	N/A	100%	96.3%

Before moving to interlocutor variety, Table 7.7 summarizes our results by regional origin and generation.

7.5. INTERLOCUTOR VARIETY

Having found no significant levels of accommodation at the generational group level, we turn now to the individual level. Was there variation in /s/ and /r̄/ realizations according to ingroup ("same") or outgroup ("different") status of the interlocutor? We saw in Table 7.3 that Mexicans produced sibilant /s/ an average of 90.9% of the time and weakened it in only 9.1% of the tokens (n = 135). Figure 7.15 shows that Mexican /s/ realizations did not vary much according to the interlocutor's dialect.

Mexicans employed high rates of sibilant /s/, with an average more than 90%. Individuals' rates of sibilant /s/ were always above 80% regardless of interlocutor. A GEE analysis for the factor interlocutor ("same" and "different") did not find significance (p = .637). Thus, we do not have evidence of accommodation on the part of Mexicans to this variable when speaking with Puerto Ricans; basically, Mexicans rarely weakened /s/ no matter if they were speaking with another Mexican or with a Puerto Rican.

It is among Puerto Ricans where we expected to find accommodation to Mexican alveolar /s/—that is, a greater use of this variant and less weakening when speaking with a Mexican interviewer. Recall that Puerto Ricans weakened /s/ at the average rate of 57.9% (Table 7.3) and that the majority of them (15 out of 24) weakened at rates more than 50% (Figure 7.1). Figure 7.16 shows Puerto Ricans' rates of weakening according to the variety of Spanish of their interlocutor.

Contrary to our predictions, Figure 7.16 shows that Puerto Rican /s/ did not vary according to whether the interviewer's Spanish was Puerto Rican ("same") or Mexican ("different"); it was close to 60% for both types of interlocutor. A GEE analysis showed that the dialect of interlocutors is not significant (p = .956). Thus, we found no evidence that Mexicans or Puerto Ricans as groups accommodated their /s/ behavior according to the dialect of their interlocutors.

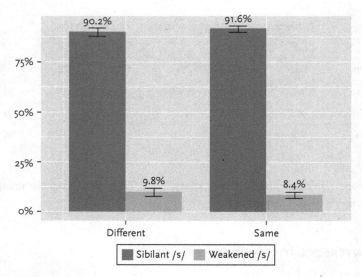

Figure 7.15. Mexican /s/ by interlocutor.

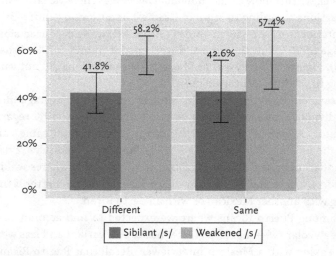

Figure 7.16. Puerto Rican /s/ by interlocutor.

Contrary to what we found with /s/, Figure 7.17 shows that for Puerto Ricans, there might have been an interlocutor effect for /ɾ/.

We see greater use of velarized /ɾ/ when Puerto Ricans were speaking with another Puerto Rican (28.7%) than when they spoke with a Mexican (8.6%). This approached but did not reach significance ($p = .055$), which may be due to the interspeaker variation described below. Yet the finding that /ɾ/ was velarized more frequently with other Puerto Ricans echoes previous claims that this variable is stigmatized and reserved for ingroup members.

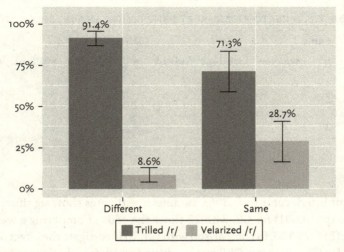

Figure 7.17. Puerto Rican /r̄/ by interlocutor.

Generation and Interlocutor

Given that we are seeking to understand whether speakers accommodate to outgroup interlocutors and whether /s/ behavior varies by generation, it would also make sense to ask whether accommodation according to speaker varies by generation. That is, were G3 Puerto Ricans more likely to use Mexican features with a Mexican interlocutor than G2 Puerto Ricans were? Unfortunately, we did not have enough speakers per cell to arrive at reliable conclusions, but we attempt to examine this question in Table 7.8 by putting speakers' behavior into the following groups:

- "Weaken" if 70% or more of the tokens were weakened.
- "Sibilant" if 70% or more of the tokens were sibilant.
- "Mixed" if the behavior was between 30% and 70%.

We chose a 70% cutoff point given that this percentage shows a predominance of the behavior and also includes the majority of our data set.

Although cell sizes are small, Table 7.8 shows no notable patterns of change with generation. What we see instead is considerable individual variation. In fact, two of the five Puerto Rican G3 speakers interviewed by Mexicans did not meet the 70% criterion: one produced sibilant /s/ 45.0% of the time, and another did so 39.5% of the time. Thus, the slight tendency seen in Figure 7.5 for G3 Puerto Ricans to weaken less frequently than G2 and G1 simply reflects individual tendencies of this small group of speakers. Nonetheless, a GEE analysis of Puerto Ricans' /s/ did find a main effect for generation ($p = .016$) and an interaction for interlocutor by generation ($p < .001$); no effect was

Table 7.8. PUERTO RICAN /S/ BY GENERATION AND INTERLOCUTOR.

	Same				Different			
	n	weaken	sibilant	mixed	n	weaken	sibilant	mixed
G1	4	2	2	0	4	3	1	0
G2	2	2	0	0	6	3	3	0
G3	3	1	2	0	5	2	1	2
Total	9	5	4	0	15	8	5	2

found for interlocutor ($p = .398$). Parameter estimates show significant odds increase ($p < 0.001$) for G2, with 23 times the odds of producing a weakened /s/, Exp(B) = 23.196, in comparison with G3. To investigate the effect of interlocutor for G2, a separate GEE was conducted which found 16 times increased odds of producing a weakened /s/ with the "same" interlocutor compared with "different" among G2 speakers, $p < 0.001$, Exp(B) = 16.021. However, recall that these findings are based on just two G2 speakers who showed greater than 70% weakening when speaking with an interlocutor of the same dialect; more data are needed to support this preliminary observation.

As we did for /s/, we now present data for /r̄/ according to generation and interlocutor combined. For this analysis, speakers were put into groups as follows:

- "Trilled" if 70% or more of the tokens were trilled.
- "Velar" if 70% or more of the tokens were velarized.
- "Mixed" if the velarized tokens were between 30% and 70%.

This summary is displayed in Table 7.9.

As was the case with /s/, we see a great deal of individual variation in /r̄/ production. This is particularly the case when Puerto Ricans spoke with Puerto Rican interlocutors, where we see three speakers with "mixed" or "velar" behavior. Among the individuals in these categories, the use of velar /r̄/ averaged 26.5% (ranging from 10.0 to 56.3). We must keep in mind that the number of tokens of /r̄/ is relatively small—averaging 14 per Puerto Rican speaker—making percentages less revealing than they were for /s/. Yet these patterns may nonetheless be indicative of accommodating behavior toward more prestigious /r̄/ when speaking with Mexicans.

A GEE analysis showed a main effect for interlocutor ($p = .035$) but no effect for generation ($p = .451$); the interaction of factors could not be analyzed because there were no instances of velarized /r̄/ among the "G1 different" group. The odds of producing a velar /r̄/ increased by nearly six times for

Table 7.9. PUERTO RICAN /R/ BY GENERATION AND INTERLOCUTOR.

	Same				Different			
	n	trilled	velar	mixed	n	trilled	velar	mixed
G1	4	3	1	0	4	4	0	0
G2	2	1	1	0	6	5	0	1
G3	3	2	0	1	5	5	0	0
Total	9	6	2	1	15	14	0	1

the "same" interlocutor, Exp(B) = 5.656, when compared with the "different" interlocutor.

It is important to note that although a given speaker may show a specific rate of velarization, individual variability may occur at the level of the lexeme. For example, a Puerto Rican G2 speaker with a 15.4% rate of velarization produced *agarró* (s/he grabbed) with a velarized /r̄/, followed less than 20 seconds later by a non-velar /r̄/ production of the same word. We also found that 41.8% of all tokens of /r̄/ produced by Puerto Rican speakers (n = 143 of 342) were contained in the word *puertorriqueño* (Puerto Rican) and its variants. However, the rate of velarization of all *puertorriqueño*-based words in the corpus was only 8.4% (n = 12 of 143), while that of words not related to *puertorriqueño* was more than two times higher (19.1%, n = 38 of 199).

7.6. CONNECTIONS BETWEEN /s/ AND /r̄/

Finally, we wondered about possible connections between /s/ and /r̄/: did speakers who reduced /s/ frequently also velarize /r̄/ frequently, and did those who rarely reduced /s/ also rarely velarize /r̄/? There are four possible patterns of combinations of these two variables:

Pattern 1: Weakened /s/ and velarized /r̄/, the most stigmatized (but "most Puerto Rican sounding") combination.

Pattern 2: Weakened /s/ and trilled variant of /r̄/, which might be considered typically Puerto Rican without being "too stigmatized."

Pattern 3: Sibilant /s/ and velarized /r̄/. We would not expect this combination, given that velar /r̄/ is more highly stigmatized than weakened /s/. Thus, a speaker who produced velar /r̄/ would also very likely produce weakened /s/.

Pattern 4: Sibilant /s/ and trilled variant of /r̄/, the most prestigious/"standard" combination.

We can visualize these relationships with /r̄/ on the y-axis and /s/ on the x-axis:

	---------/s/--------→
Pattern (2) Low use of /s/ High use of /r̄/	**Pattern (4)** High use of /s/ High use of /r̄/
Pattern (1) Low use of /s/ Low use of /r̄/	**Pattern (3)** High use of /s/ Low use of /r̄/

(↑ /r̄/)

Figure 7.18 displays a scatter diagram of all Puerto Rican speakers with one of three different shapes for each generational group (circle for G1, triangle for G2, and square for G3) according to their percentages of use of /s/ and of /r̄/. Quadrant lines appear at the 50% mark on both axes. For ease of reference, each of the four pattern numbers appears in a box within each quadrant toward the center of the figure.

Of the 24 Puerto Ricans, the largest group (*n* = 12) displayed pattern 2, low use of sibilant /s/ and high use of trilled /r̄/ variants, which arguably "sounds Puerto Rican" without being overly stigmatized. The second most common pattern was the most standard combination, pattern 4 (*n* = 9), which consists of high use of both sibilant /s/ and trilled /r̄/ variants, followed by the least common configuration, pattern 1 (*n* = 3), low use of both sibilant /s/ and trilled /r̄/ variants, the most stigmatized pattern. As predicted, there were

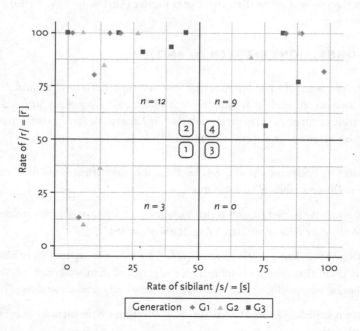

Figure 7.18. Puerto Rican percentages of /s/ and /r̄/ (*n* = 24).

[232] *Spanish in Chicago*

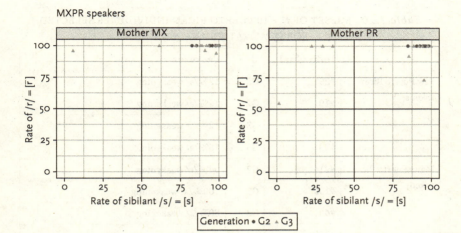

Figure 7.19. MexiRican percentages of /s/ and /r̃/, by generation and mother.

no speakers who displayed pattern 3, in which highly stigmatized velar /r̃/ is more frequent than weakened /s/. To our knowledge, this has been the first attempt to correlate /s/ and /r̃/ behavior among Puerto Rican Spanish speakers on the island or in the continental U.S. and echoes prior findings (López-Morales, 2003; Medina-Rivera, 1999) that velar /r̃/ is highly stigmatized and further suggests that it is more stigmatized than weakened /s/.

Given these interesting patterns, we did a similar analysis for the MexiRican speakers separated by mother's regional origin group. This is shown in Figure 7.19.

Unlike the Puerto Ricans, the majority of whom ($n = 12$) were in pattern 2, the majority of MexiRicans clustered in pattern 4, realizing /s/ and /r̃/ in their standard variants. In addition, nearly all the instances of patterns other than pattern 4 were produced by those with a Puerto Rican mother (except for one speaker, a G3 in the top-left quadrant of the "Mexican mother" graph) and by third-generation speakers. This could be due to the influence of the Mexican side of the family. Notably, there were no speakers in pattern 1, while there were $n = 3$ Puerto Ricans who exhibited this pattern.

7.7. QUALITATIVE EXPLORATIONS OF PUERTO RICAN VARIATION

We have seen that among the 24 Puerto Rican speakers analyzed in this study, there was a good deal of variation in proportions of /s/ weakening and /r̃/ velarization. Specifically, looking back at Figure 7.1, we saw that $n = 7$ individuals had relatively low levels of /s/ weakening (less than 20%), while $n = 11$ individuals were at the other end of the scale at 80% or greater /s/ weakening.

PHONOLOGY   [233]

Table 7.10. SUBSET OF *N* = 10 PUERTO RICAN INDIVIDUALS SELECTED FOR QUALITATIVE ANALYSIS.

	Individual	**G**	**Features**
Few Puerto Rican tokens	#39	G2	12% /s/ weakening
	#19	G2	12% /s/ weakening
	#90	G3	12% /s/ weakening
	#23	G3	18% /s/ weakening
Many Puerto Rican tokens	#21	G2	94% /s/ weakening
	#100	G3	100% /s/ weakening
	#4	G3	80% /s/ weakening
	#31	G3	44% /r̄/ velarization
	#18	G2	88% /s/ weakening and 64% /r̄/ velarization
	#54	G2	94% /s/ weakening and 10% /r̄/ velarization

As for /r̄/ velarization, we saw in Figure 7.7 that 75% of the speakers (*n* = 18) did *not* velarize /r̄/ more than 20% of the time but that *n* = 3 individuals did velarize it in 60% or more of their tokens. Finally, we saw in Figure 7.10 that *n* = 3 individuals whose /s/ weakening and /r̄/ velarization placed them in pattern 1, the "most Puerto Rican sounding."

This section aims to understand why some Chicago-raised Puerto Ricans might have more strongly Puerto Rican–marked phonological systems than other Chicago-raised Puerto Ricans. We do not examine any G1 speakers in this section because being raised on the island implies a concomitant level of Spanish input and normative pressures on its development. We are interested here in the development of these features among Chicago-raised speakers belonging to G2 and G3. We have chosen the 10 individuals displayed in Table 7.10 based on either their low or high percentage of /s/ weakening and /r̄/ velarization.

Clearly, every individual's life experiences differ, and a host of factors influence their linguistic repertoire. Most important for U.S.-raised Spanish speakers is the input they received as children from the people around them. However, we also note that not all G1s or all homeland speakers were uniform in their production of these features. A close reading of the interview transcripts allows us to speculate about factors that may help us account for some of the wide variation found in /s/ weakening and /r̄/ velarization among G2 and G3 Puerto Ricans. Two factors that seem relevant are social networks and attitudes. Considering first the four speakers with low rates of /s/ weakening (between 12% and 18%), we note that the two G2 speakers mentioned that they had a lot of contact with Mexicans. For example, one of them noted that most of the people in her neighborhood were Mexican, while the other pointed out that her partner was Mexican and she had lived among Mexicans for a long time:

> El papá de los niños es mexicano. También aquí en el barrio hay muchos latinos y han venido mucho los mexicanos de, del sur para acá. Y me he criado alrededor de todos ellos. (#39, G2 Puerto Rican female)

> The kids' dad is Mexican. Also here in the neighborhood there are lots of Latinos and lots of Mexicans have come here from, from the south. I've been raised around all of them.

Attitudes toward the different varieties of Spanish might also influence speakers' phonological realizations. When asked if she spoke Spanish to her friends, one of the G2 Puerto Ricans with a very low /s/-weakening pattern noted that she was embarrassed about her Spanish:

> I get embarrassed porque muchos de mis amigos saben español más mejor que yo y entonces, yo sé cómo, cómo decir cosas y yo lo entiendo cuando ellos lo hablan pero, me da, I'm just embarrassed. (#90, G3 Puerto Rican female)

> I get embarrassed because lots of my friends know Spanish better than me and so, I know how, how to say things and I understand it when they speak it but, it gives me, I'm just embarrassed.

She felt that Mexicans spoke more "proper" Spanish and also more frequently maintained it intergenerationally compared with Puerto Ricans:

> Creo que los mexicanos lo, lo hablan más, no sé si es mejor o es more proper y los puertorriqueños no lo hacen el mismo. Creo que it has a lot to do with generation too, like your older generations probably speak a lot more proper Spanish but it seems that los jóvenes que son puertorriqueños no hablan español mucho y los mexicanos que son jóvenes sí todavía lo están hablando y no sé por qué pero por eso no creo que los jóvenes que son puertorriqueños lo pueden hablar. Los mexicanos que son, que son jóvenes lo hablan mejor que los puertorriqueños. (#90, G3 Puerto Rican female)

> I think Mexicans, they speak it more, I don't know if it's better or it's more proper and Puerto Ricans don't do it the same. I think it has a lot to do with generation too, like your older generations probably speak a lot more proper Spanish but it seems that young people who are Puerto Rican don't speak very much Spanish and Mexicans who are young are still speaking it and I don't know why but because of that I don't think young people who are Puerto Rican can speak it. Mexicans who are, who are young speak it better than the Puerto Ricans.

This speaker lived in a majority Mexican area, so her surroundings and her linguistic insecurity concerning her own speech variety might have influenced her to model her Spanish on the Mexican variety she admired. Thus, she echoed linguistic ideologies presented in Chapter 1.

In terms of the six Puerto Ricans with high rates of /s/ weakening and /r/ velarization—speakers in the second half of Table 7.10—again, social networks and living in contexts where Puerto Rican features may be more prominent might also impact these realizations. The G3 participant with 100% /s/ weakening was born in Chicago but spent two years of high school in Puerto Rico. She was aware that she had a strong Puerto Rican accent:

> Usualmente este, nosotros los puertorriqueños no pronunciamos mucho la "r" la "s" y especialmente como un ejemplo, en el trabajo si estoy hablando, vamos a suponer con una mexicana, hablo demasiado rápido y me dice, "Mira, debes de hablar más despacio." Y allí se me cambia el acento. (#100, G3 Puerto Rican female)

> Usually, us Puerto Ricans don't pronounce "r" and "s" very much in words and especially as an example, at work if I'm talking, let's say with a Mexican woman, I speak too fast and she'll say to me, "Look, you should speak slower." And that's where my accent changes.

Unlike the example of speaker #90, speaker #100 was proud of her Puerto Rican accent. When asked if she thought one variety of Spanish was better than any other variety, she quickly responded that she preferred the Puerto Rican variety:

> No. Bueno, yo siempre voy a pensar que el mío es mejor. [Interviewer ¿Por qué?] Y es más lindo, porque es algo diferente. (#100, G3 Puerto Rican female)

> No. Well, I'm always going to think mine is better. [Interviewer: Why?] And it's prettier, because it's something different.

Thus, social networks, geographical context, and language attitudes may explain some of the variation in proportions of /s/ weakening and of /r̄/ velarization in our corpus.

7.8. SUMMARY AND CONCLUSIONS

The analyses in this chapter looked for evidence of accommodation in /s/ and /r̄/ realizations by first-, second-, and third-generation Mexican and Puerto Rican Spanish speakers in Chicago, as well as patterns of use of these two variables among MexiRicans who experienced intrafamilial dialect contact.

Overall, Mexicans did not show change in their use of either variable according to interlocutor or generation. Similarly, /s/ production of Chicago-raised Puerto Ricans—significantly different from that of Mexicans—did not change across generations or interlocutors. This seemingly contradicts the idea that weakened /s/ is stigmatized in Chicago, as was suggested by the fact presented in Chapter 1 that most speakers when criticizing Puerto Rican Spanish mentioned weakened coda /s/.

We did find tentative evidence of /r̄/ accommodation among Puerto Ricans: as a group, they used velar /r̄/ less frequently with Mexicans than they did with other Puerto Ricans. This might suggest that /r̄/ is a stigmatized variable reserved for ingroup interlocutors. However, this was based on the high velarization rates of just two speakers; more data are needed to reach firm conclusions, particularly with the same participant speaking with interviewers of different dialect backgrounds on separate occasions. We also found that social networks, geographical context, and language attitudes may underlie some phonological realizations among the 10 Puerto Rican speakers in Table 7.10 whose narratives we examined qualitatively.

Among MexiRicans, usage of /s/ and /r̄/ variants was more similar to Mexican patterns than to Puerto Rican patterns, perhaps due to the numerical predominance of Mexican Spanish in Chicago. Four out of the five MexiRican speakers who weakened /s/ at rates of 60% or higher were raised by Puerto Rican women, suggesting that having a Puerto Rican mother was necessary (but not sufficient) to develop a repertoire that produced this feature at these rates. Having a Puerto Rican mother was also related to greater use of velar /r̄/, as well as to combinations of /s/ and /r̄/ behavior that were outside of pattern 4 among G3 speakers.

Our primary suggestion for future research is to interview the same individuals twice, once with a Mexican interviewer and once with a Puerto Rican interviewer. The degree of familiarity with the interlocutor can also affect rates of some phonological realizations, so this variable should be accounted for as well. In addition, speakers' social networks should be explored, including neighborhood of residence and employment, schooling, and friends, because those who interact more frequently with outgroup members may exhibit a higher frequency of outgroup features (Hirano, 2008; Otheguy & Zentella, 2012). We also want to examine MexiRican usage of /s/ and /r̄/ variants according to interlocutor and mother. However, in the present data set, only six of the 46 MexiRican speakers were interviewed by Puerto Ricans, so this question unfortunately could not be addressed. However, in their interviews, they talked about changing their Spanish features based on their interlocutors (see Potowski, 2016). Other phonological features may show interesting patterns, including the lateralization of coda /ɾ/ (*cantar* > *cantal*) (e.g., Valentín-Márquez 2007).

Finally, factors such as gender, age, and socioeconomic status need to be explored further, since they may also contribute to the variation observed.

Yet it is relevant to recall the lack of normative pressure on Spanish in the U.S.; individuals raised and schooled entirely in the U.S. experience little to no normative pressure on their Spanish, which may alter the distribution of these features across social groups from the distributions they tend to evidence in Spanish-speaking societies. For example, we note that U.S. Supreme Court Justice Sonia Sotomayor is among the nation's intellectual elite, and her spoken and written English reflect this prestige. But her Spanish, as a G2 raised in the Bronx, New York, contains many features such as velarized /r/ and lambdacized /l/ that are stigmatized in Puerto Rico and elsewhere.[11] That is, on the U.S. mainland, Spanish features most frequently do not respond to formal education (which takes place in English) or to socioeconomic status. Thus, age, gender, and socioeconomic status may be less relevant to U.S. Spanish than they are in countries where Spanish is the language of wider society.

APPENDIX A
TOKENS OF WEAKENED /S/ AMONG MEXICAN SPEAKERS (*N* = 135)

Comparisons	Analysis, examples
By word	Tokens of 3 or more: *los* (n = 14), *muchos/as* (n = 7), *entonces* (n = 6), *es* (n = 5), *nos* (n = 4), *pues* (n = 3), *mis* (n = 3), *ellos* (n = 3).
By word context	Word-final, followed by consonant (n = 106, 78.5%); word-internal, before a consonant (n = 22, 16.3%), e.g., *mismo/a/os/as* (n = 7), *estar* (*está/n, estaba*) (n = 5), *estados* (*Estados Unidos*) (n = 3), other words (n = 7); word-final, before a pause (n = 7, 5.2%), e.g., *años, entonces, escuelas, frecuentamos, idiomas, latinos, más*.
By part of speech	Nouns (n = 27, 25.5%), verbs (n = 15, 14.2%), modifiers (quantifiers and adjectives) (n = 18, 17%), articles (n = 15, 14.2%), personal pronouns (n = 10, 9.4%), possessive pronouns (n = 8, 7.5%), other (n = 12, 11.3%).
By voicing and context	Word-final, followed by a voiced consonant (n = 81, 76.4%); word-internal, followed by a voiceless consonant (n = 15, 68.2%).

11. To hear an example, readers can search YouTube for her interview with Jorge Ramos in Spanish; the first few minutes will suffice.

Comparisons	Analysis, examples
By manner	Nasal (n = 31, 23.0%), approximant (n = 25, 18.5%), lateral (n = 21, 15.6%), fricative (n = 6, 4.4%).
By stress type	Penultimate stress (n = 67, 49.6%), monosyllabic words (n = 33, 24.4%), antepenultimate (n = 5, 3.7%), final stress (n = 1, 0.7%).
By position in relation to stress	Post-tonic position (n = 65, 48.1%), tonic position (n = 34, 25.2%), two syllables after the tonic syllable (n = 5, 3.7%), pretonic syllable (n = 2, 1.5%).

CHAPTER 8
Factors Underlying Spanish Development

8.1. INTRODUCTION

Chapters 3 through 7 explored several linguistic features produced by three generations and three regional origin groups of Spanish speakers in Chicago during hour-long sociolinguistic interviews. A main finding was that proficiency in Spanish, as measured according to the criteria put forth in Chapter 2, was connected to four of the linguistic variables studied: lexicon, discourse markers, codeswitching, and mood.[1] Specifically, we found that higher Spanish proficiency was more strongly correlated than generation with the following:

- Overall lexical familiarity score.
- Greater use of *entonces* relative to *so*.
- Lower percentage of English words and two-or-more-word codeswitches.
- Greater use of the subjunctive in obligatory and optional contexts.

Yet Spanish proficiency is more than a bundle of grammatical and lexical features. Proficiency in a language represents having participated in numerous conversations over many years, bonding with others, and expressing and reflecting cultural connections. Thus, Chapters 3–7 explored some of the "what" of Chicago Spanish, and this chapter explores the "how" behind it. Under what conditions did these individuals acquire Spanish, use it in their lives, and transmit it to their children (or not)? We are motivated here

---

1. No connection was explored between proficiency and phonological realizations.

Spanish in Chicago. Kim Potowski and Lourdes Torres, Oxford University Press. © Oxford University Press 2023.
DOI: 10.1093/oso/9780199326143.003.0008

by what Fishman (1972) called the sociology of language, which argues that we must pay attention to the social histories and geographies of speakers within their families and communities. Returning to our gemstone analogy, this chapter seeks to understand the underlying geological conditions that led to the formation of the gems that were the speech produced in our interviews.

Our interview protocol (Appendix C of Chapter 2) asked questions about topics related to Spanish learning and use. This chapter analyzes responses to these questions as well as other narratives from the 124 individuals in the CHISPA corpus. More than 15 years ago, García (2006) called attention to the shortage of ethnographic research on U.S. Spanish that bypasses traditional and static social categories such as generation (which is typical in variationist work) in favor of unearthing other less obvious categories or explanations. Studies by Guardado (2009), Mendoza-Denton (2008), and Schecter and Bayley (2002) are examples of this change in focus. While ours was not an ethnographic study, this portion of the monograph is qualitative in nature as we attempt to shed light on the factors that underlie Spanish use and intergenerational transmission among our Chicago participants. It also helps us move away from what could be called a generationally essentialist framework that relies on generation as a heuristic. While a useful concept in broad terms, particularly since we are examining intergenerational shift, generational group sometimes masks the range of linguistic experiences and outcomes among speakers of Spanish, often even within the same household. We first saw this in Chapter 2, specifically in Figure 2.1, which showed a series of dots representing the proficiency ratings of each individual in all three generational groups. This is why we presented our analyses in Chapters 3–6 according to both generational group and Spanish proficiency level, always finding that the latter was more closely tied to linguistic features (with the exception of outgroup lexicon, which was correlated with generation).

The present chapter explores the range of proficiency levels within the Chicago Spanish corpus and what factors seemed to underlie its development. We use proficiency as an imperfect but practical way to measure intergenerational Spanish-language maintenance. There is not a one-to-one relationship between language use and proficiency (Pease-Álvarez et al., 1996), and we understand that proficiency can change rather substantially across the life span. However, it seems obvious that without proficiency in a language, intergenerational transmission in that language is highly unlikely. We describe past studies of minority-language transmission before presenting the five factors that stood out most strongly in our analyses of the CHISPA interviews. We conclude with brief descriptions of the conditions that seemed related to the development of Spanish proficiency levels that were considerably higher or lower than the generational group average.

8.2. INTERGENERATIONAL SPANISH TRANSMISSION AND LOSS IN THE U.S.

The intergenerational transmission of a language from parents to children, with the subsequent use of that language in society, is common throughout the world. It only becomes remarkable when it is threatened because of the possibility of shift to another language as the primary means of communication. There are many interlaced factors contributing to language shift, and separating them into neat categories is not possible. Language shift must also be understood at both the group level and the individual level (where it is commonly referred to as language loss), because it is through individuals' speech behavior that a language is either maintained or lost in a family and in broader society. Our analysis has at its core the tenet emphasized by Fishman (1991) that language maintenance must involve intergenerational transmission of the language, that is, it must be passed on from parents to children over successive generations. If intergenerational transmission of a language ceases, it can be said that the speakers have shifted to another language.

To understand aspects of minority-language shift, it is helpful to first briefly think about multilingual situations in which shift does *not* occur. Multiple languages typically coexist due to the voluntary and involuntary migration of people and/or borders. In many multilingual nations, there is one dominant language used in wider society, while non-dominant languages coexist in a state of relatively stable multilingualism. This can happen in several ways. There can be monolingual individuals of different languages, such as monolingual French speakers and monolingual German speakers who live in Switzerland or French speakers and English speakers residing in Quebec. This is often referred to as societal bilingualism with individual monolingualism. A different situation is one with a number of bilingual individuals in a nation-state, such as Quechua-Spanish bilinguals in Peru, Hindi-English bilinguals in India, Basque-Spanish and Catalan-Spanish speakers in Spain, or multilingual individuals who speak Igbo, Hausa, English, and/or Yoruba in Nigeria. This situation is known as societal combined with individual bilingualism. In both of these situations, none of the languages is at strong risk of being lost.

A third situation, however, usually results in language shift, and its description applies to Spanish in the U.S. The pattern proceeds as follows. Adolescent or adult immigrants arrive in a country monolingual in their home language. Their children, either born in or brought very young to the new country, usually become bilingual in the home language and the societal language, which is the language in which they are schooled. Their own children—the grandchildren of the original immigrants—are frequently monolingual in the societal language, having lost all but perhaps some receptive skills in the heritage language. This pattern has been widely attested in immigrant communities around the world and has happened to virtually all languages in the U.S.[2] However, even when a language seems headed toward this fate, there are interesting outcomes one can study at various points on the way. This is what practically all studies of Spanish in the U.S. are engaged in documenting: stages of language loss, which in our color analogy from Chapter 1 is represented by the different shades of purple during the transition of blue (Spanish) to red (English). As the second most common language in the U.S., spoken by more than 41 million people, Spanish might be thought to be an exception to the pattern of shift just documented. However, quantitative studies based on the Census and large-scale language-use surveys, as well as more in-depth qualitative studies, conclude that Spanish is following a pattern of intergenerational loss, even if at a slower rate than other languages (Rumbaut et al., 2006; see Escobar & Potowski, 2015, for a review). Carreira (2013), applying a framework called Capacity, Opportunity, and Desire (COD), concluded that declining immigration, a negative climate for Spanish from the mainstream, and low rates of intergenerational transmission make the long-term sustainability of Spanish doubtful. On the other hand, a few studies find that Spanish is maintained in certain favorable contexts. These include locations with a critical mass of Spanish speakers, a steady migration stream, and a lot of transnational engagement (Linton, 2004; Linton and Jimenez, 2009; Smith, 2006). For example, many G3s develop high levels of proficiency in Spanish in communities along the border with Mexico, leading Rivera-Mills and Villa (2009) to propose a model that takes into consideration some of the circumstances that make Spanish unlike other European languages that follow a three-generation language-shift model in the U.S.

Fewer studies have examined intra-Latino differences of Spanish use. Tran (2010) looked at language proficiency data for Mexicans, Colombians, Dominicans, Cubans, Nicaraguans, and other Central and South Americans, finding that Mexicans reported the highest level of Spanish proficiency (and also had the lowest proficiency in English). Portes and Hao (1998) and Arriagada (2005) also found that Mexican American second-generation speakers tend to retain Spanish better than other Latino groups and use Spanish more frequently in the home. These studies tend to argue that the relatively high proficiency and language maintenance among Mexicans is partially due to the group's large size, which increases the opportunity for Spanish use and retention among speakers. We reported in Chapter 2 that Mexicans had higher proficiency than Puerto Ricans in all three generational groups, although the difference did not reach statistical significance. In this chapter, we look for possible differences between the language patterns of these groups.

---

2. Yiddish spoken by Hasidic Jewish communities and Pennsylvania Dutch spoken by Amish/Mennonite communities are often cited as exceptions. Some argue that Spanish in New Mexico constitutes a similar exception (Villa & Rivera-Mills, 2009).

Some basic tenets of language acquisition are key to understanding the variable outcomes of minority-language acquisition. We know that language proficiency is driven by *input*. Input is defined as language that a person hears that is meant to convey a message (Lee & VanPatten, 2003, p. 16). A critical mass of input is required for a person to develop a linguistic system in that language. Lee and VanPatten liken input to the gas that we must put in a car in order to make it go. If we are not exposed to input in a particular language, it is impossible for us to acquire it. Although input is necessary, it is not sufficient to develop productive proficiency; *output*, or producing language, is also required (to date, no quantifications have been specified regarding the amounts or the proportions of input and output necessary to acquire a language to varying degrees of proficiency). People raised monolingually are exposed to both the quantity and the quality of input, as well as the need to produce output, that are necessary to develop proficiency in their language. That is, normally developing monolingual children are unable to *not* learn the language that their parents speak to them. Our G1 speakers arrived in the U.S. having done just that in Spanish. But their G2 children, raised in the U.S. where English dominates, end up with varying proficiency levels in Spanish based on the quantity and quality of input in Spanish they received throughout their lives, as well as the need to produce spoken output in Spanish. As noted by Silva-Corvalán (2014, p. 2), the question of what constitutes "a critical mass" in bilingual first language acquisition has not been very well explored." It is with minority languages that attitudes can play a role in acquisition, to the degree that attitudes create or hamper opportunities for input and output. For example, in her work in Nebraska, Velázquez (2014) found that in households with two G1 parents, there were greater opportunities for transmission of Spanish when the mother perceived that learning it was important for their children for instrumental reasons (e.g., getting better jobs) and/or solidarity or cultural identity reasons (e.g., connecting with Mexican relatives, "being Mexican").

With this in mind, let us consider a hypothetical case of G1 parents who speak nothing but Spanish. Their first child, Isabel, grows up essentially in a monolingual household, acquiring only Spanish. When she begins kindergarten in a mainstream English-medium school, she begins spending half of her waking hours listening to and expected to produce English. Even if her parents continue to insist on Spanish input and output in the home, the proportion of Isabel's Spanish input and output has been significantly reduced. If the parents permit English output from her in the home (perhaps because they can more or less understand it), her daily proportion of Spanish output is reduced even further. It is also likely that her younger siblings will not have the benefit of the monolingual Spanish-speaking household that she herself experienced, because siblings often speak English to each other as they are acquiring it at school. The role of birth order in G3 children's Spanish input and acquisition was emphasized by Silva-Corvalán (2014, p. 6) in the study of her two grandsons:

> Overall, Nico was exposed to Spanish about one third of his waking time (30%); Brennan, the younger brother, less than one third (27%). From about age 4;0, exposure to and use of Spanish are further reduced for both children to at most a quarter of the time (20 to 25%). It is indeed remarkable that with such limited input the children are able to develop conversational proficiency in Spanish.

Although input drives the acquisition bus, where might attitudes come into play? Let's compare Isabel to another G2 girl named Marilu from a different family. Both Isabel and Marilu learned Spanish at home from their G1 parents and English at school. Isabel has positive attitudes toward Spanish because her family praises her for her abilities in the language, and she frequently interacts with her cousins in Puerto Rico (which also constitutes opportunities for Spanish input and output). If Marilu, on the other hand, does not enjoy strong relationships with cousins or any Spanish-speaking peers and/or her family makes fun of her Spanish abilities, she has fewer affective connections and little desire to use the language. Thus, attitudes can drive even young children to either seek out or avoid opportunities to use the Spanish they have acquired. Attitudes toward Spanish are also central for adults, who make decisions about which languages to use with their children and younger family members, about their choice of romantic partner (someone who dislikes Spanish would likely not date a recent immigrant with little English proficiency), and potentially about whether they pursue a job that requires regular use of Spanish.

Thus, in cases of bilingual acquisition when one of the languages is a minority/minoritized language such as Spanish in the U.S., its development can be precarious. To illustrate this point, we will make frequent reference to the following gardening analogy, which we propose based on copious research on minority languages in the U.S. and around the world. Spanish (like most non-English languages in the U.S.) is like a delicate plant. All plants require particular conditions of sunlight, water, and nutrients in order to grow. English, on the other hand, is like the kudzu plant, also known as the "foot-a-night vine" because of how quickly it grows. Once established in an area, kudzu competes with other trees and plants both for sunlight from above and for water and nutrients from the soil. The vines can directly damage existing trees by strangulation, or they may prevent the establishment of new trees and shrubs by blocking sunlight below the colonized canopy, crippling their ability to grow and reproduce. Heavy presence of kudzu can completely cover and even topple trees of almost any size and can nearly eliminate light availability within the forest canopy. In our analogy, English in the U.S. is like the kudzu plant because it is used in almost all mediums (school, entertainment, politics, etc.), and its presence is compounded by generally negative attitudes toward non-English languages among the 80% of the people in the country who report being monolingual in English. Thus, the longer amount of time Spanish is able to grow in a "kudzu-free" protected space for a child, the better the chance it will survive in an English-filled environment.

In support of this analogy, there is evidence from U.S-raised bilingual children that the later the onset of English, the stronger the Spanish they develop. For example, Anderson (1999) studied the Spanish of two sisters. When the family moved from Puerto Rico to the U.S. mainland, Beatriz was 6 years, 7 months old and had already developed some literacy skills in Spanish; Victoria was 4 years, 7 months and was beginning to learn to read in Spanish. The girls attended school in English, but the family spoke Spanish in the home. At the time of the first recording, Beatriz produced gender agreement 100% correctly, and two years later, she was producing 5.8% errors.[3] Similarly, Victoria produced almost no errors during the first recording. By the end of the data collection period, however, her production of gender errors had risen to 25%. These findings suggest that the loss of features of a minority language is more acute in children for whom English is acquired earlier, that is, whose Spanish was permitted less time to develop by itself. Similarly, Montrul and Potowski (2007) found that children who had begun learning English and Spanish simultaneously scored less accurately on a Spanish gender task than children who were sequential bilinguals who had remained monolingual in Spanish until beginning school in English at age 5. We will present data on the sequential versus simultaneous bilingualism of our participants, which, similarly to these studies, was found to be related to Spanish proficiency.

It is important to emphasize that language patterns are dynamic across the life span, so one cannot gauge with accuracy any future language use by observing child or adolescent language practices or those adults in the household at any given moment. For example, even among Spanish monolingual adults, the presence of English-speaking children in the home may affect the language that parents come to speak with their children. Also, while children may come to prefer English once they start going to school, this may change depending on their social network as they enter young adulthood. In this regard, the Language Policy Task Force (Pedraza, 1980, p. 29) refers to a "life cycle of language change": as a child enters adolescence, a dormant language may "reactivate" if the context changes, for example, if a young person is politicized, chooses a Spanish-dominant partner, is integrated into adult Spanish-speaking networks, or engages with more native speakers from the ancestral country.

---

3. "Error" here refers to a grammatical gender mismatch, such as *la casa rojo*.

We have reviewed here findings that input, attitudes, regional origin, and age of onset of English can all affect the development of a minority language. This chapter seeks to clarify some of the factors that influenced the acquisition of Spanish among our participants in Chicago, where it is a minority language vis-à-vis English. We first focus on those individuals in the CHISPA corpus whose Spanish proficiency level was within the average range for their generational group and then consider those whose proficiency was either a good deal stronger or weaker than the average of their generational group. While it is impossible to monitor closely and over the 18 years of childhood and adolescence the linguistic input and output of 124 individuals in order to report on it reliably,[4] in this chapter we explore what the participants said about different life circumstances that contributed to Spanish input and output for themselves and for their children.

8.3. PROFICIENCY INLIERS

The average proficiency levels for each generational group in the CHISPA corpus were reported in Chapter 2: the G1 average was 4.87, for G2 it was 3.76, and for G3 it was 2.77, and this decline was statistically significant. In this section, we explore the narratives of the 93 individuals (representing 75% of the entire CHISPA corpus) whose Spanish proficiency fell within the average range of their generational group, whom we call proficiency inliers (we are thus not using this word in a statistical sense). They are represented in the shaded cells in Table 8.1.

Of the proficiency inliers, 23 were G1 speakers. This was 100% of the G1 speakers in the CHISPA corpus, which was expected; although it is certainly possible for a person who immigrated from Mexico or Puerto Rico at age 12 or later[5] to decline in their Spanish proficiency, we were not surprised to find that this in fact had not happened to any of our G1 speakers. Questions about home language environment and schooling are not as relevant for these individuals for our purposes, because they were raised in Mexico or in Puerto Rico monolingually in Spanish. Instead, we focus on how they raised their own children, their thoughts about bilingual education, and their experiences as grandparents. We also report on their attitudes toward Spanish and their use of Spanish at work, because these factors help shape Chicago as a Spanish-speaking location. Next, 36 proficiency inliers belonged to the

---

4. Silva-Corvalán (2014) is a rare longitudinal study of the development of two bilingual children over a period of 6 years. The fact that they were her grandchildren contributed to the feasibility of gathering such copious childhood data.
5. This was the youngest age of arrival among our G1 participants (see Chapter 2, Appendix C).

Table 8.1. SPANISH PROFICIENCY INLIERS (SHADED CELLS, *N* = 93).

Proficiency	n, G1 avg 4.87	n, G2 avg 3.76	n, G3 avg 2.77
5	20	(11)	(2)
4	3	18	(10)
3	0	18	17
2	0	(3)	17
1	0	0	(5)
Total	23	36	34

G2 group (which constituted 72% of all G2 speakers). G2 inliers had their Spanish proficiency rated as level 4 or 3, close to the group average of 3.76. As for G3 speakers, there were 34 proficiency inliers in this group (67% of all G3s in the corpus). These individuals had a Spanish proficiency level rated at 3 or 2, close to the group average of 2.77. For both G2 and G3 speakers, questions about home language use and schooling are of primary concern here, as well as questions about attitudes, bilingual education, Spanish at work, and so on.

We read through the transcripts of all 93 proficiency inliers looking for content that suggested factors that led to their development of Spanish proficiency. We include quotes from participants, some edited for clarity and length but otherwise presented verbatim and including what some readers might consider infelicitous uses of Spanish. Five main themes emerged with consistent frequency, which will serve as the organization for the remainder of this chapter:

- Attitudes about Spanish
- Language use in the home and in social networks
- Order of acquisition
- Bilingual education
- Travel to Mexico or Puerto Rico

Some of these categories overlap. For example, having positive attitudes toward Spanish intersects with choosing to speak it with one's children. But a parent can hold positive attitudes toward Spanish yet use English with their children, and, as explained earlier, without input and output, the children will not acquire Spanish. In another example of overlapping themes, the order of acquisition of Spanish and English, specifically whether they were acquired simultaneously or if English was introduced when the child began school, directly impacts whether the child qualified for bilingual education services, as we will see.

Having established the principal tenets that (1) a critical mass of input and output is necessary for language proficiency to be developed, (2) Spanish in the U.S. is not afforded the same conditions for growth as English and in fact is often lost in favor of English, and (3) there are many factors that influence how and how much a person uses Spanish across their life span, we now turn to what our participants said about the importance of Spanish and how they learned and (in the case of parents and grandparents) transmitted it, with the goal of understanding more about the "how" behind the linguistic features explored in Chapters 3–6.

8.3.1. Attitudes about Spanish

This section describes attitudes our participants held about the importance of the Spanish language in general.[6] The section analyzes responses to the following questions:

- ¿Crees que los latinos en Estados Unidos deben mantener el español? ¿Por qué? ¿Quién tiene la responsabilidad de enseñarles el español a los niños? (Do you think Latinos in the U.S. should maintain the Spanish language? Whose responsibility is it to teach the children Spanish?)
- ¿Decían tus padres algo acerca de la importancia de algún idioma? ¿Qué decían?[7] (Did your parents say anything about the importance of a language? What did they say?)

Almost every single person said that they and their families thought Spanish was important and that Latinos should maintain it. This was often stated alongside the importance of English:

> Oh, sí, [decían] "tienes que hablar español y inglés, tienes que hablar los dos. No nomás el inglés y no se te vaya olvidar el español." Siempre mitad y mitad. (#86, G2 Puerto Rican male)

> Oh, yes, they would say "you have to speak Spanish and English, you have to speak them both. Not only English and don't forget how to speak Spanish." Always half and half.

---

6. We already described in Chapter 2 participants' opinions about different varieties of Spanish, specifically Mexican and Puerto Rican Spanish, and also whether they considered any particular variety "better" than others.
7. For this question, we report the responses of G2 and G3 individuals only, because G1 individuals were raised monolingually in Mexico or Puerto Rico.

Eh, decían que era importante saber de los dos. Porque yo soy latina y debo de saber español y . . . yo nací aquí en los Estados Unidos y debo de saber inglés. (#38, G2 Puerto Rican female)

Um, they would say that it was important to know both of them. Because I am Latina and I should know Spanish and . . . I was born here in the U.S. and should know English.

However, we continue to emphasize that believing Spanish is important is not sufficient to ensure its transmission. For example, this 19-year-old G3 Mexican male with a proficiency rated at level 2 said (with some difficulty, repeated verbatim here) that his mother insisted that Spanish was important:

Um mi . . . mi mamá tra . . . trajo . . . or, how do you say they tried? Trató, trata enseñar español para yo . . . pero es que aprendió español cuando tenía dos años, tres años y . . . y uh, sabio muy bien. Pero hasta tenía, hasta empezar escuela, I got uh, like when I started school, um, me olvidó cómo hablar en español. Y no más, es, no más habló en inglés. Pues mis padres nunca me, men dijo or me dijon . . . me dijeron que, de que español está más importante inglés o inglés está más importante español. So I just learned English. (#98, G3 Mexican G3 male)

Um my . . . my mother . . . tri- . . . or, how do you say they tried? She tried, tries to teach Spanish for I . . . but it's that [third person] learned Spanish when I was two or three, three and . . . and uh, I knew it very well. But until I was, until begin school, I got uh, like when I started school, um, I forgot how to speak Spanish. And I, it's, [third person] only spoke English now. Well my parents never told—said to me that, that Spanish was more important English, or English was more important Spanish. So I just learned English.

Another fairly uniform response across the corpus was that parents are the ones primarily responsible for their children learning Spanish, although some people added that schools should contribute as well:

Primero los padres para que, mm, sigan su idioma y su cultura y todo. Pero, también le corresponde a los maestros, porque . . . ah, porque la mitad del día los niños están en la escuela. So, si nada más lo aprenden en la casa y después van para la escuela [. . .] se le olvidaría. So, yo pienso que es de los dos, los maestros y los padres, pero primero los padres. (#19, G2 Puerto Rican female)

First parents for me for, mm, follow their language and their culture and everything. But it is also up to the teachers, because . . . ah, because half the day the children are in school. So, if they only learn it at home and then they go to school . . . they would forget it. So, I think it is both of them, the teachers and the parents, but first the parents.

A G1 Puerto Rican offered an anecdote from when he was in the U.S. Army and encountered Latinos who knew little Spanish as an argument that schools should support home language efforts. He insisted that if parents do not transmit enough Spanish at home ("grow" it, in our analogy), then Spanish classes in school may be too late: "Si el muchacho no sabe hablar español y cuando va y le ofrece la clase de español, no va a querer tomarla porque no quiere hacer el ridículo delante de los otros amigos siendo él de herencia latina." (If the child doesn't know how to speak Spanish and when you go and offer the Spanish class he doesn't want to take it because he doesn't want to seem stupid in front of his other friends because he is of Latino heritage).

No one reported having parents who said Spanish was unimportant, but several described that their immigrant parents' primary concern was their children's English development. It is understandable that an individual who faced challenges due to their own lack of English proficiency would do whatever they felt necessary to ensure that their children learned English quickly and well in order to avoid similar problems. This 24-year-old G3 MexiRican woman alluded to what her father experienced when he began school in the U.S. having been raised speaking only Spanish:

> Cuando yo nací ellos me dijeron que no podía hablar español, y mi papá dijo a mi abuela que no, que yo no podía aprender cómo hablar porque vas a hacer problemas en high school, en las escuelas porque él tenía problemas so. (#126, G3 MexiRican female)

> When I was born, they told me that I couldn't speak Spanish . . . my father told my grandmother not to, that I couldn't learn how to speak it because I was going to have problems in high school, in schools because he had problems so.

Similarly, this G3 Puerto Rican woman described her mother's experiences as an English as a second language (ESL) learner:

> Cuando ella vino para acá . . . ella no sabía nada en inglés, so you know los niños . . . ya hablaban en en inglés, se burlaban y ella estaba en ESL classes y cosas así. So creo que es un otro razón que cuando yo vine de escuela de preschool llorando que no entendía la idioma ella se sentía mal. So me empezó you know a enseñar inglés. (#8, G3 Puerto Rican female)

> When she came here . . . she didn't know any English, so you know the kids . . . they already spoke in English, they teased her and she was in ESL classes and things like that. So I think it's another reason that when I came

home from preschool crying that I couldn't understand the language she felt bad. So she started you know to teach me English.

The following G2 woman arrived from Puerto Rico at age 8, and her youngest brother was born in Chicago 7 years later. She recalled her mother insisting:

[En casa] teníamos que hablar inglés. Cuando él estaba chiquito, y yo le estaba hablando en español, mi mamá me dijo "Háblale en inglés porque eso es lo que él necesita aprender. El español él lo aprenderá pero el inglés es lo que tiene que hablar para cuando se vaya para la escuela." So, para mi mamá lo más importante era hablar inglés. (#21, G2 Puerto Rican female)

[At home] we had to speak English. When he was little, and I would speak to him in Spanish, my mom told me "Speak to him in English because that is what he needs to learn. He will learn Spanish but he needs to speak English for when he goes to school." So, for my mom the most important thing was speaking English.

She said that her own son's Spanish was "horrible" and attributed this to his marrying a non-Spanish-speaking spouse and living in an area where there were few Spanish speakers, but we suspect he may have received relatively little input as the youngest of three children and the only boy (see Zentella, 1997, about boys spending less time at home with opportunities to develop Spanish compared with girls).

Only a handful of individuals out of the 93 proficiency inliers emphasized the importance of English over Spanish without citing difficulties they or their parents had experienced as the motive. That is, very few claimed that English was more important for ideological reasons. This woman was among those who did feel that way:

El inglés es la lengua principal en América. No es el español. Es la que tú necesitas pa' moverte para aquí pa' allá pa' buscar trabajo. Este, llegar a hablar con el policía, para llamar a los bomberos. English is the first language. (#61, G3 MexiRican female)

English is the main language in America. It is not Spanish. It's the one you need to move ahead everywhere to find work. Um, to speak with the police, to call the fire fighters. English is the first language.

We have seen that when asked who was responsible for children learning Spanish, the majority of participants replied that it was the parents. Despite this almost universal belief, we will see throughout this chapter that raising a child with proficiency in a non-English language in the U.S. is no easy task when the parents are fluent in English.

A number of participants mentioned a link between language and ethnicity, commenting that for them, Spanish was an important living symbol of their culture. A G2 Puerto Rican noted that Spanish was an essential part of her cultural identity:

> Es parte de quien eres. Para mí es parte de quien soy. Si voy a sentarme aquí y decir que soy puertorriqueña, I better be able to speak Spanish. You know? Yo creo que es importante saber de tu cultura y eso incluye su idioma. (#77, G2 Puerto Rican female)

> It is part of who you are. For me, it is part of who I am. If I am going to sit here and say I am Puerto Rican, I better be able to speak Spanish. You know? I think it is important to know your culture and that includes your language.

This same woman spoke Spanish to her nieces and nephews because she valued the language and wanted to preserve it, noting: "Si ellos no hablan español, ¿qué va a pasar con los niños de ellos? No van a hablar español tampoco. Y se va a perder." The following young man was able to benefit from a connection with his great-grandmother in Puerto Rico because of his Spanish proficiency:

> Cuando fui a Puerto Rico mi bisabuela no podía hablar con muchos de mis primos 'cause they would not talk Spanish. Me dijo "¿Sabes qué? Tú eres mi favorito porque no hablan español, I do not understand anything they say." And I looked at that and I thought, it's sad. Not for me. (#69, G2 MexiRican male)

> When I went to Puerto Rico my great-grandmother couldn't speak with many of my cousins because they couldn't speak Spanish. She said to me "Do you know what? You are my favorite because they don't speak Spanish, I do not understand anything they say." And I looked at that and I thought, it's sad. Not for me.

Many speakers indicated that their reason for valuing Spanish went beyond cultural or ethnic affiliation. This G3 speaker discussed both her affective and instrumental connections to Spanish:

> Creo que sí sería bonito saber el español, saber tu idioma, el idioma de tus papás. Saber dos lenguajes. Porque hay más, uhm, uh, *privileges*, tiene más *privileges* que alguien que nada más sabe un, un lenguaje. Como, a veces, si andas buscando trabajos, te preguntan, "Oh, ¿eres bilingüe?" Y creo

que siempre es mejor saber otro lenguaje que el inglés. (#97, G3 Mexican female)

I think it would be beautiful to know Spanish, know your language, the language of your parents. Know two languages. Because there are more, uhm, uh, privileges, one has more privileges than someone that only knows one, um, one language.

Knowing Spanish for future employment was mentioned frequently among all three generational groups. In addition, some G1 speakers mentioned the importance for their Chicago-raised G2 children to talk with their grandparents in Latin America. Even some individuals who struggled with Spanish recognized the need to speak it for both affective and instrumental reasons, including these two G3 speakers:

I regret . . . how do you say I regret not learning it? Como . . . como . . . como está con mi . . . uh mi abuela, estaba hablando con . . . yo estaba hablando con mi abuelo o otra familia like me preguntan algo y no puedo en . . . I can't answer that or . . . o cuando, um, cuando when I try, like when I go to a grocery store. Y trato, or . . . orden like, como comida, like me preguntan en español and like no puedo like, how do you say answer? [Interviewer: Contestarles.] Yeah, no puedo contestarlos. So . . . it, it's like algo . . . I just wish I could . . . like speak it better. And understand it a little better. (#98, G3 Mexican male)

I regret . . . how do you say I regret not learning it? Like, like, like was with my, uh my grandmother, I was talking with . . . to my grandfather and other family like they asked me something and I can't ah . . . I can't answer that or . . . or when, um, when I try, like when I go to a grocery store. I try, or . . . order like, like food, like they ask me in Spanish and like I can't like, how do you say answer? [Interview: Answer them.] Yeah, I can't answer them. So . . . it, it's like something . . . I just wish I could . . . like speak it better. And understand it a little better.

I know how to answer, I just don't know how to word it right. Para mí, no solamente porque somos latinos, um, I think that, tenemos, yo creo que nos va a, affect us, for the fact that you know, we're Hispanic or Latinos, okay, and yo creo que es importante que nosotros, in a way, know where we came from and we need to know Spanish. Because like me, es duro para mí hablar español, comunicar con otro gente. Yo creo que eso es lo más importante, enseñar, us, you know, latinos, los Hispanics, you know, Spanish, where we came from. So we can comunicar mejor con otra persona, you know, tener un trabajo bueno because ahora los trabajos quieren bilingual. And it's hard si nosotros no sabemos español. (#6, G3 MexiRican female)

I know how to answer, I just don't know how to word it right. For me, not only because we are Latinos, um, I think that, we have, I think it's going to, affect us, for the fact that you know, we're Hispanic or Latinos, okay, and I think it is important that we, in a way, know where we came from and we need to know Spanish. Because like me, it is hard for me to speak Spanish, communicate with other people. I think that it is the most important thing, to teach, us, you know, Latinos, the Hispanics, you know, Spanish, where we came from. So we can communicate better with another person, you know, have a good job because because now jobs want bilingual. And it's hard if we don't know Spanish.

The majority of CHISPA participants reported that they used Spanish at their jobs. These positions included retail, lifeguard, Sunday school teacher, delivery services, factory supervisors, hospital billing department, Hispanic publicity agencies, insurance companies, and bank tellers. Fewer than 10 people in the entire corpus said that they either did not use Spanish at all (including a beauty salon receptionist, a postal worker in the suburbs, an employee at a law firm, and a university facilities manager) or used it only with cooks in the kitchens of the restaurants where they worked. It seems obvious that basic proficiency in Spanish had to have been developed *before* beginning a job in order to use it reasonably competently there. However, it is also the case that interacting with others regularly in Spanish on the job serves to bolster one's proficiency in the language, creating a cycle of use that sustains proficiency and leads to potentially greater use. Thus, living in an area like Chicago with many opportunities to use Spanish at work contributes to the maintenance of Spanish proficiency among G2 and G3 speakers. Some studies suggest that bilinguals earn more than monolinguals (Saiz & Zoido, 2005), but it is unfortunately often the case that Spanish speakers in the U.S. are hired for jobs that require knowledge of both English and Spanish, but they are not compensated more than their monolingual coworkers, a circumstance about which one participant complained quite bitterly.

Some G1 parents said they felt separated from their Chicago-raised children when the children began learning English, causing the parents to feel pressure to learn it themselves:

Lo sentí como una urgencia, que si yo quería poder, quería mantener la relación con mis hijas, comunicarme con ellas, entender qué hacían y, y mantenerme en una posición de trabajo más o menos aceptable tenía que hablar el idioma. (#24, G1 Mexican female)

I felt it urgently, that if I wanted to be able to, if I wanted to maintain a relationship with my daughters, communicate with them, understand what they were doing and, and maintain myself in a more or less acceptable job position I had to learn the language.

A similar sentiment was expressed by a G2 daughter:

Mi mamá se enoja siempre porque ya se me olvidó casi el español. [. . .] Mi papá, pues se enojaba también, porque entre yo y mis hermanos nada más hablábamos el inglés y ellos como que sentían que "Oh ¿están hablando de nosotros?" O "¿qué estarán diciendo?" Y no nos entendían. So, si hablábamos inglés era entre nosotras, yo y mi hermanos y dejábamos a mis padres away from it. (#19, G2 Puerto Rican female)

My mother would always get mad because I had already almost lost Spanish. [. . .] My father, well he would also get mad, because my siblings and I would only speak in English to each other and they felt like, "Oh are you talking about us? Oh what could they be saying?" And they didn't understand us. So, if we spoke English it was between us, me and my brothers and we left our parents away from it.

As noted by Velázquez (2014), whether or not Spanish is passed on to the next generation depends in part on Latinos' belief that Spanish has relevance in their lives, the quality and amount of Spanish exposure, and the opportunity for children to use Spanish. All of our participants had very positive attitudes toward maintaining Spanish, and they tended to believe both family and schools were responsible for doing so. While it is noteworthy that all of our participants had such a positive orientation toward Spanish, actual use must coincide with positive feelings to actually impact language development and maintenance. In addition, we note that attitudes likely have the greatest relevance for G2 and G3 parents, because they have a choice whether to use Spanish or English, while G1 parents are usually constrained to Spanish. The attitudes of children younger than 5 have little importance, because during this period, they are naturally acquiring any language(s) to which they are exposed. We turn now to discuss circumstances and factors that condition language use, which is the engine that drives the acquisition of Spanish and thus impacts the vitality of the Spanish language in the lives of our participants.

8.3.2. Language Use in the Home and in Social Networks

This section focuses on home language use, which typically constitutes the primary setting for input and output in the minority language. As we have emphasized in this chapter, if children do not hear and speak Spanish, they cannot acquire it, no matter how positive their family's attitudes. We focus in this section on the conditions for Spanish acquisition of G2 and G3 speakers, because these individuals were raised in English-speaking Chicago; our G1 speakers were raised monolingually in Spanish in Mexico or Puerto Rico and thus acquired Spanish as all other children did in those locations. We divide this section into two main themes discussed by our participants: explicit language policies and the composition of the household. We also describe changes in participants' social networks, such as a new job or a Spanish-speaking partner, that led to opportunities for increased Spanish use.

Un Cocotazo si Hablábamos Inglés": Explicit Language Policies

Spolsky (2009, p. 24) and others have explored in detail the various strategies employed by parents to increase their children's exposure to the parents' language, such as dictating what language(s) will be used in the home and planning interaction with speakers of the target language(s). In a number of our participants' Chicago households, caretakers tried to enforce a Spanish-supporting language policy, expressed vividly by this G2 Puerto Rican female when asked whether Spanish was important in her home: "¡Era importante siempre! Nos daban un cocotazo[8] si hablábamos inglés" (It was always important! They use to rap us on the head with their knuckles if we talked English) (#124, G2 Puerto Rican female).

In some households, one parent would try to always use Spanish, while the other would speak English:

> Umm con mi mamá siempre fue en español y con mi papá en inglés y porque aquí en Chicago, mi papá tenía mucha familia, tenía muchos tíos y tías aquí mis primos so uh casi toda mi familia del lado de mi papá hablan inglés so no hablan mucho español. (#19, G2 Puerto Rican female)

> Umm with my mother it was always in Spanish and with my father in English and because here in Chicago, my father had a lot of family, he had a lot of uncles and aunts here my cousins so uh almost all my family on my father's side spoke English so they don't speak much Spanish.

Although there is no way to gauge the degree to which these families adhered to such policies, they indicated a conscious effort to provide Spanish-language input for the children. Several G2 individuals indicated that a home Spanish policy was implemented only after they had began learning English in school, such as this 32-year-old Mexican man who said that his mother would get angry because she could not understand the English that he and his siblings would speak to her when they came home from school:

---

8. *Cocotazo* = rap to the head with the knuckles.

Entonces cuando vino mi papá del trabajo un día, él dijo que mientras nosotros estemos en la casa, siempre vamos a hablar español. [...] Porque él dijo que el español no quería que se nos olvidara. Y ... y sí, trabajó, eso fue muy bueno para nosotros. (#10, G2 Mexican G2 male)

And then when my father came home from work one day, he said while we were in the house, we were always going to speak Spanish. [...] Because he said that he didn't want us to forget Spanish. And ... and yes, it worked, that was very good for us.

He went on to say that he had a Mexican-origin coworker who could not speak any Spanish, and thus "ese sentido, estoy muy contento que mi papá puso esa regla en la casa, que nosotros nada más habláramos puro español (in that sense, I am very happy that my dad put that rule in the house, that we would only speak pure Spanish)." In the terms of our plant metaphor, these parents sought to keep kudzu (English) out of the home, which gave Spanish the chance to grow. He then explained that he had recently established a similar "only Spanish in the home" policy with his own two-and-a-half-year-old son but that it was challenging to implement because his wife and the boy's older brother were used to speaking to him in English, and there were no children's television shows in Spanish. Both of these challenges were mentioned frequently in the CHISPA corpus.

An additional note about child care is relevant here. At least through the mid-2000s, it was not easy to locate public child care in Spanish in Chicago. One of the authors (Potowski) sought Spanish-speaking day care for her children when they were ages 2 and 4. A common route for locating child care was to contact a group called Illinois Action for Children, which for a small fee would mail a list of state-approved home day cares in up to five different zip codes. Potowski called approximately 15 of the Latino surnames on the list mailed to her and spoke to the women in Spanish. She asked in what language they spoke to the children in their care, and without exception, they replied that they used English because "that's what families wanted," including Spanish-speaking families. She finally did find a Puerto Rican woman who said she would commit to speaking to her children in Spanish while using English with the other children. Since that time, new options have fortunately been established in the city, including a day-care facility called Rayito de Sol which provides "Spanish immersion day care and preschool," presumably also to non-home-Spanish-speaking children, and at least two others (Narcisa's Daycare and Lucila's Home Daycare). It remains to be seen in what ways the Covid-19 pandemic may have disrupted for some families and bolstered for others the use of Spanish with children, given that many day cares were closed, many children were completing schooling from home online, and parents may have been at home working or out of work instead of away from the home, in addition to the tragic loss of lives within Latino communities.[9]

Spanish use can be supported or hindered by the members living and spending time in the household. When participants talked about a parent who stayed at home to be with young children or when they themselves were the parent who had done so, it was always the mother. The following quote from a G1 Mexican woman was fairly representative of this theme. She had stayed at home until the youngest of her four children went to school:

Bueno, mi hijo el mayor fue el que tuvo más problema porque él hablaba solamente español cuando entró a la escuela. Entonces él lloraba porque no entendía. Entonces me empezaron a decir que le pusiera mucho los programas en inglés y que el *Sesame Street* y todo eso. Y entonces él fue el que sufrió más. Y yo también porque no le pude ayudar. (#52, G1 Mexican female)

Well, my son the oldest was the one who had the most problems because he only spoke Spanish when he started school. So he cried because he didn't understand. And so they told me to put on a lot of English-language programs and *Sesame Street* and all of that. And so he was the one who suffered the most. And me too because I couldn't help him.

Despite her son's difficulties, he grew up to thank her for insisting on Spanish in the home:

En ese tiempo yo no sabía qué importante iba a ser para ellos, que ellos también aprendieran español, hasta que ya fueron al colegio.[10] Porque todavía en secundaria el hijo más grande me reclamaba, me decía, "Mamá, tú... ustedes porque no nos insistieron a hablar el inglés, ahora tenemos el inglés muy pronunciado; y no me gusta, no quiero tener acento." Pero después cuando entró al colegio, nos dijo, "Mamá, gracias. Porque de veras ahora sé el valor que tiene para mí hablar dos idiomas. (#52, Mexican G1 female)

At that time I didn't know how important it was going to be for them, that they also learn Spanish, until they already went to college. Because still in high school my oldest son would reproach me, he would say, "Mom, you, you because you didn't insist we speak English, now we have a highly accented English; and I don't like it, I don't want to have an accent." But then when he started college, he told us, "Mom, thanks. Because now I really understand the value for me of speaking two languages."

---

9. As of November 2020, Chicago's Latino Covid death rate was 10.6 per 10,000 residents, compared with 9.2 for whites and 16.1 for African Americans.

10. As mentioned in Chapter 5, in our corpus, *colegio* typically refers to college (university).

We see in #52's narrative that her oldest son had more difficulties adjusting to school in English compared with her subsequent children. There is a fair amount of evidence that birth order influences language use (Hakuta & D'Andrea, 1992), and in the U.S. it is common for the first- and second-born children to have stronger levels of Spanish compared with later-born children, which was found by Parada (2013) in Chicago. This came up repeatedly among G2s in our corpus.[11] For example, this Puerto Rican woman described what happened when her older twin sisters began school two years before she did:

[En casa hablábamos] español. Pero después que mis hermanas mayores fueron a la escuela y hablaban inglés. So yo aprendí a hablar inglés con ellas. Cuando yo empecé la escuela sí hablaba inglés. Cuando ellas empezaron la escuela no. (#77, G2 Puerto Rican female)

[At home we spoke] Spanish. But then my older sisters went to school and they would speak English. So I learned to speak English with them. When I started school yes I spoke English. When they started school they did not.

In fact, many participants described cases of family members who did not speak any Spanish, and although this was often a cousin or a niece or nephew, sometimes it was their own younger sibling. This 20-year-old G3 Puerto Rican woman described how her own experiences influenced those of her younger sister:

Hablé español hasta cuando tení como cinco años, creo, como preschool, kindergarten. [. . .] Empecé a hablar inglés porque obviamente era difícil estar en preschool and kindergarten y no poder hablar con la maestra con los niños y yo vine de, venía de la escuela llorando. So mi mamá me enseñaba y me estaba hablando más en ingles, y lo que pasó es el inglés como . . . sacó el español. So sólo hablaba inglés. Mi hermana no habla nada en español, nada nada. Entiende más, pero para hablar, nada. (#8, G3 Puerto Rican female)

I spoke Spanish until I was about five, I think, like preschool, kindergarten. [. . .] I started speaking English because obviously it was difficult to be in preschool and kindergarten and not be able to speak with the teacher with the children and I came from, I would come home crying from school. So my mother would teach me and she was speaking to me more in English, and what happened is the English like took out the Spanish. So I only spoke

---

11. Unfortunately, we do not have reliable data from all CHISPA G2 and G3 participants about their birth order, so we are unable to analyze all of our participants' proficiency according to this variable.

English. My sister doesn't speak any Spanish, none, none. She understands more, but speaking, nothing.

Another 23-year-old Mexican woman said she had to remind her mother to speak in Spanish to her 13-year-old sister, who was growing up with very different linguistic circumstances from those she herself had. Their mother had separated from their father seven years before and was with a new partner who did not speak Spanish. Her mother also worked evenings and thus was not able to spend much time with her younger daughter. Similarly, this G3 Puerto Rican had a sister who was 14 months younger, but of her Spanish, she said:

No lo habla muy bien, lleva acento. Habla . . . como una güera hablando español. Oh, it's terrible to listen to. Algunas veces la oigo and I'm like "Ouch, man do I sound this bad when I speak—ouch!" [*laughs*]. But you know I don't wanna, no le quiero dar vergüenza so I keep my mouth shut y le sigo hablando. (#4, G3 Puerto Rican female)

She doesn't speak it very well, she has an accent. She speaks . . . like a white girl speaking Spanish. Oh, it's terrible to listen to. Sometimes I hear her and I'm like "Ouch, man do I sound this bad when I speak—ouch!" [*laughs*]. But you know I don't wanna, I don't want to shame her so I keep my mouth shut and I keep talking with her.

Some participants lamented that their siblings were raising children (their own nieces or nephews) who were not learning any Spanish:

Yo tengo una hermana ahorita que tiene un hijo y vive en el suburbio, no sabe nada de español. Y, allí es donde comete, como padres, el error de que, de no enseñarle de la raíces de donde vino. Él es latino, el papá es tejano, ella es boricua, debe de tener el español. (#39, G2 Puerto Rican female)

I have a sister now who has a son and he lives in the suburbs, he doesn't know any Spanish. And, that is where they commit, the parents, the error of, of not teaching him about his roots, where he is from. He is Latino, his father is a Texan, she is Boricua, she should speak Spanish.

Such G3 children, once they grow into adulthood, would very likely be unable to participate in a Spanish interview for this project as their G2 aunts, uncles, and parents did. Although it was rare in our corpus, even G1s are not guaranteed to transmit Spanish to their children in the U.S.: #85 arrived from Puerto Rico at age 13 and at age 36 said that his children "hablan pues nada más que el inglés (they speak nothing more than English)."

An important factor in intergenerational transmission of a minority language is the fact that preteens and adolescents frequently push back on all manner of their parents' attempts to steer them, which includes the speaking of non-English languages. Literature from the field of heritage languages makes clear that the children and grandchildren of families in the U.S. who speak languages including Spanish, Chinese, Hmong, Arabic, and a host of others go through periods in which they resist speaking these languages, preferring to respond to their parents and others in English. Many parents in the CHISPA corpus described how their children resisted Spanish. This G3 Puerto Rican woman complained that she paid thousands of dollars in college tuition—presumably to study Spanish—when she could have learned it at home. But even this regret was not a strong enough motivator for her to use Spanish with her son:

Ahora teniendo mis hijos sabiendo lo que sé—lo que me pasó a mí que yo tenía que pagar treinta mil dólares para tener una educación que yo tenía gratis en casa cuando yo era pequeña, quiero enseñarles a ellos. Pero desafortunadamente, yo no lo hago tampoco, you know. Y ahora el hijo mío me mira y me dice "Why do I have to speak Spanish? No quiero hablar español. Háblame en inglés, que yo no te entiendo." Si yo hablo español me dice que no me entiende. (#4, G3 Puerto Rican female)

Now having my children knowing what I know—what happened to me was that I had to pay thirty thousand dollars to get an education that I had free at home when I was a child, I want to teach them. But unfortunately, I don't do it either, you know. And now my son looks at me and says "Why do I have to speak Spanish? Speak to me in English, I don't understand you." If I speak Spanish he tells me he doesn't understand me.

Some individuals acknowledged that as children, they had pushed back on their parents' Spanish use. This G3 woman said she felt her G2 mother should have insisted on using Spanish with her despite her resistance:

Mi mamá, ella pudo hablar los dos muy, muy bien. Yo no sé qué pasó conmigo, I mean, yo sé que... I don't remember, pero ugh, I get so upset. [...] [She tells me] "Es por tu culpa que tú no puedas hablar." I'm like "pero yo tengo tres años, ¿cómo es posible que yo puedo?, you know, I mean, you're mom! Just tell me no. (#40, G3 Puerto Rican female)

My mother, she could speak them both very very well, I don't know what happened with me, I mean, I know what... I don't remember, but ugh, I get so upset. [...] [She tells me] "It's your fault that you can't speak." I'm like "but I am three years old, how is it possible that I can, you know, I mean, you're mom! Just tell me no.

It is importantly to note that there was very frequent mention of grandparents as a primary source of Spanish input for G2 and G3 participants. Particularly for those G3 individuals whose parents were both dominant in English, a grandparent was often the sole source of Spanish input both when they were children and as adults. For example, this Mexican G3 woman was rated with a fairly low proficiency level of 2 (which was, however, close to the G3 group average of 2.77). She said that her household was almost entirely English-speaking but that:

> Mi abuelita, cuando venía, ella era la que me hablaba en español. Y yo aprendí mi español through her. Y ella me leía libros and, es donde yo aprendí mi español. [. . .] I feel like she took the role, que no quería que yo me olvidara de Spanish, you know porque, soy mexicana. (#41, G3 Mexican female)

> My grandma, when she would come, she was the one who would speak to me in Spanish. And I learned my Spanish through her. She would read books to me and, it's where I learned my Spanish. [. . .] I feel like she took the role, she didn't want me to forget Spanish, you know because I'm Mexican.

She said that her parents did want her to learn both languages, but since they had been raised in Chicago, they were accustomed to speaking English in the home. When they divorced, she went to live with her father and his second wife, who knew little English, thus leading to a dramatic increase in her Spanish use but one that she was a bit resentful of: "Me enojaba porque a veces it was like, '¿Cómo vas a decir que yo hable español all of a sudden, cuando tú nunca me hablabas en español?' Es muy difícil para que yo haga ese transition con él" (I would get mad because sometimes it was like, How are you going to say that I should speak Spanish all of a sudden when you never spoke to me in Spanish? It is very difficult for me to make that transition with him) (#41, G3 Mexican female).

The following G3 Puerto Rican woman had a close relationship with her grandmother, who lived in the apartment below hers while she was growing up. Similarly to speaker #41 just discussed, her proficiency was rated at level 2. We see that the onset of her grandmother's dementia caused a shift in language use which promoted greater Spanish use:

> Every time I was hungry, I would go downstairs when I didn't like what my mom cooked and I would go "Wela,[12] did you cook?" And it was always the same thing my mom cooked: arroz blanco con habichuelas y bistec. [. . .] Cuando mi abuela empecé con Alzheimer's, ella no puede hablar

---

12. *Abuela* (Grandma).

inglés nada, es como te olvidadoaron [sic] de todo el idioma, y la familia tiene que hablar español. Y con mucho práctica y todo eso, yo puedo hablar. (#31, G3 Puerto Rican female)

Every time I was hungry, I would go downstairs when I didn't like what my mom cooked and I would go "Wela, did you cook?" And it was always the same thing my mom cooked: white rice with beans and steak. [. . .] When my grandma got Alzheimer's, she couldn't speak any English, it's like you forget all the language, and the family has to speak Spanish. And with a lot of practice and all of that, I can speak Spanish.

The Spanish of the following G3 MexiRican G3 was also rated level 2. If it had not been for her grandparents, she would not have learned Spanish at all, and now she was able to enjoy friendships with people who knew only Spanish. She stated that she learned Spanish "con mi abuela, con mi abuelo porque ellos hablan español. So, tengo que hablar en, tú sabes, en español también. Yo tengo muchos, muchos um, amistades que, tú sabes, you know, solamente hablan en español, no entienden papa de inglés" (with my grandmother, with my grandfather because they speak Spanish. So, I have to speak in, you know, in Spanish also. I have many, many, um, friends who, you know, you know, only speak in Spanish, they don't understand any English) (#6, G3 MexiRican female).

Several participants were raised almost entirely by their grandparents, usually the grandmother, including this G3 Puerto Rican woman whose relatively long quote we include because it describes family and neighborhood dynamics that contributed to her Spanish development:

Cuando yo era chiquita mi abuela fue quien me crió porque mi mamá me tuvo bien joven, estaba terminando high school y entonces trabajando. Mi primer idioma fue inglés y lo aprendí por mi mamá. Yo aprendí español porque, well, mi abuela fue quien me creció pero ella me hablaba en español, yo la entendía pero no podía hablar. Y cuando yo tenía como cinco años había una muchacha que se mudó a lado a mí y ella venía de Puerto Rico y ella no hablaba inglés y yo no hablaba español. Pero ella era la única, uhm, mujer en el bloque y mi mamá no me dejaba jugar con los muchachos porque las nenas no se vayan con los varones y por eso nosotros fuimos . . . las únicas amigas y ella me enseñó español y yo lo enseñé el inglés. (#29, G3 Puerto Rican female)

When I was little my grandma was the one who raised me because my mom had me very young, she was finishing high school and also working. My first language was English and I learned it from my mom. I learned Spanish because, well, my grandma was the one who raised me but she would speak to me in Spanish, I understood her but couldn't speak. And when I was about five there was a girl who moved next to me and she came from Puerto

Rico and she didn't speak English and I didn't speak Spanish. But she was the only, umh female on the block and my mom didn't let me play with the boys because girls don't go with males and because of that we were . . . the only girlfriends and she taught me Spanish and I taught her English.

We are reminded here of Zentella's (1997) descriptions of the Puerto Rican neighborhood of *el bloque* in New York City, where the girls had to stay by the house and were not permitted to ride their bikes away like the boys. In another point reminiscent of Zentella's *el bloque*, #29 stated that she had many cousins who did not learn Spanish, but this was not a problematic issue in her family: "La importancia del idioma nunca fue stressed en mi familia, como si lo sabías lo sabías, si no, no. Como todos mis primos con quien crecí, ellos casi no hablan español, yo soy la única." (The importance of the language never was stressed in my family, like if you knew it, you knew it, if not, no. Like all of my cousins who I grew up with, they almost don't speak Spanish, I am the only one.)

Thus, grandparents often played a key role in the development of Spanish among G3 individuals with inlier proficiency levels. There were also some G2 individuals with inlier Spanish proficiency who, surprisingly, had learned the language not from their parents but from their grandparents. This is somewhat curious, because by definition, both parents of a G2 are G1 individuals who had spent their childhoods in Latin America. However, there are cases in which one or both of the G1 parents had immigrated relatively young. For example, #82's mom arrived at age 10 (the younger end of the G1 spectrum) and her father at age 20. She claimed that "mis abuelos me enseñaron a mí, no mi mamá." She was also expecting a baby, and when asked whether she would teach her child Spanish, she replied with a somewhat tentative "¡Ojalá que sí!" (I hope so). But as we see throughout this chapter, G2 and G3 individuals' positive attitudes and intentions to transmit Spanish were frequently not sufficient to actually make it happen. This G2 Puerto Rican mother, for example, said it was simply "easier" to speak English with her children:

En la casa, I use [Spanish] here . . . I would say forty percent of the time, cuarenta, porque mi esposo nomás que habla español, you know. [. . .] You know it's sad. Los niños, ahora están aprendiendo inglés. I failed [*laughs*]. Empecé con español y terminé en inglés. It's kinda hard. Es duro cuando una—yo era madre soltera por siete años. So, um, les hablaba español cuando iba para casa de mami, o en la iglesia, pero en la casa, como que se me olvidaba y hablaba inglés. [. . .] It's like easier. (#43, G2 Puerto Rican female)

In the house, I use [Spanish] here . . . I would say forty percent of the time, forty, because my husband only speaks Spanish, you know. [. . .] You know it's sad. The kids are now learning English. I failed [*laughs*]. I started with Spanish and ended with English. It's kinda hard. It is hard when one—I was a single mother for seven years. So, um, I would speak to them in Spanish when I would go to my mom's house, or in church, but in the house, like I would forget and I would speak English. [. . .] It's like easier.

She raised them alone for seven years, and although marrying a man who did not know much English increased her Spanish use in the home, a pattern of English use had already been established with her children. Perhaps realizing that they themselves lived their daily lives almost entirely in English and thus being doubtful of their ability to transmit Spanish to their children, several G2 speakers claimed that they would put their own mothers in charge of their future children's Spanish acquisition, thus creating a future *abuela* situation as explained by this Mexican woman: "Siempre le digo a mi mamá que ella va a cuidar a mis hijos cuando están pequeños, porque quiero que ellos saben español. So, quiero que su abuela le enseñen el español" (I always tell me mother that she will take care of my kids when they are little, because I want them to know Spanish. So I want their grandmother to teach them Spanish) (#12, G2 Mexican female). Similarly, this G3 Puerto Rican female relied on her G2 mother's Spanish for her own daughter (who is a G4), in part because she felt her own Spanish was not strong enough to impart it "correctly," a fear articulated by several young women:

Se queda con mi mamá una o dos veces a la semana, tienen una relación bien buena las dos so, uhm, ella aprende con mi mamá. Porque mi español no es muy bueno, no le quiero . . . estoy asustada que voy a enseñar algo, uhm, malo o incorrecto. So yo estoy solamente enseñándole cosas como números y letras, los colores. (#123, G3 Puerto Rican female)

She stays with my mom once or twice a week, they have a great relationship so, uhm, she learns with my mom. Because my Spanish is not very good, I don't want to . . . I am scared that I will teach her something, uhm, wrong or incorrect. So I am only teaching her things like numbers and letters, the colors.

This G3 Mexican described how she and her boyfriend never used Spanish together except when they would occasionally challenge each other to see who could use it the longest, "Y [*laughs*], we never last that long. It's funny porque es cuando realmente te pones a pensar que es muy difícil to just hablar español y no decir nada. (And [laughs] we never last that long. It's funny because it is when you really start to think that it is very difficult to just speak Spanish and not say anything.)" She went on to say:

We're kind of scared que no le vamos a dar la ventaja, our kids, you know, in the future, que sepan muy, muy bien el español. [. . .] Queremos que sepan [las dos lenguas] porque, una, you know, it's really good to be bilingual, y dos, es parte de quién ellos son. Ellos son mexicanos, y no quiero que sean como esos mexicanos, they're like "Oh, no sé nada de español, yo soy de aquí." My grandparents fueron de México, y tienen que respetar eso. Tienen que respetar cuando van a México, you know, cómo hablar y comunicarse con gente que son mexicanos igual que ellos. (#41, G3 Mexican female)

We're kind of scared that we are not going to give our kids, the advantage you know, in the future, that they know Spanish very very well. [. . .] We want them to know [the two languages] because, one, you know, it's really good to be bilingual, and two, it is part of who they are. They are Mexicans, and I don't want them to be like those Mexicans, they're like "Oh, I don't know any Spanish, I am from here." My grandparents were from Mexico, and they have to respect that. They have to respect when they go to Mexico, you know, how to talk and communicate with Mexican people the same as them.

When the interviewer asked how she was going to achieve her goal of wanting her future children to know Spanish, she replied that she would have to "focus on" and "esforzarse" (make an effort) to speak Spanish instead of English. But our data suggest that this will be very challenging. She mentioned that two additional important factors were schooling and being vigilant against the child's resistance to speaking Spanish:

También, uhm, meterlo en maybe you know en bilingual or something para que escuche el idioma. Y pues también estar muy, muy, uhm, careful you know, que cuando, "Oh, no quiero hablar tanto español." (#41, G3 Mexican female)

Also, uhm, putting them in maybe you know in bilingual or something so they can hear the language. And also be very, uhm, careful you know, that when, "Oh, I don't want to speak so much Spanish."

The idea to "meterlo en bilingual" (put him in bilingual education) is a good one, but will her future child have access to such a program? Transitional bilingual education programs (to be discussed in Section 8.3.4) are typically only for children who are limited in their English abilities. An excellent option would be a dual-language program that teaches 50% to 90% of the day in Spanish, and as of 2023, there were 33 such programs in the Chicago public school system (which we will discuss in Chapter 9). However, most are neighborhood schools that admit children from the immediate area only. Thus, while this future mother seemed aware of the challenges involved in raising children proficient in Spanish, it is an open question how well she will be able to achieve her goals, particularly given that English is her stronger language. As noted by this G2

Puerto Rican woman, "Hablo español con mis hijos, pero me sale el inglés también y no me gusta. Creo que es una costumbre" (I speak Spanish with my kids, but English comes out also and I don't like that. I think it is just a habit.) (#124, G2 Puerto Rican female).

Some G1 participants were grandparents and said their adult children insisted that they use Spanish with the grandchildren but that it was challenging to maintain a Spanish-only policy in their homes because the kids did not speak it very well:

> Y ellos me insisten que les hable español a sus hijos, o sea mis nietos cuando vienen aquí. Desde que entran ellos saben que nosotros no hablamos inglés aquí. Aquí se habla español. [Pero no lo hablan] muy bien. Porque ya son más grandecitos. Yo les digo a mis hijos, "Ustedes como les empezaron a hablar en inglés, ahora ellos ya no les aceptan a ustedes que les hablen en español." Nada más sus abuelitos son los únicos que hablan español. Entonces ellos han perdido mucho este . . . lenguaje." (#52, G1 Mexican female)

> And they would insist that I speak Spanish to their kids, in other words my grandkids when they came here. From the time they enter they know we don't speak English here. Here we speak Spanish. [But they don't speak it] very well. Because they are already a bit older. I tell my kids, "Because you started to speak to them in English, now they don't accept that you speak to them in Spanish." Only their grandparents speak to them in Spanish. So they have lost that language a lot.

Overall, it seems very likely that had it not been for their grandparents, a fair number of G3 participants in our study would not have developed a level of Spanish proficiency that fell within the average for their generational group. That is, they either would have been proficiency outliers (with a proficiency level of 1) or they would not have been able to participate in a Spanish interview at all. This *"abuela* factor" has important implications for Spanish maintenance among G3 individuals, whose *abuelas* were G1s. However, when G2 individuals become the *abuelas*, it is very likely that they will not impart Spanish to the G4 grandchildren. Indeed, this is what national data show, as we describe in the conclusions to this chapter.

It is important to note that if it can be challenging for immigrant G1 parents who are dominant in Spanish (and began learning English as adults) to raise children with Spanish in Chicago, it is even more challenging to do so when one or both of the parents were themselves raised in Chicago and have English as their dominant language. This 23-year-old G3 Puerto Rican woman had a unique plan: "I'm going to get me a Spanish nanny [*laughs*]. No no no, uhm, yo tengo un prima de mi mamá que ella cuida niños. Yo sé que ella va empezar con español y yo con, what I know, y mi novio con lo que él sabe, puedo hablar en los dos" (No, no, no uhm, I have a cousin of my mother who takes care of kids. I know she will begin with Spanish and me with, what I know, and my boyfriend with what he knows, I can speak in both of them.) (#31, G3 Puerto Rican female). Another Puerto Rican woman also mentioned a Spanish-speaking nanny (who, she insisted, could not know any English). She herself had a Spanish proficiency level rated at 2 and described the scenario she had imagined for her future children's language input, which included a Latino husband as well:

> Okay, eso es porque yo estoy tomando clases de español ahora, porque yo quiero que mis niños de principio que aprenden español primero y después inglés, that's my dream. [. . .] Yo voy a hablar con ellos en español y su niñera, ella va a hablar español también. Pero como que ella no puede hablar inglés, que ella no sabe cómo hablarlo, eso es lo que yo quiero. Y yo y mi esposo, él tiene que ser latino para que esto puede, you know, it can happen. (#40, G3 Puerto Rican female)

> Okay, that is why I am taking Spanish classes now, because I want my kids from the start to learn Spanish first and then English, that's my dream. [. . .] I am going to speak to them in Spanish and their nanny, she is also going to speak Spanish. But like she can't speak English, she doesn't know how to speak it, that is what I want. And me and my husband, he has to be Latino so this can, you know, it can happen.

It is remarkable that she had put such a degree of thought into a language plan for her future children, in particular her insistence on a monolingual nanny. As we have repeated throughout this chapter, Spanish is in a precarious situation vis-à-vis English in the U.S. It may in fact take this kind of investment to be successful, particularly for a G3 individual with a relatively low level of Spanish proficiency as this young woman had. Those who take for granted that their children will learn Spanish are frequently frustrated to discover that this does not happen. Such would seem to be the fate of #82, a G2 Puerto Rican who said she did not speak Spanish with her husband or her friends but that she "would try" to speak to her future children in Spanish but "wasn't sure" whether she could: "Yo sé que no va a ser mucho. Quizás en escuela. Quizá con la televisión y el ayuda con mi mamá, porque ella quiere que los, que mi niña sabe el español también" (I know it is not going to be a lot. Maybe in school. Maybe with the television and with my mother's help, because she wants that, that my daughter know Spanish also).

Several participants had chosen romantic partners who were Spanish-dominant themselves and/or whose families were, which led to opportunities to revitalize their Spanish. This 20-year-old G3 Puerto Rican woman (#8) said that she did not use Spanish with any of her friends but that "Cuando estoy con la familia de mi novio, que muchos de ellos hablan sólo español, so tengo que hablar más español . . . like los padres de él no hablan tanto inglés" (When I am with my boyfriend's family, a lot of them only speak Spanish, so I have to speak more Spanish . . . like his parents don't speak much English). When asked what she would do if she did not marry a Latino, she replied that she would still ask her family to teach her future children Spanish: "Le decía a mi familia, 'Sólo habla a mí niño, you know, español y yo en inglés,' porque you know, mi español no es tan perfecto so no quiero enseñar a mi niño, you know, hablar mal" (I used to tell my family, 'Only speak to my child, you know, Spanish, and me in English,' because you know, my Spanish is not so perfect so I don't want to teach my child, you know, to speak incorrectly). Several other young women felt secure in the knowledge that their future children would "learn English easily at school" and that it was important to use Spanish in the home.

Thus, even though some of our participants did not enjoy childhood conditions that fostered a level of proficiency of Spanish that they felt comfortably strong with, new conditions can arise that encourage a reconnection with the language. This 24-year-old G3 Puerto Rican woman (#31) explained how both her mother's insistence and her own belief in the value of Spanish on the job market convinced her to use Spanish with her daughter and to enroll her in a dual-language school: "Mi mamá me está enseñando la importancia de [hablarle en español. Me dice] 'Tú no sabes lo que tú le estás haciendo a esa nena. Va a crecer y no va a saber nada de español y eso va ser toda tu culpa" (My mom is teaching me the importance of [speaking in Spanish. She tells me] 'You don't know what you are doing to that girl. She is going to grow up and she is not going to know any Spanish, and that's going be your fault). She then described a friend who didn't know Spanish: "Ella odia que no puede hablar español y dice que es puertorriqueña pero gente le dicen 'pero tú no hablas español' you know, como quita un poco de tu, cómo se dice, tu orgullo para decir que 'soy puertorriqueña pero no sé hablar español,' you know" (She hates that she can't speak Spanish and she says that she is Puerto Rican but that people tell her 'but you can't speak Spanish,' you know, like it takes a little bit away from you, like how do you say, you are proud to say 'I am Puerto Rican but I can't speak Spanish,' you know).

To conclude this section, it is important to recognize that while childhood language socialization practices have a substantial impact on language maintenance, language practices throughout young adulthood and beyond are also crucial. As Porcel (2011, p. 640) noted about research efforts, "The mere fact that [language maintenance and language shift] are ongoing processes, whose directionality can change at any given moment, implies that we are trying to capture an unstable equilibrium of forces." In our corpus, those who did not yet have children expressed hope, such as this 19-year-old G2 male (#14), who said he would ensure his future children knew Spanish by "hablando más español

Table 8.2. ORDER OF ACQUISITION AND SPANISH PROFICIENCY LEVELS, ALL G2 INDIVIDUALS.

Order of acquisition	Average Spanish proficiency
Sequential (n = 40)	3.9
Simultaneous (n = 8)	3.1

en la casa, como hicieron mis papás" (speaking more in Spanish at home, like my parents did). However, his parents had little choice in the matter because they had immigrated from Mexico in their 20s monolingual in Spanish. Those participants who already had children recognized the challenges in providing them with the circumstances required to develop Spanish proficiency.

8.3.3. Order of Acquisition

We divided all of our G2 CHISPA participants into two categories based on the order in which they began acquiring Spanish and English.[13] *Simultaneous* bilinguals had exposure to both Spanish and English in the home, while *sequential* bilinguals learned mostly or only Spanish at home and began learning English when they started school. There were 40 sequential and only eight simultaneous bilinguals among all our G2 speakers, suggesting that many G2s in Chicago are exposed predominantly to Spanish in the home. Table 8.2 compares the average Spanish proficiency of the simultaneous and sequential groups.[14] Mexicans, Puerto Ricans, and MexiRicans were equally distributed across these two categories, meaning that order of acquisition is not an underlying factor related to the slightly higher proficiency of Mexicans noted in Chapter 2.

We see that the sequential bilinguals showed slightly higher levels of Spanish proficiency as adults than their simultaneous bilingual peers who were exposed to English alongside Spanish. This difference was statistically significant: A Welch's two-sample t-test (which accounts for uneven sample sizes across comparison groups) indicated that sequential bilinguals had higher proficiency (M = 3.88, SD = 0.88) than simultaneous bilinguals (M = 3.13, SD = 0.64), $t(12.98) = 2.82$, $p = .015$, with a large effect size ($d = 0.88$) as per

---

13. Unexpectedly, there were three G3 individuals who were sequential bilinguals, but we do not include them here, because the vast majority of G3s (49 out of 52, or 94%) were simultaneous bilinguals, rendering a comparison of sequential versus simultaneous bilinguals among G3s of little value.

14. There were two G2 individuals for whom we could not reliably determine their order of acquisition.

Cohen (1988). This finding is in line with research cited earlier (Anderson, 1999; Montrul & Potowski, 2007) and supports our garden analogy of bilingualism in the U.S.: the longer Spanish is allowed to exist by itself, the stronger it grows. Clearly, this is not absolute, because even among sequential bilinguals, exposure to English can occur at different ages and to different degrees. Nor is this the only factor involved in developing proficiency in a minority language, given that proficiency can change rather substantially even once an individual enters adulthood. Although we have not measured by any scale the English proficiency of our G2 participants, the English they used during their interviews suggests that they were fully proficient in English. What we mean to suggest here is that delaying the onset of English input until the beginning of the school years did not seem to negatively affect their ultimate English attainment. This information is key to communicate to parents who are making decisions about home language use and school programs that teach through Spanish.

8.3.4. Bilingual Education

Valdés (2011) has argued that because G3 individuals have so little exposure to the minority language at home and within the community, the direct involvement of educational institutions is essential if these youth are to have the opportunity to develop competence in the language. This can also be true for G2 children, particularly those who have older siblings who introduced English into the home and/or parents who arrived at the U.S. mainland during early adolescence and thus likely developed functional English proficiency. Several studies support the idea that bilingual education, even transitional programs lasting only a few years in the early grades, have been shown to lead to higher levels of Spanish proficiency than all-English-based programs (August & Shanahan, 2006).

A detailed history of bilingual education in the U.S. can be found in Baker and Wright (2017); a brief summary is presented here. When children in the U.S. first enroll in public school and qualified staff determine that their level of English is not strong enough for them to be successful in the mainstream classroom—that is, they are English learners, or ELs—it has since 1974 been a federal law that they must have access to some kind of assistance. The two most common programs for EL children are English as a second language (ESL) and transitional bilingual education (TBE). ESL programs provide 100% of classroom instruction in English, but a portion of it is tailored to the needs of ELs, usually with the students being pulled out of the classroom for a portion of each day. ESL is typically the only option when there are fewer than 20 EL children who speak the same language. In another popular program model, TBE, a portion of each school day is taught in the children's home language, also often in a pull-out format. However, as the "T" for *transitional* in

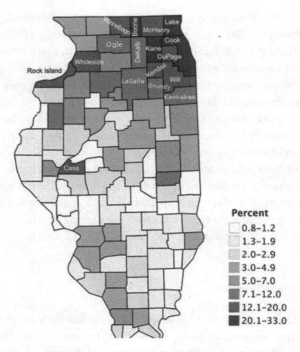

Figure 8.1. Percentage Latino population, Illinois counties. (Source: U.S. Census estimates, 2019.)

the program name clearly indicates, the goal is to transition students to the mainstream all-English classroom as soon as possible, meaning that the descriptor *bilingual* refers to a method and not a goal. The transition out of bilingual education typically takes place after three years, in fourth grade. After this point, most students never engage academically with Spanish again until high school. In some states, an additional two years in a TBE program can be requested.

When there are 20 or more children who speak the same language, at least six states (Connecticut, Illinois, New Jersey, New York, Texas, and Wisconsin) require the school district to find a teacher who speaks that language and offer TBE instead of ESL. Given the concentration of Latinos in Illinois (see Figure 8.1), it is no surprise that TBE in Spanish is offered in a large number of schools around the state. However, as we will see, many parents mistakenly believe that bilingual programs "confuse" children or slow down their English acquisition and that all-English programs are a better option, which reflects a wider monoglossic ideology that is common around the world and particularly in the U.S.

The Chicago area is located in Cook County, which has been approximately 25% Latino for years, and many of our G2 participants were in TBE programs as children. It is important to keep in mind that in Illinois public schools, TBE programs are offered when a child's family indicates that a language other than English is spoken in the home and the child's English is determined to be below a particular level. Given the patterns of home language use described in the previous section, it makes sense that the majority of speakers in our corpus who participated in TBE programs were G2s. This is because G2 children have two G1 immigrant parents who usually spoke only Spanish in the home, resulting in the fairly common outcome that their children arrive in kindergarten with relatively little English proficiency. However, not all G2 children arrive in school as ELs. For example, it is possible for a first- or second-born G2 child to place into a TBE program in kindergarten, learn English during their first years at school, and speak it at home to their younger (also G2) siblings; when these younger siblings arrive in kindergarten, it is possible that they, unlike their older siblings, have acquired sufficient English proficiency to avoid an EL determination and resulting TBE placement. We have seen this in some of our participants' quotes. In other cases, a G2 child may have learned sufficient English from sources other than the home, such as in a preschool program or with a day-care provider. Finally, we mention that private schools are not required by federal law to offer any programmatic support for EL children, and we will see in our corpus that a fair number of G2 participants had been ELs as children but did not attend a TBE program because they were enrolled in private Catholic elementary schools.

It is possible, but far less common, for a G3 kindergarten-age child to have a low enough level of English proficiency to qualify for TBE. Recall from Chapter 2 that G3 individuals have one or two parents who are G2. When both parents are G2—raised largely or entirely in Chicago—the G3 child was very likely spoken to in English in the home by both parents, and thus it would be very unlikely for such a child to place into TBE (but we will see a handful of individuals for whom this was the case). On the other hand, if the G3 child has one G1 parent—that is, they are what we have labeled a G3:1—and that G1 parent was the primary caregiver during the early years and spoke only in Spanish to the child, it is possible that this child at age 5 would still not have acquired sufficient English proficiency to test into the mainstream classroom. There are several such examples in the CHISPA corpus. One is a 24-year-old Mexican woman (#105) whose father arrived in Chicago at age 5 but whose mother arrived at age 24. It is interesting to note that her Spanish proficiency was rated at level 5, much higher than the G3 average;[15] as we have noted, these mismatches between generational group and Spanish proficiency motivated our decision to look at Spanish proficiency and generation separately

---

15. This means that she is what we call a proficiency outlier, so her circumstances will be described in a later section of this chapter.

in all of our linguistic analyses. Finally, we note that participation in a bilingual program is usually directly connected with sequential bilingualism. That is, children who receive evaluations as ELs are usually those who were not exposed to much English before age 5. However, it is technically possible for a child to be a simultaneous bilingual—exposed to both Spanish and English in the home—and still arrive in school with levels of English low enough to warrant placement in TBE.

We first present findings about all CHISPA participants who attended bilingual education programs, before focusing on the proficiency inliers. Two caveats are necessary when presenting our bilingual education findings. First, 14 individuals were inadvertently not asked whether they had participated in bilingual education. Second, we do not have reliable details on individuals' childhood EL status or on the type of program they attended and for how long. Some people remembered bilingual education as consisting of lessons in both languages, while others described classes solely in Spanish. Some said they attended for only two years, while other quoted five years.

Overall, approximately half of the G2 speakers who were asked this question (22 out of 42) had participated in a bilingual program as children. Of the 20 G2 individuals who said they had not been in bilingual education, six said they had attended Catholic schools, which are not required to provide these programs and typically do not do so. The remaining five were older than 50 and said that bilingual programs were not offered when they were in kindergarten. Of these 11 individuals who did not have access to a bilingual program, based on what they reported in their interviews, at least eight would very likely have tested as EL had they attended public schools (for example, #11 stated, "Yo recuerdo cuando tuve cinco años que entré al kindergarten en la escuela católica Yo estaba en una escuela que era gente—no había muchos hispanos en ese tiempo y la maestra era monja. Me criticaba porque hablaba con un acento" I remember when I was five I started kindergarten in catholic school. I was in a school where people—there weren't many Hispanics at that time and the teacher was a nun. She criticized me because I spoke with an accent). The remaining nine G2 individuals who did not participate in bilingual education either did not qualify as ELs or their parents chose not to enroll them.

As predicted, because G3s are typically simultaneous bilinguals, of the 45 G3 speakers asked, only eight said they had attended a bilingual program. Also as predicted, half of these were G3:1s, meaning that they had one G2 parent, that is, someone more likely to use Spanish in the home. In addition, two G3:2 individuals who had participated in bilingual education had one parent who had arrived in Chicago at age 8, meaning that this parent was one year shy of qualifying as a G1. It also means that this parent had lived monolingually in Spanish for eight years, developing a Spanish proficiency level much stronger than that of most G2 individuals raised in Chicago. Thus,

Table 8.3. BILINGUAL EDUCATION AND SPANISH PROFICIENCY LEVELS, SEQUENTIAL BILINGUALS (N = 43).

Bilingual education	Average Spanish proficiency
Yes (n = 25)	3.0
No (n = 14)	4.3

it makes a bit more sense that their child could have shown up to kindergarten with limited English proficiency. One G3:2 individual had attended the dual-language program profiled in August and Shanahan (2006), which is an enrichment program, meaning that children do not require an EL designation to enroll. She was the only individual in our corpus to have attended such a school where half or more of the day was taught in Spanish; we will return to the potentially crucial role of dual-language education in promoting Spanish proficiency in Chapter 9. This leaves just one G3:2 individual out of nine who had participated in bilingual education for whom we could not identify an explanation for having received an EL designation and subsequent bilingual education services.

Before returning our focus to the proficiency inliers, we examine for all CHISPA sequential bilinguals (both proficiency inliers and outliers) whether having participated in bilingual education appeared to have contributed to Spanish proficiency. We display this information in Table 8.3.[16]

We see that, contrary to findings cited earlier (August & Shanahan, 2006), the sequential bilingual individuals who had participated in bilingual education did not have stronger Spanish proficiency as adults than their cohort members who had not gone through bilingual education. However, we consider our findings unreliable because, as mentioned earlier, we do not have access to information on EL status or on type of program attended and length of attendance. We also separated the proficiency inliers to examine their bilingual education. Approximately half of the proficiency inlier G2s had been in bilingual education, and most of the G3s had not. Thus, it is not the case that proficiency inliers were either more or less likely to have participated in TBE.

Opinions about bilingual education in the CHISPA corpus ranged widely from very positive to highly negative. Some of the positive opinions

---

16. There were three individuals for whom we unfortunately could not determine the order of acquisition of their Spanish and English and an additional four G2 sequential bilinguals for whom we did not have information on whether they had participated in bilingual education.

underscored how essential it was for children to have access to teachers and to instruction they could understand:

> Pienso que es importante para los niños que vienen de México o Puerto Rico y no saben inglés, cuando llegan aquí se sienten como tímidos y no saben como aprochar al maestro. Y, así si tiene a un maestro que sabe hablar español, se sienten más cómodos en hablarle y decirle en qué tienen problemas. (#19, G2 Puerto Rican female)
>
> I think it is important for the kids who come from Mexico and Puerto Rico and don't know English, when they get here they feel like timid and they don't know how to approach the teacher. And if they have a teacher who knows Spanish, they feel more comfortable speaking to them and telling them with what they are having problems.
>
> Pienso que es algo esencial. Yo he visto muchas ventajas que tiene la educación bilingüe para niños que vienen de México. Y, cuando tienen educación bilingüe es como un, un escalón que les facilita llegar hacia más arriba. (#59, G2 Mexican male)
>
> I think it is essential. I have seen a lot of advantages that bilingual education brings to the children who come from Mexico. And when they have bilingual education it's like a step up that allows them to achieve more.

Others felt that bilingual education would contribute to Spanish proficiency or at least help prevent its decline:

> Se necesita algo de eso. Creo que, uhm, es gente, like myself, se le olvida el español cuando andan en la escuela, ay, es puro inglés, so yeah. (#34, G3 Mexican female)
>
> Some of that is necessary. I think that, uhm, it's people, like myself, who forget Spanish when they get to school, ay, it is only English, so yeah.
>
> Creo que es muy bueno, I mean, I would have loved to, like, yo sé que ahora mi español no es tan bueno porque yo no quería hablar español cuando yo era nena. Yo no sé por qué, pero no quería hablarlo. (#40, G3 Puerto Rican female)
>
> I think it is very good, I mean, I would have loved to, like, I know that now my Spanish isn't that good because I didn't want to speak it when I was a young girl. I don't know know why, but I didn't want to speak it.

However, there were also very negative opinions held by some participants and/or their parents about bilingual education, reflecting a belief that these programs slow down the acquisition of English. Speaker #34, quoted above suggesting that she could have benefited from bilingual education, said it was her mother's choice not to enroll her despite her qualifying as an EL:

Entré a kindergarten y me querían meter en programas bilingües y, am, mi mamá no quería eso, so me cambiaron a clases regulares. [. . .] Porque ella sabía que me iba a retrasar, que no iba a, como que, yeah, they were going to teach me a little slower than if I was in regular class. (#34, G3 Mexican female)

I started kindergarten and they wanted to put me in bilingual programs and, am, my mother didn't want that, so they changed me to regular classes. [. . .] Because she knew it would slow me down, that I was not going to, like, yeah, they were going to teach me a little slower than if I was in regular class.

Echoing #34's mother's concerns, this 23-year-old G2 Puerto Rican woman felt that she was not taught English quickly enough:

Yo creo que no deben de meter todos los latinos en una clase donde les enseñan todo en español y supuestamente es bilingüe. Yo creo que deben de hablar más inglés porque es el idioma más que se usa aquí. So, yo creo que ellos tuvieron que enseñar mejor, porque cuando yo me fui a otra escuela, se me hizo bien difícil aprender el inglés cuando yo ya lo debería de saber, yo tenía nueve años. (#36, G2 Puerto Rican female)

I don't think they should put all the Latinos in a class where they teach them everything in Spanish and that is supposedly bilingual. I think they should speak more English because it is the language that is most used here. So, I think that they had to teach better, because when I went to another school, it was very difficult for me to learn English when I should have already known it, I was already nine years old.

A handful of participants like this 52-year-old woman felt that some individuals took advantage of bilingual education programs:

Cuando yo vine a la escuela, there was no such thing as bilingual learning. Yo era la única latina en mi clase. It was sink or swim [*pause*] and I swam. Nadie hablaba español so tuve que aprender. Por eso a veces yo no tengo paciencia con la gente que pide tanto cuando ya tienen tanto. Y yo pienso que estamos haciendo la gente vaga porque yo vi un niño de ocho años nacido aquí que no hablaba inglés, ¡qué barbaridad! (#21, G2 Puerto Rican female)

When I came to the school, there was no such thing as bilingual learning. I was the only Latina in my class. It was sink or swim [*pause*] and I swam. No one spoke Spanish so I had to learn. That is why sometimes I have no patience with the people who ask for so much when they already have so much. I think we are making people lazy because I saw a nine-year-old kid born here who didn't know English. That's outrageous!

Finally, there were several more nuanced opinions that bilingual education was necessary for recently arrived children but that English needed to be emphasized more, particularly for older arrivals:

Llegas a este país y tienes que aprender la lengua y es bueno que te ayuden pero hasta cierto tiempo determinado porque si no, qué sentido tiene que vengas a este país y te estén dando las clases en tu idioma y no te estás forzando para aprender el idioma que aquí se habla. [Tengo] amigos que entraron conmigo a la high school, iban dos años en el programa y para tiempo de graduación no, no hablaban inglés porque todas sus clases eran en español. (#56, G1, Mexican male)

You arrive in this country and you have to learn the language and it is good that they help you but only for a period of time because if not, what sense does it make to come to this country and they are giving you classes in your native language and you are not making the effort to learn the language that is spoken here. [I have] friends who started with me in high school, they had been in the program two years and at graduation time, they didn't, they didn't speak English because all their classes were in Spanish.

Overall, we see that either a majority of G2s participated in bilingual education or we feel reasonably confident that they began kindergarten with EL status and would have qualified for bilingual education. It is far less likely for a G3 to arrive in kindergarten with a level of English proficiency low enough to qualify for bilingual education; in the rare cases where this happened, one of the parents was almost always a G2. The majority of opinions about bilingual education across generational groups were positive, but there were some strong negative opinions as well. We also saw that having participated in a bilingual education program was not related to average Spanish proficiency levels. However, it may be the case that some of our proficiency inliers described in this chapter reached their level of Spanish proficiency in large part due to having participated in bilingual education and that it might have been lower had they not done so.

8.3.5. Travel to Mexico or Puerto Rico

For the fifth and final factor, proficiency in Spanish can be strongly impacted by visits to a Spanish-speaking location to interact in domestic and community spaces with extended family. Although unfortunately not every participant was asked about this, many said they had been to Mexico and/or Puerto Rico. Some went at least once a year for a week or two, while others traveled to their parents' home country not very frequently but for relatively extended stays of a month or more. This young woman credited a month in Puerto Rico in fifth grade with her current interest in her culture:

> En quinto grado pasé un mes en Puerto Rico con mi madre y mis abuelos y . . . I don't know, cuando regresé era un poco distinto porque allá todo el mundo hablaba español. Allá es donde empecé a interesarme un poquito más, you know, porque antes [. . .] yo no estaba tan pendiente de mi cultura, you know . . . [. . .] no le hacía mucho caso. (#4, G3 Puerto Rican female)

> In fifth grade I spent a month in Puerto Rico with my mom and my grandparents and . . . I don't know, when I returned it was a bit different because over there everyone spoke Spanish. That is where I started to get interested a bit more, you know, because before [. . .] I wasn't so aware of my culture, you know . . . [. . .] I didn't pay a lot of attention to it.

While in Puerto Rico, she watched the telenovela called *Amor en silencio* with her grandfather, and she watched it again when it aired later in the U.S. She said that the trip also enabled her to connect with her mother's language and music:

> Yes girl, I got double the novela. Um, and you know what, funny enough, I think, eso es donde yo empecé también en oír a mi mamá hablar español, oír la música que ella ponía para limpiar. Es donde me, um . . . I picked up— . . . hablar en español.

> Yes girl, I got double the soap opera. Um, and you know what, funny enough, I think, that is where I also began to hear to my mom speak Spanish, hearing the music she used to put on to clean. It is where I, um . . . I picked up— . . . speaking in Spanish."

Her Spanish proficiency was rated at level 2; it is reasonable to posit that her Spanish would have been even weaker at the time of the interview had she not spent that month in Puerto Rico. This is probably also true of #123 (rated at level 4):

> Mi mamá me hablaba en español porque ella nació en Puerto Rico y estaba allí hasta los dieciocho. [. . .] Para mi papá, él estaba mas cómodo hablando inglés so estábamos como en una batalla, y inglés ganó porque estamos en los Estados Unidos so yeah no había mucha chanza. Pero cada verano nosotros íbamos con mi mamá a Puerto Rico, tenía que hablar español como tres semanas . . . al año."

My mom spoke to me in Spanish because she was born in Puerto Rico and was there until she was eighteen. [. . .] For my dad, he was more comfortable speaking English so we were like in a battle, and English won because we are in the United States so yeah there wasn't much chance. But every summer we would go to Puerto Rico with my mom, I would have to speak Spanish like three weeks . . . a year.

A 45-year-old G1 father echoed how difficult it was for bilingual parents to raise bilingual children in Chicago. His two older children did not want to speak Spanish with him, "y ya me cansé de tratar," and his youngest "tiene un acento en el español y no le gusta hablar el español, pero [. . .] ahora lo mandamos pa' Puerto Rico por tres semanas so allá tenía que hablar español. Y vino más, cómo se llama . . . le gustaba, hablarlo más" (and then I got tired of trying, and his youngest has an accent in Spanish and he doesn't like to speak in Spanish, but [. . .] now we send him to Puerto Rico for three weeks so over there he had to speak Spanish. And he came back, how do call it . . . he liked speaking it more) (#55, G1 Puerto Rican male). And this 18-year-old G2 Mexican female described how her social life in Mexico changed once her Spanish proficiency improved:

Yo siempre iba a México cada año y no podía comunicarme con mis primas y no me gustaba. So un año que regresamos de México, le dije a mi mamá, "enséñame el español, nomás puro español, no inglés." [. . .] Yo siempre era muy callada, muy tímida, y nunca hablé con mis primas o mis primos y siempre me quedaba, como en el brazo de mi amá. Y ahora cuando estoy en México voy a los bailes con mis primas, me quedo en su casa y, todos mis primos y mis tíos dicen que yo he cambiado mucho. [. . .] Ahora puedo hablar de puros secretos con mis primas, ahora puedo ir a los bailes y hablar con muchachos. Antes yo nunca hablaba con ellos. Siempre cuando iba a México yo siempre buscaba a un muchacho que era Dallas o era de Houston que sabía el inglés. Pero ahora me junto con todos, con los muchachos de México los mis primas, mis primos. Ahora sí puedo hablar con ellos y sí nos llevamos bien. (#12, G2 Mexican female)

I always went to Mexico every year and I couldn't communicate with my cousins and I didn't like it. So one year when we returned from Mexico, I said to my mom, "teach me Spanish, only Spanish, no English." [. . .] I was always very quiet very timid and never spoke with my cousins and I always stayed like attached to my mom. And now when I am in Mexico I go to dances with my cousins, I stay at their homes and, all of my cousins and my uncles say that I have changed a lot. [. . .] Now I can share secrets with my cousins, now I can go to dances and talk with the guys. Before I never talked with them. Always when I went to Mexico I always looked for this guy who was from Dallas or Houston who knew English. But now I get together with all of them, with the guys from Mexico my cousins. Now I can talk with them and yes we get along well.

We offer these final observations about visits to Mexico or Puerto Rico, but because not all participants were asked about it (or they were not asked in the same way), they are speculative in nature. We noticed the following trends:

- More G2s traveled to their family's region of origin than G3s did.
- Slightly more Mexicans visited Mexico than Puerto Ricans visited Puerto Rico.
- MexiRicans had the highest rates of travel, perhaps because they had two locations in which to visit family.

Periods of time that bilingual Spanish-speakers spend abroad typically lead to linguistic gains during both short and long stays (Pozzi, Quan, & Escalante 2021). It stands to reason that extensive contact with monolingual speakers positively affected the Spanish proficiency of our participants.

8.4. PROFICIENCY OUTLIERS

In this final section, we discuss the 31 speakers we refer to as proficiency outliers—speakers whose Spanish proficiency was either higher or lower than the average for their generational group. This refers to G2s with a Spanish proficiency level of 5 or 2 and G3s with a high 4 or 5 or with a low 1. The numbers of individuals in each of these five categories appear in the shaded cells in Table 8.4.

Many of the factors identified for the proficiency inliers were important for the outliers as well. For example, having an *abuela* in the house contributed positively to Spanish proficiency for inliers, but it did so even more for outliers. We divide this section into two parts. The first presents the narratives

Table 8.4. SPANISH PROFICIENCY OUTLIERS (SHADED CELLS, *N* = 31).

Proficiency	*n*, G2 avg 3.76	*n*, G3 avg 2.77
5	11 above	2 above
4	(18)	10 above
3	(18)	(17)
2	3 below	(17)
1	0	5 below
Total	14	17

of individuals who had higher proficiency than their generational group's average, and the second looks at speakers whose Spanish proficiency was lower than their generational group's average.

8.4.1. High-Proficiency Outliers (*n* = 23)

Here we examine the narratives of 23 individuals: the 11 G2 speakers with a Spanish proficiency level of 5 and the 12 G3 speakers with levels of 5 or 4.

G2 Speakers with a High Proficiency of Level 5 (*n* = 11)

Eleven G2 speakers out of 50 in the CHISPA corpus (22%) were rated as having a Spanish proficiency level of 5. They were fairly equally spread across the regional origin groups—five Mexicans, three Puerto Ricans, and three MexiRicans—suggesting that regional background is not related to this outcome in any important way. In the CHISPA corpus, this maximum proficiency rating was typically applied to G1 speakers only; it is remarkable that people raised in the U.S. should develop such strong levels of Spanish. How did they do so, when the group average was a much lower 3.76?

For nine of these 11 speakers, some demographic information provided plausible explanations for their high proficiency. Recall from Chapter 2 that all G2s have G1 parents who immigrated at age 12 or later, but G2s can be born on the U.S. mainland or brought there by the age of 5. We explained that the five individuals in our corpus who arrived between the ages of 6 and 8, frequently called G1.5, were grouped with the G2s. Seven of these high-proficiency outlier G2 individuals were born abroad, and of these, four had arrived in the U.S. before age 5, and three arrived between ages 3 and 8. One of the 3-year-old arrivals had also spent a year of high school in Puerto Rico. Every year spent in Mexico or Puerto Rico was another year of input and interaction only in Spanish. In fact, none of the 10 G2 individuals in the CHISPA corpus who were born abroad had proficiency levels lower than 4 or 5. As for the other two of these 11 individuals, they had spent significant time in Latin America; one had completed two years of high school in Puerto Rico, and the other had spent ages 4–6 in Mexico.

In addition to being born abroad, several of these individuals lived with a monolingual Spanish-speaking grandparent while growing up. For example, this is how #18 (who arrived from Puerto Rico at age 3) described the opposite language conditions in her childhood home (Spanish) versus her school (English):

[En casa hablábamos] español, porque mi abuelita no hablaba nada nada, nadie hablaba inglés. En el tiempo que yo me crié, estudié la escuela . . . no había nada de de español, no había ningún programa, nada, todo era en inglés. No le podíamos hablar [inglés] a mi abuelita, porque mi abuelita no nos entendía. (#18, G2 Puerto Rican female)

[At home we spoke] Spanish, because my grandma didn't speak any, no one spoke English. At the time I was raised, I studied in school . . . there was no Spanish, there wasn't any program. Nothing, everything was in English. We couldn't speak [English] to my grandma, because my grandma didn't understand us.

Regarding the final two individuals in this category, we had to extrapolate from their narratives how they might have developed such strong levels of Spanish. Speaker #111 was a 23-year-old MexiRican female raised on the North Side of the city who was hoping to become a neonatal nurse. Her mother, who began working at Burger King and eventually became a cosmetologist, had arrived from Mexico at age 15, and her father, who worked in construction and in trucking prior to a back injury, came from Puerto Rico at 13. The family spent four months every summer in Mexico with her mother's family until her parents divorced when she was 8 years old, after which time they still went annually but for only one to two months. At the time of the interview, she was working as an insurance salesperson and said she used Spanish on the job very frequently because she was the only person in the large office who spoke it. She held another job as a swimming instructor at a public park and spoke Spanish with the cleaning crew because they did not know English. Her husband did not know English, so she said she used Spanish in her home. This combination of factors—regular extended periods in Mexico as a child, using Spanish on the job, and a monolingual Spanish-speaking husband—help us understand her high level of Spanish proficiency. Unfortunately, she dropped her high school Spanish class because she was made to believe that her Spanish was inferior. Although she was against bilingual education and was glad her parents had not enrolled her in such a program because she believed it confused children, she held highly positive attitudes about Spanish maintenance within families, evident through her criticisms of one of her aunts for not speaking Spanish with her children. When asked whether her 5-month-old son would know Spanish as well as she did when he became her age, she said that she hoped so and very much wanted him to. She had already brought him to visit her father (the baby's *abuelo*) at his ranch in Mexico, continuing the tradition that she herself had lived as a child.

The remaining G2 speaker with a Spanish proficiency level of 5 was another MexiRican, a 42-year-old woman whose mother, a hotel cleaning-service worker, arrived from Mexico at age 14 and whose father, a chef, came from Puerto Rico as a young adult. She had been to each parent's hometown only once, for approximately three weeks each. She used Spanish at her job at a window-framing company because:

> Cuando es alguien que yo veo que es hispano, uso el español, no soy fantoche. Me gusta que cuando, si es una persona hispana, hablar el español, no el inglés. (#107, G2 MexiRican female)
>
> When it's someone that I can tell is Hispanic, I use Spanish, I am not a show-off. I like it when, if it's a Hispanic person, speak in Spanish, not in English.

She said her childhood home was Spanish-speaking only and that "yo siempre soy una de esas personas que en la casa, aunque sean nacidos uno aquí, es español. El inglés se usas en la escuela o donde es necesario" (I always am one of those people that in the house, even if you were born here, it's Spanish). However, following through on this decision was clearly not easy, because she later said of her own sons' Spanish: "Saben bien. Se saben defender, o sea, en la casa usábamos los dos idiomas. Con mi hijo el grande usaba el inglés, pero yo lo regañaba más: 'Háblame español, yo no soy gringa. Tu inglés háblalo con tus amigos, en tus trabajos, en donde tú quieras, pero aquí en la casa es puro español'" (They know it well. They know how to defend themselves, in other words, at home we use both languages. With my son the eldest when he used English, but I scolded him the most: 'Speak to me in Spanish, I am not a gringa. Your English use it with your friends, at your jobs, wherever you want, but here in the house it's Spanish only).

G3 Speakers with a High Proficiency of Level 4 or 5 (n = 12)

Out of 51 G3 speakers in the CHISPA corpus, there were 12 (24%) high-proficiency outliers, two whose Spanish proficiency was rated at level 5 and 10 rated at level 4. Four were Mexican, and six were MexiRican; just two were Puerto Rican. First we looked for demographic factors that might suggest greater amounts of Spanish use. Overall, eight of the 12 (two-thirds) were G3:1, meaning that they had one parent who had arrived in Chicago as an adult and thus were Spanish-dominant. Two of them had even a bit more possible Spanish support because their U.S.-raised parent had arrived in Chicago at age 5 rather than being born there. We note about the two G3 speakers rated at Spanish proficiency level 5 that both were G3:1; one had a G2 parent who had arrived at age 5, and one had spent two years of high school in Puerto Rico, thus bolstering her Spanish proficiency significantly.

What about the four G3:2 speakers in this category, who seemed to have the most against them for developing strong levels of Spanish (most importantly, two U.S.-raised parents)? One of them, a 35-year-old male who had studied anthropology, had an Irish American mother (who did not speak Spanish), a Mexican father who had been raised in Chicago, and an older brother. He said that when his G2 father was in school in the 1940s, the nuns used to hit students for speaking Spanish; how did his son arrive at a proficiency level of 4? Nothing in his upbringing revealed any circumstances connected to this strong level. He said his house was mostly English-speaking and that only his paternal grandparents used Spanish there, but they worked outside of the home. The only time he felt obligated to use Spanish was during brief family visits to Mexico and in Chicago with his Mexican friends' parents who did not know English. He said he always felt ashamed of what he felt was his very weak Spanish; he said his family in Mexico frequently laughed at him. The secret to his Spanish proficiency appears to be that he lived and worked in Mexico for "many years" as an adult. He spoke extensively about his family, friends, and even a godchild there. When asked about his own future children's possibilities of knowing Spanish, he replied:

> He pensado mucho en eso pero no tengo la solución. Quiero que aprendan los dos idiomas. Si me caso con una mexicana pues . . . tal vez. Si me caso con una mexico-americana, un poquito menos pero tal vez. Si me caso con una mujer de aquí que no habla el español pues . . . no sé, no tengo la solución, pues. (#44, G3 Mexican male)

> I have thought about that a lot but I don't have a solution. I want them to learn both languages. If I marry a Mexican well . . . maybe. If I marry a Mexican American, a bit less but maybe. If I marry a woman from here who doesn't speak Spanish well . . . I don't know, I don't have a solution, so.

The second G3:2 individual with a proficiency level of 4 was #95, a 22-year-old man raised in the McKinley Park area on the South Side of Chicago who was studying criminal justice and hoped to work for the FBI. His mother arrived from Mexico at age 5, and he did not know his father. He had only been to Mexico once when he was 2 years old, for three months. He used Spanish at his job at a security company. He said that Spanish was the primary language in his home, which was somewhat unusual given that his mother was raised in Chicago, but he said "mis tíos, mi abuela, mi abuelo me hablaban en español. Todos me hablaban en español. El inglés yo creo que lo aprendí en la escuela o mirando tele." (my uncles, my grandmother, my grandfather spoke to me in Spanish. They all spoke to me in Spanish. I think I learned to speak English in school or watching TV.) He also worked in La Villita, a highly Mexican neighborhood mentioned in Chapter 2. There are no other clues in his interview to explain his strong Spanish proficiency, although we note that his mother lived monolingually in Mexico until the age of 5, and his Chicago-raised father, who as the other G2 parent may have been a predominately English speaker, was not in fact present in the home.

The third person, #22, was a 23-year-old MexiRican woman who lived in the North Side neighborhood of Logan Square until her parents divorced, when she moved to Puerto Rico for three years with her father. This explains her strong level of Spanish. She said:

> Cuando me fui para Puerto Rico, yo sabía más inglés y era un poco difícil porque todo el mundo se burlaban de mí, me decían la gringa o hacían comentarios que mi español no era muy bueno. So mientras los años pasaban empecé a hablar más y adaptarme más al idioma. So cuando me vine de nuevo para acá, básicamente era lo mismo, you know, mi español era mejor que el inglés. Y la gente se confundían porque no me entendían bien o no podía pronunciar las palabras adecuadamente. (#22, G3 MexiRican female)

> When I went to Puerto Rico, I knew more English and it was a bit difficult because everyone made fun of me, they called me the gringa or made comments that my Spanish wasn't very good. So as the years passed I started to speak more and adapt myself to the language. So when I came back here again, basically it was the same thing, you know, my Spanish was better than my English. And people would get confused because they didn't understand me very well or I couldn't pronounce the words adequately.

She held a degree in animal health from a community college and was working in customer service at an electronics store, where she used Spanish frequently because she was one of the few people working there who spoke it.

Finally, #113 was a 27-year-old MexiRican female raised in Cicero, a heavily Mexican township right outside of Chicago, who was a medical technician studying to become a nurse. Both her Mexican mother and her Puerto Rican father had been raised in Chicago, and she said her father barely knew Spanish. Her maternal grandmother, who knew no English, lived downstairs while she was growing up, about which she said: "Yo podía bajar con ella y ella siempre me hablaba de sus historias, de cuando era niña y diferente cosas" (I could go down with her and she always told me her stories, about when she was a child and different things). She also used to spend three months in Mexico every summer until approximately age 15 (she had been to Puerto Rico twice, for one or two weeks each time). As a medical assistant, she used a lot of Spanish on the phone with patients, because only she and one other woman in the office spoke Spanish. She said she felt a strong sense of unity with her Mexican family and that knowledge of Spanish was important. She and her G2 Mexican husband used both Spanish and English with their 7-year-old son. She said that her son's school tested his English (per the policies of U.S. public schools explained earlier), but it was strong enough that he did not qualify for bilingual education. This meant that unless his parents sought out and located a dual-language school to enroll him in, all of his schooling would be in English. In sum, it was likely living with her Mexican grandmother and the regular summers in Mexico that enabled her to develop her strong level of Spanish proficiency, which she continued to maintain at work and with her bilingual husband. In fact, we note that three of the four G3:2 high-proficiency outliers had lived relatively extensive periods of time in Puerto Rico or Mexico.

8.4.2. Low-Proficiency Outliers (*n* = 8)

We turn now to the eight cases that are less encouraging when examining Spanish vitality in Chicago. There were three G2 speakers rated with a Spanish proficiency level of 2, which is outlying from the group average of 3.76, and five G3 speakers with a proficiency of 1, outlying from the group average of 2.77. We note that only one speaker out of the eight was Mexican, echoing findings from Chapter 2 about higher levels of Spanish proficiency among Mexicans but not a large enough trend to warrant strong conclusions. At first blush, one might be heartened by the fact that we found only eight low-proficiency outliers out of 124 speakers in the CHISPA corpus. However, this is misleading, because there are plenty of G3 individuals (and perhaps G2s as well) who would not have agreed to participate in an hour-long interview in Spanish because they felt their Spanish was not strong enough. Yet we also note that proficiency can change across a lifetime, and such individuals could very likely increase their Spanish proficiency should they be willing and able to create the necessary linguistic input and output opportunities.

G2 Speakers with a Low Proficiency of Level 2 (n = 3)

There were three G2 speakers whose Spanish proficiency was rated at level 2. Two were MexiRican, and one was Puerto Rican; none was Mexican. What circumstances might have led the children of Spanish-speaking immigrants to develop Spanish proficiency that was this limited? Speaker #80 was a 20-year-old MexiRican male. His mother arrived from Mexico and his father from Puerto Rico, both as young adults; she worked as a technician in a factory, and he taught history. Speaker #80 had been to Puerto Rico once at age 4 and to Mexico five times for short periods. He said he did not use Spanish at his job as a processor at a bank. Although he said he used only Spanish with his mother because she did not speak English (his father did), he had trouble understanding some of the interview questions and answered many of them in English. Because he was MexiRican, he was asked a series of specific questions about each variety of Spanish, and when asked what others had said about how his Spanish sounded, he laughed and replied, "Que necesito a practicar." (That I need to practice.) In sum, we could not discern any clear explanations for why his Spanish proficiency was so low, particularly since he claimed to have been speaking Spanish with his mother his entire life.

Speaker #109 was a 28-year-old MexiRican female raised on the North Side of Chicago. Her mother arrived from Puerto Rico at age 13 after a short period in New York. Her father arrived from Mexico in high school, which he completed in Chicago and where he met his future wife. She said that her father did not speak English very well and that her mother spoke it better than he did. Both parents worked in factories, and she often spoke Spanish with her grandmother who lived three blocks away. She did not use Spanish at her accounting job but had positive attitudes toward it, saying that Latinos should maintain it. Her case is particularly curious because she was raised by two immigrants, she lived for six months in Puerto Rico when she was 10 years old, and her mother put her in bilingual education from first through third grades: "I felt like I didn't fit in, but mi mamá me puso ahí porque quería que aprendiera el español. But it was weird" (but my mom put me there because she wanted me to learn Spanish.). Yet her proficiency level was rated at 2. We were unable to locate any convincing explanations.

Finally, #115 is another curious case, a 21-year-old Puerto Rican female also raised on the North Side of the city in the Puerto Rican neighborhood of Humboldt Park. Her mother arrived in Chicago from Puerto Rico at age 23 (after a period of living on the mainland from ages 12–17) and worked in factories, stores, and ultimately as a school secretary; her father remained on the island. She did not use Spanish at her job as a receptionist, and she was studying to be an art teacher. She said that Spanish was her first language, and she was even in a bilingual education program from first through sixth grades. Although she responded affirmatively that U.S. Latinos should maintain Spanish, she was not hopeful about her own possibilities. When asked whether her future children would know Spanish as well as she did, she said no, because she would be speaking mostly English, and she mentioned that her younger sister did not know much Spanish, either.

G3 Speakers with a Low Proficiency of Level 1 (n = 5)

Finally, we analyze the five individuals with the lowest levels of Spanish proficiency in the CHISPA corpus. As one might predict, all were G3:2 except for one, #35. One was Mexican, one was Puerto Rican, and three were MexiRican. While a proficiency level of 1 was below the 2.77 average for the G3s in this corpus, we note that this level indicates an ability to hold a conversation in Spanish. In this chapter, we have heard from participants who claimed their

G3 family members (nieces and nephews, cousins, and even younger siblings) did not speak Spanish at all. While we do not have direct evidence of the proficiency of those individuals, there is little reason to doubt our participants' assessments. Thus, a Spanish proficiency level of 1 may in fact be on par with or even higher than the average of all G3s in Chicago.

We begin with the three MexiRicans. Speaker #28 was an 18-year-old male who had been raised by his mother, who was born in Mexico and came to the U.S. at age 5. He had lived in Texas for two years with his Spanish-dominant grandmother and aunt, who "speak only a little bit of English, but you know, not so much. So, you know, I try to do my part and try to speak Spanish." He said he learned Spanish during that time: "Mi tía dizo que 'yo hablo español o no como'" (I had to speak Spanish or I don't eat). But his Spanish contained multiple misconjugated verbs (including *dizo*, above). He had not visited Puerto Rico or Mexico. In sum, we did not locate any particular evidence that might point to a reason for his low proficiency.

Next, #46 was a 24-year-old MexiRican female. We present here a relatively lengthy excerpt from her interview to demonstrate not only her spoken Spanish (which we have edited slightly for length but otherwise rendered how she produced it, including pauses) but also some insight into her acquisition circumstances and her motivations for "relearning" Spanish:

> Well, hay una presencia de inglés más en mi casa porque mis abuelitos y mis padres, uhm, crean que para su—suceder en este país, necesita la lengua de este país. Entonces especialmente para mis abuelitos es muy importante que sus—que sus niños tienen la habilidad para hablar en inglés y con una—una acento que es muy angloamerican, no es un—no—ellos no—no quieren que sus niños hablan con un acento de español. Y because of that, hay una importancia que está—que está placed onto, uhm, inglés. Pero yo creo que es muy importante para, uhm, guardar su lengua porque yo creo que, uhm, es una asimilación de lenguas, es una ejemplo de colonialism y porque en esto yo—yo creo que es muy importante que yo, uhm, relearn mi lengua porque es obvio que—que tengo muchas dificultades con mi lengua y es una—es una otra manera que el gobierno y los capitalistos—¿cómo se llama?—y la gente que está—que está muy poderosa y muy . . . ricos, tiene, es una manera para like, uhm, muerte cultural, cultural death porque es una—es una manera para, uhm, para tiene poder sobre una—una comunidad o una—un—una grup—un grupo de gente como latinos o como—or como gente que están—que están de color. Hay mu—muchos ejemplos de esto situación. Entonces es muy importante para mí para relearn mi español. (#46, G3 MexiRican female)
>
> Well, there is more of a presence of English in my house because my grandparents and my parents, uhm, think that to su—succeed in this country,

you need the language of this country. So especially for my grandparents it is very important that their—that their kids have the ability to speak in English and with an—a very American accent, it is not a, not them, they don't want their kids to speak with a Spanish accent. And because of that, there is an importance that is, that is placed onto, uhm, English. But I think it is very important to uhm, preserve your language because I think that, uhm, it is an assimilation of languages, it is an example of colonialism and because about that I—I think it is very important that I, uhm, relearn my language because it is obvious that—that I have a lot of difficulties with my language and it is one—it is one way the government and the capitalists—how do you say it?—and the people that are—that are very powerful and very . . . rich, have, it is a way for them to like, uhm, cultural death, cultural death but it is a—it is a way for, uhm, to have power over a—a community or a—a—a grou—a group of people like the Latinos or like or like people who are—people of color. There are ma—many examples of this situation. So it is very important for me to relearn my Spanish.

The third person was #78, a 21-year-old MexiRican female whose father had arrived from Puerto Rico at age 8 and whose mother was born and raised in Chicago. However, we could not identify any salient reasons that might explain her low Spanish proficiency. She said she spoke both languages as a small child and that while her Puerto Rican grandparents spoke mostly in Spanish, her Mexican grandparents used both Spanish and English. She answered all of the attitudinal questions in ways that supported Spanish maintenance: her parents stressed the importance of knowing two languages, she thought it was important to maintain the language for cultural reasons, she felt that both parents and schools are responsible for teaching it, and she wanted her future children to speak Spanish. She claimed to use Spanish at her job with Medicare, but she had never traveled to Puerto Rico or Mexico. Hers was one of the shortest interviews in the corpus. She was asked every single question, and the interviewer—a Mexican American woman roughly the same age as the interviewee—was one of the most successful members of our team at eliciting narratives. Despite several attempts to get her to talk, #78's responses were no longer than the following excerpt and were usually shorter. When asked whether she used different terms to identify herself ethnically when asked by a white, Black, or Latino person, she replied, "Ah, yo cambio. Aha. Porque cuando es blanca, les digo que es hispanic, pero yo uso latina. Pero cuando está hablando con las personas, los latinos, que eres latina pero con los blancos, Hispanic" (I change. Uh-huh. Because when it's a white person, I say [is] Hispanic, but I use Latina. But when [is] talking with people, the Latinos, that [you're] Latina, but with whites, Hispanic). Although we have no extensive stretches of Spanish from her, the combination of very short responses plus her subject-verb agreement issues, in particular the use of third-person singular instead of first-person singular (*es* instead of *soy* and *está* instead of *estoy* when referring to herself) and her use of second-person *eres* instead of *soy*, led us to the rating of 1.

Speaker #84 was a 23-year-old Puerto Rican female. Her attitudes toward Spanish were positive, and her parents told her it was important to learn two languages, but they never actually spoke to her in Spanish:

> Siempre me dijo que, que aprender y saber el español es importante. Pero no, no . . . me enseñaron. So, es algo raro porque siempre me dicen, "Oh, tú no puedes hablar en español, tú tienes que aprender español," pero, ustedes me hablan en inglés, so, ¿cómo voy a aprender? So, me dice, pero, no le hace [*laughs*]. (#84, G3 Puerto Rican female)

> They always told me that learning and knowing Spanish is important. But they didn't teach me. So, it's strange because they always tell me "Oh, you can't speak Spanish, you need to learn Spanish," but they always talk to me in English, so how am I going to learn it? So they tell me, but they don't do it.

This frustration defined the tone of #84's conversation about her Spanish: although knowing Spanish was important to her and her family, it was not an ability that she could achieve on her own. We note here her use of *dijo* where she probably meant *dijeron* (referring to her parents) as well as her simple sentence structure, repetitions, and pauses. She said that she learned English first and was exposed to Spanish through her great-grandmother:

> De mi bisabuela, como ella me habló en español, uhm, pero, como ella también entendió la inglés, no, no hablé con ella en español. Pero, yo le entendí. Aprendí el español como en la secundaria, uhm, y después, también en el colegio. Uhm, y todavía tengo problemas hablar en español. (#84, G3 Puerto Rican female)

> From my great-grandmother, because she spoke to me in Spanish, uhm, because she also understood English, I didn't speak to her in Spanish. But, I understood her. I learned Spanish like in high school, uhm, and then, also in college. Uhm, and I still have problems speaking in Spanish.

Thus, hers seemed like a clear case of lack of input in Spanish during childhood.

Finally, unlike the other four speakers in this category, 20-year-old Mexican #35 was not a G3:2 but a G3:1. He had considerable difficulty understanding some of the interview questions and, like #78 seen earlier, his answers were typically very short. It is unclear whether he was generally a taciturn young man, or if his lack of abilities in Spanish led him to make the choice to speak so little rather than codeswitch into English. His longest stretch of speech came in response to the question of what he would do if he won a million dollars:

> Me compraré un coche primero, y dar y lo demás. . . . ¡No! No, y otra parte le pagaré pa'tras a mis papás un poquito, y el otro porciento lo guardaré para que aumentara umm like the you know how you put it in the bank and you get some what do you call it? (#35, G3 Mexican male)

> I would buy a car first, and give and the rest. . . . No! No, and another part I will pay back my parents a bit, and the other percentage I will save it so that it increases umm like the you know how you put it in the bank and you get some what do you call it?

His mother was born in California, but his father arrived from Zacatecas, Mexico, at age 15. He was raised in Calumet City (at the southern edge of the city of Chicago, also within Cook County) until age 17, when his family moved 20 miles west to the suburb Tinley Park. He said he learned Spanish first and started using it less when he began learning English. He traveled to Mexico every other year and spoke Spanish with his family there. The only factor we could identify was that he grew up in a neighborhood with lots of white and non-Spanish-speaking people. In the 1990s, Calumet City had a Latino population of just 11%, much lower than that of Chicago. Despite his low proficiency, he said he would transmit Spanish to his future children.

Our five low-proficiency outliers were able to articulate some specific reasons for what they felt had hindered their Spanish development, but there is no sole "smoking gun" behind the lack of intergenerational transmission. Given what we know about the loss of Spanish after G2, it might be more reasonable to assume that transmission will not happen and then look for explanations when it does.

8.5. SUMMARY AND CONCLUSIONS

Although it is not feasible from a one-hour interview to have a complete sense of the circumstances that existed across the life span of an individual that would lead to their linguistic development in two languages, in this chapter we have tried to present convincing accounts, using participants' own words, to paint a portrait of Spanish-language socialization practices across Chicago Latino communities. While the data overall point clearly toward language shift, outcomes for each individual depend on a complex interplay of past, present, and future conditions. For many G2 speakers, developing Spanish proficiency was the default, because their parents did not know English and they did not have older siblings. They were sequential bilinguals who were raised in homes that were largely monolingual in Spanish and who did not begin acquiring English until starting school. In our garden analogy, their Spanish had "protected space to grow" before the acquisition of English began. G2s with older siblings, however, as well as G3 individuals, were often simultaneous bilinguals. While it is certainly possible to develop strong Spanish proficiency alongside English, the trend in our data as well as those of other studies is that English, like the kudzu plant, "takes over the garden," and Spanish proficiency is not developed to the same degree as among sequential bilinguals. It merits underscoring that two of our G2 participants had begun kindergarten dominant in Spanish (evidenced by their participation in a transitional bilingual program, which requires being evaluated as an EL), yet at the time of our interview, their Spanish proficiency was at level 2. This suggests that even when children spend the first few years of their lives practically monolingual in Spanish, they can still lose a great deal of proficiency if the "plant" is not continually watered and cared for.

We noted in Chapter 2 that those G3:1 individuals with one G1 parent had significantly stronger Spanish proficiency as a group than their G3:2 counterparts (who had two G2 parents). This is congruent with our findings in the present chapter that U.S.-raised individuals frequently did not speak Spanish with their own children. Despite positive attitudes toward Spanish and a desire for their children to speak it, our data show that in the U.S., it is extremely challenging for bilinguals to raise bilinguals. G2 parents very frequently defaulted to speaking English in the home, and even some G1 parents commented that their children resisted Spanish and/or that they themselves had simply given up trying to use it with their G2 children. The central role of grandparents in the development of Spanish proficiency among Chicago-raised Latinos cannot be overstated. The presence of consistently Spanish-speaking adults plays such a large role in proficiency that we are even more disinclined to rely on analyses of U.S. Spanish solely based on generational category. We propose that future studies using oral corpora for analysis attempt to conduct some measure of Spanish proficiency. Future research could also interview individuals belonging to three generations within the same families to flesh out different perspectives. These could be additionally supported by ethnographic observations (à la Zentella, 1997), but such work requires enormous time commitment and access to families.

TBE classes may have played a role in the proficiency of the (almost always) G2s who had participated in them. Although in this corpus having attended bilingual education was not connected with stronger adult Spanish proficiency, it could be that the Spanish of bilingual program graduates would have been lower had they not been in these programs. It is also notable that the majority of individuals in our corpus reported using Spanish at their jobs, which not only promotes maintenance of proficiency but can in fact improve communicative abilities in Spanish. However, echoing findings among Chicago high school students (Gorman & Potowski, 2009), most G2s and G3s said that they rarely used Spanish with peers, and only those who had chosen a Spanish-preferring partner used it with their partners.

We noted in Chapter 2 that Mexicans had higher average Spanish proficiency than Puerto Ricans in all three generational groups. Although we were unable to corroborate this via our analyses of participants' narratives, it may be that a greater number of Mexicans were impacted by the presence of a Spanish monolingual in the household and frequent visits to the home country for extended periods; rates of sequential language acquisition did not differ between Mexicans and Puerto Ricans. We also noted in Chapter 2 that the Mexican participants in our corpus tended to:

- Link Spanish to Mexican identity more strongly than Puerto Ricans.
- Live in more concentrated Latino neighborhoods than Puerto Ricans (who commonly lived alongside African Americans), which may promote denser Spanish-speaking social networks.
- Consider Mexican Spanish more prestigious (many Puerto Ricans did so as well).

This combination of factors may create the conditions for Mexicans to retain Spanish to a stronger degree. MexiRicans tended to be somewhat equally divided between participants who benefited from these factors and those who did not.

We have noted repeatedly that only those G3 individuals who felt their Spanish was strong enough to do so agreed to participate in an hour-long interview in Spanish for this study; many G3s in Chicago and around the U.S. do not develop basic conversational levels of proficiency in Spanish. We do not know what proportion of G3 individuals in Chicago have a level of Spanish proficiency within the range of what we found in our corpus and what proportion do not, but national surveys have shown the following:

- Slightly less than half (47%) of third-generation and higher individuals say they speak Spanish "very well" or "pretty well," a third (29%) say they are "bilingual," and 69% say they are English-dominant (Pew Research Center, 2012).
- It is estimated that a third (34%) of Hispanics will speak only English at home by 2020, up from a quarter (25%) in 2010 (Ortman & Shin, 2011).
- The Spanish-speaking populations in the nation's metropolitan areas with the top five largest Latino populations—Los Angeles, New York, Miami, Houston, and Chicago—all showed a decrease in the percentage of

individuals who reported speaking Spanish in the home between 2006 and 2015 (all declined between 2 and 7 percentage points).

One thing that is striking to us about our analyses is that all participants who were asked expressed a clear desire that their current or future children be bilingual in Spanish and English, and the narratives of how and why this did not come to pass expressed elements of regret and loss. As cited at the beginning of this chapter, positive attitudes toward a language can create conditions that increase the likelihood that it is used (Velázquez, 2019), and inversely, negative attitudes can contribute to language loss. However, regardless of attitudes, there must be a sufficient quantity of meaningful input and output in Spanish for a child to acquire it. Put simply, without input and output, there is no language acquisition. If before having children a couple tends to interact almost entirely in English, using Spanish with their children seems to happen relatively rarely; the G1 grandparents often end up being the sole Spanish-input providers (but again, we note that even some G1 grandparents were unsuccessful at transmitting Spanish to their Chicago-raised grandchildren because they did not interact with them frequently enough). When Chicago-raised G2 and G3 individuals become grandparents, there seems to be little chance that they will speak Spanish to their grandchildren; Spanish will have been lost in the family unless other sources of Spanish input and requirements to produce output are put in place. We will make suggestions along these lines in Chapter 9.

CHAPTER 9
Conclusions

9.1. INTRODUCTION

In the introductory chapter, we presented an analogy of language and dialect contact experienced by many Spanish speakers in the U.S. that involves the combination of different colors to make new ones. For this project, we carried out sociolinguistic interviews in Spanish with 124 individuals in Chicago from different regional origins and generational backgrounds to get a clearer sense, in our analogy, of the varying amounts of red, blue, and purple in their Spanish. We examined overall Spanish proficiency as well as five linguistic features in order to elucidate trends suggestive of both kinds of contact, as well as those underlying the Spanish of individuals who experienced intrafamilial dialect contact.

Then, to approach our goal of viewing "language in society and society in language" (García et al., 2017, p. 2; motivated by Fishman, 1972), we also looked at what participants said about their linguistic development and that of their children and grandchildren for those who had them. In this chapter, we summarize our findings and make some suggestions for the continued vitality of Spanish in Chicago and in the United States more generally.

9.2. SPANISH PROFICIENCY: HOW TO MEASURE IT AND WAYS TO SUPPORT IT

We rated the Spanish produced during these interviews for global proficiency according to a 5-point scale based on criteria we developed and explained in Chapter 2. Evaluating bilingual individuals' abilities in one of their languages based on a single, individually administered sociolinguistic interview

Spanish in Chicago. Kim Potowski and Lourdes Torres, Oxford University Press. © Oxford University Press 2023.
DOI: 10.1093/oso/9780199326143.003.0009

is fraught with imperfection, yet we felt the attempt was worthwhile. Looking at the samples provided in Chapter 2's Appendix B, it is obvious that Chicago Spanish speakers have a wide range of communicative abilities in the language, and we sought a way to be able to refer to individuals along this range. Future work with speech samples such as ours can continue to hone useful details corresponding to levels of expressive ability such that the field can more easily discuss and compare speakers. Of their New York City corpus, for example, Erker and Otheguy (2020, p. 10) noted: "Our participants . . . represent a group of people who could largely restrict their linguistic interactions to Spanish should they desire to do so." Yet there is likely a range of abilities that fit this description. Furthermore, clearly not all U.S. Spanish speakers fit this description. For example, the following G2 speaker in the CHISPA corpus (#38) is the daughter of immigrants. It does not seem to us very likely that she could "largely restrict her linguistic interactions to Spanish":

Interviewer: ¿Hay problemas entre los latinos y los blancos o los negros?

#38: No, no, donde vivo no.

Interviewer: En general, ¿crees que hay problemas?

#38: Sí, yo creo que sí. I mean, a veces, um, como dice, los morenos, um, a lo mejor . . . I don't know how to say it . . . um . . . okay, a veces, um, como morenos son los minority y también los latinos como ellos, siempre están, como dice, como los americano le hacen burla de ellos, entonces, los morenos hacen burla de los latinos, tú sabes.

Interviewer: Are there problems among Latinos and whites and Blacks?

#38: No, not where I live, no.

Interviewer: In general, do you think there are problems?

#38: Yes, I think so, yes. I mean, sometimes, um, how do you say, the Blacks, um, sometimes . . . I don't know how to say it . . . um . . . okay, sometimes, um, like Blacks are the minority and also the Latinos like them, they are always, how do you say, like the Americans make fun of them, so the Blacks make fun of the Latinos, you know.

We consider it a positive finding that most of our Chicago G2s had acquired quite strong levels of Spanish: 94% of them were at level 3 or higher. Yet, as has been shown around the U.S., we found that average proficiency in Spanish declined significantly from G2 to G3: only 57% of our G3 sample scored at level 3, and this did not include the many G3 individuals in the city who would not have agreed to give an hour-long interview in Spanish because it would be too difficult for them. However, there were also 12 G3 speakers (24% of our G3 sample) who were high proficiency outliers: two whose Spanish proficiency was rated at level 5 and 10 at level 4.

Thus, in Chicago, as in the rest of the U.S., the ability to communicate in Spanish is being lost across generations. While we have no argument with Erker and Otheguy's (2020) methodology or analyses, their conclusions are based on a relatively highly proficient subset of U.S. Spanish speakers. Intergenerational loss of Spanish is happening, and the fact that linguistic constraints are similar between G1 and G2 speakers on any number of features does not change this. Our goal is to sound an alarm by documenting the loss of Spanish and seeking to understand more about how it happens, in order to empower communities to carry out whatever activities they may wish to engage in to support Spanish development in schools, families, and wider society such that it can continue to be spoken intergenerationally alongside English. We saw earlier that most of our participants wanted their current and/or future children to be able to speak Spanish, and they believed that parents were responsible for its transmission. However, raising a child with proficiency in a non-English language in the U.S. is a daunting task. How can Chicago Latinos promote intergenerational Spanish transmission? It is unclear whether conditions for stable bilingualism are ultimately achievable anywhere in the U.S., such as that of Quechua-Spanish bilinguals in Peru or Catalan-Spanish speakers in Spain referenced in Chapter 1, but based on what we learned from our participants, combined with our decades of living in Chicago, we offer several suggestions for supporting Spanish proficiency.

Bilingualism Public Informational Campaign

There are many common misconceptions about language. A public campaign that educates the Spanish-speaking community and people in general about several relevant points would be useful, including these:

- Speaking in two languages does not "confuse" children or negatively affect their English acquisition in rate, ultimate attainment, or accent, even those children who experience learning or speech/hearing challenges.
- Bilingual parents often face difficulties in raising their children to be bilingual in the U.S.; it is not a given. Families are advised to plan how they will ensure that sufficient input is provided to their children. The more "protected spaces" can be cultivated in the early years, the better the chance for Spanish to take root and grow. It can frequently be revitalized in later years, so establishing early roots is highly beneficial.

- Even if adults feel their Spanish is not as strong as they would like it to be, they should not feel afraid to speak it to the children in their families and communities. They will not harm children's linguistic development in any way by doing so.
- As will be described, dual-language programs that teach 50% to 90% of the day in Spanish consistently result in stronger Spanish proficiency, English proficiency, and overall academic development for all students.

Such a campaign has been launched by the Bilingual Advantage, a collaboration between the University of Illinois at Urbana–Champaign and the University of Illinois at Chicago, which includes a color brochure and a two-minute video[1] in a variety of different languages. The Spanish version will be proposed to consular offices (particularly but not only the Mexican consulate) to be played in waiting rooms where there are many Spanish-speaking adults. Spanish-language news outlets will also be targeted to run a shorter version. The Chicago branch of Bilingualism Matters also works to promote knowledge and resources among local families.

We also note that the linguistic climate in the U.S. has not been conducive to speaking Spanish or other minority languages in general. Cases of linguistic repression and bullying, such as those documented at http://potowski.org/resources/repression, include public harassment, physical violence, and even a Texas judge who threatened to withdraw custody from a mother who spoke Spanish to her daughter. It is thus unsurprising that some families might not prioritize the maintenance of Spanish or that they might choose to abandon it altogether. We urgently call upon researchers whose work relies on the linguistic systems of U.S. Spanish speakers to invest their power and energy in assisting Spanish-speaking communities, in ways that community members themselves request, in language-maintenance efforts, and in fighting monolingual, xenophobic ideologies at all levels. We also wish to amplify Zentella's (2018) call to create possibilities for Latino undergraduate students to become linguists and engage in studying their own communities. To do so effectively, we can seek funding to create channels from schools in grades K–8 through high school and into undergraduate study and then graduate school.

Day Care and Children's Television Programming in Spanish

Birth through age 8 are crucial for a child's language development. Particularly among parents who prefer to communicate in English, giving input to their

1. https://bilingualadvantage.uillinois.edu/

children in Spanish is important if they wish for them to acquire it. We noted in Chapter 8 the relatively few public Spanish day-care options in Spanish. A network of parents, community members, and university members could work together to increase offerings around the city. This needs to go hand in hand with a publicity campaign for parents to understand the benefits of such an approach; recall from Chapter 8 the quote from the day-care provider insisting that "families want English."

There is also a need for children's television programming in Spanish. Television cannot teach language directly, but it can support its growth through providing input that children enjoy and engage with. While the internet now provides greater access to cartoons and other shows directly from Latin America—for example, Cartoon Network L.A. offered via YouTube a free 24-hour livestream to support families staying at home during the Covid pandemic—but not all families have reliable online access. Thus, the country's larger Spanish-language television stations such as Univisión and Telemundo might collaborate to offer a free dedicated children's cable channel in Spanish that includes high-quality educational programming. This investment would ideally result in future adult viewers of content in Spanish.

Dual-Language Public School Programs

As noted by Valdés (2011), the direct involvement of educational institutions is essential if U.S.-raised youth are to develop competence in Spanish. Thus, K–8 schools, including private Catholic schools, can be called upon to support Spanish maintenance. Around the U.S., dual-language programs that teach 50% to 90% of the school day in Spanish have repeatedly been shown to be the best model both for promoting EL children's English (see Thomas & Collier, 2009, in California; Lindholm-Leary, 2001, in Houston; and Steele et al., 2017, in Portland) as well as their Spanish (Lindholm-Leary, 2013).

We take a moment to briefly share some detailed findings about dual-language Spanish outcomes in Chicago. Potowski and Marshall (under review) examined the Spanish of two groups of home-Spanish-speaking students attending the same K–8 school. In one group, there were 32 children enrolled in the mainstream English program (where, if they were classified as ELs, they received ESL services; these programs were described in Chapter 8). The other group consisted of 102 children enrolled in the dual-language program taught in Spanish 80% of the day in grades K–4, 60% in grades 5 and 6, and 50% in grades 7 and 8. Scores on all four Spanish skill tests of the Language Assessment Scales (De Avila & Duncan, 2005) were statistically higher for the dual-language students, but it was the tests of reading and writing where the

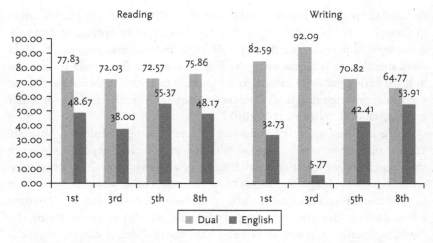

Figure 9.1. Average percentage accuracy on Spanish reading and writing tests, dual language versus English-only students. (Potowski & Marshall, under review.)

largest differences were evidenced (Figure 9.1). This makes sense when we consider that although all of these children hear and respond to Spanish at home with family members, they usually do not engage in writing and reading it at home.

Figures 9.2 compares four specific short writing samples. Two of the students were in first grade, and two were in fifth grade. Students were asked to describe the drawings or respond to the prompt in Spanish.

It is clear that in both grade levels, the dual-language students' texts are longer, lexically richer, and more morphosyntactically complex; the authors found this trend for all students. Yet in our CHISPA corpus, out of 101 G2s and G3s, only one stated that they had attended a dual-language program. There are currently more than 30 dual-language programs in the Chicago public school district, and an additional 10 districts around the state offer these programs. In a stellar example for the state and the nation, the Elgin school district (40 minutes northwest of Chicago) recently eliminated all TBE programs for Spanish-speaking EL children, replacing them with dual-language. The Illinois State Board of Education should continue to invest in these programs via teacher development, materials, and other means. We also note that there is currently only one postsecondary education program in the state, at Roosevelt University in Chicago, that prepares teachers to become dual-language educators. We are hopeful that dual-language programs and corresponding teacher preparation degrees will increase around the nation under the direction of U.S. Secretary of Education Dr. Miguel Cardona, who has claimed his support for these programs (Offgang, 2021).

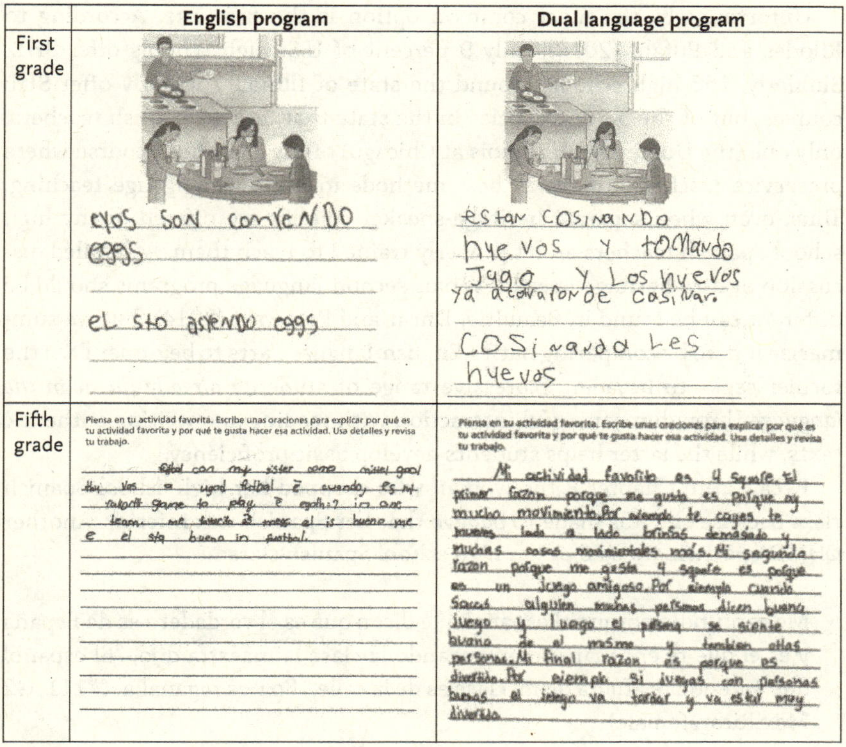

	English program	Dual language program
First grade	eyos son comYeNDO eggs el sto asYeNDO eggs	estan COSiNaNDo hyevos y toMando Jugo y Los hyevos Ya acavaron de Cosinar. COSinando Les hyevos
Fifth grade	[handwritten English text about playing soccer with sister]	Mi actividad favorita es 4 square. Tu primer razón porque me gusta es porque hay mucho movimiento. Por ejemplo te corres te mueves lado a lado brincas demasiado y muchas cosas movimentales más. Mi segunda razón porque me gusta 4 square es porque es un juego amigoso. Por ejemplo cuando saces alguien muchas personas dicen bueno juego y luego el persona se siente bueno de sí mismo y también otras personas. Mi final razón es porque es divertido. Por ejemplo si juegas con personas buenas el juego va tardar y va estar muy divertido.

Figure 9.2. Spanish written production. (Potowski & Marshall, under review.)

High School and University Spanish Heritage Language Programs

When home-Spanish-speaking children get to high school, one of two things usually happens:

- They are placed into a basic "Spanish as a second language" course with students learning it for the first time. There they are often bored, sometimes accused of wanting an "easy A" (a complaint no one levies against English-speaking students in English courses), and frequently told that the way they speak Spanish is "incorrect" because it is informal, belongs to a stigmatized dialect, and/or has English influence.
- They are placed into a "Spanish for heritage speakers" (SHL) class. This is a much better option, because these classes are specially designed to take home-developed communicative competence into account. However, in many cases, SHL teachers received no specific training in how to work with heritage speakers, which usually leads to similar frustrations—being erroneously "corrected," having curricular goals that are not a good match for students' skills and interests, and so on.

CONCLUSIONS [305]

Unfortunately, the most common option is the first one. According to Rhodes and Pufahl (2010), only 9 percent of U.S. high schools offer SHL. Similarly, 158 high schools around the state of Illinois currently offer SHL courses, but of the 33 universities in the state that license Spanish teachers, only one (the University of Illinois at Chicago) offers a methods course where preservice teachers can study best methods in heritage-language teaching. Thus, even when separate heritage-speaker courses are offered, many high school Spanish teachers aren't properly trained to teach them. A detailed discussion of how heritage-speaker versus second-language programs should be different can be found in Beaudrie, Ducar and Potowski (2014), but we summarize it here by comparing native English-language arts to beginner ESL: the former seeks to broaden expressive range of students *already fluent in the language* through meaningful interaction with reading and writing authentic texts, while the latter helps students develop basic proficiency.

Recall from Chapter 8 the woman who dropped her high school Spanish class because she was made to believe that her Spanish was inferior. Another CHISPA participant said of her high school Spanish class:

> Me confundía porque el español que dicen que es el verdadero es de España y es el que te enseñan. So empezando la clase la maestra dijo, "El español que aprendiste afuera de mi clase es de la calle." So nos regañaba. (#111, G2 MexiRican female)

> I would get confused because the Spanish they said is the real one is from Spain and that is the one they teach you. So starting the class the teacher said, "The Spanish you learned out of my class is of the street." So she would scold us.

Similar problems exist in university Spanish classes, ranging from program goals that do not match student profiles to outright linguistic violence as expressed in this quote. Heritage Spanish courses should be taught by professionals with the proper preparation, which ideally includes knowledge of what the Spanish of local communities looks like (based in part on samples like what we have described and analyzed in this volume) and how local varieties of Spanish can inform pedagogical decisions that simultaneously embrace U.S. Spanish and promote its strengthening.

Visits to Spanish-Speaking Places of Origin

This is not always possible due to financial and legal considerations, but visits to Puerto Rico or Mexico when youngsters are between 4 and 18 years of age can have noticeable benefits. We stress this age range because after age 3, children typically understand and produce a wider range of language and can benefit more from long periods of monolingual interactions in Spanish.

9.3. SUMMARY OF FIVE LINGUISTIC FEATURES

We studied our 124 Chicago speakers' lexical familiarity, proportional use of *so* versus *entonces*, number of codeswitches and percentage of English use, production of subjunctive morphology in obligatory and variable contexts, and two phonological features, the weakening of coda /s/ and the velarization of /r̄/. Table 9.1 presents a summary of our findings.

The three features where Puerto Ricans and Mexicans were different enough in G1 to warrant looking for evidence of dialect leveling in subsequent generations were outgroup lexicon, codeswitching, and the two phonological features. However, we found that on none of these features did Puerto Ricans become more like Mexicans or did Mexicans become more like Puerto Ricans across generational groups. For outgroup lexicon, both groups increased in their scores from G1 to G2, but one group did not do so more than the other, and both groups declined in outgroup (and ingroup) lexical familiarity scores in G3. Thus, while Puerto Ricans were shown to know more Mexican lexicon than vice versa, this did not change across generations. Rather, the loss of Spanish proficiency led to the decline in lexical familiarity for both groups.

Our analysis of codeswitching led to a similar conclusion: although Puerto Ricans codeswitched more frequently than Mexicans in G1, both increased in their amount of codeswitching across generations. Codeswitching is quite clearly an area in which English plays a key role, slightly more among Puerto Ricans, who in G3 used on average almost twice as many codeswitches as Mexicans. Finally, on /s/ and /r/, unlike Erker and Otheguy (2016), we found no differences in the use of /s/ weakening or /r/ velarization across generations for either regional origin group, although we had tentative signs that some Puerto Ricans may use fewer tokens of velarized /r/ when speaking with Mexicans. This latter finding highlights the value of looking at individual behavior even if generational groups do not show differences and also suggests that accommodation might be occurring at the individual level even if it is not detected at the group level. In any case, none of these three features suggested evidence of dialect leveling.

On the remaining two features, discourse markers and the subjunctive, Puerto Ricans and Mexicans were not very different in G1. Both groups in G1 used *so* between 21% and 34% of the time, and while Mexicans increased slightly in their proportions in G2 and G3, Puerto Ricans increased considerably more, particularly in G3. Finally, the proportions of subjunctive use in both obligatory and variable contexts were similar for Mexicans and Puerto Ricans in G1 and then declined for both groups into G2 and G3,

Table 9.1. SUMMARY OF MEXICAN AND PUERTO RICAN LINGUISTIC ANALYSES, CHAPTERS 3–7.

Feature	Were regional origin groups different in G1?	General findings	Generation vs. proficiency stronger?	Evidence of dialect leveling?	Evidence of convergence with English?
Lexicon	Yes, Puerto Ricans know more outgroup lexicon	G2 ~ G1 > G3 on outgroup lexicon G1 > G2 > G3 on ingroup and overall lexicon	Generation for outgroup lexicon Proficiency for ingroup/overall lexicon	No, Puerto Ricans retain same "lead" in outgroup scores across generations	No
Proportion of *so*	Not much (22% vs. 31%)	G3 > G2 > G1 Puerto Ricans increase much more than Mexicans across generations	Proficiency	No	Yes
Number of codeswitches	Yes, Puerto Ricans used more	G3 > G2 > G1 Puerto Ricans retain "lead," which increases in G3	Proficiency	No	Yes
Percentage of English	Yes, Puerto Ricans higher %	G3 > G2 > G1	Proficiency	No	Yes
Subjunctive	Not much	G1 > G2 > G3	Proficiency	No	Yes
/s/ and /r/	Yes, Puerto Ricans weaken /s/ and velarize /r/ more	No changes cross-generationally	Not examined	No	No

although, again, the decline was steeper for Puerto Ricans. Thus, we might say that Puerto Ricans converged onto English intergenerationally more than Mexicans on these two features.

Overall, the groups' Spanish is not becoming more similar. To return to our opening analogy, the situation seems to be like that depicted in Figure 1.7 (repeated here): the blue and the yellow are not influencing each other but rather are each engaged in their own path to red.

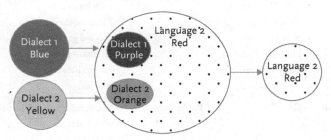

Despite Puerto Rican speakers being vastly outnumbered by Mexican speakers, Puerto Rican Spanish dies with its Boricua flag waving; speakers across generations do not replace Puerto Rican lexicon, phonology, or G1 codeswitching patterns with Mexican variants or patterns. Thus, in this situation of what Otheguy and Zentella (2012, p. 219) called "chronologically relatively shallow contact," we find among both groups what De Genova and Ramos-Zayas (2003, p. 168) termed a "shared erosion of Spanish."

As for the MexiRicans, they arguably have an even greater cognitive load, because they are usually exposed to two Spanish dialects from birth in addition to English. Table 9.2 summarizes the linguistic findings for these 45 speakers.

We saw similar patterns for MexiRicans regarding lexicon and use of *so* across generations to what we saw for Mexicans and Puerto Ricans. We also found several points where the mother's regional origin seemed to exert influence on MexiRican features, in particular the lexicon, the proportion of *so* use, and the weakening of coda /s/.

9.4. PROFICIENCY PREFERABLE TO GENERATION WHEN EXAMINING CHANGES IN U.S. SPANISH

We note that for all five of these features except for outgroup lexicon, proficiency was more strongly correlated with linguistic features than generational group was. This makes sense because, as we saw in Chapters 2 and 8, a speaker's Spanish proficiency level was not always directly correlated with their generational group. Thus, measuring informal oral proficiency in reliable ways is important; the field should continue to develop and test instruments.

Table 9.2. SUMMARY OF MEXIRICAN LINGUISTIC ANALYSES, CHAPTERS 3-7.

Feature	General findings	Generation vs. proficiency stronger?	Evidence of "mother factor"?	Evidence of convergence with English?
Lexicon	More familiarity with Mexican than Puerto Rican lexicon, but more Puerto Rican lexicon than Mexicans had	N/A	Yes, speakers with Puerto Rican mothers showed greater familiarity with Puerto Rican lexicon	No
Proportion of *so*	G2 ~ G3	Proficiency	Yes, speakers with Puerto Rican mothers used *so* more than those with Mexican mothers	Yes
Number of codeswitches	G3 > G2	Proficiency	N/A	Yes
Percentage of English	G2 > G3	Proficiency	N/A	Yes
/s/ and /r/	G3 weakened /s/ more than G2	N/A	Yes, 5 out of the 6 speakers who weakened /s/ 60% or more had Puerto Rican mothers	No

Such measures must take care to avoid circularity; for example, a proficiency measure cannot include the use of subjunctive versus indicative morphology and then, based on speakers' scores on the measure, make claims about correlations between proficiency and mood morphology.

An abbreviated version of the written Diploma del Español como Lengua Extranjera (DELE) has become de rigueur in psycholinguistically oriented studies of U.S. Spanish features as a measure of Spanish proficiency. It is frequently used to create "matched proficiency" groups for the purpose of comparing speakers. The exam consists of 50 multiple-choice items focused principally on lexical knowledge. Some research has shown that although heritage speakers (U.S.-raised bilinguals) and L2 learners are "matched" for proficiency based on their scores on the DELE, they in fact exhibit very different behaviors on specific language tasks (Montrul 2005). In addition, the written nature of the exam suggests that it would not be a reliable measure for oral communicative ability. Tomsiček and Potowski (in progress) administered, on different days, the DELE and the ACTFL Oral Proficiency Interview (OPI) to 22 heritage speakers and 15 L2 Spanish students. They found that scores on the two measures were significantly correlated for L2 students, $r(13) = .59$, $p = .021$, with a large effect size as per Cohen's (1988) guidelines. However, for heritage speakers, the DELE–OPI correlation was not significant, $r(20) = .36$, $p = .095$. These preliminary results suggest that the DELE does not adequately represent the oral proficiency of U.S.-raised, Spanish-speaking bilinguals.

9.5. AREAS FOR FUTURE RESEARCH

As noted by Erker and Otheguy (2016, p. 145), in studies of U.S. Spanish:

> It will be crucial to examine a broader range of linguistic features. . . . Of particular value will be variables that show clear regional differentiation in Latin America, that are high in social salience, and that in principle could be realigned so as to converge toward aspects of English. Finally, it would be ideal to complement the present study and others similar to it with longitudinal data capable of assessing contact induced change across the lifetime of speakers.

There are many additional ways that Puerto Rican and Mexican Spanish have been shown to differ, including subject pronoun expression (both general quantity and their position in interrogatives), pragmatics, prosody, and additional phonological features including lambdacisms. Filled pauses are also a very interesting area for the study of U.S. Spanish; Erker and Brusso (2017) found that U.S.-raised bilinguals are more likely to fill their pauses while speaking Spanish with the more centralized English-like vowels in [a(m)] and [ə(m)] rather than with [e(m)], which is seen as evidence of contact-induced change.

Chicago is well suited for these endeavors and can inform studies in other parts of the U.S. and wherever Spanish is a minority language, including Australia and Aoteaora-New Zealand (Jones Díaz & Walker, 2018), Italy (Bonomi & Sanfelici, 2018), Switzerland (Sánchez Abchi, 2018), Sweden (Parada, 2018), and Canada and the U.K. (Guardado, 2018).

REFERENCES

Aaron, J. E. (2004). So respetamos un tradición del uno al otro. *Spanish in Context*, *1*(2), 161–179.

Aaron, J. E., & Hernández, J. E. (2007). Quantitative evidence for contact-induced accommodation: Shifts in /s/ reduction patterns in Salvadoran Spanish in Houston. In K. Potowski & R. Cameron (Eds.), *Spanish in contact: Policy, social and linguistic inquiries (Impact: Studies in Language and Society 22)* (pp. 329–344). John Benjamins.

Acevedo, R. (2000). Perspectiva histórica del paradigma verbal en el español de California. In A. Roca (Ed.), *Research on Spanish in the United States: Linguistic issues and challenges* (pp. 110–120). Cascadilla Press.

Agrelo, J., Rice, K., Bayne, M., & Lydersen, K. (2019). *Puerto Ricans in Chicago: The stories of struggle and survival go on*. Centro de Periodismo Investigativo.

Aguado, G. (1988). Valoración de la competencia morfosintáctica en el niño de dos años y medio. *Infancia y Aprendizaje*, *11*(43), 73–96.

Alamo (2007).

Alba, O. (2009). *La identidad lingüística de los dominicanos*. Ediciones Librería La Trinitaria.

Andersen, E. S., Brizuela, M., Dupuy, B., & Gonnerman, L. (1999). Cross-linguistic evidence for the early acquisition of discourse markers as register variables. *Journal of Pragmatics*, *31*, 1339–1351.

Anderson. (1999).

Anderson, T. K., & Toribio, A. J. (2007). Attitudes towards lexical borrowing and intrasentential code-switching among Spanish-English bilinguals. *Spanish in Context*, *4*(2), 217–240.

Anderson, V. M. (2014). *Bidialectism: An unexpected development in the obsolescence of Pennsylvania Dutchified English*. Duke University Press.

Aparicio, F. R. (1999). Reading the "Latino" in Latino studies: Toward re-imagining our academic location. *Discourse*, *21*(3), 3–18.

Aparicio, F. R. (2019). *Negotiating Latinidad: Intralatina/o lives in Chicago*. University of Illinois Press.

Arriagada, P. A. (2005). Family context and Spanish-language use: A study of Latino children in the United States. *Social Science Quarterly*, *86*(3), 599–619.

August, D., & Shanahan, T. (2006). *Developing literacy in second-language learners: Report of the National Literacy Panel on Language Minority Children and Youth*. Lawrence Erlbaum.

Bada, X. (2014). *Mexican hometown associations in Chicagoacán: From local to transnational civic engagement*. Rutgers University Press.

Bailey, B. (2000). Language and negotiation of ethnic/racial identity among Dominican Americans. *Language in Society*, 29(4), 555–582.

Baker, C., & Wright, W. E. (2017). *Foundations of bilingual education and bilingualism*. Multilingual Matters.

Barrera-Tobón, C. (2013). *Contact-induced changes in word order and intonation in the Spanish of New York City bilinguals*. City University of New York. ProQuest LLC.

Beaudrie, S., Ducar, C., & Potowski, K. (2014). *Heritage language teaching: Research and practice*. McGrawHill.

Becker, K. R. (1997). Spanish/English bilingual codeswitching: A syncretic model. *Bilingual Review/La Revista Bilingüe*, 22(1), 3–30.

Bentahila, A., & Davies, E. E. (1995). Patterns of code-switching and patterns of language contact. *Lingua*, 96(2–3), 75–93.

Blake, R. (1980). *The acquisition of mood selection among Spanish-speaking children: Ages 4 to 12* [Doctoral dissertation]. University of Texas–Austin.

Blake, R. (1983). Mood selection among Spanish-speaking children ages 4 to 12. *Bilingual Review/La revista bilingüe*, 10(1), 21–32.

Boersma, P., & Weenink, D. (2020). *Praat*: Doing phonetics by computer, version 6.1.29. www.praat.org

Bolonyai, A. (1998). In-between languages: Language shift/maintenance in childhood bilingualism. *International Journal of Bilingualism*, 2(1), 21–43.

Bonomi, M., & Sanfelici, L. (2018). Spanish as a heritage language in Germany. In K. Potowski (Ed.), *The Routledge handbook of Spanish as a heritage language* (pp. 479–491). Routledge.

Bookhamer, K. (2013). *The variable grammar of the Spanish subjunctive in second-generation bilinguals in New York City*. City University of New York. ProQuest LLC.

Brizuela, M., Andersen, E., & Stallings, L. (1999). Discourse markers as indicators of register. *Hispania*, 82(1), 128–141.

Brody, J. (1987). Particles borrowed from Spanish as discourse markers in Mayan languages. *Anthropological Linguistics*, 29(4), 507–521.

Brody, J. (1995). Lending the "unborrowable": Spanish discourse markers in indigenous American languages. In C. Silva-Corvalán (Ed.), *Spanish in four continents: Studies in language contact and bilingualism* (pp. 132–147). Georgetown University Press.

Bullock, B. E., & Toribio, A. J. (2004). Introduction: Convergence as an emergent property in bilingual speech. *Bilingualism: Language and Cognition*, 7(2), 91–93.

Bullock, B. E., & Toribio, A. J. (2009). *The Cambridge handbook of linguistic codeswitching*. Cambridge University Press.

Bullock, B. E., Toribio, A. J., & Amengual, M. (2014). The status of s in Dominican Spanish. *Lingua*, 143, 20–35.

Cameron, D. (2000). Styling the worker: Gender and the commodification of language in the globalized service economy. *Journal of Sociolinguistics*, 4(3), 323–347.

Carreira. (2013). The vitality of Spanish in the United States. *Heritage Language Journal*, 10(3), 396–413.

Cashman, H. R. (2018). *Queer, Latinx, and bilingual: Narrative resources in the negotiation of identities*. Routledge.

Center for Latin American, Caribbean, and Latino Studies (2016). *The Latino population of New York City 1990–2015*. Center for Latin American, Caribbean, and Latino Studies, Graduate Center, City University of New York. http://clacls.gc.cuny.edu

Chambers, J. (1992). Dialect acquisition. *Language, 68*(4), 673–705.

Cisneros, R., & Leone, E. (1983). Mexican American language communities in the Twin Cities: An example of contact and recontact. In Lucía Elías-Olivares (Ed.), *Spanish in the US setting: Beyond the Southwest* (pp. 181–210). Rosslyn, VA: National Clearinghouse for Bilingual Education.

Cohen, J. (1988). *Statistical power analysis for the behavioral sciences* (2nd ed.). Erlbaum.

Cohen, J. (1992). A power primer. *Psychological Bulletin, 112*, 155.

Condon, T. (2005). Difference between North and South Sides. https://www.chicagotribune.com/news/ct-xpm-2005-10-14-0510140037-story.html

Cooper, G. F. (2013). An exploration of intentions and perceptions of code-switching among bilingual Spanish-English speakers in the Inland Northwest. *Journal of Northwest Anthropology, 47*(2), 215–225.

Cortés, M., & Vila, I. (1991). Uso y función de las formas temporales en el habla infantil. *Infancia y aprendizaje, 14*(53), 17–43.

Crespo del Río, C. (2022). Panorama de los estudios sobre el subjuntivo en el castellano peruano. In L. A. Ciudad & S. Sessarego (Eds.), *Los castellanos del Perú: Historia, variación y contacto lingüístico* (pp. 243–254). Routledge.

Cruz, W. (2007). *City of dreams: Latino immigration to Chicago*. University Press of America.

Dávila, A. (2002). Talking back: Spanish media and U.S. Latinidad. In M. Romero & M. Habell-Pallán (Eds.), *Latino/a Popular Culture* (pp. 25–37). New York University Press.

De Avila, E., & Duncan, S. (2005). *Language Assessment Scales*. McGraw-Hill.

De Genova, N., & Ramos-Zayas, A. Y. (2003). *Latino crossings: Mexicans, Puerto Ricans, and the politics of race and citizenship*. Routledge.

Delgado-Díaz, G., & Galarza, I. (2015). ¿Qué comiste [x]amón? A closer look at the neutralization of /h/ and posterior /r/ in Puerto Rican Spanish. In E. W. Willis, P. Martín-Butragueño, & E. Herrera (Eds.), *The 6th Conference on Laboratory Approaches to Romance Phonology* (pp. 70–82). Cascadilla Proceedings Project.

Delvaux, V., & Soquet, A. (2007). The influence of ambient speech on adult speech productions through unintentional imitation. *Phonetica, 64*(2–3), 145–173.

Elías-Olivares, L., González-Widel, M., & Vargas, L. (1985). *Variational use of the subjunctive in Chicago's "La Villita"* [Unpublished manuscript]. University of Illinois–Chicago.

Erker, D., & Brusso, J. (2017). Filled pauses as a site of contact-induced change in Boston Spanish. *Language Variation and Change, 29*(2), 205–244.

Erker, D., & Otheguy, R. (2016). Contact and coherence: Dialectal leveling and structural convergence in NYC Spanish. *Lingua, 172–173*, 131–146.

Erker, D., & Otheguy, R. (2020). American myths of linguistic assimilation: A sociolinguistic rebuttal. *Language in Society*, 1–37.

Escobar, A. M., & Potowski, K. (2015). *El español de los Estados Unidos*. Cambridge University Press.

Farr, M. (Ed.). (2005). *Latino language and literacy in ethnolinguistic Chicago*. Lawrence Erlbaum.

Farr, M. (2006). *Rancheros in Chicagoacán: Language and identity in a transnational community*. University of Texas Press.

Fernández, L. (2012). *Brown in the windy city: Mexicans and Puerto Ricans in postwar Chicago*. University of Chicago Press.

Fernández, S. (1997). *Interlengua y análisis de errores en el aprendizje del español como lengua extranjera*. Edelsa Grupo Discalia.

Fernández Parera, Antoni (2017). Lexical influences and perceptions of Miami Cuban Spanish. In A. Cuza (Ed.), *Cuban Spanish dialectology* (pp. 211–227). Washington, DC: Georgetown University Press.

Feuer, W. (2003). Little but Language in Common; Mexicans and Puerto Ricans Quarrel in East Harlem. *The New York Times*, September 6. https://www.nytimes.com/2003/09/06/nyregion/little-but-language-in-common-mexicans-and-puerto-ricans-quarrel-in-east-harlem.html

Fishman, J. A. (1972). *The sociology of language*. Newbury House.

Fishman, J. A. (1991). *Reversign language shift: Theoretical and empirical foundations of assistance of threatened languages*. Multilingual Matters.

Flores-Ferrán, N. (2014). So pues, entonces: An examination of discourse markers in oral narratives of personal experience of English dominant New York City–born Puerto Ricans. *Journal of Sociolinguistic Studies*, 8(1), 57–83.

Foreman, A. (2003) *Pretending to be someone you're not: A study of second dialect acquisition in Australia* [Doctoral dissertation]. Monash University.

Fuller, J. M. (2001). The principle of pragmatic detachability in borrowing: English-origin discourse markers in Pennsylvania German. *Linguistics*, 39(2), 351–370.

Fuller, J. M. (2003). The influence of speaker roles on discourse marker use. *Journal of Pragmatics*, 35(1), 23–45.

Gallego, M. (2016). An analysis of subjunctive frequency and semantic predictors of mood in Central Argentinian Spanish. In A. Cuza, L. Czerwionka, & D. J. Olsen (Eds.), *Inquiries in Hispanic linguistics: From theory to empirical evidence* (pp. 301–316). John Benjamins.

García, M. (2006). Contemporary Spanish sociolinguistics: Stop the insanity! In L. Martin-Estudillo, F. Ocampo, & N. Spadaccini (Eds.), *Debating Hispanic studies: Reflections on our disciplines* (pp. 127–131). *Hispanic Issues On Line*, 1(1). Retrieved from http://spanport.cla.umn.edu/publications/HispanicIssues/hispanic-issues-online/ hispanic%20issues%20online-1.htm/garcia.pdf

García, L. (2012). *Respect yourself, protect yourself: Latina girls and sexual identity*. New York University Press.

García, L., & Rúa, M. (2007). Processing latinidad: Mapping Latino urban landscapes through Chicago ethnic festivals. *Latino Studies*, 5, 317–339.

García, O., Flores, N., & Spotti, M. (Eds.). (2017). *The Oxford handbook of language and society*. Oxford University Press.

García Bedolla, L. (2003). The identity paradox: Latino language, politics and selective dissociation. *Latino Studies*, 1, 264–283.

Gardner-Chloros, P. (2009). *Code-switching*. Cambridge University Press.

Gelb, R. (2005). The magic of verbal art: Juanita's santería initiation. In M. Farr (Ed.), *Latino language and literacy in ethnolinguistic Chicago* (pp. 323–350). Lawrence Erlbaum.

Ghosh-Johnson, E. (2005). Mexiqueño? A case study of dialect contact. *Penn Working Papers in Linguistics*, 11(2), 91–104.

Gilbertson, G. A., Fitzpatrick, J. P., & Yang, L. (1996). Hispanic intermarriage in New York City: New evidence from 1991. *International Migration Review*, 30(2), 445–459.

Giles, H. (1970). Evaluative reactions to accents. *Educational Review*, 22(3), 211–227.

Gorman, L., & Potowski, K. (2009). Is there Spanish "recontact" between U.S. born and recent arrival Latinos in Chicago? [Paper presentation]. 22nd Conference on Spanish in the U.S., Coral Gables, FL.

Goss, E. L., & Salmons, J. C. (2000). The evolution of a bilingual discourse marking system: Modal particles and English markers in German-American dialects. *International Journal of Bilingualism, 4*(4), 469–484.

Grosjean, F. (1998). Transfer and language mode. *Bilingualism: Language and Cognition, 1*(3), 175–176.

Guardado, M. (2009). Speaking Spanish like a Boy Scout: Language socialization, resistance, and reproduction in a heritage language Scout troop. *Canadian Modern Language Review, 66*(1), 101–129.

Guardado, M. (2018). Spanish as a minority/heritage language in Canada and the UK. In K. Potowski (Ed.), *The Routledge handbook of Spanish as a heritage language* (pp. 537–554). Routledge.

Gudmestad, A. (2010). Moving beyond a sentence-level analysis in the study of variable mood use in Spanish. *Southwest Journal of Linguistics, 29*(1), 25–51.

Guerra, J. C. (1998). *Close to home: Oral and literate practices in a transnational Mexicano community*. Teachers College Press.

Guitart, J. M. (1982). On the use of the Spanish subjunctive among Spanish-English bilinguals. *Word, 33*(1–2), 59–67.

Gutiérrez, M. J. (2003). Simplification and innovation in US Spanish. *Multilingua, 22*, 169–184.

Hakuta, K., & d'Andrea, D. (1992). Some properties of bilingual maintenance and loss in Mexican background high-school students. *Applied Linguistics, 13*(1), 72–99.

Halekoh, U., Højsgaard, S., & Yan, J. (2006). The R package geepack for generalized estimating equations. *Journal of Statistical Software, 15*(2), 1–11.

Hazen, K. (2001). An introductory investigation into bidialectalism. *University of Pennsylvania Working Papers in Linguistics, 7*(3), 85–95.

Hernández, J. E. (2002). Accommodation in a dialect contact situation. *Filología y Lingüística, 28*(2), 93–110.

Hernández, J. E. (2009). Measuring rates of word-final nasal velarization: The effect of dialect contact on in-group and out-group exchanges. *Journal of Sociolinguistics, 13*(5), 583–612.

Hernández, J. E., & Maldonado, R. A. (2012). Reducción de /s/ final de sílaba entre transmigrantes salvadoreños en el sur de Texas. *Lengua y Migración, 4*(2), 43–67.

Hernández-Campoy, J. M. (2010). Dialect contact and accommodation in a standard context. *Sociolinguistic Studies, 4*(1), 201–225.

Hernández-Pina, F. (1984). *Teorías psico-sociolingüísticas y su aplicación a la adquisición del español como lengua materna*. Siglo XXI.

Hidalgo, M. (1986). Language contact, language loyalty and language prejudice on the Mexican border. *Language in Society, 15*(2), 193–220.

Hidalgo, M. (1988). *Perceptions of Spanish-English code-switching in Juarez, Mexico*. Latin American Institute Research Paper Series. University of New Mexico.

Hill, J. H., & Hill, K. C. (1986). *Speaking Mexicano: Dynamics of syncretic language in central Mexico*. University of Arizona Press.

Hirano, K. (2008). L1 dialect contact in an L2 setting: Intervocalic /t/ in the anglophone community of Japan. *Essex Graduate Student Papers in Language & Linguistics, 10*, 45–75.

Hirano, K. (2010). Dialect contact in the anglophone community of Japan: Modifications in the pronunciation of TRAP and BATH vowels by American English speakers. In B. Heselwood & C. Upton (Eds.), *Proceedings of Methods XIII: Papers from the*

13th International Conference on Methods in Dialectology, 2008 (pp. 341–350). Peter Lang.

Hlavac, J. (2006). Bilingual discourse markers: Evidence from Croatian-English code-switching. *Journal of Pragmatics, 38*(11), 1870–1900.

Holliday, N. (2014). *You black or what?* [Paper presentation]. Critical Mixed Race Studies Conference, DePaul University, Chicago.

Hualde, J. I. (2014). *Los sonidos del español*. Cambridge University Press.

Huerta-Macias, A., & Quintero, E. (1992). Code-switching, bilingualism, and biliteracy: A case study. *Bilingual Research Journal, 16*(3–4), 69–90.

Irizarri van Suchtelen, P. (2016). *Spanish as a heritage language in the Netherlands: A cognitive linguistic exploration* [Doctoral dissertation]. Netherlands Graduate School of Linguistics.

Jones Díaz, C., & Walker, U. (2018). Spanish in the Antipodes: Diversity and hybridity of Latino/a Spanish speakers in Australia and Aotearoa-New Zealand. In K. Potowski (Ed.), *The Routledge handbook of Spanish as a heritage language* (pp. 463–478). Routledge.

Keller, R. (1994). *On language change: The invisible hand in language*. Psychology Press.

Kern, J. (2020). *Like* in English and *como, como que*, and *like* in Spanish in the speech of Southern Arizona bilinguals. *International Journal of Bilingualism, 24*(2), 1–24.

Kerswill, P. (2002). Koinization and accommodation. In J. K. Chambers, P. Trudgill, & N. Schilling-Estes (Eds.), *The handbook of language variation and change* (pp. 669–702). Blackwell.

Kerswill, P., & Williams, A. (2000). Creating a new town koine: Children and language change in Milton Keynes. *Language in Society, 29*(1), 65–115. 10.1017/S0047404500001020.

Kraha, A., Turner, H., Nimon, K., Reichwein Zientek, L., & Henson, R. K. (2012). Tools to support interpreting multiple regression in the face of multicollinearity. *Frontiers in Psychology, 3*. https://www.frontiersin.org/articles/10.3389/fpsyg.2012.00044/full

Kroll, J. (2014). *A new hypothesis about second language learning: What bilingualism teaches us about the mind and the brain*. http://web.international.ucla.edu/cwl/article/140218

Labov, W. (1966). Hypercorrection by the lower middle class as a factor in linguistic change. In W. Bright (Ed.), *Sociolinguistics* (pp. 84–113). Mouton.

Labov, W. (1984). Field methods of the project on language change and variation. In J. Baugh & J. Sherzer (Eds.), *Language in use: Readings in sociolinguistics* (pp. 28–53). Prentice-Hall.

Labov, W. (1998). Co-existent systems in African-American English. In S. S. Mufwene, J. R. Rickford, G. Bailey, & J. Baugh (Eds.), *African-American English: Structure, history, and use* (pp. 110–153). Routledge.

Lamboy, E. M. (2004). *Caribbean Spanish in the metropolis: Spanish language among Cubans, Dominicans, and Puerto Ricans in the New York City area*. Routledge.

Lee, J. F., & VanPatten, B. (2003). *Making communicative language teaching happen*. McGraw-Hill.

Language Policy Task Force. (1980). *Social dimensions of language use in East Harlem*. Centro de Estudios Puertorriqueños.

Lee, S. (2006). Love sees no color or boundaries? Interethnic dating and marriage patterns of Dominican and CEP (Colombian, Ecuadorian, Peruvian) Americans. *Journal of Latino/Latin American Studies, 2*, 84–102.

Lenth, R. 2020. Emmeans: Estimated marginal means, aka least-squares means. R package version 1.4.5. http://CRAN.R-PROJECT.org/package=emmeans

Lindholm-Leary, K. J. (2001). *Dual language education* (Vol. 28). Clevedon, UK: Multilingual Matters.

Lindholm-Leary, K. (2013). Bilingual and biliteracy skills in young Spanish-speaking low-SES children: Impact of instructional language and primary language proficiency. *International Journal of Bilingual Education and Bilingualism*, 17(2), 144–159.

Lindsey, B. (2006). Language loss and recovery in heritage language learner Spanish: A study on code-switching. *Divergencias: Revista de Estudios Lingüísticos y Literarios*, 4(1), 3–22.

Linton, A. (2004). Learning in two languages: Spanish-English immersion in US public schools. *International Journal of Sociology and Social Policy*, 27(7/8), 46–74.

Linton, A., & Jimenez, T. R. (2009). Contexts for bilingualism among US-born Latinos. *Ethnic and Racial Studies*, 32(6), 967–995.

Lipski, J. M. 1985. *Linguistic aspects of Spanish-English language shifting*. Latin American Studies Center, Arizona State University.

Lipski, J. M. (1988). Central American Spanish in the United States: Some remarks on the Salvadoran community. *Aztlán*, 17(2), 91–123.

Lipski, J. M. (1989). Salvadorans in the United States: Patterns of intra-Hispanic migration. http://www.personal.psu.edu/jml34/salv-usa.pdf

Lipski, J. M. (1994). *Latin American Spanish*. Longman.

Lipski, J. M. (2005). Code-switching or borrowing? No sé so no puedo decir, you know. In L. Sayahi & M. Westmoreland (Eds.), *The Second Workshop on Spanish Sociolinguistics* (pp. 1–15). Cascadilla Press.

Lipski, J. M. (2009). "Fluent dysfluency" as congruent lexicalization: A special case of radical code-mixing. *Journal of Language Contact*, 2(2), 1–39.

Lipski, J. M. (2011). *El español de América* (7th ed.). Cátedra.

Lipski, J. M. (2014). Spanish-English code-switching among low-fluency bilinguals: Towards an expanded typology. *Sociolinguistic Studies*, 8(1), 23–55.

López-Morales, H. (2003). *Los cubanos de Miami: Lengua y sociedad*. Ediciones Universal.

López Ornat, S., Fernández, A., Gallo, P., & Mariscal, S. (1994). *La adquisición de la lengua española*. Siglo XXI.

Luna, K. V. (2010). *The Spanish of Ponce, Puerto Rico: A phonetic, phonological, and intonational analysis* [Doctoral dissertation]. University of California–Los Angeles.

Lynch, A. (2008). The linguistic similarities of Spanish heritage and second language learners. *Foreign Language Annals*, 41(2), 252–381.

Lynch, A., & Potowski, K. (2014). La valoración del habla bilingüe en los Estados Unidos: Fundamentos sociolingüísticos y pedagógicos en "Hablando bien se entiende la gente." *Hispania*, 97(1), 32–46.

Ma, R., & Herasimchuk, E. (1971). The linguistic dimensions of a bilingual neighborhood. In J. A. Fishman, R. L. Cooper, & R. M. Newman (Eds.), *Bilingualism in the Barrio* (pp. 349–464). Indiana University Press.

MacGregor-Mendoza, P. (1999). *Spanish and academic achievement among Midwest Mexican youth: The myth of the barrier*. Psychology Press.

Martínez-Mira, M. I. (20090. Spanish heritage speakers in the southwest: Factors contributing to the maintenance of the subjunctive in concessive clauses. *Spanish in Context*, 6(1), 105–126.

Matthei, E., & Roeper, T. (1985). *Understanding and producing speech*. Universe.

Medina-Rivera, A. (1999). Variación fonológica y estilística en el español de Puerto Rico. *Hispania*, *82*(3), 529–541.

Megenney, W. W. (1978). El problema de R velar en Puerto Rico. *Thesaurus: Boletín del Instituto Caro y Cuervo*, *33*(1), 72–86.

Mendoza-Denton, N. (1999). Sociolinguistics and linguistic anthropology of US Latinos. *Annual Review of Anthropology*, *28*(1), 375–395.

Mendoza-Denton, N. (2008). *Homegirls: Language and cultural practice among Latina youth gangs*. Wiley. 10.1002/9780470693728.

Milroy, J. (2001). Language ideologies and the consequences of standardization. *Journal of Sociolinguistics*, *5*(4), 530–555.

Montrul, S. (2005). Second language acquisition and first language loss in adult early bilinguals: Exploring some differences and similarities. *Second Language Research*, *21*(3), 199–249.

Montrul, S. (2007). Interpreting mood distinctions in Spanish as a heritage language. In K. Potowski & R. Cameron (Eds.), *Spanish in contact: Policy, social and linguistic inquiries* (pp. 23–40). John Benjamins.

Montrul, S. (2008). *Incomplete acquisition in bilingualism: Re-examining the age factor*. John Benjamins.

Montrul, S. (2009). Knowledge of tense-aspect and mood in Spanish heritage speakers. *International Journal of Bilingualism*, *13*(2), 239–269.

Montrul, S. (2017). Developmental continuity in morphosyntactic attrition. *Linguistic Approaches to Bilingualism*, *7*(6), 739–743.

Montrul, S., & Potowski, K. (2007). Command of gender agreement in school-age Spanish-English bilingual children. *International Journal of Bilingualism*, *11*(3), 301–328.

Moreno-Fernández, F. (2005). Anglicismos en el léxico disponible de los adolescentes hispanos de Chicago. In K. Potowski & R. Cameron (Eds.), *Spanish in contact: Policy, social and linguistic inquiries* (pp. 41–58). John Benjamins.

Mougeon, R., & Beniak, E. (1986). *Linguistic consequences of language contact and restriction*. Oxford University Press.

Mougeon, R., & Beniak, E. (1991). *Linguistic consequences of language contact and restriction: The case of French in Ontario, Canada*. Oxford University Press.

Muysken, P. (2000) *Bilingual speech: A typology of code-mixing*. Cambridge University Press.

Myers-Scotton, C. (1992). Comparing codeswitching and borrowing. *Journal of Multilingual & Multicultural Development*, *13*(1–2), 19–39.

Myers-Scotton, C. (1993). *Dueling languages: Grammatical structure in codeswitching*. Oxford University Press.

Nagy, N. (2011). Lexical change and language contact: Faetar in Italy and Canada. *Journal of Sociolinguistics*, *15*, 366–382.

Navarrete, C. B., & Soares, F. C. (2020). *dominanceanalysis*: Dominance Analysis, R package, version 1.3.0. https://www.rdocumentation.org/packages/dominance analysis/versions/2.0.0

Navarro Tomás, T. (1967). *Manual de pronunciación española* (6th ed.). Hafner.

Nordenstam, K. (1979). *The Swedish language in Norway: Language variation among Swedish immigrants in Bergen*. Gothenburg: Acta Universitatis Gothoburgensis.

Norteir, J. (1990). *Dutch-Moroccan Arabic code switching among Moroccans in the Netherlands*. Foris.

Offgang, E. (2021) Secretary of Education nominee Miguel Cardona expected to support dual language schools. *Tech & Learning: Tools and Ideas to Transform*

Education. https://www.techlearning.com/news/secretary-of-education-nominee-miguel-cardona-expected-to-support-dual-language-schools

O'Rourke, E., & Potowski, K. (2016). Phonetic accommodation in a situation of Spanish dialect contact: /s/ and /r/ in Chicago. *Studies in Hispanic and Lusophone Linguistics, 9*(2), 355–399.

Ortman, J., & Shin, H. (2011). Language projections: 2010 to 2020. https://www.census.gov/content/dam/Census/library/working-papers/2011/demo/2011-Ortman-Shin.pdf

Otheguy, R., & García, O. (1993). Convergent conceptualizations as predictors of degree of contact in U.S. Spanish. In A. Roca & J. M. Lipski (Eds.), *Spanish in the United States: Linguistic contact and diversity* (pp. 135–154). Mouton de Gruyter.

Otheguy, R., & Zentella, A. C. (2012). *Spanish in New York: Language contact, dialectal leveling, and structural continuity*. Oxford University Press.

Padilla, E. (1947). *Puerto Rican immigrants in New York and Chicago: A study in comparative assimilation* [Master's thesis]. University of Chicago.

Padilla, F. M. (1985). *Latino ethnic consciousness: The case of Mexican Americans and Puerto Ricans in Chicago*. University of Notre Dame Press.

Pallares, A., & Flores-González, N. (2010). *¡Marcha! Latino Chicago and the immigrant rights movement*. University of Illinois Press.

Parada, M. (2013). Sibling variation and family language policy: The role of birth order in the Spanish proficiency and first names of second-generation Latinos. *Journal of Language, Identity & Education, 12*(5), 299–320.

Parada, M. (2018). Chilean Spanish speakers in Sweden: Transnationalism, trilingualism, and linguistic systems. In K. Potowski (Ed.), *The Routledge handbook of Spanish as a heritage language* (pp. 517–536). Routledge.

Paral, R., Ready, T., Chun, S., & Sun, W. (2004). *Latino demographic growth in metropolitan Chicago*. Institute for Latino Studies, University of Notre Dame.

Pease-Álvarez, L., Hakuta, K., & Bayley, R. (1996). Spanish proficiency and language use in a California Mexicano community. *Southwest Journal of Linguistics, 15*(1–2), 137–151.

Pedraza, C., & Ortiz López, L. (2016). *Dialect contact in migratory contexts: Linguistic perceptions and attitudes toward Dominican Spanish in Puerto Rico* [Paper presentation]. Sociolinguistics Symposium 21, Murcia, Spain.

Pedraza, P. (1980). *Rethinking diglossia* (Vol. 9). Language Policy Task Force, Centro de Estudios Puertorriqueños, CUNY.

Penny, R. (2000). *Variation and change in Spanish*. Cambridge University Press.

Pérez, G. (2003). "Puertorriqueñas rencorosas y mejicanas sufridas": Gendered ethnic identity formation in Chicago's Latino communities. *Journal of Latin American Anthropology, 8*(2), 96–124.

Pérez, G. (2004). *The near northwest side story: Migration, displacement, and Puerto Rican families*. University of California Press.

Pesqueira, D. (2008). Cambio fónico en situaciones de contacto dialectal: El caso de los inmigrantes. *Fonología instrumental: Patrones fónicos y variación, 5*, 171.

Pesqueira Barragán, D. (2012). *Acomodación y cambio lingüístico en situaciones de contacto dialectal* [Doctoral dissertation]. El Colegio de México.

Pew Research Center. (2012). *Language use among Latinos*. April 4. https://www.pewresearch.org/hispanic/2012/04/04/iv-language-use-among-latinos/

Polinsky, M. (2006). Incomplete acquisition: American Russian. *Journal of Slavic Linguistics, 14*(2), 191–262.

Polinsky, M. (2008). Gender under incomplete acquisition: Heritage speakers' knowledge of noun categorization. *Heritage Language Journal, 6*(1), 40–71.

Poplack, S. (1980). Sometimes I'll start a sentence in Spanish y termino en español. *Linguistics, 18,* 581–618.

Poplack, S. (1982). Bilingualism and the vernacular. In A. Valdman & B. Hartford (Eds.), *Issues in international bilingual education: The role of the vernacular* (pp. 1–24). Plenum.

Poplack, S., Sankoff, D., & Miller, C. A. (1988). The social correlates and linguistic processes of lexical borrowing and assimilation. *Linguistics, 26*(1), 47–104.

Poplack, S., Torres Cacoullos, R., Dion, N., de Andrade Berlinck, R., Digesto, S. Lacasse, D., & Steuck, J. (2018). Variation and grammaticalization in Romance: A cross-linguistic study of the subjunctive. In W. Ayres-Bennet & J. Carruthers (Eds.), *Manuals in linguistics: Romance sociolinguistics* (pp. 217–252). De Gruyter.

Porcel, J. (2011). Language maintenance and language shift among US Latinos. In M. Díaz-Campos (Ed.), *The handbook of Hispanic sociolinguistics* (pp. 623–645). Wiley.

Porter, B. A., & Kennison, S. M. (2010). Differences in men's and women's knowledge of and memory for names. *North American Journal of Psychology, 12*(3), 433–444.

Portes, A., & Hao, L. (1998). E pluribus unum: Bilingualism and loss of language in the second generation. *Sociology of Education, 71*(4), 269–294.

Potowski, K. (2002). Experiences of Spanish heritage speakers in university foreign language courses and implications for teacher training. *ADFL Bulletin, 33,* 35–42.

Potowski, K. (2004). Spanish language shift in Chicago. *Southwest Journal of Linguistics, 23*(1), 87–116.

Potowski, K. (2008). "I was raised talking like my mom": The influence of mothers in the development of MexiRicans' phonological and lexical features. In M. Niño-Murcia & J. Rothman (Eds.), *Bilingualism and identity: Spanish at the crossroads with other languages* (pp. 201–220). John Benjamins.

Potowski, K. (2015). Ethnolinguistic identities and ideologies among Mexicans, Puerto Ricans, and "MexiRicans" in Chicago. In R. Márquez-Reiter & L.M. Rojo (Eds.), *A sociolinguistics of diaspora: Latino practices, identities and ideologies* (pp. 13–30). Routledge.

Potowski, K. (2016). *Inter-Latino language and identity: MexiRicans in Chicago.* Benjamins.

Potowski, K., & Gorman, L. (2011). Hybridized tradition, language use, and identity in the U.S. Latina *quinceañera* ritual. In K. Potowski & J. Rothman (Eds.), *Bilingual youth: Spanish in English-speaking societies* (pp. 57–87). John Benjamins.

Potowski, K., & Marshall, M. (under review). The Spanish proficiency of Latino dual immersion students compared to peers in an all English program: A pseudo-longitudinal study across multiple domains.

Pozzi, R., Escalante, C., & Quan, T. (Eds.). (2021). *Heritage speakers of Spanish and study abroad.* New York: Routledge.

Ramirez, J. D. (1991). Longitudinal study of structured English immersion strategy, early-exit and late-exit transitional bilingual education programs for language-minority children. Final report. Vols. 1 and 2. https://eric.ed.gov/?id=ED330216

Ramírez, L. G. (2011). *Chicanas of 18th Street: Narratives of a movement from Latino Chicago.* University of Illinois Press.

Ramos-Pellicia, M. F. (2007). Lorain Puerto Rican Spanish and "r" in three generations. In J. Holmquist, A. Lorenzino, & L. Sayahi (Eds.), *Selected proceedings of the Third Workshop on Spanish Sociolinguistics* (pp. 53–60). Cascadilla Proceedings Project.

Ramos-Pellicia, M. F. (2012). Retention and deletion of /s/ in final position: The disappearance of /s/ in the Puerto Rican Spanish spoken in one community in the U.S. Midwest. *Southwest Journal of Linguistics*, 31(1), 161–176.

Ramos-Zayas, A. (2003). *National performances: Class, race, and space in Puerto Rican Chicago*. University of Chicago Press.

Raña Risso, R. (2013). *A corpus-based sociolinguistic study of subject pronoun placement in Spanish in New York* [Doctoral dissertation]. City University of New York. ProQuest LLC.

Raymond, G. (2004). Prompting action: The stand-alone "so" in ordinary conversation. *Research on Language and Social Interaction*, 37(2), 185–218.

Rhodes, N. C., & Pufahl, I. (2010). *Foreign language teaching in US schools: Results of a national survey*. Center for Applied Linguistics.

Riggenbach, H. (1991). Toward an understanding of fluency: A microanalysis of non-native speaker conversations. *Discourse Processes*, 14(4), 423–441.

Rivera-Mills, S. V. (2011). Use of voseo and Latino identity: An intergenerational study of Hondurans and Salvadorans in the western region of the US. In Luis A. Ortiz-López (Ed.), *Selected proceedings of the 13th Hispanic Linguistic Symposium* (pp. 94–106). Cascadilla Proceedings Project.

Rivera-Mills, S. V., & Villa, D. (2009). An integrated multigenerational model for language maintenance and shift: the case of Spanish in the Southwest. *Spanish in Context*, 6(1), 26–42.

Roberts, J. (1997). Hitting a moving target: Acquisition of sound change in progress by Philadelphia children. *Language Variation and Change*, 9(2), 249–266.

Rodríguez Cadena, Y. (2006). Variación y cambio en la comunidad de inmigrantes cubanos en la ciudad de México: Las líquidas en coda silábica. *Líderes Lingüísticos: Estudios de Variación y Cambio*, 7, 61.

Rodríguez Muñiz, M. (2010). Grappling with Latinidad: Puerto Rican activism in Chicago's pro-immigrant rights movement. In A. Pallares & N. Flores-Gonzalez (Eds.), *¡Marcha! Latino Chicago and the immigrant rights movement* (pp. 237–258). University of Illinois Press.

Ronquest, R., & Rao, R. (2018). Heritage Spanish phonetics and phonology. In K. Potowski (Ed.), *The Routledge handbook of Spanish as a heritage language* (pp. 164–177). Routledge.

Rooij, V. A. de. (2000). French discourse markers in Shaba Swahili conversations. *International Journal of Bilingualism*, 4(4), 447–469.

Rosa, J. (2019). *Looking like a language, sounding like a race: Raciolinguistic ideologies and the learning of Latinidad*. Oxford University Press.

Rumbaut, R. G., Massey, D. S., & Bean, F. D. (2006). Linguistic life expectancies: Immigrant language retention in Southern California. *Population and Development Review*, 32(3), 447–460.

Said-Mohand, A. (2008). Aproximación sociolingüística al uso del marcador del discurso como en el habla de jóvenes bilingües en la Florida. *Revista Internacional de Lingüística Iberoamericana*, 2(12), 71–93.

Saiz, A., & Zoido, E. (2005). Listening to what the world says: Bilingualism and earnings in the United States. *Review of Economics and Statistics*, 87(3), 523–538.

Sánchez Abchi, V. (2018). Spanish as a heritage language in Switzerland. In K. Potowski (Ed.), *The Routledge handbook of Spanish as a heritage language* (pp. 504–516). Routledge.

Sánchez-Muñoz, A. (2007). Style variation in Spanish as a heritage language: A study of discourse particles in academic and non-academic registers. In K. Potowski

& R. Cameron (Eds.), *Spanish in contact: Policy, social and linguistic inquiries* (pp. 153–172). John Benjamins.

Sankoff, D., & Poplack, S. (1981). A formal grammar for code-switching. *Papers in Linguistics, 14*(1), 3–45.

Schecter, S. R., & Bayley, R. (2002). *Language as cultural practice: Mexicanos en el Norte*. Lawrence Erlbaum.

Schreffler, S. B. (1994). Second-person singular pronoun options in the speech of Salvadorans in Houston, TX. *Southwest Journal of Linguistics, 13*, 101–119.

Schwenter, S. A., & Hoff, M. (2020). Cross-dialectal productivity of the Spanish subjunctive in nominal clause complements. In S. Sessarego, J. J. Colomina-Almiñana, & A. Rodriguez-Riccelli (Eds.), *Variation and evolution: Aspects of language contact and contrast across the Spanish-speaking world* (pp. 11–32). John Benjamins.

Serrano, J. (2002). *Dialectos en contacto: Variación y cambio lingüístico en migrantes sonorenses* [Bachelor's thesis]. Escuela Nacional de Antropología e Historia.

Siegel, J. (2010). *Second dialect acquisition*. Cambridge University Press.

Silva-Corvalán, C. (1983). Code shifting patterns in Chicano Spanish. In J. Amastae & L. Elías-Olivares (Eds.), *Spanish in the United States: Sociolinguistic aspects* (pp. 69–87). Cambridge University Press.

Silva-Corvalán, C. (1994). *Language contact and change: Spanish in Los Angeles*. Oxford University Press.

Silva-Corvalán, C. (1995). The study of language contact: An overview of the issues. In C. Silva-Corvalán (Ed.), *Spanish in four continents: Studies in language contact and bilingualism* (pp. 3–14). Georgetown University Press.

Silva-Corvalán, C. (2014). The acquisition of Spanish by third generation children. *Informes del observatorio/Observatorio Reports*. https://cervantesobservatorio.fas.harvard.edu/sites/default/files/005_informes_csc_acquisition_spanish_third_generation.pdf

Simonet, M., Rohena-Madrazo, M., & Paz, M. (2008). Preliminary evidence for incomplete neutralization of coda liquids in Puerto Rican Spanish. In L. Colantoni & J. Steele (Eds.), *The 3rd Conference on Laboratory Approaches to Spanish Phonology* (pp. 72–86). Cascadilla Proceedings Project.

Smith, J., & Durham, M. (2012). Bidialectalism or dialect death? Explaining generational change in the Shetland Islands, Scotland. *American Speech, 87*(1), 57–88.

Smith, R. C. (2006). *Mexican New York: Transnational lives of new immigrants*. University of California Press.

Solomon, A. (2009). Two sides of Chicago: In the Windy City, there's a great distinction between North and South. *Twin Cities Pioneer Press*, August 1. https://www.twincities.com/2009/08/01/two-sides-of-chicago-in-the-windy-city-theres-a-great-distinction-between-north-and-south/

Solomon, J. (1995). Local and global functions of a borrowed native pair of discourse markers in a Yucatan Mayan narrative. In J. Ahlers, L. Bilmes, J. S. Guenter, B. A. Kaiser, & J. Namkung (Eds.), *The 21st annual meeting of the Berkeley Linguistic Society, Feb. 17–20: General session and parasession on historical issues in sociolinguistics* (pp. 287–298). Berkeley Linguistics Society.

Spielman, F. (2017, October 2). Mayor: Chicago welcomes Puerto Ricans fleeing their destroyed homes. *Chicago Sun Times*. https://chicago.suntimes.com/2017/10/2/18397817/mayor-chicago-welcomes-puerto-ricans-fleeing-their-destroyed-homes

Spolsky, B. (2009). *Language management*. Cambridge University Press.

Steele, J. L., Slater, R. O., Zamarro, G., Miller, T., Li, J., Burkhauser, S., & Bacon, M. (2017). Effects of dual-language immersion programs on student achievement: Evidence from lottery data. *American Educational Research Journal*, *54*(1 suppl), 282S–302S.

Tagliamonte, S. A. (2012). *Variationist sociolinguistics: Change, observation, interpretation*. Wiley-Blackwell.

Tagliamonte, S. A. (2014). *New perspectives on analyzing variation* [Paper presentation]. 7th International Workshop on Spanish Sociolinguistics, University of Wisconsin–Madison.

Paul Taylor, Mark Hugo Lopez, Jessica Martinez & Gabriel Velasco. "When labels don't fit: Hispanics and their views of identity." Pew Research Center. (2012). https://www.pewresearch.org/hispanic/2012/04/04/when-labels-dont-fit-hispanics-and-their-views-of-identity/

Terrell, T. D. (1977). A natural approach to second language acquisition and learning. *Modern Language Journal*, *61*(7), 325–337.

Thomas, W., & Collier, V. (2009). *Educating English learners for a transformed world*. Dual Language Education of New Mexico/Fuente Press.

Thomason, S. G., & Kaufman, T. (1988). *Language contact, creolization, and genetic linguistics*. University of California Press.

Timm, L. A. (1975). Spanish-English code-switching: El porqué y how-not-to. *Romance Philology*, *28*(4), 473–482.

Tomsiček, A., & Potowski, K. (in progress). Probing the DELE as measure of Spanish proficiency.

Toro-Morn, M., & García, I. (2019). *Puerto Ricans in Illinois*. Southern Illinois University Press.

Torres, L. (1989). Code-mixing and borrowing in a New York Puerto Rican community: A cross-generational study. *World Englishes*, *8*, 419–432.

Torres, L. (2002). Bilingual discourse markers in Puerto Rican Spanish. *Language in Society*, *31*, 65–83.

Torres, L., & Potowski, K. (2008). A comparative study of bilingual discourse markers in Chicago Mexican, Puerto Rican, and MexiRican Spanish. *International Journal of Bilingualism*, *12*(4), 263–279.

Torres, L., & Potowski, K. (2016). Hablamos los dos in the Windy City: Codeswitching among Puerto Ricans, Mexicans and MexiRicans in Chicago. In R. E. Guzzardo Tamargo, C. M. Mazak, & M. C. Parafita Couto (Eds.), *Spanish-English codeswitching in the Caribbean and the US* (pp. 83–105). John Benjamins.

Tran, V. C. (2010). English gain vs. Spanish loss? Language assimilation among second-generation Latinos in young adulthood. *Social Forces*, *89*(1), 257–284.

Travis, C. E. (2005). *Discourse markers in Colombian Spanish: A study in polysemy*. De Gruyter.

Trudgill, P. (1983). *Sociolinguistics: An introduction to language and society*. Penguin.

Trudgill, P. (1984). *Language in the British Isles*. Cambridge University Press.

Trudgill, P. (1986). *Dialects in contact*. Blackwell.

Trudgill, P. (2004). *New-dialect formation: The inevitability of colonial Englishes*. Oxford University Press.

Tse, S.-M., & Ingram, D. (1987). The influence of dialectal variation on phonological acquisition: A case study on the acquisition of Cantonese. *Journal of Child Language*, *14*(2), 281–294.

U.S. Census Bureau. (1970–2010). Decennial Census. www.census.gov

U.S. Census Bureau. (2011a). American Community Survey 5-Year Estimates of Selected Social Characteristics in the United States, Table DP02. https://data.census.gov/cedsci/table?q=2011%20custodial%20divorced%20parents&g=

0400000US17_1600000US1714000&d=ACS%205-Year%20Estimates%20Data%20Profiles&tid=ACSDP5Y2011.DP02&hidePreview=false

U.S. Census Bureau. (2011b). American Community Survey 1-Year Estimates of Characteristics of People by Language Spoken at Home, Chicago, Table S1603, generated using American FactFinder. http://factfinder.census.gov

U.S. Census Bureau. (2016). American Community Survey. https://www.census.gov/

U.S. Census Bureau. (2018). American Community Survey 1-Year Estimates Language Spoken at Home, Table S1601. https://data.census.gov/cedsci/table?q=language%20spoken%20at%20home%20chicago%202018&tid=ACSST1Y2018.S1601&hidePreview=false

U.S. Census Bureau. (2019a). American Community Survey 1-Year Estimates Language Spoken at Home, Table S1601. https://data.census.gov/cedsci/table?q=language%20use&tid=ACSST1Y2019.S1601&hidePreview=false

U.S. Census Bureau (2019b). Population estimates, July 1, 2019 (V2019). QuickFacts. https://www.census.gov/quickfacts/fact/table/chicagocityillinois/RHI725219

Valdés, G. (1976). Social interaction and code-switching patterns: A case study of Spanish/English alternation. *Bilingual Press/Editorial Bilingüe*, 209–229.

Valdés, G. (1989). Teaching Spanish to Hispanic bilinguals: A look at oral proficiency testing and the proficiency movement. *Hispania*, 72(2), 392–401.

Valdés, G. (2011). Ethnolinguistic identity: The challenge of maintaining Spanish-English bilingualism in American schools. In K. Potowski & J. Rothman (Eds.), *Bilingual youth: Spanish in English-speaking societies* (pp. 113–146). John Benjamins.

Valencia, M., & Lynch, A. (2019). The mass mediation of Spanish in Miami. In Andrew Lynch (Ed.), *The Routledge handbook of Spanish in the global city* (pp. 73–100). Routledge.

Valentín-Márquez, W. (2007). *Doing being Boricua: Perceptions of national identity and the sociolinguistic distribution of liquid variables in Puerto Rican Spanish* [Doctoral dissertation]. University of Michigan.

Valentín-Márquez, W. (2015). Doing being *Boricua* on the island and in the U.S. Midwest: Perceptions of national identity and lateralization of /r/ in Puerto Rican Spanish. In S. Sessarego & M. González-Rivera (Eds.), *New perspectives on Hispanic contact linguistics in the Americas* (pp. 327–345). Vervuert.

Varra, R. M. (2013). *The social correlates of lexical borrowing in Spanish in New York City* [Doctoral dissertation]. City University of New York.

Velázquez, I. (2014). Maternal attitudes toward Spanish transmission in the US Midwest: A necessary but insufficient condition for success. *Sociolinguistic Studies*, 7(3), 225–248.

Velázquez, I. (2019). *Household perspectives on minority language maintenance and loss: Language in the small spaces*. Multilingual Matters.

Verhoeven, J., De Fauw, G., & Kloots, H. (2004). Speech rate in a pluricentric language: A comparison between Dutch in Belgium and the Netherlands. *Language and Speech*, 47, 297–308.

Villa, D. J., & Rivera-Mills, S. V. (2009). An integrated multi-generational model for language maintenance and shift: The case of Spanish in the Southwest. *Spanish in Context*, 6(1), 26-42.

Villegas, B., Luque, A., Potowski, K., & Torres, L. (submitted). Spanish subjunctive use by Mexicans and Puerto Ricans in Chicago: A comparison of generational groups and proficiency levels.

Viner, K. M. (2016). Second-generation NYC bilinguals' use of the Spanish subjunctive in obligatory contexts. *Spanish in Context*, *13*(3), 343–370.

Viner, K. M. (2017). Subjunctive use in the speech of New York City Spanish heritage language bilinguals: A variationist analysis. *Heritage Language Journal*, *14*(3), 307–333.

Viner, K. M. (2018). The optional Spanish subjunctive mood grammar of New York City heritage bilinguals. *Lingua*, 210–211, 79–94.

Viner, K. M. (2019). Comment clauses and mood choice in New York City Spanish: Generational constraints and innovations. *Linguistic Approaches to Bilingualism*, *10*(5), 728–744.

Whiteside, S. P. (1996). Temporal-based acoustic-phonetic patterns in read speech: Some evidence for speaker sex differences. *Journal of the International Phonetic Association*, *26*, 23–40.

Wolfram, W., & Schilling-Estes, N. (2006). Language evolution or dying traditions? The state of American dialects. In W. Wolfram & B. Ward (Eds.), *American voices: How dialects differ from coast to coast* (pp. 1–10). Wiley-Blackwell.

Woods, M. R., & Rivera-Mills, S. V. (2010). Transnacionalismo del voseante: Salvadoreños y hondureños en los Estados Unidos. *Lengua y migración*, *2*(1), 97–112.

Woods, M. R., & Rivera-Mills, S. V. (2012). El tú como un "mask": Voseo and Salvadorean and Honduran identity in the United States. *Studies in Hispanic and Lusophone Linguistics*, *5*(1), 191–216.

Woods, M., & Shin, N. L. (2016). Fíjate . . . sabes que le digo yo. In M. Moyna & S. V. Rivera-Mills (Eds.), *Forms of address in the Spanish of the Americas* (pp. 305–324). John Benjamions.

Wordreference.com. (2006). https://forum.wordreference.com/threads/birthday-cake-torta-tarta-pastel-bizcocho.225364/

Yan, J. (2002). Geepack: Yet another package for generalized estimating equations. *R News*, *2*, 12–14.

Yan, J., & Fine, J. (2004). Estimating equations for association structures. *Statistics in Medicine*, *23*, 859–874.

Yuan, J., Liberman, M., & Cieri, C. (2006). *Towards an integrated understanding of speaking rate in conversation* [Paper presentation]. International Conference on Spoken Language Processing (Interspeech 2006), Pittsburgh. http://ldc.upenn.edu/myl/llog/icslp06_final.pdf

Zentella, A. C. (1987). Language and female identity in the Puerto Rican community. In J. Penfield (Ed.), *Women and language in transition* (pp. 167–179). State University of New York Press.

Zentella, A. C. (1990). Lexical leveling in four New York City Spanish dialects: Linguistic and social factors. *Hispania*, *73*(4), 1094–1105.

Zentella, A. C. (1997). *Growing up bilingual*. Blackwell.

Zentella, A. C. (2007). "Dime con quién hablas y te diré quién eres": Linguistic (in)security and Latino unity. In J. Flores & R. Rosaldo (Eds.), *A companion to Latina/o studies* (pp. 25–39). Blackwell.

Zentella, A. C. (2018). "LatinUs and linguistics: Complaints, conflicts, contradictions—the anthro-political linguistics solution" In Naomi L. Shin & Daniel Erker (Eds.), *Questioning theoretical primitives in linguistic inquiry (Papers in honor of Ricardo Otheguy)*. John Benjamins.

Zimmerman, M. (Ed.). (2018). *The Mexican experience in Chicago: Early memories and echoes in our time*. CreateSpace.

INDEX

For the benefit of digital users, indexed terms that span two pages (e.g., 52–53) may, on occasion, appear on only one of those pages.

Tables and figures are indicated by *t* and *f* following the page number

Aaron, J. E., 116–18
accommodation, 6
African American English, 6–7, 10–11, 211
Alamo, Hector, 22–24, 30
Anglicisms, 31, 75–76
Appalachian English, 6–7
Australian English, 211
Ayala, Carmen, 304

Beaudrie, S., 306
bidialectal, 6–7
bilingual education, 268–69, 273–80, 277*t*
    TBE, 273–76, 277, 295–96, 304
bilingualism public informational campaign, 301–2
bilinguals and bilingualism, 2, 6–7, 42–44, 53, 57, 84
    codeswitching and, 146–50, 148*t*, 170*t*, 174, 175
    discourse markers and, 111–20, 113*t*, 141
    language acquisition, 245–47, 249–50
    multilingualism and, 243
    Puerto Ricans, 25, 116, 146
    sequential bilingualism, 272, 272*t*, 275–76, 277, 277*t*, 294–95
    simultaneous bilingualism, 247, 249–50, 272–73, 272*t*, 275–77, 294–95

Capacity, Opportunity, and Desire (COD), 243–44

Cardona, Miguel, 304
Caribbean Spanish, 73–76
Chambers, J., 71, 75, 81–82, 109
Chicago, Spanish in. *See* Spanish-speakers, study participants
children's television programming, in Spanish, 303
CHISPA corpus, 27, 35, 36, 38–39. *See also* Spanish-speakers, study participants
    by generational groups and regional origins, 36–41, 36*t*
chronologically relatively shallow dialect contact, 8–9
Cintrón, Ralph, 21
COD. *See* Capacity, Opportunity, and Desire
codeswitching, 3, 12–13, 57, 145. *See also* Spanish-speakers, study participants, codeswitching
    by bilinguals, 146–50, 148*t*, 170*t*, 174, 175
    congruent lexicalization and, 147
    discourse markers and, 114, 115, 116
    Spanish-English, 146–55, 156–73, 174–76
    subjunctive use and, 202, 203*t*
Colombian Spanish, 74*t*, 75–76, 77
colonization, 5
congruent lexicalization, 147, 148
Covid-19 pandemic, 303
Croatian, 114

Cuban Spanish, 74t, 76, 77
day cares, 302–3
De Genova, N., 24–25, 26–29, 30, 77, 309
DELE. *See* Diploma del Español como Lengua Extranjera
dialect, language and, 3–4
dialect contact, 1–2, 4, 30–31, 309
  chronologically relatively shallow contact, 8–9
  Erker and Otheguy research on, 9–10, 9t
  intrafamilial, 6–7, 10–11, 11f, 35, 71, 236–37, 299
  lexical outcomes of, 71–79
  of Mexicans and Puerto Ricans in Chicago, 76–77
  new settlement, 4–5, 5f, 8–9
  phonological accommodation in situations of Spanish, 205–10
  Spanish, 30–31, 75, 205–10
dialect immigration, monolingual, 5f, 5
dialect leveling, 1, 4, 9–10, 12–13
dialects
  English, 6–7, 10–11
  immigrant, 7–9, 8f, 10f, 10
  Spanish, 3–4, 7–12, 8f, 9t, 28, 84
  Spanish, phonology and, 210–11, 210t, 211t
  2+, 6–7, 7f
Diploma del Español como Lengua Extranjera (DELE), 310–11
discourse markers, 111–12. *See also* Spanish-speakers, study participants, discourse markers
  bilingualism and, 111–20, 113t, 141
  codeswitching and, 114, 115, 116
  coexistence and similar functions, 112–13
  functions of, 137f, 137–40, 138f, 139f, 140f
  language contact and, 115–16
  MexiRican, 115–16, 119
  partial or total replacement, 114–20
  Spanish, 112–14, 113t, 115–20, 117t
Dominican Spanish, 74t, 76, 77
dual-language public school programs, 303–4, 304f, 305f
Ducar, C., 306

English. *See also* Spanish, English and
  African American, 6–7, 10–11, 211
  Appalachian, 6–7
  Australian, 211
  British and Canadian, 75, 81–82
  Croatian and, 114
  dialects, 6–7, 10–11
  German and, 114
English as a second language (ESL), 252, 273–74, 303–4, 306
English learners (ELs), 273–76, 277, 278–79, 280, 294–95, 303–4
Erker, D., 3–4, 12–13
  Otheguy and, 4, 9–10, 9t, 12–13, 207, 222, 299–300, 301, 311
ESL. *See* English as a second language

Fishman, J. A., 241–42, 243
Flores-Ferrán, N., 119
Foreman, A., 211
French, 112, 114–15

Gallego, M., 181–82
German, 114
Gorman, L., 32–33
Gutiérrez, Luis, 26

Hernández, J. E., 206–7, 209, 211
high school and university Spanish heritage language programs, 305–6
homeland speakers, 85–89, 86t, 87t, 88f, 94f, 94t
Houston, Spanish in, 7–8, 8f, 206–7, 211

Illinois Action for Children, 259–60
Illinois State Board of Education, 304
immigrant dialects, 7–9, 8f, 10f, 10
immigrant languages, in US, 2–4, 3f, 6, 243–44
immigration, monolingual dialect, 5f, 5
Ingram, D., 11
input and output, in language proficiency, 245
intergenerational Spanish transmission and loss, 243–48, 301
intrafamilial dialect contact, 6–7, 10–11, 11f, 35, 71, 236–37, 299

Kern, J., 119
Kerswill, P., 5
koine, 5

[330] Index

L2. *See* second-language learners
Labov, W., 76
language acquisition
　by bilinguals, 245–47, 249–50
　order of, 272–73, 272t, 294–95
　Spanish proficiency and, 257–58, 267, 278–79, 291–92, 295–96
　subjunctive in, 179
language contact, 1–3, 3f, 9–11, 9t, 299
　discourse markers and, 115–16
language loss, 1–2, 243–48, 301
Language Policy Task Force, 247
language shift, 25, 243–44, 271–72
latinidad, 24, 25–26, 26f, 29–30, 59
Latino Chicago, 1, 13–23, 14f, 15t, 16f, 16t, 17f, *See also* Spanish-speakers, study participants
　growth of, 16f, 19f
　Hispanic populations, percentage by origin, 20f
　La Villita neighborhood, 19–22, 22f
　Mexican and Puerto Rican neighborhoods, 19–23, 20f
　Spanish in, 13–23, 25, 28–31
Latino population, of Illinois, 274f, 274–75
La Villita neighborhood, Chicago, 19–23, 22f
lexical familiarity, 71. *See also* Spanish-speakers, study participants, lexical familiarity of
lexical outcomes of dialect contact, 71
linguistic convergence, 2–3, 9–10, 12–13
Lipski, J. M., 118, 146–48

Marshall, M., 303–4, 304f, 305f
Mexican Americans, codeswitching by, 146–47
Mexicans and Puerto Ricans, in Chicago, 35. *See also* Spanish-speakers, study participants
　complex relationship of, 23–31, 26f, 30f
　dialect contact, 76–77
　discourse markers, 119
　latinidad and, 25–26
　negative social and linguistic attitudes, 31f
　neighborhoods, 19–23, 20f
　Spanish of, 28–31, 32–33, 34, 71, 76–79, 119, 120
Mexican Spanish, 75

MexiRican, 35. *See also* Spanish-speakers, study participants
　generational and parental characteristics, 40–41, 41t
　Spanish, 10–11, 76–77
monolingual dialect immigration, 5f, 5
Montrul, S., 183–84, 202, 247
multilingualism, 243

Náhuatl, 112–13, 113t
new settlement dialect contact, 4–5, 5f, 8–9
New York City, Spanish in, 8–9, 11–12, 30–31, 75–76, 77
Nordenstam, K., 72

OPI. *See* Oral Proficiency Interview scale
Oral Proficiency Interview (OPI) scale, 42, 310–11
Otheguy, R., 8–9, 125, 184
　Erker and, 4, 9–10, 9t, 12–13, 207, 222, 299–300, 301, 311
　Zentella and, 6, 30–31, 51–52, 125, 309

Padilla, E., 24
Padilla, F., 24
Pérez, G., 23–25, 28
phonological accommodation, in situations of Spanish dialect contact, 205–10
Pilsen neighborhood, 19–21, 22
Poplack, S., 146–47, 157–58, 170–71, 174, 182, 191
Porcel, J., 271–72
Potowski, K., 27–28, 30, 35, 96, 216–17, 303–4
　Beaudrie, Ducar and, 306
　Gorman and, 32–33
　Marshall and, 303–4, 304f, 305f
　Montrul and, 247
　Tomsiček and, 310–11
　Torres and, 31, 119, 126, 137–38
Puerto Ricans. *See also* Spanish-speakers, study participants
　bilinguals, 25, 116, 146
　in New York, codeswitching by, 146
Puerto Rican Spanish, 58, 75, 76
　discourse markers, 119, 120
Pufahl, I., 306

quinceañera celebrations, 32–33

Index [331]

Ramos-Zayas, A. Y., 24–25, 26–29, 30, 77, 309
Rhodes, N. C., 306

Said-Mohand, A., 118
Salvadorans and Mexicans, in Houston, Spanish of, 7–8, 8f, 206–7, 211
second-language (L2) learners, 42, 310–11
sequential bilingualism, 272, 272t, 275–76, 277, 277t, 294–95
SES. *See* socioeconomic status
Shaba Swahili, 114–15
SHL. *See* Spanish heritage language programs
Silva-Corvalán, C., 146, 182–83, 186, 193, 245–46
simultaneous bilingualism, 247, 249–50, 272–73, 272t, 275–77, 294–95
socioeconomic status (SES), of study participants, 55f, 55–57
sociology of language, 241–42
Spanglish, 28–29
Spanish, 1, 2, 3–4, 11–12
  Caribbean, 73–76
  in Chicago, prior studies of, 31–33
  Colombian, 74t, 75–76, 77
  colonization of Latin America by, 5
  Cuban, 74t, 76, 77
  day care and children's television programming in, 302–3
  dialect contact, 30–31, 75, 205–10
  dialect leveling, 12–13
  dialects, 3–4, 7–12, 8f, 9t, 28, 84
  dialects, phonology and, 210–11, 210t, 211t
  discourse markers, 112–14, 113t, 115–20, 117t
  Dominican, 74t, 76, 77
  English and, 1–3, 3f, 9–11, 42–44, 53, 57, 73–76, 74t, 115–18
  intergenerational transmission and loss of, 243–48, 301
  intra-Latino differences of use, 244
  Latin American, varieties of, 3–4
  in Latino Chicago, 13–23, 25, 28–31
  linguistic convergence, 12–13
  media broadcasts, 77–78
  Mexican, 75
  Mexican and Puerto Rican, in Chicago, 28–31, 32–33, 34, 71, 76–79, 119, 120

  MexiRican, 10–11, 76–77
  Náhuatl and, 112–13, 113t
  in New York City, 8–9, 11–12, 30–31, 75–76, 77
  phonological accommodation, dialect contact and, 205–10
  proficiency, measuring and supporting, 299–307
  Puerto Rican, 58, 75, 76, 119, 120
  of Salvadorans and Mexicans in Houston, 7–8, 8f, 206–7, 211
  subjunctive in, 179, 180–86
  Yucatec Maya and, 113–14
Spanish, English and. *See also* bilinguals and bilingualism
  codeswitching, 146–55, 156–73, 174–76
  day-care options and, 302–3
  discourse markers and, 112, 113–14, 116–20, 117t, 121–26, 123t, 126f
  dual-language public school programs, 303–4, 304f, 305f
  language acquisition, 245–47, 249–50
Spanish heritage language (SHL) programs, 305–6
Spanish-speakers, study participants
  age of, 53, 54f
  in dual-language programs, 304
  gender of, 54
  generational groups of, 36–40, 36t, 37t, 39t, 44–48, 45t, 46f, 48f, 54f
  on high school Spanish classes, 306
  homeland speakers of Mexicans and Puerto Ricans and, 85–89, 86t, 87t, 88f, 94f, 94t, 100t
  interviews with, 57–59, 58t, 59t, 79–85, 80t, 85t
  Mexican and Puerto Rican Spanish of, 79–82, 80t, 83–84
  Mexicans and Puerto Ricans, linguistic analyses, summary of, 307–9, 308t
  MexiRicans, linguistic analyses, summary of, 309, 310t
  regional groups of, 40–41, 41t, 51f
  SES of, 55f, 55–57
Spanish-speakers, study participants, codeswitching
  intersentential, 153–55, 167, 168f, 168–70, 169f, 170f, 170t, 175

[332] Index

intrasentential, 151–53, 167, 168f, 168, 170t, 175–76
numbers of, 162–67, 163f, 164f, 165f, 166f, 167f
overall quantity of English in, 156–62
by proficiency level, 159f, 159–62, 160t, 161f, 161t, 162f, 165f, 165–67, 166f, 172–74, 173f, 174t, 175–76
by regional origin and generation, 148–50, 150t, 156–59, 156t, 157f, 158f, 160t, 161t, 162f, 162–65, 163f, 164f, 166f, 168f, 168–73, 169f, 170f, 171f, 173f, 174–76, 202, 203t, 307
types of, 167–73, 168f, 169f, 170f, 170t, 171f, 173f

Spanish-speakers, study participants, discourse markers
functions of, 137f, 137–40, 138f, 139f, 140f
of Mexicans and Puerto Ricans, 126–32, 127f, 128f, 140–41
of MexiRicans, 120, 127–29, 128f, 131–32, 140–41
proficiency and, 132–37, 133f, 134t, 135f, 136t, 139–40, 140f
regional origin and generation in, 126–33, 127f, 128f, 129f, 131f, 134, 134t, 135f, 139f, 139
so and *entonces* as, 119–26, 121t, 123t, 126f, 127–41, 129f, 134t, 136t, 137f, 138f, 139f, 140f

Spanish-speakers, study participants, lexical familiarity of, 77, 79, 83–85
by generational groups, 79, 91, 93, 93t, 95f, 96f, 102–8, 103t, 107t, 108t, 109
homeland speakers and, 85–89, 86t, 87t, 88f, 94t, 100t
Mexicans, scores on individual lexical items, 99, 100t, 103t
Mexicans and Puerto Ricans, 89–98, 89t, 90f, 92f, 92t, 97f, 104–6, 108–10
Mexicans and Puerto Ricans, scores on individual lexical items, 104–6
MexiRicans, 96–98, 97f, 98f, 105–6, 109
proficiency and, 106–8, 107f, 107t, 108t, 109

Puerto Ricans, scores on individual lexical items, 99–102, 101t, 103t
scores, outgroup and ingroup, 89–96, 89t, 90f, 92f, 92t, 95f, 96f, 307
scores on individual lexical items, 98–106, 100t, 101t
total scores, 93–96, 93t, 94f, 94t, 106–8, 107f

Spanish-speakers, study participants, outgroup and ingroup lexicons, 76–77, 83–84
individual lexical items and, 99–102, 100f, 101t, 102f, 103t
ingroup lexical familiarity scores, 91–93, 92f, 92t, 95f
ingroup lexical familiarity scores, correlation to generation *versus* proficiency, 107–8, 108t
outgroup lexical familiarity scores, 89–91, 89t, 90f, 95f
outgroup lexical familiarity scores, correlation to generation *versus* proficiency, 106–8, 107t

Spanish-speakers, study participants, phonology
dialects and, 210–11, 210t, 211t
interlocutors and, 227–31, 228f, 230t, 231t
of Mexicans and Puerto Ricans, 210, 210t, 213–15, 214t, 215f, 217–18, 218f, 218t, 221f, 221–22, 222f, 225f, 227–33, 227t, 228f, 230t, 231t, 232f
of MexiRicans, 210, 211t, 216f, 216–17, 216t, 217f, 218–21, 219f, 219t, 220f, 223f, 223–27, 224f, 225f, 226f, 227t, 233f, 233
qualitative analysis of Puerto Rican variation, 233–36, 234t
regional origin and generation in, 213–27, 217f, 221f, 222f, 225f, 227t, 229–31, 230t, 231t
/r̄/ in, 213, 217–21, 218f, 218t, 225f, 225–26, 226f, 227t, 228, 229f, 230–37, 231t, 232f, 233f, 234t, 307
/s/ in, 213–15, 214t, 215f, 216f, 216–17, 216t, 217f, 221f, 221–22, 222f, 223f, 223–27, 224f, 225f, 227t, 228f, 229–30, 230t, 231–37, 232f, 233f, 234t, 307

Index [333]

Spanish-speakers, study participants,
proficiency of, 42–53, 43t, 45t, 46f,
48f, 241–42, 244
attitudes about Spanish and, 250–57,
293, 295
bilingual education and, 275–80, 277t
codeswitching and, 159f, 159–62, 160t,
161f, 161t, 162f, 165f, 165–67, 166f,
172–74, 173f, 174t, 175–76
cultural identity and, 254–55
discourse markers and, 132–37, 133f,
134t, 135f, 136t, 139–40, 140f
employment and, 255–56
English and, 249–51, 252–54, 256–57,
258–62, 266–67, 268–71, 272–73,
275–80, 286–87, 291–96, 297
generational groups, 248–49, 249t,
263, 269, 275–76, 283t, 284–97,
300–1, 309–11
generational groups, ingroup lexical
familiarity scores and, 107–8, 108t
generational groups, outgroup lexical
familiarity scores and, 106–8, 107t
grandparents and, 264–66, 269, 283–
85, 291–93, 297
high-proficiency outliers, 284–89
inliers, 248–83, 249t
language acquisition and, 257–58,
267, 278–79, 291–92, 295–96
language use in home and social
networks, 257–72
lexical familiarity and total lexical
scores, 106–8, 107f, 107t, 108t, 109
low-proficiency outliers, 289–94
measuring and supporting, 299–301
order of acquisition in, 272–73, 272t,
294–95
proficiency outliers, 283–94, 283t
subjunctive use and, 197–203, 198f,
198t, 199f, 200f, 201f, 203t
transmission in, 250, 251–52, 263
travel to Mexico or Puerto Rico in, 280–83
WPM and, 44, 48–53, 49t, 50f, 51f
Spanish-speakers, study participants,
subjunctive use
indicative use and, 191f, 192f, 192–94,
195f, 196f, 198f, 198, 199f, 200f,
202, 203
obligatory subjunctive contexts, 187–90,
188t, 192–96, 194f, 195f, 198f, 198,
199f, 200f, 200–1, 202

proficiency and, 197–203, 198f, 198t,
199f, 200f, 201f, 203t
by regional group and generation,
187–90, 187t, 191f, 191, 192f,
192–93, 193f, 194f, 194–95, 196f,
196–97, 198f, 198–201, 199f, 200f,
202–4, 203t, 307–9
variable subjunctive contexts, 187–90,
189t, 192–93, 194f, 196f, 196–97,
198f, 198, 199f, 201f, 201–2
Spolsky, B., 258
subjunctive. See also Spanish-speakers,
study participants, subjunctive use
codeswitching and use of, 202, 203t
in first language acquisition, 179
indicative and, 180–82, 183–84, 187,
190, 191f, 192f, 192–94, 195f, 196f,
198f, 198, 199f, 202, 203
obligatory subjunctive contexts, 187–90,
188t, 192–96, 194f, 195f, 198f, 198
, 199f, 200f, 200–1, 202
use across generations, 182–86, 185t
in U. S. Spanish, 179, 180–86
variable subjunctive contexts, 187–90,
189t, 192–93, 194f, 196f, 196–97,
198f, 198, 199f, 201f, 201–2

TBE. See transitional bilingual
education
Tomsiček, A., 310–11
Torres, L., 31, 116–18, 119, 126, 137–38,
182, 186
transitional bilingual education (TBE),
273–76, 277, 295–96, 304
Travis, C. E., 119, 122, 123t, 137
Trudgill, P., 6, 72, 76, 78
Tse, S.-M., 11

Valdés, G., 273, 303
Velázquez, I., 257
Viner, K. M., 184–86, 185t

words per minute (WPM), 44, 48–53,
49t, 50f, 51f

Yucatec Maya, 113–14

Zentella, A. C., 8–9, 72–77, 74t, 104,
108, 109, 147, 184, 266, 302
Otheguy and, 6, 30–31, 51–52, 125,
309